METROPOLITAN STADIUM:
MEMORABLE GAMES AT MINNESOTA'S DIAMOND ON THE PRAIRIE

EDITED BY STEW THORNLEY
ASSOCIATE EDITORS LEN LEVIN, BILL NOWLIN, AND CARL RIECHERS

Society for American Baseball Research, Inc.
Phoenix, AZ

Metropolitan Stadium: Memorable Games at Minnesota's Diamond on the Prairie

Edited by Stew Thornley
Associate editors Len Levin, Bill Nowlin, and Carl Riechers

Society for American Baseball Research, Inc.
Phoenix, AZ

Copyright © 2021 Society for American Baseball Research, Inc.
All rights reserved. Reproduction in whole or in part without permission is prohibited.
978-1-970159-67-7   Metropolitan Stadium ebook
978-1-970159-68-4   Metropolitan Stadium paper
Library of Congress Control Number: 2022903120
Front cover image by Minnesota Historical Society
Book design: Rachael Sullivan

Cronkite School at ASU
555 N. Central Ave. #416
Phoenix, AZ 85004
Phone: (602) 496-1460
Web: www.sabr.org
Facebook: Society for American Baseball Research
Twitter: @SABR

CONTENTS

1. INTRODUCTION 9

2. PLAY OF FOUR DECISIONS ENSURES BALLPARK'S DEBUT IS MEMORABLE 13
   April 24, 1956: Wichita Braves 5, Minneapolis Millers 3
   By Joel Rippel

3. MAYS HOMERS TWICE IN SHOWCASE EXHIBITION GAME 16
   June 7, 1956: New York Giants 6, Minneapolis Millers 4
   By T.S. Flynn

4. A GRATE THROW PRECEDES MILLERS' WIN OVER OMAHA 19
   August 27, 1956: Minneapolis Millers 2, Omaha Cardinals 0
   By J. G. Preston

5. BRAVES AND MILLERS PUT ON A COLD-WEATHER EXHIBITION 22
   April 13, 1957: Milwaukee Braves 4, Minneapolis Millers 3
   By Joel Rippel

6. THE BABY "BABY BULL" 24
   April 30, 1957: Minneapolis Millers 12, Louisville Colonels 8
   By Bob Tholkes

7. THE WEIRDEST INNING METROPOLITAN STADIUM HAS SEEN IN ITS BRIEF HISTORY 26
   May 26, 1957: Minneapolis 9, Wichita 8 (Game One of Doubleheader)
   By Alan Cohen

8. A HARBINGER OF THINGS TO COME 29
   August 5, 1957: Detroit Tigers 6, Cincinnati Reds 5
   By Joel Rippel

9. GREEN SURVIVES PARADE TO LEAD MILLERS TO OPENING DAY WIN 31
   April 22, 1958: Minneapolis Millers 11, Louisville Colonels 6
   By Dave Mona

10. AN INDIAN HOMER BINGE 34
    June 15, 1958: Indianapolis Indians 8, Minneapolis Millers 0 (Game One of Doubleheader)
    By Alan Cohen

11. BOTH TED WILLIAMS AND PUMPSIE GREEN STAR IN RED SOX-MILLERS EXHIBITION GAME 37
    June 16, 1958: Minneapolis Millers 14, Boston Red Sox 10
    By Bill Nowlin

12. SEPTEMBER 29, 1958: MILLERS WIN THEIR SECOND JUNIOR WORLD SERIES 39
    Minneapolis Millers 7, Montreal Royals 1
    By Rich Arpi

13. ART SCHULT HITS FOR THE CYCLE IN WIN 42
    April 29, 1959: Minneapolis 9, Houston 5
    By Alan Cohen

14. YAZ DEBUT DOESN'T COUNT; MILLERS STILL PREVAIL OVER OMAHA 45
    September 15-16, 1959: Minneapolis Millers 4, Omaha Cardinals 3 10 innings (nullified game)
    Minneapolis Millers 5, Omaha Cardinals 3 (7 innings)
    Minneapolis Millers 3, Omaha Cardinals 2 (12 innings)
    By Dave Mona

15. MILLERS WIN SECOND CONSECUTIVE AMERICAN ASSOCIATION CHAMPIONSHIP 48
    September 25, 1959: Minneapolis Millers 4, Fort Worth Cats 2
    By Brian M. Frank

16. THE LAST MINOR-LEAGUE POSTSEASON GAME AT METROPOLITAN STADIUM 50
    September 28, 1959: Minneapolis Millers 6, Havana Sugar Kings 5 (Second Game of Junior World Series)
    By Alan Cohen

17. MILLERS PLATE 10 IN SECOND GAME OF DOUBLEHEADER, FINALLY SOLVE COLONELS 53
    May 8, 1960: Minneapolis Millers 10, Louisville Colonels 2
    By Mike Lynch

18. LAST MILLERS GAME AT MET STADIUM 56
    September 8, 1960: St. Paul Saints 7, Minneapolis Millers 0 (Game 2)
    By Joe O'Connell

19. TWINS LOSE FIRST HOME OPENER 59
    April 21, 1961: Washington Senators 5, Minnesota Twins 3
    By Dave Lande

20. ORIOLES' JIM GENTILE BLASTS TWO GRAND SLAMS ON CONSECUTIVE PITCHES 62
    May 9, 1961: Baltimore Orioles 13, Minnesota Twins 5
    By Mike Huber

21. JULIO BECQUER HITS FIRST PINCH-HIT AND WALK-OFF HOME RUN IN MINNESOTA TWINS HISTORY 65
    June 20, 1961: Minnesota Twins 5, Baltimore Orioles 4
    By Bruce Harris

22. BECQUER'S SUDDEN JULY FOURTH SHOT 68
    July 4, 1961, Game 1: Minnesota Twins 6, Chicago White Sox 4
    By Gene Gomes

23. THE FIRST INSIDE-THE-PARK HOME RUN IN TWINS HISTORY 71
    July 4, 1961 – Game 2: Minnesota Twins 4, Chicago White Sox 2
    By Gene Gomes

24. ALLISON AND KILLEBREW HIT FIRST-INNING GRAND SLAMS AS TWINS ROUT INDIANS 74
    July 18, 1962: Minnesota Twins 14, Cleveland Indians 3
    By Paul Hofmann

25. JACK KRALICK ALMOST PERFECT IN FIRST NO-HIT GAME FOR TWINS 77
    August 26, 1962: Minnesota Twins 1, Kansas City Athletics 0
    By Tim Otto

26. PASCUAL REACHES 20-WIN GOAL IN SEASON FINALE 80
    September 30, 1962: Minnesota Twins 1, Baltimore Orioles 0
    By Richard Cuicchi

27. NEW TWINS RELIEVER SAVES THE DAY AIDED BY MELE'S MARAUDERS 83
    May 26, 1963: Minnesota Twins 5, Chicago White Sox 2
    By Sarah Johnson

28. CHICAGO'S LANDIS AND ROBINSON HIT BACK-TO-BACK HOMERS IN NINTH AS WILHELM SHUTS DOWN TWINS IN RELIEF 86
    August 31, 1963: Chicago White Sox 2, Minnesota Twins 0
    By Mike Huber

29. TWINS RALLY FROM 7-1 DEFICIT 89
    May 9, 1964: Minnesota Twins 10, Kansas City Athletics 8
    by Rich Arpi

30. CLINTON'S THROW TO RETIRE BATTEY AT FIRST HELPS ANGELS SHUT OUT TWINS 92
    July 17, 1964: Los Angeles Angels 1, Minnesota Twins 0
    By Ralph Caola

31. TWINS WIN IN EXTRA INNINGS ON OPENING DAY 95
    April 12, 1965: Minnesota Twins 5, New York Yankees 4 (11 Innings)
    By Steve West

32. KILLEBREW BELTS TWO HOMERS, INCLUDING GAME-WINNER IN EIGHTH 98
    May 12, 1965: Minnesota Twins 4, Los Angeles Angels 3
    By Gregory H. Wolf

33. TEBBETTS'S TECHNICALITY TURNS TIDE FROM TWINS TO TRIBE AFTER KAAT'S WARDROBE MALFUNCTION 100
    June 9, 1965: Cleveland Indians 2, Minnesota Twins 1
    By Nathan Bierma

34. HARMON KILLEBREW CLOUTS WALKOFF HOME RUN TO BEAT YANKEES 103
    July 11, 1965: Minnesota Twins 6, New York Yankees 5
    By Gregory H. Wolf

35. SENIOR CIRCUIT TAKES CHARGE IN MINNESOTA'S FIRST ALL-STAR GAME 105
    July 13, 1965: National League 6, American League 5
    By Greg Erion

36. TWINS TAKE GAME ONE OF WORLD SERIES IN KOUFAX'S ABSENCE 109
    October 6, 1965: Minnesota Twins 8, Los Angeles Dodgers 2
    By Norm King

37. TWINS BEAT DODGERS AT THEIR OWN GAME TO TAKE COMMANDING SERIES LEAD 111
    October 7, 1965: Minnesota Twins 5, Los Angeles Dodgers 1
    By Norm King

38. MUDCAT TIES THE SERIES WITH PITCHING, HITTING IN GAME SIX 113
    October 13, 1965: Minnesota Twins 5, Los Angeles Dodgers 1
    By Norm King

39. KOUFAX HAS NOTHING TO ATONE FOR IN GAME SEVEN MASTERPIECE 115
    October 14, 1965: Minnesota Twins 5, Los Angeles Dodgers 1
    By Norm King

40. DEAN CHANCE, JACKIE WARNER, AND BASERUNNING BLUNDERS DOOM THE TWINS 117
    April 16, 1966: California 3 Minnesota 2
    By Thomas E. Merrick

41. TWINS COME FROM BEHIND TO DEFEAT A'S 9-4 BEHIND FIVE HOME RUNS IN THE SEVENTH 120
    June 9, 1966: Minnesota Twins 9, Kansas City Athletics 4
    By Bob Webster

42. JIM KAAT OUTDUELS EARL WILSON FOR 25TH WIN 123
    September 25, 1966: Minnesota Twins 1, Detroit Tigers 0
    by Steve Ginader

43. KILLEBREW BLASTS TWO TAPE-MEASURE HOME RUNS ON CONSECUTIVE DAYS 125

    June 3 and 4, 1967: Minnesota Twins 8, California Angels 6; Minnesota Twins 8, California Angels 7
    By Thomas J. Brown Jr.

44. DEAN CHANCE IS PERFECT FOR FIVE INNINGS ... 128

    August 6, 1967: Minnesota Twins 5, Boston Red Sox 0 (5 Innings)
    By Stew Thornley

45. RELIEVER'S 10 SHUTOUT INNINGS HELP SENATORS OUTLAST TWINS 130

    August 9, 1967: Washington Senators 9, Minnesota Twins 7 (20 Innings)
    By Andrew Sharp

46. THE GAME WITH ALMOST EVERYTHING 133

    June 18, 1968: Minnesota Twins 9, Washington Senators 8
    by Rich Arpi

47. CÉSAR TOVAR PLAYS ALL NINE POSITIONS, LEADS TWINS TO VICTORY 136

    September 22, 1968: Minnesota Twins 2, Oakland Athletics 1
    by Mike Huber

48. BILLY MARTIN'S HOME DEBUT 139

    April 18, 1969: Minnesota Twins 6, California Angels 0
    By Dave Mona

49. TOVAR AND CAREW STEAL HOME IN THE SAME INNING 142

    May 18, 1969: Detroit Tigers 8, Minnesota Twins 2
    By Thomas J. Brown Jr.

50. EARLY FIREWORKS DOOM A'S IN BIG SERIES OPENER 145

    July 4, 1969: Minnesota Twins 10, Oakland Athletics 4
    by Steve Ginader

51. KILLEBREW DOES IT AGAIN: TWO-RUN GAME-WINNING HOMER; TWINS COME FROM BEHIND TO DEFEAT A'S 7-6 147

    July 6, 1969: Minnesota Twins 7, Oakland Athletics 6
    By Bob Webster

52. METROPOLITAN STADIUM POSTPONEMENTS 150

53. REESE PINCH-HIT SLAM ENDS MCNALLY'S STREAK 159

    August 3, 1969: Minnesota Twins 5, Baltimore Orioles 2
    By Stew Thornley

54. PERRY'S 20TH VICTORY PUSHES TWINS NEARER PENNANT 161

    September 20, 1969: Minnesota Twins 3, Seattle Pilots 2
    By Doug Skipper

55. KILLEBREW'S PERFECT DAY NOT ENOUGH TO BEAT PILOTS AND CLINCH DIVISION TITLE 165

    September 21, 1969: Seattle Pilots 4, Minnesota Twins 3
    By Mike Lynch

56. OCTOBER 6, 1969: TWINS PLAY FIRST PLAYOFF GAME IN METROPOLITAN STADIUM 168

    Baltimore Orioles 11, Minnesota Twins 2
    By Thomas J. Brown Jr.

57. EARL WILSON NEARLY ACHIEVES A "LITTLE LEAGUE HOME RUN" AFTER STRIKING OUT 171

    April 25, 1970: Minnesota Twins 4, Detroit Tigers 3
    By Chad Moody

58. WILLIAMS AND QUILICI PICK OFF A WIN VERSUS CLEVELAND 174

    April 29, 1970: Minnesota Twins 1, Cleveland Indians 0
    By Tom Hawthorn

59. BOMB THREAT PROVIDES EXTRA EXCITEMENT IN TWINS-RED SOX GAME 177

    August 25, 1970: Boston Red Sox 1, Minnesota Twins 0
    By Stew Thornley

60. ROYALS' SIX-RUN NINTH INNING RUINS PERRY'S CHANCE FOR A 25-WIN SEASON 180

    September 29, 1970: Kansas City Royals 14, Minnesota Twins 13 (12 Innings)
    By Bob Webster

61. SLAM, ERRORS GIVE ORIOLES PLAYOFF OPENER 182

    October 3, 1970: Baltimore Orioles 10, Minnesota Twins 6
    By Stew Thornley

62. ORIOLES' BATS BLAST TWINS TO TAKE 2-0 ALCS LEAD 184

    October 4, 1970: Baltimore Orioles 11, Minnesota Twins 3
    By Stew Thornley

63. TORNADOES DON'T TWIST TWINS' FORTUNES 187

    June 4, 1971: Cleveland Indians 4, Minnesota Twins 2 (6 Innings)
    By Gordon Gattie

64. BLUE'S 13 STRIKEOUTS AND MITTERWALD'S ERRANT THROW SPARK OAKLAND WIN 190

    June 21, 1971: Oakland Athletics 3, Minnesota Twins 2
    By Gordon Gattie

65. QUIET AS KITTENS AGAINST KAAT, NEW YORK ROARS BACK AGAINST MINNESOTA PEN TO BEST TWINS 193

    July 30, 1971: New York Yankees 11, Minnesota Twins 9
    By Mark S. Sternman

66. WILLIE MAYS AND HARMON KILLEBREW DELIGHT TWINS FANS 195

    August 9, 1971: Minnesota Twins 5, San Francisco Giants 2
    By Thomas E. Merrick

67. KILLEBREW ENDS HOME RUN DROUGHT BY JOINING 500 CLUB 197

    August 10, 1971: Baltimore Orioles 4, Minnesota Twins 3
    By Richard Cuicchi

68. KILLEBREW'S PINCH-HIT GRAND SLAM PROPELS TWINS TO 9-4 WIN OVER ATHLETICS 199

    September 3, 1971: Minnesota Twins 9, Oakland Athletics 4 (Game 1)
    By Doug Skipper

69. RED ROSES, BLUE BUTTONS, AND A MITTERWALD WALK-OFF 201

    September 3, 1971: Minnesota Twins 2, Oakland Athletics 1 (Second Game of Doubleheader)
    By Gordon Gattie

70. BREWERS, TWINS TAKE TWO DAYS, 22 INNINGS TO FINISH 204

    May 12-13, 1972: Milwaukee Brewers 4, Minnesota Twins 3 (22 Innings)
    By Stew Thornley

71. JULY 7, 1972: KILLEBREW'S HOMER WINS QUILICI DEBUT 207

    Minnesota Twins 5, New York Yankees 2
    By Dana Yost

72. YANKEES' BERNIE ALLEN DOES IN FORMER TEAMMATES 210

    July 8, 1972: New York Yankees 1, Minnesota Twins 0 (11 Innings)
    By Stew Thornley

73. REESE'S PINCH GRAND SLAM LEAVES TWINS SHORT OF VICTORY 212

    July 9, 1972: New York Yankees 9, Minnesota Twins 6
    By Stew Thornley

74. EDDIE BANE MAKES MAJOR-LEAGUE DEBUT FOR TWINS IN INDEPENDENCE DAY SELLOUT 214

    July 4, 1973: Kansas City Royals 5, Minnesota Twins 4
    By Steve Smith

75. KAAT DEFEATS FORMER TEAMMATES IN COMPLETE-GAME DUEL WITH ALBURY 216

    June 22, 1974: Chicago White Sox 3, Minnesota Twins 1 (10 Innings)
    By Richard Cuicchi

76. HISLE HOMER HELPS BLYLEVEN OVERCOME RANGERS ON INDEPENDENCE DAY 219

    July 4, 1974: Minnesota Twins 3, Texas Rangers 1
    By Frederick C. Bush

77. THREE EXTRA-INNING COMEBACKS AND WIN FOR LOCAL PITCHER IN BIG-LEAGUE DEBUT 222

    September 10, 1974: Minnesota Twins 8, CHICAGO WHITE SOX 7 (15 Innings)
    By Gordon Gattie

78. PETE MACKANIN SAVES OFFICIAL SCORER'S DILEMMA 225

    October 1, 1974: Minnesota Twins 6, Texas Rangers 0
    By Stew Thornley

79. JENKINS FOILS HUGHES'S NO-HIT BID AS RANGERS TAKE 1974 FINALE FROM TWINS 227

    October 2, 1974: Texas Rangers 2, Minnesota Twins 1
    By Frederick C. Bush

80. MAY 4, 1975: TWINS RETIRE KILLEBREW'S NUMBER BEFORE BEATING ROYALS 230

    Minnesota Twins 6, Kansas City Royals 3
    By Thomas J. Brown Jr.

81. CAREW STEALS HOME AS HUGHES OUTDUELS PERRY IN WHITEWASH OF INDIANS 232

    May 14, 1975: Minnesota Twins 3, Cleveland Indians 0
    By Frederick C. Bush

82. KILLEBREW HITS FINAL HOME RUN 235

    September 18, 1975: Kansas City Royals 4, Minnesota Twins 3
    By Paul Hofmann

83. TWINS FANS BOO BLYLEVEN IN FINAL START BEFORE TRADE, BLYLEVEN MAKES OBSCENE GESTURE 237

    May 31, 1976: California Angels 3, Minnesota Twins 2
    By Mike Lynch

84. YOUTH IS SERVED AS TIGERS TOP TWINS 7-3 240

    June 20, 1976: Detroit Tigers 7, Minnesota Twins 3
    By Bill Schneider

85. BLYLEVEN TRIUMPHANT IN RETURN TO THE MET 243

    July 26, 1976: Texas Rangers 3, Minnesota Twins
    By Bob Wood

86. SINGER SETS STAGE FOR BAD NIGHT WITH ANTHEM FLUB 245

    August 17, 1976: Baltimore Orioles 10, Minnesota Twins 3
    By J. G. Preston

87. LATE SEASON OFFICIAL SCORING CONTROVERSY ENDED BY NINTH-INNING HIT 247

    September 25, 1976: Minnesota Twins 6, California Angels 0
    By Sarah Johnson

88. ADAMS'S EIGHT RBIS, CAREW'S FIVE RUNS LEAD TWINS IN SLUGFEST 250

   June 26, 1977: Minnesota Twins 19, Chicago White Sox 12
   By Jim McKernon

89. LARRY HISLE'S BUNT HELPS DAVE GOLTZ BEAT NOLAN RYAN 253

   July 21, 1977: Minnesota Twins 3, California Angels 2
   By Thomas E. Merrick

90. JULY 27, 1978: CUBBAGE HITS FOR THE CYCLE; PERZANOWSKI GETS HIS ONLY COMPLETE-GAME VICTORY 256

   Minnesota Twins 6, Toronto Blue Jays 3
   By Dan Levitt

91. DISCO DAN'S BLUNDER HANDS TROUT FIRST MAJOR-LEAGUE VICTORY 258

   September 5, 1978: Chicago White Sox 4 Minnesota Twins 3
   By Paul Hofmann

92. ALL ABOUT RODNEY 261

   April 17, 1979: California Angels 6, Minnesota Twins 0
   By Bob Tholkes

93. KOOSMAN REACHES 20-WIN PLATEAU FOR SECOND TIME 264

   September 30, 1979: Minnesota Twins 5, Milwaukee Brewers 0
   By Brian Wright

94. GROUND GEOFF 267

   July 5, 1980: Minnesota Twins 2, Texas Rangers 1
   By Bob Tholkes

95. CLUTCH HOMERS BY HATCHER AND SMALLEY LEAD TWINS TO WIN OVER RED SOX 269

   May 12, 1981: Minnesota Twins 4, Boston Red Sox 3 (10 Innings)
   By Brian M. Frank

96. TWINS DOWN A'S TO TAKE '81 'REOPENER' 271

   August 10, 1981: Minnesota Twins 6, Oakland Athletics 1
   By Peter Seidel

97. TWINS OVERSHADOWED BY THE PAST 273

   August 15, 1981: Seattle Mariners 6, Minnesota Twins 0
   By Bob Tholkes

98. THE MET CLOSES WITH A LOSS 275

   September 30, 1981: Kansas City Royals 5, Minnesota Twins 2
   By Joe O'Connell

99. CONTRIBUTOR BIOGRAPHIES 279

INTRODUCTION

Metropolitan Stadium was the result of a civic-business-political collaboration to bring major-league baseball to Minnesota. It was born in concept when the Boston Braves of the National League moved to Milwaukee before the 1953 season, the first movement of a major-league team in 50 years. With a half-century of inertia broken, fans in other Midwestern cities developed hope for a team of their own.

Minneapolis formed a committee to land a major-league team and soon determined that a new stadium would be needed. They tried to lure the St. Louis Browns for the 1954 season, offering to expand a spartan stadium on the city park board's Parade Grounds on the western edge of downtown Minneapolis until a new stadium could be built. The Browns instead went to Baltimore, and the Minneapolis baseball committee set its sights on building a new ballpark before focusing on attracting another team.

Minneapolis did the heavy lifting – city government working with business and civic leaders – to finance a stadium with the sale of bonds to investors and through public subscriptions. The Minneapolis interests didn't even plan to locate the new stadium within their city limits, instead choosing a site in a village to the south called Bloomington. The placement wasn't to assuage or lure those in a city to the east, St. Paul. (They were neither assuaged nor lured.) The selection of a suburban location fit with a postwar trend to get to open areas, sites with good highway access and plenty of parking.

The groundbreaking, on a former cornfield, took place on June 20, 1955, before a crowd of spectators and dignitaries, including Minneapolis Mayor Eric Hoyer but not St. Paul Mayor Joseph Dillon, who had already said his city would not support this stadium site. In late September, Matty Schwab was brought in to oversee the laying of sod and work on the infield. Schwab was the groundskeeper at the Polo Grounds – the home of the New York Giants, the parent club of the Minneapolis Millers, who would be the tenants in the new ballpark until a major-league team came along.

The first load of structural steel didn't arrive until mid-January in 1956. At the same time, the brickwork began. The structure rose quickly over the next month. Steel erection for the second and third decks began on February 10 with the placement of the first seats in the lower deck starting a week later.

On Sunday, February 26, an explosion rocked the site, setting off a fire on the third-base side of the grandstand that made it necessary to rebuild one section of it. The placement of the concrete had just been completed, and butane heaters were being used to warm the concrete as it cured. "Exploding tanks ripped through the concrete floor and one bomb-like tank landed a few feet from the left-field fence, almost the first home run in the new stadium," said narrator Dick Enroth in a film made by WCCO Radio and Television soon after the stadium opened. Another fire struck a set of storage shacks barely three weeks later although this did not affect the stadium itself.

Despite the setbacks, construction remained on track and on Tuesday, April 24, 1956 – barely 10 months after groundbreaking – the Minneapolis Millers played the Wichita Braves. The facility was still without an official name, which did not come until that July when it was announced that it would be called Metropolitan Stadium. The distances down the line to right and left were 316 feet 3 inches, and the distance to center field was 405 feet; the outfield fences were 8 feet high.

A good-luck baseball signed by the Minneapolis Millers was dropped into the first batch of concrete for Met Stadium.

METROPOLITAN STADIUM

A large sign – proclaiming Metropolitan Sports Area – was by the main entrance/exit on Cedar Avenue.

A triple-decked permanent grandstand extended only to the end of each of the dugouts, although portable seating expanded the capacity, and a crowd of 18,366 attended the first game.

One of the most significant components of Met Stadium was not what it had, but what it didn't have: posts to support the upper decks as the Met became the first baseball stadium in the country to take advantage of cantilever construction.

It took five years, but Met Stadium eventually achieved the goal set for it, drawing a major-league team. In October 1960 Calvin Griffith announced he was moving his American League Washington Senators franchise to Minnesota, and the Minnesota Twins took the field the following spring.

Met Stadium needed expanding for its new tenants. Bloomington, no longer a village and now a city of more than 50,000, was content to let its benefactors in Minneapolis continue doing the work. Although irritated by Bloomington's resistance to paying a part of the renovation and maintenance expense, the Minneapolis City Council used its credit rating to endorse a financing plan to cover the expansion costs.

Originally, the triple-decked grandstand extended only around the infield. With the arrival of the Twins, the first two decks were extended beyond the foul pole in right field, although a similar extension was not done in the other direction. A section of reserved seats, made up of blue folding chairs, with wooden bleachers farther up, filled the gap down the left-field line. For many years, fans with a general-admission ticket could choose to sit either in these bleachers or in the outfield.

Of course, many who paid the dollar-and-a-half for general admission upgraded themselves by roving into the permanent grandstand, a practice that stopped in 1977 when Griffith confined all general-admission buyers to the outfield. Before that, the Andy Frain gendarmes made little effort to keep the general-admission fans out of the good seats.

Some intrepid fans didn't even bother with tickets. The Met had multicolored bricks on the exterior with open beams, which offered a route to non-acrophobic freeloaders. Those who could shinny up an I-beam and then a set of crossbeams could get to a gap between the first and second decks. The most out-of-the-way spot for such an ascent was toward the right-field corner. The downside was that this was also in the vicinity of the police room. A fan once got up to the gap, glanced down, and saw two police officers, who barked, "Get down here!" Feigning deafness, the fan ignored the order and slithered into the stadium.

To accommodate the stadium's other primary tenant, the Minnesota Vikings of the National Football League, the bleachers in left field were replaced by a double-decked grandstand in 1965. (Work on the grandstand was continuing as the season opened, and one of the construction workers was able to corral a home-run ball hit into the stands by Elston Howard of the New York Yankees in the season opener.)

The new grandstand allowed more fans to sit along the sidelines for football games. The Twins also benefited from the extra capacity provided by the grandstand as they hosted two major events in 1965. The first was the All-Star Game in July. An added bonus was the World Series as Minnesota won the American League pennant. The Twins lost the World Series to the Los Angeles Dodgers in seven games with the final game drawing 50,596, the only time a baseball crowd exceeded 50,000 at Met Stadium.

Even the double-decked addition didn't make the Met a good venue for football. The gridiron ran from right field toward third base, with barely enough room to squeeze in the playing field and end zones. The space between the sidelines and the stands was vast for football (only half-vast for baseball).

In 1967 the Met Stadium gained a neighbor – the Metropolitan Sports Center (later known as Met

MEMORABLE GAMES AT MINNESOTA'S DIAMOND ON THE PRAIRIE

Center) – built for the arrival of the Minnesota North Stars of the National Hockey League. The heading on the large sign by the parking lot's main entrance on Cedar Avenue was changed from Metropolitan Stadium to Metropolitan Sports Area. Inside the parking lot, the different sections were identified with signs containing the name and logo of the other teams in the American League.

Bloomington native Steve Rushin, in *The 34-Ton Bat*, wrote that Baltimore's Boog Powell walked through the parking lot after games to get to the team hotel, just to the north of the sports area, and he sometimes got waylaid by gregarious revelers. Rushin said Powell told him he once failed to make it back to the hotel, instead bunking in the Winnebago of some fans who had offered him refreshments.

From 1961 to 1970, the Twins had mostly competitive teams and drew at least 1 million fans, then considered a benchmark for success. The team plunged in the standings and also in attendance in 1971 and stayed down for many years. The drop in fortunes corresponded with the rise of the Minnesota Vikings, and the moribund Twins were even outdone by a new soccer team, the Kicks, in 1976. Tailgating was a trademark of the Vikings and Kicks but – aside from Boog Powell's experiences – it didn't catch on with baseball fans until later in the 1970s.

With the Minnesota Vikings becoming the hottest item on the Minnesota sports scene, talks began regarding remodeling Met Stadium to improve the sight lines for football or even building a brand-new stadium for just the Vikings. It was expected that since Minneapolis interests had sold the bonds for the original stadium construction, funding for an upgrade for the Met would come, once again, from Minneapolis.

But this time the Minneapolis business community decided that, if it was going to foot the bill, it might as well have a stadium within its own city limits. Amy Klobuchar in *Uncovering the Dome*, a book that resulted from her senior thesis at Yale College, wrote that Minneapolis took the stance of, "Why should we use the city's money to subsidize a hot shot, ungrateful ex-cow town? Why not use the city's money to help the city?"

One of the first proposals was for a domed football stadium on the northwestern edge of downtown Minneapolis, although this plan was eventually derailed. In 1977 the Minnesota Legislature passed a no-site stadium bill, one that was initially palatable even to the anti-Minneapolis contingent in the state. This action by itself did not mean the end of Metropolitan Stadium, because the options included a remodeling of the Met for baseball with a new football stadium built adjacent to it. However, the new stadium commission, which was formed by the legislation, opted for a multipurpose covered facility on the eastern edge of downtown Minneapolis.

The Twins, in their final years at Met Stadium, twice more topped 1 million in attendance, in 1977 and 1979. The 1977 season was exciting for fans because of the play of the team, which was in the title race for much of the season, and because of Rod Carew, who finished the season with a .388 batting average and was named the American League Most Valuable Player.

The biggest day of the season came on Sunday, June 26, as the Twins played the Chicago White Sox. With first place in the West Division at stake and the fans receiving a replica Carew jersey as a giveaway, a crowd of nearly 47,000 turned out for a wild game. Glenn Adams provided the early fireworks with a grand slam en route to a team-record eight runs batted in. The Twins took an 8-1 lead, only to have the White Sox cut the gap with six runs in the third inning. The parade across the plate continued for both teams, unimpeded by even an alcohol-laced fan who interrupted the game in the bottom of the fourth by climbing to the top of the foul pole in left field. The Twins won the game, 19-12. Carew had four hits, scored five runs, and drove in six runs, capping his performance in the last of the eighth inning with a home run that raised his batting average to .403 and drew another long ovation from the fans.

In 1979 the Twins stayed in the race until the final week of the season and drew 1 million fans for the second time since 1970 and for the last time at Met Stadium.

The final baseball game at the Met was played on September 30, 1981, with the Kansas City Royals beating the Twins 5-2. Roy Smalley popped out to end the game and an era of baseball on the former cornfield. The final event at the Met was a Vikings football game on Sunday, December 20, 1981. After the game, fans in search of souvenirs ravaged the stadium, taking what wasn't bolted down and many things that were.

Met Stadium remained partially dismantled for several years before being totally demolished, and it stayed a vacant site for several more years before a shopping center was built. A plaque marking the spot of home plate was installed in an amusement-park area in the middle of the shopping center.

METROPOLITAN STADIUM

SOURCES

Several publications provided general information on Metropolitan Stadium and the Metrodome: *Metropolitan Sports Area Stadium: Stadium Souvenir*, published by the Metropolitan Sports Area Commission in 1956: 10; *A Decade at the Met*, by the Minneapolis Chamber of Commerce (1966); *History of the Metropolitan Stadium and Sports Center*, by Charles Johnson (Minneapolis: Midwest Federal, 1970); and *Once There Was a Ballpark*, by Joe Soucheray (Edina, Minnesota: Dorn Books, 1981).

A film, Metropolitan Stadium, was produced by WCCO Radio and Television shortly after the opening of Met Stadium in 1956. Narrated by Dick Enroth, this is essentially a film promoting the new stadium as well as the Twin Cities metropolitan area for the purpose of luring major-league baseball to the area. However, it contains footage of the final game of Nicollet Park and its demolition, the groundbreaking of the Bloomington stadium, the fire during construction in February 1956, and the first game on April 24, 1956. The film is available at the Minnesota Historical Society.

General resources on the Metrodome include *The Hubert H. Humphrey Metrodome Souvenir Book*, compiled by Dave Mona (Minneapolis: MSP Publications, 1982), and *Uncovering the Dome: Was the Public Interest Served in Minnesota's 10-year Political Brawl over the Metrodome?*, by Amy Klobuchar (Minneapolis: Bolger Publications, 1982).

Additional sources of information on Metropolitan Stadium and the Metrodome include *Stadiums and Major League Sports: The Twin Cities*, by James Quirk (a publication of the Brookings Institute, 1997), and Stadium Games by Jay Weiner (Minneapolis: University of Minnesota Press, 2000).

OTHER SOURCES:

Beebe, Bob. "Triple-Decked Stadium Is a Construction 'Miracle,'" *Minneapolis Tribune*, April 22, 1956: 16.

Cowles, John Jr. "City Gets Stadium Bond Go-Ahead," *Minneapolis Tribune*, July 1, 1954: 1.

Cullum, Dick. "First Step Taken Toward Bringing Big League Baseball to Twin Cities," *Minneapolis Tribune*, March 24, 1952: 1.

Hall, Halsey. "Baseball Backers Dig Up Bloomington Diamond in Rough," *Minneapolis Star*, June 20, 1955: 1.

Hertz, Will. "Work Starts on New Baseball Stadium," *Minneapolis Tribune*, June 21, 1955: 1.

Rushin, Steve. *The 34-Ton Bat: The Story of Baseball as Told through Bobble Heads, Cracker Jacks, Jockstraps, Eye Black, and 375 Other Strange and Unforgettable Objects* (New York: Little, Brown and Company, 2013).

"National League Moves Braves to Milwaukee," *Minneapolis Tribune*, March 19, 1953: 1

"Fire Sweeps Stadium in Bloomington," *Minneapolis Tribune*, February 27, 1956: 1.

Stadium Damage Estimated at $50,000," *Minneapolis Star*, February 27, 1956: 1.

"2nd Fire Strikes New Stadium," *St. Paul Pioneer Press*, March 20, 1956: 1.

"Take Me Out to the Ball Park," *Construction Bulletin*, May 3, 1956: 52-55.

"'Metropolitan Stadium' Is Now Official Name," *Minneapolis Tribune*, July 20, 1956: 15.

"New Look in Minneapolis," *Sports Illustrated*, August 20, 1956: 36.

"You Can't Sit Behind Posts in New Stadium," *Minneapolis Tribune*, April 22, 1956: 16.

PLAY OF FOUR DECISIONS ENSURES BALLPARK'S DEBUT IS MEMORABLE

APRIL 24, 1956: WICHITA BRAVES 5, MINNEAPOLIS MILLERS 3[1]

By Joel Rippel

The first game played in a new ballpark is always noteworthy. Minneapolis Millers manager Eddie Stanky helped ensure that the Millers' debut in their new home in suburban Bloomington was memorable.

After playing the first six games of the 1956 American Association season on the road, the Millers returned home to christen the yet-to-be named ballpark in a game against the Wichita Braves.

The Millers, who had won the American Association title and the Junior World Series in 1955, featured a young lineup. Stanky's batting order for the home opener had an average age of 24. Three of the starters – Joey Amalfitano, Bill White, and Willie Kirkland – were 22. Starting pitcher Jim Constable, who was starting his third consecutive Millers home opener, was 23.

Wichita, which was in its first season in the American Association after relocating from Toledo, brought a 2-5 record into the game. The Millers were 3-3.

On a sunny Tuesday afternoon (it was 56 degrees at the game's 2:30 P.M. start), an American Association record crowd of 18,366 was "thoroughly entertained, however, by more than umpires' decisions."[2]

The Minneapolis Millers line up before the first game at the new stadium in Bloomington.

METROPOLITAN STADIUM

Wichita left-hander Charlie Gorin, who was 10-12 with a 4.15 earned-run average for Toledo in 1955, pitched a complete game in the Braves' 5-3 victory. Gorin allowed just six hits and two earned runs to earn his first victory of the season. He struck out five while overcoming seven walks.

The Braves, who had 10 hits off Constable and four Millers relievers, opened the scoring in the first inning on a double to right-center by Vin Garcia and a single by Bob Thorpe.

The Millers got the run back in the third inning when Amalfitano walked, stole second, and scored on White's single to right.

The Braves scored twice in the tumultuous fifth inning. Bob Hazle walked and Joe Koppe reached on an error by Millers third baseman Ozzie Virgil on a potential double-play grounder. Garcia struck out but Hazle scored and Koppe took third on Thorpe's single to right.

With Billy Queen batting, Koppe broke for home. Millers catcher Vern Rapp took Constable's pitch "and made a great glove-hand stab to tag out Koppe."[3]

Home-plate umpire Bob Phillips initially signaled Koppe out. That brought Wichita manager George Selkirk out of the dugout. After conferring with third-base umpire John Mullen, Phillips changed his call and signaled that Koppe was safe.

Stanky rushed out to argue. Phillips and Mullen conversed again, and Phillips reversed his call and again ruled Koppe out.

That brought a return of Selkirk. The two umpires again conversed, and Phillips again changed his call. This ruling was final: Koppe was safe, which gave the Braves a 3-1 lead.

That brought Stanky, who had been ejected 27 times during his 11-year major-league playing career and 16 times during his time (1952-55) as manager of the St. Louis Cardinals, for an encore that eventually saw him "set the record for drop-kicking his baseball cap after he had slammed it to the ground."[4]

Stanky and catcher Rapp were both ejected by Phillips.

"I hated to get run out of my first game in Minneapolis, but I couldn't help it," said Stanky.[5]

Apparently the disagreement was fueled when Phillips misheard Selkirk's original argument.

"I protested on the basis of catcher Vern Rapp of Minneapolis dropping the ball, and Phillips thought I was asking for a balk to be called," Selkirk said.[6]

That is why Phillips changed his call the first time. After Stanky objected to that, Phillips said, "Then I went down to ask John [Mullen] if he had called a balk."[7]

Mullen told Phillips he hadn't called a balk, so Phillips called Koppe out again.

Selkirk then told Phillips, "I didn't say he balked, he dropped the ball."[8]

Phillips went back to Mullen and asked him if Rapp had dropped the ball. Mullen said he had.

After the game, Mullen said, "Phillips wasn't in a position to see the ball, so I reversed the decision when I saw that Rapp dropped the ball."[9]

Rapp acknowledged that he had dropped the ball, "but after I held it long enough for the putout."[10]

Stanky, who had managed the St. Louis Cardinals for 3½ seasons before being fired in late May of 1955, said after the game, "I hate indecision on the baseball field. I can excuse young umpires for indecision, but we had an experienced group, including chief umpire John Mullen. I hate passing the buck. I'm glad this happened in the presence of league president Ed Doherty."[11]

The Millers regrouped and scored two runs in the sixth inning to tie the score. After Virgil reached on an error, Jake Jensen, who had replaced Rapp after Rapp was ejected, hit a long home run to left center. It was his first home run of the season.

The Braves regained the lead with two runs in the eighth inning. Ed McHugh singled and eventually scored on a wild pitch, and Ben Taylor singled and eventually scored on a squeeze-play bunt by Koppe.

Gorin shut down the Millers over the final three innings.

"Charlie Gorin had good stuff," said Selkirk, who spent nine seasons in the major leagues with the New York Yankees. "He used his fastball and curve to advantage; this was his first start since coming down from Milwaukee. We used him in relief for an inning last week against Omaha. Gorin never had much luck against Minneapolis in that bandbox at Nicollet Park. But it's a lot different pitching in this beautiful park. We used to throw the bunt and squeeze out the window at Nicollet. Here you can play baseball like it should be played."[12]

Gorin said, "I pitched only 2⅔ innings in spring training with Milwaukee, so I'm a little wild. This is a great place to pitch in, quite a bit different than Nicollet Park.[13]

Thorpe had three hits and Hazle had two for the Braves. Jenkins, the only Miller with more than one hit, was 2-for-2.

MEMORABLE GAMES AT MINNESOTA'S DIAMOND ON THE PRAIRIE

Doherty, who spent nearly 50 years in professional baseball including 7½ as the president of the American Association before becoming the first general manager of the "second" Washington Senators, enjoyed the day despite the controversy. He said, "This is one of the greatest days in my life, a chance to see stands filled with baseball fans cheering for two minor league teams."[14]

Longtime Minneapolis sportswriter Halsey Hall summed up the day by mentioning perhaps the oldest fan in attendance: "Probably no one in the crowd or anywhere else could match the record held by John McHugh, who lives at the Masonic home. McHugh, formerly of Red Wing, [Minnesota,] is a jolly 98 and he played in the first game he ever saw. That, mind you, was in 1878. 'I was a catcher,' he recalled in his ground floor box seat right in back of home plate. 'See.' And, with a chuckle he showed twisted fingers. 'Yes, it's better now, certainly for the catchers. We didn't have much protection.'"[15]

SOURCES

In addition to the sources cited in the Notes, the author consulted Baseball-Reference.com, Newspapers.com, Retrosheet.org, and sabr.org.

NOTES

The Play of Four Decisions still fell short of a greater rhubarb at the Millers' previous home: *October 5, 1932: Minneapolis Millers Come up Short on 'Play of Six Decisions,'* https://sabr.org/gamesproj/game/october-5-1932-minneapolis-millers-come-up-short-on-play-of-six-decisions.

1. The new stadium did not become Metropolitan Stadium until July 1956.
2. Tom Briere, "Gorin Stingy with 6 Hits," *Minneapolis Tribune*, April 25, 1956: 13.
3. Briere: 15.
4. Briere: 15.
5. Bob Beebe, "Umpire Claims Two Decisions," *Minneapolis Star*, April 25, 1956: 69.
6. "Voice-by-Voice on Play at Plate," *Minneapolis Tribune*, April 25, 1956: 16.
7. "Voice-by-Voice on Play at Plate."
8. "Voice-by-Voice on Play at Plate."
9. Sid Hartman, "Umps Indecision Irritates Stanky," *Minneapolis Tribune*, April 25, 1956: 14.
10. Hartman, "Umps Indecision."
11. Hartman, "Umps Indecision."
12. Sid Hartman, "Selkirk Hails the Return of 'Baseball,'" *Minneapolis Tribune*, April 25, 1956: 15.
13. Hartman, "Selkirk Hails the Return of 'Baseball.'"
14. "One of Greatest Days of My Life: Doherty," *Minneapolis Tribune*, April 25, 1956: 16.
15. Halsey Hall, "Major Openers," *Minneapolis Star*, April 25, 1956: 70.

MAYS HOMERS TWICE IN SHOWCASE EXHIBITION GAME

JUNE 7, 1956: NEW YORK GIANTS 6, MINNEAPOLIS MILLERS 4

By T.S. Flynn

Six weeks after Opening Day at their new $4.5 million ballpark in Bloomington, Minnesota, the Minneapolis Millers hosted the New York Giants for an exhibition game. Local newspaperman Jim Klobuchar described the still unnamed facility as "an ornate blend of steel, affectionate dreams and civic pride."[2] His colleague Bob Beebe hailed it as "a construction miracle" for going from concept to baseball-ready in just 19 months. But crews were still scrambling to complete the project before the June exhibition after an explosion and fire in the third-base grandstand on February 26 necessitated significant reconstruction of the affected area, a six-week (and counting) inconvenience.[3] Only 21,690 of the planned 30,000 seats were installed in time for the game. Undaunted, Millers business manager George Brophy expressed confidence that fans would buy as many as 2,000 standing-room tickets to congregate behind the chain-link outfield fences for the third annual Giants-Millers showdown.[4] Alas, just 142 fans invested in the $1.10 SRO ducats, including a group who took in the action while seated on wooden crates behind the right-field boundary.[5] In all, 21,832 fans paid to see the game. Workers spent the days and hours before the game touching up paint and preparing for the largest crowd ever to assemble for a baseball game in the Upper Midwest.[6] The final number for the $100,000 scoreboard was put in place just an hour before the first pitch.[7]

The towering, triple-decked stadium didn't rise from 164 acres of farmland[8] to accommodate the Triple-A Millers. They were merely short-term tenants whose residency (and existence) might expire at any time. The easily expandable ballpark was erected to sell Major League Baseball on the viability of Minneapolis as a major-league city, and the exhibition was a chance to show how good it looked with big-league talent on the field. Giants owner Horace Stoneham vented publicly about his displeasure with his club's New York home, the Polo Grounds, and, like Brooklyn Dodgers owner Walter O'Malley, he lobbied for a new ballpark while threatening relocation. A move to Minneapolis made sense. The Giants owned the Millers, so supplanting them would be a simple in-house transaction. On a boozy night in a Minneapolis hotel suite in January of 1954, he allegedly told Brophy and other Millers employees that he had plans to move the Giants to Minneapolis as part of a scheme that would also relocate the Cincinnati Redlegs to New York.[9] A year and a half later, Minnesota's major-league-ready ballpark beckoned.

A move to the Minneapolis metropolitan area was an enticing proposition for many reasons in 1956. With a population approaching 1.5 million, the Twin Cities

Willie Mays had played for the Minneapolis Millers in 1951.

Minnesota Historical Society

metropolitan area was growing quickly and had established its baseball bona fides, supporting two top-notch American Association clubs for more than 50 years. The Millers won the American Association pennant and the Junior World Series in 1955. The University of Minnesota baseball team was on a roll in 1956, too. Just days before the Giants-Millers game, the Gophers defeated Ohio University to advance to the College World Series, a tournament they would win a week later. Minnesota's politicians and titans of business lobbied aggressively for the Twin Cities to join the roster of major-league cities. Newspaper coverage of the exhibition made it clear that the Giants were the primary target of the campaign to replace the Millers.

Stoneham had flown into Bloomington for Opening Day in April, the first game ever played at the new ballpark, and he would return for its dedication game on June 27, but he skipped the exhibition. Instead, the Giants sent a clutch of executives to Bloomington to attend the game and attend to some urgent business beforehand. Vice president Chub Feeney, farm director Carl Hubbell, and chief scout Tom Sheehan met up with rookie Giants manager Bill Rigney the day before the exhibition. The group huddled with Millers general manager Rosy Ryan for much of the afternoon to discuss potential trades. The Giants needed help. They'd slumped into Minnesota as losers of nine of their previous 12 games, in sixth place, nine games under .500, and 8½ games behind the first-place Cardinals, Pirates, and Redlegs.[10] The exhibition provided the New York club a brief but much-needed respite from major-league competition.

Eager though the fans may have been to see the Giants, "it was a late crowd that came from all over the state" for the 8:00 P.M. start, according to *Minneapolis Star and Morning Tribune* executive sports editor Charles Johnson. "There were slowdowns in traffic and some late arrivals in the stands, but the combined efforts of police, sheriffs, civilian defense, Shriners and private individuals took it in stride to move more than 9,000 cars into the huge parking area with much less delay than anyone expected."[11] Once settled in their seats, they witnessed a good game.

The Millers initiated the scoring with a long Gail Harris home run to right off Ramon Monzant in the second inning. In the fourth, Al Dark doubled for the Giants and Willie Mays followed with "a towering blast which cleared the left field fence and landed at the base of the outer fence up a high embankment," according to Bob Beebe. It was the farthest Mays had hit a ball in 1956 and his first home run since May 15.[12]

Mays famously spent a little more than a month with the Millers five years earlier, abusing American Association pitching to the tune of a .477/.524/.799 slash line in 35 games to force his ascension to the Giants at age 20. On this night, of the 16 Giants to appear in the game, the "Say Hey Kid" was one of 13 who had previously played for the Millers.[13] Additionally, rookie Giants manager Rigney was the Millers player-manager in 1954-55 and Sheehan pitched for the team in 1931 and managed them from 1939 to 1943 and in 1946-47.

Most in the crowd had come to watch Mays, and he delivered again in the sixth, crushing his second circuit clout of the game to punctuate the two-run inning. The Millers responded in the seventh, plating three runs to tie via Willie Kirkland and Bob Lennon singles, a fielder's choice grounder by Willie Harris, and Jake Jenkins's homer. The Giants answered with a run in both the eighth and ninth innings, and knuckleballer Hoyt Wilhelm stymied the Millers to lock down the 6-4 win for the big leaguers.

Although the Minneapolis club lost on the field, its new home won over all the right people and secured a victory for the future of baseball in the Twin Cities. Joe King of the *New York World Telegram* asserted from his seat in the press box, "If Horace Stoneham had this Bloomington stadium in New York, just as it is, mind you, he'd draw over 1,250,000 people" per season. "Nobody likes to go to the Polo Grounds," he continued. "It's a freak and it's rather old and run down."[14] Giants players were likewise impressed, stopping short of besmirching their New York home while drawing a clear distinction. "Great lights," said outfielder Dusty Rhodes. His compatriot George Wilson completed the sentiment, "Yeah, easy to pick up the ball in the outfield."[15] In the next morning's *Minneapolis Tribune,* sportswriter Sid Hartman quoted King, who echoed what Twin Cities locals insisted: "The folks here are in the big league business now because they have the stadium. If the Giants aren't forced to come here, another team may gratefully take advantage of the facilities."[16]

NOTES

1. The new stadium did not become Metropolitan Stadium until July 1956.
2. Jim Klobuchar, "Bloomington Stadium Nears Readiness for Miller Opener," *St. Cloud* (Minnesota) *Times*, April 9, 1956: 5.
3. Bob Beebe, "Triple-Decked Stadium Is a Construction 'Miracle,'" *Minneapolis Sunday Tribune*, April 22, 1956: 16.
4. Donald Brostrom, "Record 23,000 to See Millers Play Giants," *Minneapolis Star*, June 7, 1956: 1.

METROPOLITAN STADIUM

5   Bonham Cross, photographer, "Giants Fill Stadium – and Then Some," *Minneapolis Morning Tribune*, June 8, 1956: 18.

6   Charles Johnson, "21,832 See Stadium Pass Another Test," *Minneapolis Morning Tribune*, June 8, 1956: 1D.

7   Bob Beebe, "White: Never Can Let Down in Major League," *Minneapolis Star*, June 8, 1956: 4D.

8   Pat Borzi, "The Giants Almost Headed Not Quite So Far West," *New York Times*, June 17, 2005.

9   Jay Weiner, *Stadium Games: Fifty Years of Big League Greed and Bush League Boondoggles* (Minneapolis: University of Minnesota Press, 2000), 11.

10 Chris Kieran, "Wanted: Some Hits! Giants in the Market," *New York Daily News*, June 7, 1956: C24.

11 Charles Johnson, "21,832 See Stadium Pass Another Test," *Minneapolis Morning Tribune*, June 8, 1956: 43.

12 Bob Beebe, "Millers, Giants Both Profit from Game," *Minneapolis Star*, June 8, 1956: 43.

13 Bob Beebe, "White: Never Can Let Down in Major League."

14 Halsey Hall, "Stadium, as Is, Would Attract 1,296,000 in New York," *Minneapolis Star*, June 8, 1956: 1D.

15 Hall.

16 Sid Hartman, "Stadium Praised; Move Speculated," *Minneapolis Morning Tribune*, June 8, 1956: 24, 26.

A GRATE THROW PRECEDES MILLERS' WIN OVER OMAHA

AUGUST 27, 1956: MINNEAPOLIS MILLERS 2, OMAHA CARDINALS 0

By J. G. Preston

As the first season of play at Metropolitan Stadium neared its end in 1956, the Minneapolis Millers continued a tradition from Nicollet Park days by holding an "Appreciation Night" on August 27, when they played the Omaha Cardinals. In previous years the event showed appreciation for the team members by presenting them with gifts, but this time it was billed as "Stadium Appreciation Night," with fans urged to turn out "in appreciation of the 1956 Millers and also in appreciation of the first season in the new stadium."[1]

The ballpark didn't receive any gifts that night, but all the players and team staff members did, with such goodies as a box of fishing plugs (given to manager Eddie Stanky), an electric frying pan (Ed Bressoud, Ozzie Virgil), socks (Dick Strahs), and a steam iron (business manager George Brophy).[2] That was part of a 90-minute pregame show that included a celebrity slow-pitch softball game (in which Minneapolis Lakers basketball great George Mikan hit a home run), a 100-yard race between Millers outfielder Gil Coan and a horse (given a 20-yard head start, Coan held on to win), an exhibition by golf trick-shot artist Chuck Lewis and his daughter Linda, an award of a plaque to Dick Siebert, coach of the University of Minnesota's 1956 College World Series champions, and the presentation of a $1,000 savings bond to Patricia Healy in honor of her winning essay in the "Name-the-Stadium" contest.[3] One event had to be called off: Millers catcher Vern Rapp was slated to try to catch a baseball dropped out of a Navy helicopter from 600 feet above the field, but the chopper was sidelined with "motor trouble."[4]

One of the pregame events went into the history books, if only briefly, as Millers outfielder Don Grate extended his own world record for the longest baseball throw.

Grate was a two-sport star at Ohio State during World War II. He was twice named second-team All-America in basketball and was selected for the 1944 US Olympic team (although the Olympics were canceled because of World War II). He also played baseball for the Buckeyes and signed with the Philadelphia Phillies after his junior year in 1945, going straight to the big leagues as a pitcher.

Grate was hit hard in his first two appearances in the majors and was sent to the minors, but he returned to the Phillies in September and got another call-up in September 1946. In what turned out to be his final big-league appearance in 1946, "something snapped" in his pitching shoulder.[5] He bounced around the minors for

Before the August 27, 1956 game, Minnesota Gophers coach Dick Siebert was awarded a plaque for winning the 1956 College World Series. Under Siebert, the Gophers won the College World Series again in 1960 and 1964.

University of Minnesota

19

four years after that, then got a job as a high-school teacher and basketball coach and filed his voluntary retirement from baseball.

But Grate changed his mind and gave baseball another shot after the school year ended, when he was acquired by Chattanooga of the Southern Association. Not long after joining the team in 1951, he asked for a chance to play the outfield, and when he hit two inside-the-park home runs in his first game in the garden, his days on the mound were essentially over.[6]

Despite the injury that diminished his pitching ability, Grate still had a fine arm, which he showed off before Chattanooga's final game of the season in 1952. In a pregame exhibition he made a throw measured at 434 feet, 1 inch, the longest ever recorded. And he extended his record the next year with a heave of 443 feet, 3½ inches.

Grate spent five seasons in Chattanooga before moving up to Louisville of the American Association in 1956. In June of that year he was traded to Minneapolis, and on August 27, his 33rd birthday, the Millers gave him a chance to break his own record again.

"Tell the folks I can't be sure [about breaking the record]," Grate told the *Minneapolis Star*. "I've been pitching a lot of batting practice lately and working off that mound is very different from the outfield throw."[7]

The center-field fence was 405 feet from home plate. A gate in the wire fence was opened to give Grate a six-step running head start on his throws. "Don fired two almost to the stands," Halsey Hall wrote in the next day's *Minneapolis Star*. "And then he hurled one that landed in Chuck Lewis' golf bag dead against the box seat backstop."[8]

The throw was measured at 445 feet, 1 inch – a new record. But the fact that it landed in the golf bag may have kept it from going even farther. "That [throw] hit eight or ten feet up on the backstop," Grate said years later. "They only measured it to the bottom of the backstop. You should probably add another 10 or 15 feet to it."[9]

Grate may have been exaggerating how much farther his throw would have gone, but for the rest of his life he remained convinced he was the rightful holder of the longest-throw record, even after another American Association outfielder, Glen Gorbous, broke the mark by 9 inches with a throw of 445 feet, 10 inches in Omaha on August 1, 1957. (No one has attempted to top Gorbous's record since.) "I felt I threw it further even though it wasn't the official record," Grate said in 2006.[10]

MACADAM ROAD RACE CLASSIC

Different events – from wrestling matches to a Beatles concert – were held inside Metropolitan Stadium, but a regular event outside the stadium was the Macadam Road Race Classic. Sports cars traversed a 1.5-mile track on the perimeter roads that encircled the parking area and stadium. Sanctioned by the Land O'Lakes Sports Car Club of America, the race featured sharp turns, long and short straightaways, and obstacle areas. A 1,300-foot straightaway along Cedar Avenue, on the west side of the Met, allowed drivers to reach speeds of 120 MPH. Approximately 3,500 fans watched from the inside of the track in the initial race, held on Sunday, October 14, 1956. The race continued annually through the end of the 1950s.

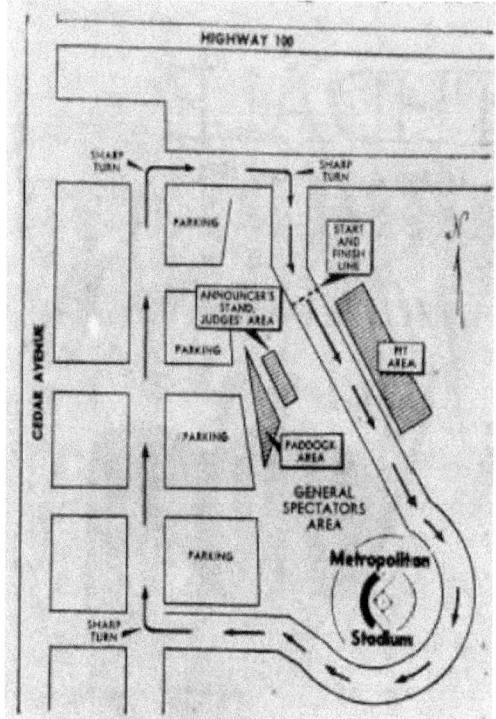

The Macadam Road Race Classic was held in the 1950s outside Met Stadium.

For the record, Don Grate's gifts on "Appreciation Night" were slacks and walking shorts.

Once the golf bag and the horse and the frying pans had cleared the field, the 10,620 fans settled in to watch the Millers' Roger Bowman pitch a five-hit shutout in a 2-0 win. Bowman, a 29-year-old veteran with 50 major-league appearances under his belt, had been purchased from Buffalo of the International League two weeks earlier.[11]

"I did that the hard way," Bowman said. "Seemed like I was always behind the hitters three and nothing and three and one [he walked four in the game]." He primarily threw his curveball and slider: "I could count the fastballs I threw on my two hands."[12]

The Millers scored twice against Omaha's Ed Mayer. Singles by Gail Harris and Willie Kirkland and a sacrifice fly by Jake Jenkins produced the first run in the second inning. Then in the fifth, Bowman led off with a double, moved to third on a single by Wayne Terwilliger, and scored on a single by Rapp, pinch-hitting for Coan.

The Cardinals brought the tying run to the plate in the ninth inning, but the Millers' third double play of the night ended the game. That put the Millers two games ahead of Omaha for third place in the American Association, although that lead soon disappeared; Omaha went 11-3 the rest of the way to finish third, and the Millers were 6-10 down the stretch.

SOURCES

Game stories from the *Minneapolis Tribune* and *Minneapolis Star* were accessed via Newspapers.com. The author has written more about Don Grate in a blog post, "The history of the record for baseball's longest throw, a tale that involves John Hatfield, Honus Wagner, Sheldon Lejeune, Hugh McMullan, Don Grate, Rocky Colavito and Glen Gorbous, among others" prestonjg.wordpress.com/2009/12/04/the-history-of-the-record-for-baseballs-longest-thrown-a-tale-that-involves-john-hatfield-honus-wagner-sheldon-lejeune-don-grate-rocky-colavito-and-glen-gorbous-among-others.

NOTES

1. "Grate Eyes New Mark at 'Appreciation Night,'" *Minneapolis Tribune*, August 16, 1956: 19.
2. The full list of gifts appears in "Grate Breaks Own Baseball Toss Mark," *Minneapolis Tribune*, August 28, 1956: 14.
3. Halsey Hall, "Grate Was Set to 'Try for 400,'" *Minneapolis Star*, August 28, 1956: 11B. The full program was outlined in "Arm, Running Debate 'Settled,'" *Minneapolis Star*, August 27, 1956: 13B.
4. "Grate Breaks Own Baseball Toss Mark," *Minneapolis Tribune*, August 28, 1956: 14. The helicopter stunt was an attempt to break a record set in 1908, when Gabby Street of the Washington Senators caught a ball that was thrown from the top of the Washington Monument, 555 feet high.
5. Kevin T. Czerwinski, "Chattanooga outfielder had Grate-est arm." milb.com/news/minor-leaguer-don-grate-had-historically-great-arm-311376544.
6. Wirt Gammon, "Grate Hits Two Homers, but Chicks Pound Five Triples for 15-7 Victory," *Chattanooga Times*, July 11, 1951: 13. See also Shirley Povich, "Nats High on Lofty Grate as Outfielder," *The Sporting News*, March 12, 1952: 4.
7. "Arm, Running Debate 'Settled,'" *Minneapolis Star*, August 27, 1956: 13B.
8. Halsey Hall, "Grate Was Set to 'Try for 400.'" Hall also contributed to *The Sporting News*, and in the September 5 issue of that publication he wrote that Grate made five throws before breaking the record. Halsey Hall, "Grate Throws Ball 445 Feet, One Inch to Set New Record," *The Sporting News*, September 5, 1956: 30. Hall also served as master of ceremonies for the "Appreciation Night" proceedings.
9. Steven P. Gietschier, "The Longest Throw," greenfieldhistoricalsociety.org/The%20Longest%20Throw.pdf.
10. Kevin T. Czerwinski, "Chattanooga Outfielder Had Grate-est Arm." milb.com/news/minor-leaguer-don-grate-had-historically-great-arm-311376544. This post is dated November 1, 2019, but it's a repost of a story that was first posted in 2006, when Grate threw out the first pitch at a Florida Marlins game on the 50th anniversary of his longest throw; note that Grate, born in 1923, was referred to as being 83 years old. Grate had lived in Miami since 1963 and died in 2014.
11. Tom Briere, "Millers Buy Vet Bowman of Buffalo," *Minneapolis Tribune*, August 12, 1956: S1.
12. Bob Beebe, "Bowman 'Does It Hard Way' for Clutch Miller Shutout," *Minneapolis Star*, August 28, 1956: 11B.

BRAVES AND MILLERS PUT ON A COLD-WEATHER EXHIBITION

APRIL 13, 1957: MILWAUKEE BRAVES 4, MINNEAPOLIS MILLERS 3

By Joel Rippel

The Milwaukee Braves and the Minneapolis Millers were both optimistic heading into their 1957 seasons.

The Braves, who had finished one game behind National League champion Brooklyn in 1956, were the favorite to win the 1957 pennant, according to an Associated Press poll.

"The club looks good," said Braves manager Fred Haney, "I feel we have a club that can win this year."[1]

The Millers, who finished fourth in the American Association in 1956 – their first season at Metropolitan Stadium, were looking for improvement in 1957 with a lineup that featured Felipe Alou, Orlando Cepeda, and Jim Davenport.

Three days before the Braves and Millers were scheduled to open their respective seasons on the road – the Braves in Chicago and the Millers in Indianapolis – they stopped by Metropolitan Stadium for an exhibition tune-up.

The Braves, who trained in Bradenton, Florida, broke their training camp on April 2 and played exhibitions in Jacksonville, San Antonio, Houston, Dallas, Fort Worth, Oklahoma City, Tulsa, Wichita, and Topeka before reaching Minnesota with a 19-10 exhibition record. The Braves were the third major-league team – following the New York Giants and Cleveland Indians in 1956 – to play an exhibition game against the Millers at Metropolitan Stadium.

The Millers, who trained in Sanford, Florida (just outside of Orlando), were 12-6-2 in Florida exhibitions – a record that was highlighted by Alou's .360 batting average and Cepeda's .356 average with 20 runs batted in.

The Braves had a simple approach going into the Saturday afternoon game against the Millers.

"It was a cold day," said Braves pitcher Lew Burdette. "Our big interest was trying to get the game over as fast as we could."[2]

With a game-time temperature of 36 degrees, the Braves used their regular lineup except for third baseman Eddie Mathews, who was in New York for a promotional date. The Braves were managed in Minneapolis by coach Charlie Root because Haney was at his home in Milwaukee recuperating from the flu.

The teams met Burdette's goal by playing the game in an efficient, 1 hour 57 minutes.

Braves pitchers Bob Buhl, Warren Spahn. and Burdette combined to hold the Millers hitless for 8⅓ innings before hanging on for a 4-3 victory.

Buhl, a right-hander who had a won-lost record of 18-8 with a 3.32 earned-run average for the Braves in 1956, breezed through the first three innings, allowing two baserunners, issuing walks to Cepeda in the second and Alou in the third.

Spahn, who was 20-11 in 1956 (his seventh season of winning 20 or more games since 1947), allowed just one baserunner in the middle three innings. He walked Davenport with one out in the fourth inning but then coaxed Carlos Paula to hit an inning-ending double-play grounder.

Burdette, who was 19-10 with a 2.70 ERA and NL-leading six shutouts in 1956 and was 62-37 with the Braves since they relocated from Boston before the 1953 season, took over in the seventh. The Millers got a baserunner after a Braves error with two outs in the seventh, but Cepeda flied out to right for the third out.

Burdette retired the Millers in order in the eighth and retired pinch-hitter Lee Tate on a fly ball to left for the first out in the ninth.

Millers shortstop Eddie Bressoud then topped a ball down the third-base line and beat third baseman Felix Mantilla's throw for Minneapolis's first hit, then went to second on Mantilla's throwing error. Wayne Terwilliger reached on infield hit, and Bressoud took third.

MEMORABLE GAMES AT MINNESOTA'S DIAMOND ON THE PRAIRIE

Davenport's sacrifice fly to center scored Bressoud to make the score 4-1. Paula then drove a low slider from Burdette over the left-field fence and it was 4-3, Braves.

Burdette regrouped and got Cepeda to ground out for the final out.

"Actually, we weren't paying any attention to the fact they didn't have a hit," Burdette said. "The no-hitters don't mean anything in spring training and especially when three pitchers have thrown."[3]

Burdette said the pitch to Paula was a mistake.

"Funny thing about Paula's home run," he said. "[Catcher] Carl Sawatski signaled for a curveball. As I started to wind up, I forgot what he had asked for. So, I let go of a nothing ball and Paula hit it out of the park."[4]

The Braves built their 4-0 lead off Millers starter Joe Shipley, who was a month shy of his 22nd birthday and was 8-19 in 1956 with Johnstown in the Class A Eastern League, and veteran Mike Blyzka.

The Braves opened the scoring with a run in the first on successive doubles by Henry Aaron, who had led the NL with a .328 batting average in 1956, and Bobby Thomson. The Braves extended their lead to 3-0 in the fourth inning on Johnny Logan's single and Bill Bruton's 330-foot home run over the right-field screen.

Wes Covington's line-drive home run to right in the seventh inning made it 4-0.

Blyzka allowed only two hits and one run in three innings before Webbo Clarke pitched the ninth for Minneapolis. Clarke allowed one hit.

Bruton, who was 2-for-4, and Thomson, who was 2-for-2, paced Milwaukee's 11-hit attack.

Despite the loss, Millers first-year manager Red Davis was not disappointed by his team.

"Don't forget," Davis said, "we were looking at the three best pitchers in the National League. There's no disgrace to be shut out by those guys. And we came back in the ninth to scare 'em. I still like our club."[5]

Millers general manager Rosy Ryan was pleased with the game and the crowd.

"Imagine close to 10,000 people (9,972) turning out on a day as cold as this," said Ryan. "I felt we'd be lucky if 5,500 showed up.

"The Milwaukee club kept every promise. They pitched Burdette, Spahn, and Buhl, the three aces, and they put on a real good show. Our club? I was very satisfied. It was a good start for us, and I think the fans liked what they saw."[6]

After the game, the Braves returned to Milwaukee for an exhibition game the next day against the Cleveland Indians. Cleveland won, 5-4.

Spahn pitched the Braves to a 4-1 victory over the Cubs in their regular-season opener. The Braves opened the season with five victories and 12 victories in their first 15 games, and went on to win the NL pennant with a 95-59 record. The Braves finished eight games ahead of the second-place St. Louis Cardinals.

The Millers did show improvement in their second season in Metropolitan Stadium. They went 85-69 (seven more victories than in 1956) to finish in third place in the American Association. Wichita, the Braves' top minor-league affiliate, won the AA title with a 93-61 record. The Denver Bears, a New York Yankees farm team, finished in second with a 90-64 record. The Millers were swept by Denver in the playoffs.

One of the highlights for the Millers in 1957 was the play of Cepeda. The 19-year-old first baseman hit .309 with 25 home runs and 108 RBIs. Cepeda moved up to the San Francisco Giants in 1958, the start of a 17-season Hall of Fame career.

SOURCES

In addition to the sources cited in the Notes, the author consulted Baseball-Reference.com, Newspapers.com, Retrosheet.org and sabr.org.

NOTES

1. Associated Press, "Haney: Braves Ready to Win," *Minneapolis Star*, April 13, 1957: 12A.
2. Sid Hartman, "Thompson Here; Majors Is Aim," *Minneapolis Sunday Tribune*, April 14, 1957: 33.
3. Hartman.
4. Hartman.
5. Hartman.
6. Hartman.

THE BABY "BABY BULL"

APRIL 30, 1957: MINNEAPOLIS MILLERS 12, LOUISVILLE COLONELS 8

By Bob Tholkes

Polled in the April 30, 1957, issue of the *Minneapolis Tribune*[1] about the Minneapolis Millers' prospects for the season, six fans split down the middle: Three were optimistic, two pessimistic, and one said it was too early to tell. (The Millers had played 13 games at the time, winning six.) The optimists were more correct, as the club placed third in the Triple-A American Association at 85-69. The pessimist who noted their lack of pop with the bat had a last laugh: They scored only six runs in four games in the first round of the postseason league playoffs and were swept by Denver.

More prescient yet was the fan who liked the look of 19-year-old first baseman Orlando Cepeda, who was making the jump from the Giants' Class C affiliate at St. Cloud, Minnesota, to Minneapolis, the top of New York's chain. The kid had started the season 1-for-18 but then had adjusted and was hitting .318, with power.[2]

The Millers' immediate prospects were about to improve – the first-place Wichita Braves, who had just taken two of three, were leaving town, and the last-place Louisville Colonels, losers of eight of their first 10, were coming in.

Metropolitan Stadium had opened on April 24, 1956, on its Bloomington ex-cornfield, and with more cornfields still adjacent. Its seating capacity of 18,200 was a fraction of the 45,000 to which it would eventually be expanded,[3] but the 2,325 who made the trip to the 'burbs on April 30, an unseasonably warm Tuesday night (80 degrees at the 8:00 P.M. game time), would find it spacious.

Millers starter Al Corwin was 30 years old and in the second, declining half of a professional career spanning 13 seasons. Unbeknownst to him, his big-league career, spent entirely with the Giants, had concluded in 1955 with a cumulative record of 18 wins and 10 losses in 117 games in which he pitched 289⅓ innings and posted a 3.98 earned-run average.[4] Corwin had thrown a complete-game, 14-1 win at the Colonels the previous week in Louisville. His mound opponent, Marion "Murph" Murszewski, another minor-league vet, would shuffle between three stops in 1957, pitching only five games in Louisville before demotion to Double A.

Recent history was in this case a poor guide to predicting the course of the game of April 30. The Colonels roughed up Corwin. Clarence Moore's lead-off triple in the first inning turned into a run when the outfield relay got away from Millers third baseman Jim Davenport. Three consecutive singles and a double-play grounder brought in two more in the second. A walk, a single, another triple by Moore, and a final single in the fourth finished Corwin. Murszewski meanwhile allowed only Don Grate's solo home run through the first four.

Second baseman Wayne Terwilliger began the Millers comeback in the fifth, doubling home two, and two more in the sixth finished Murszewski's night and cut the Millers' deficit to one run. Reliever Harry Fisher surrendered the tying run in the seventh on a walk, a sacrifice, and a single before Cepeda homered over the 405-foot sign in center field, the deepest part of the ballpark. Joe Shipley, a 22-year-old making the jump from Class A Springfield (Massachusetts), was meanwhile in the course of four innings of shutout relief for the Millers.

Two more unsuccessful relievers allowed four more Millers runs in the eighth, two on another Terwilliger double, which perhaps allowed the veteran infielder to consider his two errors on the night as balanced out. Working with a 12-6 lead in the ninth, Shipley started the inning with a walk and a hit batsman, and both runners came in on a single and pair of infield outs before he closed out the inning and the game.[5]

With the Kentucky Derby coming up, the *Louisville Courier-Journal* of May 1 dolefully reported the blown lead but gave no space to commentary on the Colonels' showing. The *Minneapolis Star* was naturally far more

MEMORABLE GAMES AT MINNESOTA'S DIAMOND ON THE PRAIRIE

upbeat: "Millers Kids Star in Rally for 12-8 Victory,"[6] referring to Shipley and Cepeda, with additional kudos for 25-year-old shortstop Ed Bressoud, who handled 11 chances and started three double plays. Staff writer Bob Beebe's game summary dubbed Cepeda "Feets" (a shoe-size reference?) and noted that the young slugger now had three hits in the last week that gave the Millers late-inning leads. Columnist Charles Johnson was especially impressed with "Feets":

> "Orlando Cepeda boomed a line drive home run over the centerfield fence at Metropolitan stadium Tuesday night. It was one of the hardest hit balls smacked in the new plant. His batting performance on this occasion could become typical of his nightly efforts. He boasts tremendous brute strength. When he gets his bat on the ball, it travels. Last night's home run fairly exploded."[7]

With the *Star* also reporting that injured regulars Carlos Paula and Bob Schmidt were now fit to play, and that general manager Rosy Ryan expected the parent Giants to shortly send pitching help, all was on the upswing for the Millers.

Not everyone was a fan of Metropolitan Stadium, however, as the *Star* also reported. Bloomington's streets were not ready for prime time:

> "Steps to meet the traffic problem which develops in Bloomington when some 4,500 cars leave Metropolitan stadium at once are being studied by stadium and village officials. ... The traffic problem at the new stadium is complicated because the suburb's street program is in a rapid state of change and expansion."[8]

Frequent complaints about stadium traffic from nearby residents produced promises by the village of Bloomington to upgrade and expand surrounding commercial avenues and protect residential streets with barriers, and by the stadium's officials to provide information to fans on parking, streets, and exit routes.

Six springs after a 20-year-old Willie Mays had wowed Millers fans in his brief sojourn in a Minneapolis uniform, Cepeda, though the Giants decided he needed an entire Triple-A season under his belt, displayed the "can't miss" talent that made him the 1958 National League Rookie of the Year.

NOTES

1. "Just Ask: Do the Minneapolis Millers Look Like a Pennant Contender?" *Minneapolis Tribune,* April 30, 1957: 18.
2. Bob Beebe, "Cepeda's Hitting Surge Bright Spot for Millers," *Minneapolis Star,* April 30, 1957: 13B.
3. stadiumsofprofootball.com/stadiums/metropolitan-stadium/.
4. baseball-reference.com/players/c/corwial01.shtml.
5. Bob Beebe, "Colonels Blow Big Early Lead, Bow to Minneapolis 12 to 8," *Louisville Courier-Journal,* May 1, 1957: Sec.2, 4.
6. Bob Beebe, "Shipley Earns More Work; Three 'Wins' for Cepeda," *Minneapolis Star,* May 1, 1957: 1F.
7. Charles Johnson, "Lowdown on Sports," *Minneapolis Star,* May 1, 1957: 1F.
8. "Solution Is Sought for Stadium Traffic," *Minneapolis Star,* May 1, 1957" 1C.

THE WEIRDEST INNING METROPOLITAN STADIUM HAS SEEN IN ITS BRIEF HISTORY[1]

MAY 26, 1957: MINNEAPOLIS 9, WICHITA 8 (GAME ONE OF DOUBLEHEADER)

By Alan Cohen

Hard-changing Minneapolis pulled to within a half-game game of first-place Wichita by sweeping the Braves in a doubleheader at Metropolitan Stadium on May 26.

It was a spring day in name only as the cold rain and wind held the crowd down to 2,359.

In the first game, Wichita, the Triple-A affiliate of the Milwaukee Braves, struck first and often, scoring eight runs in the first inning against Gene Bearden and Joe Shipley. Shipley calmed down and shut down the Braves after the first inning. He also led a comeback with his bat.

Wichita's Joe Koppe led off the game with a walk. After Harry Hanebrink doubled to right field, Ray Shearer struck out. Wes Covington's wind-blown double to right field scored the two runners. Bobby Malkmus homered to left field, making it 4-0. A triple by Bob Talbot and the second two-run homer of the inning, this one by Earl Hersh, made the score 6-0 and finished off Bearden. Minneapolis manager Red Davis summoned Shipley into the game and, at first, he poured kerosene on the fire. After getting Mike Roarke for the second out of the inning, he walked pitcher Bob Trowbridge and gave up a single to Koppe. Hanebrink's second double of the inning brought Trowbridge home, and Shearer singled Koppe home with Wichita's final tally.

Minneapolis, the top farm club of the New York Giants, started to chip away at the lead in the bottom of the second inning. With Bob Schmidt and Jim Davenport on base, Shipley came to the plate and homered off Trowbridge. An inning later, Bill Taylor singled and came home on Schmidt's homer. Later in the third inning, Shipley singled Eddie Bressoud home to make the score 8-6, and Trowbridge was finished for the day.

Wichita manager Ben Geraghty brought in Bobby Ross, who retired the side without any further scoring. But Minneapolis tied the game in the fourth inning. With Taylor at bat, catcher Roarke was unable to handle strike three and Taylor raced to first base. He was forced at second by Orlando Cepeda, who came home on Schmidt's second homer in as many innings.

Shipley and Ross then got down to business and there was no scoring from the fifth inning through the ninth. However, each team did threaten. In the sixth inning, Henry Thompson of the Millers tried to score from first on a double by Taylor but was thrown out at home when Koppe at shortstop relayed center fielder Talbot's throw to catcher Roarke. In the ninth, Wichita seemed to have an opportunity when Talbot doubled to right field with Malkmus on first base. Malkmus rounded third and tried to score but was gunned down as Thompson's throw was relayed to catcher Schmidt by Wayne Terwilliger.

"It was so cold and rainy in the outfield I wanted to end it. I hit the first pitch; I think it was supposed to be a breaking ball, but it was up high."

– Minneapolis outfielder Don Grate[2]

The game went into extra innings. Shipley put up another goose egg in the top of the 10th and the Millers came to bat. Ross retired Davenport and Carlos Paula, batting for Shipley. Up stepped Don Grate, who was cold and wanted to go to the warmer confines of the clubhouse. He settled the encounter with a homer on the first pitch.

The win went to Shipley and was his third of the season against no losses. The 22-year-old appeared in 18 games with Minneapolis, only three as a starter, going 4-1, before being optioned to Springfield of the Class A Eastern League on June 21. With Springfield he started 16 of his 17 appearances and went 5-8. Over the next three seasons he was up and down between the Giants and the minors, getting into 26 games without a decision. In 1961 and 1962 he bounced around the minor leagues, briefly getting back to the majors with the White Sox in 1963, going 0-1 in three appearances.

Ross took the loss, bringing his record to 1-2. His career in Organized Baseball had begun at the tender age of 16 in 1945. Like Shipley, he was in the big leagues for just a short while, pitching parts of three seasons and going 0-2 in 20 games. By 1957 he was no longer a prospect. He finished the season with a 2-6 record at Wichita. Three years later, he was out of baseball.

In the second game, the Millers again came from behind to win the seven-inning game, getting their first hits and scoring two runs in the last of the seventh to win 2-1 against Wichita's Joey Jay, who had pitched a perfect game through six innings.

Minneapolis manager Davis was a career minor leaguer, except for 21 games at third base with the New York Giants in 1941. He broke in with Greensburg, Pennsylvania, in the Class D Pennsylvania State Association in 1935 and was still playing minor-league ball in 1954. He had become a player manager in 1949 and was still at it in 1976, putting together a won-lost record of 1,927-1,845.

Wichita manager Ben Geraghty began his professional career at the major-league level, playing for the Dodgers right out of Villanova University in 1936. An infielder, he played parts of three seasons in the majors. He was with Spokane on June 24, 1946, when a life-changing moment occurred. The team bus was involved in a horrific crash that killed nine members of the team. Geraghty was named the team manager, replacing Mel Cole, who had perished in the crash.

SABR biographer Rory Costello tells us, "In the disaster's aftermath, he developed unusual psychological gifts, rooted in his trauma. 'This deepened perception was what made Ben Geraghty a great manager and a great man,' [Pat] Jordan wrote [in *A False Spring*]." His best year as a manager was 1953, when he led a Jacksonville team that included 19-year-old Hank Aaron to a 93-44 record in the South Atlantic League. But the cost of Geraghty's success was high. "To remain a manager, he had to do what scared him most – continue to ride buses." In May 1959, a bus brought him to Minneapolis. A heart attack killed him in 1963, aged just 50.[3]

Sharing the sports page in the *Minneapolis Star* that evening in May was a story that would have a significant impact on several of the players in the games played on May 26. It was reported that the New York Giants would move to San Francisco, the Brooklyn Dodgers would move to Los Angeles, and the Cincinnati Reds would move to New York.[4] Although the Reds stayed put, the other moves did take place.

In 1958 three Millers players who spent the 1957 season in Minneapolis would take the field in San Francisco on Opening Day.

Bob Schmidt, who homered twice in the win over Wichita and had nine homers at Metropolitan Stadium in 1957, was behind the plate for the Giants and played three full seasons in San Francisco. In 1961 he was traded to Cincinnati for Ed Bailey. Later in his career, he was with Washington and on June 1, 1962, returned to Metropolitan Stadium and homered off Jim Kaat.

Jim Davenport, who went 1-for-5, was anchored at third base for 13 seasons. In his best season, 1962, he batted .297, was named to the All-Star team, and won a Gold Glove as the Giants played in the World Series for the first time since moving to San Francisco.

Although Orlando Cepeda went 0-for-5 against Wichita, he did hit 14 homers at Metropolitan Stadium in 1957. He went on to a great major-league career. He was the National League's Rookie of the Year in 1958, was chosen for the National League All-Star team in seven seasons, and in his MVP season of 1967 led the St. Louis Cardinals to the World Series championship. He was inducted into the Hall of Fame in 1999.

Of the Wichita players, perhaps Covington had the most noteworthy career. He had first played with the Braves in 1956, batting .283 in 75 games. In 1957 he got off to a terrible start with Milwaukee. The Braves had no room for him in their outfield, and he was batting .143 in limited pinch-hitting opportunities. On May 12 he was sent to Wichita and, after batting .265 in 32 games, returned to Milwaukee. He played 11 major-league seasons, his best year being with the Philadelphia Phillies, with whom he batted .303 with 17 homers and 64 RBIs in 1963.

The Millers, after getting to within a half-game of the league lead, were not able to sustain the momentum. However, Red Davis's squad finished third in the standings and advanced to the league playoffs. They were swept by the Denver Bears in four games.

The next season, 1958, the Giants moved their Triple-A team to Phoenix, and Minneapolis became the home of the Boston Red Sox Triple-A affiliate for three seasons.

SOURCES

In addition to Baseball-Reference.com, the author used the sources cited in the notes and the following:

Briere, Tom. "Millers Beat Wichita 9-8, 2-1; Half Game Out of First," *Minneapolis Morning Tribune*, May 27, 1957: 28.

NOTES

1. Bob Beebe, "Shipley Hero; Millers Near Top in Fantastic Twin Bill," *Minneapolis Star*, May 27, 1957: 17B.
2. "Chilled Grate Turns on 'Heat' for Victory," *Minneapolis Morning Tribune*, May 27, 1957: 28.
3. Rory Costello, "Ben Geraghty," SABR BioProject.
4. "N.L. Airs Three-Club Shift on Tuesday?" *Minneapolis Star*, May 27, 1957: 28.

A HARBINGER OF THINGS TO COME

AUGUST 5, 1957: DETROIT TIGERS 6, CINCINNATI REDS 5

By Joel Rippel

Before the Minneapolis Millers' inaugural game in Metropolitan Stadium in 1956, New York Giants President Horace Stoneham was asked if he agreed that the ballpark was a good facility for minor-league baseball.

"Minor league nothing," Stoneham replied. "This is a real major league park, and you'll have major league ball here in the near future."[1]

A major-league tenant was still four years in the future but in August 1957, the ballpark moved closer to that result when it played host to two major-league teams for the first time. In the first two seasons in Bloomington, the Millers had played four exhibition games against major-league teams (the New York Giants in 1956 and 1957, the Cleveland Indians in 1956, and the Milwaukee Braves in April 1957).

In a harbinger of things to come, the Cincinnati Reds and Detroit Tigers visited Met Stadium in August 1957 for the first game in twentieth-century Minnesota featuring two major-league teams.

The Reds and Tigers each came to town as fourth-place teams. The Reds (58-46), who were 4½ games behind the National League-leading St. Louis Cardinals, had played a doubleheader with the New York Giants at home the previous day. The Giants won the first game, 7-6, in 14 innings before the Reds salvaged a split with a 3-2 victory in the second game.

The Tigers (50-52), who were a distant 18½ games behind the first-place New York Yankees, had lost to the Washington Senators, 8-4, in Washington the previous day.

Met Stadium in the early years, before the large scoreboard in right-center field was installed.

After the doubleheader split, the Reds were 4-5 in their last nine games and the Tigers had lost three straight and five of seven heading into the exhibition.

A Minneapolis columnist wrote before the game, "While both will receive tidy guarantees for their efforts, they were reluctant to take on an exhibition game at this important stage of their pennant races."[2]

But the two teams made a favorable impression on the crowd of 21,689 – a record for a baseball game played in Minnesota – as the Tigers, managed by Jack Tighe, outlasted the Reds, managed by Birdie Tebbetts, 6-5.

The game featured 10 players who had played in the All-Star Game the previous July 9 in St. Louis, won by the American League, 6-5. Tigers pitcher Jim Bunning was the winning pitcher.

"Too often, major league clubs in exhibitions just go through the motions of playing the game, taking the public's money and giving the minimum in effort. Not Detroit and Cincinnati. They went all out. The two managers got every player of note into action before the nine innings were up," observed a sportswriter.[3]

The Reds opened the scoring in the bottom of the second inning. Rookie outfielder Joe Taylor doubled off Tigers starter Billy Hoeft and scored on Don Hoak's two-out single. The Reds wouldn't score again until the ninth inning as Tigers relievers Duke Maas and Al Aber limited the. to two hits over the next six innings.

Reds starter Art Fowler, a one-time Miller, held the Tigers hitless into the fifth before running into trouble. With one out in the fifth the Tigers tied the score on consecutive singles by Red Wilson and future Twins Bill Tuttle and Reno Bertoia.

The Tigers were just getting started. They had 11 hits in their final four at-bats. The Tigers chased Fowler in the sixth inning with six consecutive singles, which delivered three runs and gave them a 4-1 lead.

The Tigers extended their lead to 6-1 with two runs in the top of the ninth on an RBI single by Harvey Kuenn and a two-out single by John Groth.

A Reds comeback in the bottom of the ninth fell one run short.

Pinch-hitter Ed Bailey drew a walk from Aber, who was beginning his fifth inning of relief. Jerry Lynch's double scored Bailey. After Wally Post lined out for the first out, Lynch scored on Pete Whisenant's single to make it 6-3. George Crowe followed with a two-run home run and pulled the Reds to within 6-5.

Frank Lary relieved Aber and ended the threat by striking out Smoky Burgess and retiring Alex Grammas on a fly to left.

"I knew Detroit's 6-1 lead wasn't safe against our club," said Tebbetts. "We can explode any time. I thought we'd win it until Lary got Smoky Burgess, a really tough hitter, on that curveball in the ninth."[4]

Groth had three hits and Kuenn had two for the Tigers, who outhit the Reds 14-7. All of the Tigers' hits were singles. Seven players each had one hit for the Reds.

Minneapolis Tribune columnist Dick Cullum wrote, "There was only one reason why the Detroit Tigers and Cincinnati Redlegs accepted the invitation to play a midseason game in Minneapolis. They wanted to do something for baseball."[5]

The Tigers also did something for their themselves during their one-day stay in town. They signed University of Minnesota shortstop George Thomas. Thomas, who was a sophomore for the Gophers in 1957, agreed to a $25,000 bonus, which would be paid over the next three years.

The Tigers told Thomas, the younger brother of Jerry Thomas, who was a key member of the Gophers pitching staff when they won their first College World Series title in 1956, that he would be placed on their active roster on September 1. Commissioner Ford Frick had recently issued a directive that bonus signees didn't have to join their clubs immediately (as former Gopher Jerry Kindall did when he signed in 1956).

SOURCES

In addition to the sources cited in the Notes, the author consulted Baseball-Reference.com, Newspapers.com, Retrosheet.org, and sabr.org.

NOTES

1   Sid Hartman, "Stoneham Praises Stadium, Predicts Major League Ball Soon," *Minneapolis Tribune*, April 24, 1956: 14.

2   Charles Johnson, "Lowdown on Sports," *Minneapolis Star*, August 5, 1957: 11B.

3   Johnson, "Major Leaguers Go All Out to Please," *Minneapolis Star*, August 6, 1957: 10B.

4   "Kuenn Will Play Leftfield," *Minneapolis Tribune*, August 6, 1957: 17.

5   Dick Cullum, "Tigers, Redlegs Boost Baseball," *Minneapolis Tribune*, August 6, 1957: 17.

GREEN SURVIVES PARADE TO LEAD MILLERS TO OPENING DAY WIN

APRIL 22, 1958: MINNEAPOLIS MILLERS 11, LOUISVILLE COLONELS 6

By Dave Mona

Pumpsie Green's successful Millers debut was nearly set back when the car in which he was riding in a morning parade down Nicollet Avenue in downtown Minneapolis ran out of gas.[1]

The parade was the idea of the Minneapolis Chamber of Commerce as a way to introduce fans to an entirely new 1958 Millers team.

When the Millers' parent club, the New York Giants, announced they were moving to San Francisco for the 1958 season, the Boston Red Sox swapped ownership of their top farm team, the San Francisco Seals of the Pacific Coast League, for the Millers, enabling the Giants to move into San Francisco.

Gone with that club were such familiar names as Orlando Cepeda, Jim Davenport, Ed Bressoud, Bobby Hofman, Wayne Terwilliger, Foster Castleman, Hank Thompson, Felipe Alou, Stu Miller, Pete Burnside, and Al Corwin.

The new Millers, who complied a 5-2 road record before coming home to Minneapolis, featured a mix of veterans and promising rookies including Dean Stone, Lou Clinton, Bill Monbouquette, Tom Umphlett, Faye Throneberry, Art Schult, Ed Sadowski, Jerry Zimmerman, and Green, a 6-foot, 175-pound 23-year-old shortstop from the San Francisco Bay area.

Green, born in Boley, Oklahoma, and named Elijah Jerry at birth, came from an athletic family. His brother, Cornell, was a longtime starting safety for the Dallas Cowboys in their early years in the National Football League. The family moved to Richmond, California, when he was a child.

By the time he reached Minnesota, Green had already made stops in Wenatchee, Washington; Stockton, California; Albany, New York; Oklahoma City, and San Francisco. He was purchased from Stockton by the Red Sox in 1955 and immediately showed good fielding skills and a strong arm while playing mostly at shortstop.

He spent most of the 1957 season at Oklahoma City, where he hit .258 with 3 home runs, 38 runs batted in, and 10 stolen bases.

The Minneapolis Chamber of Commerce and the Minneapolis Minutemen, a local sports booster group, reflected the general disdain of local fans in their dislike for the Giants, who were being strongly courted to relocate to the new Metropolitan Stadium (opened in 1956) in suburban Bloomington. The stadium was built to attract a major-league team, and the logical team was the Giants.

The Chamber and the Minutemen wanted to show the major leagues that they had snubbed a logical candidate for either expansion or relocation. With the strong support of the local media, they mounted an aggressive drive for a large Opening Day crowd.

Millers business manager George Brophy said more than 10,000 tickets were sold for the opener, but the combination of cold weather and a strong wind held actual attendance to a league-best 8,513. For the season the Millers drew a total attendance of 152,533, an average of 1,994 per game.

The most direct route from Minneapolis to the ballpark went past Lake Nokomis and down Cedar Avenue, through Richfield into Bloomington. Most of the land between 66th Street and the ballpark was still farmland. Fans headed for the game listened to the number one hit on WDGY (1130 AM), "He's Got the Whole World in His Hands," by British 14-year-old Lorrie London.

Meanwhile, at the ballpark, Gene Mauch, a 32-year-old in just his second stint as a manager, worked on his starting lineup against Louisville Colonel lefty Ron Babkoff.

Despite a slow start at the plate, Mauch (2-for-28) penciled his own name into the starting lineup, batting sixth and playing third base.

Umphlett, a fleet center fielder, was the leadoff hitter, followed by Green at shortstop, Throneberry in right field batting third, first baseman Frank Kellert fourth, and slugger Schult in right field batting fifth in front of Mauch.

Second baseman Harry Malmberg hit seventh, followed by catcher Sadowski and starting pitcher Jack Spring.

As the Millers were called from the dugout for the pregame introductions, the largest ovation, according to local columnist Dick Cullum, was directed at Green.[2]

African-American players were not unusual in Millers starting lineups. Future Hall of Famers Ray Dandridge, Willie Mays, and Monte Irvin had all spent time starring for the Millers since Jackie Robinson broke the baseball color barrier in 1947.

By 1957 most major-league teams featured Black players in their starting lineups. Larry Doby, a Cleveland outfielder, became the first Black player in the American League in 1947.

Ten years later it was a rarity for a major-league team to not have a Black player, but the Red Sox were beginning to draw attention for their lack of color. It was not a question of if so much as when, and a look at the Red Sox minor-league system quickly identified Green as the most logical prospect.

That speculation proved correct when Green was called up in midseason of 1959, making the Red Sox the final major-league team to integrate. Green made his major-league debut on July 21, 1959, as a pinch runner for Vic Wertz. Less than a week later, his Millers teammate, African-American starting pitcher Earl Wilson, was called up to join Green with the Red Sox.

Things got off to a bad start for the Millers in the 1958 opener. After a scoreless first inning Louisville took advantage of starter Jack Spring's wildness. Louisville shortstop Frank Di Prima's double gave his team a 4-0 lead.

The damage could have been worse in the third when Spring walked two batters and was clearly struggling with his control.

Mauch summoned veteran Harry Dorish from the bullpen. Outfielder Jim Pyburn lined a Dorish pitch to the outfield gap, but Umphlett made a diving catch that Louisville manager Del Wilber later called the defensive play of the game.[3]

Hitless in two innings against Babkoff, the Millers loaded the bases in the third on a double by Sadowski, a walk to Dorish, and Umphlett's single. Not wanting to walk in a run, Babkoff grooved a pitch that Green lined solidly over the 380-foot sign in left-center to tie the game.

"First bases-loaded homer I've ever hit," Green told reporters after the game. "I was guessing fast ball all right, and I knew it was good for a base hit between the outfielders … but I didn't think it was going over the fence."[4]

An inning later Malmberg gave the Millers a 5-4 lead with his first home run of the season.

The Millers added a sixth run in the fifth on a single by Throneberry, a hit-and-run single by Kellert, and Schult's fielder's-choice grounder to third.

In the sixth the Millers put the game out of reach with four more runs. Malmberg reached base on the second error by Louisville third baseman Bob Barron. Sadowski followed with a single, and Dorish drove in a run with a sacrifice fly. Umphlett doubled to right and Green's infield hit scored Sadowski. Throneberry was walked intentionally. A balk, a walk to Kellert, and a double by Schult gave the Millers a 10-4 lead.

The Millers went on to win the game 11-6. Umphlett, Green, and Sadowski had two hits each, and Green led the attack with five runs batted in.

Dorish pitched six innings in relief, giving up on four hits and two earned runs while walking one and striking out three. Tom Hurd relieved a tiring Dorish in the ninth and recorded the final two outs.

After the game Wilber told *Minneapolis Tribune* sportswriter Sid Hartman that he would pick the Millers as the favorite to win the American Association title. "These Millers have power," he said. "They showed it to you today. To have a good club you need speed, defense, pitching and power. Minneapolis has them all."[5]

MILLER NOTES:

Wilber's prediction turned out to be accurate. The Millers finished with an 82-71 record. They defeated the Wichita Braves four games to two in the first round of the playoffs and swept the Denver Bears four games to none in the final round.

Under close scrutiny by the Red Sox, Green finished the season with a .253 batting average, 6 home runs, and 43 runs batted in. He did show an excellent batting eye, leading the league with 107 walks. He was hitting .320 in 98 games when he was called up in 1959.

Mauch made his major-league managing debut at age 34 in 1960 with the Philadelphia Phillies. His major-league managing career spanned 26 years, including a return to Met Stadium as the Twins manager from 1976 to 1980.

Hall of Famer Jimmie Foxx, one of Mauch's coaches, had some first impressions of Metropolitan Stadium. In the course of his major-league career he had a .325 batting average with 534 home runs. His last plate appearance was in 1945. Asked

MEMORABLE GAMES AT MINNESOTA'S DIAMOND ON THE PRAIRIE

what he thought of the Met, he told *Minneapolis Star* sportswriter Jim Byrne, "I'd like to hit in this ballpark, especially when the wind is blowing like it was today. Now, I guess it'd be better if I did the hittin' and let someone else do the runnin'."[6]

NOTES

1. "Pumpsie's Car Runs Out of Gas," *Minneapolis Tribune,* April 23, 1958: 19.
2. Dick Cullum, "Cullum's Column: Millers Have First-Raters," *Minneapolis Tribune,* April 23, 1958: 19.
3. "Hurlers 'Surround' Tom – Umphlett Pitcher's Friend," *Minneapolis Star,* April 23, 1958: 1F.
4. "Grand Slam Is Green's First," *Minneapolis Tribune,* April 23, 1958: 19.
5. Sid Hartman, "Umphlett Save Was Key, Claims Wilber," *Minneapolis Tribune,* April 23, 1958: 19.
6. Jim Byrne, "Miller 'Musclemen' Happy; Foxx Wants to Hit," *Minneapolis Star,* April 23, 1958: 1F.

AN INDIAN HOMER BINGE

JUNE 15, 1958: INDIANAPOLIS INDIANS 8, MINNEAPOLIS MILLERS 0 (GAME ONE OF DOUBLEHEADER)

By Alan Cohen

The 1958 season was one of change in minor-league baseball, especially at the highest level. With the migration of the two New York National League teams to California, there was a realignment of locations and affiliations. New Pacific Coast League teams were established in Spokane, Phoenix, and Salt Lake City. Minneapolis of the American Association changed its affiliation from the New York Giants (now with Phoenix) to the Boston Red Sox (formerly with San Francisco in the PCL).

June 15 was both Father's Day and the trading deadline, and the Minneapolis Millers hosted the Indianapolis Indians in a doubleheader at Metropolitan Stadium. In front of 3,069 spectators, the teams split two games. Indianapolis won the opener, 8-0, before Minneapolis discovered home plate in time to win the nightcap, 8-4.

"The kid had a good slider today. He was difficult to hit."

– Minneapolis center fielder Tom Umphlett, speaking of Indianapolis pitcher Carl Thomas[1]

In the first game, Carl Thomas was on the mound for Indianapolis, then affiliated with the Chicago White Sox. It was as if the team's manager, Walker Cooper, used a roulette wheel to determine his starting pitcher. Twenty-one different pitchers were used in 1958 by Indianapolis, and seven pitchers started 10 or more games. Thomas had lost his prior four decisions. The offense was a blend of young and old from 19-year-old Johnny Callison to 43-year-old player-manager Cooper. And the roster included a player on loan from the Washington Senators. (The Senators did not field a Triple-A team in 1958.) But on this day, Thomas went all the way, shutting out Minneapolis, making it 25 consecutive scoreless innings for the Millers' batters.

Thomas's Indianapolis mates supported him with 13 hits, including four home runs.

Bert Thiel was on the mound for the Millers. The 32-year-old had been around since 1947, and Minneapolis was his eighth minor-league stop. He had pitched very briefly with the Boston Braves in 1952. His major-league career consisted of four appearances and a total of seven innings pitched.

It didn't take long for Indianapolis to solve Thiel. Second-inning homers by John Romano and Harmon Killebrew staked Thomas to a 2-0 lead, and the Indians added another run in the third on a single by Callison. Callison drove in Ted Beard, who had reached base with one of his three hits in the twin bill. Romano's homer broke a 0-for-20 slump. Thiel left the game for a pinch-hitter, Lou Clinton, in the bottom of the third inning.

Killebrew, a future Hall of Famer, was having a bad season so far. Wrote *The Sporting News*, "the [Indianapolis] Indians finally gave up on Harmon Killebrew."[2] For Killebrew, on loan from the Senators, it was only his second homer of the

Harmon Killebrew homered at Met Stadium even before he was with the Twins.

season. His batting average was .215 in 38 games, and by the end of the day the one-time bonus baby had been sent to Chattanooga, Washington's affiliate in the Double-A Southern Association, in exchange for third baseman Stan Roseboro. Killebrew was a victim of the Bonus Rule of 1953-57, under which talented players signed to bonus contracts wound up sitting on major-league benches. Roseboro had been around for a while. He first gained notice as a sandlot player in the Pacific Northwest in 1945, playing in an All-Star game to determine Seattle's representative for the annual Esquire's All-American Boys Baseball Game in New York. He was not selected. He had started playing professionally in 1951.

The Indians piled it on in the middle innings. They victimized Al Schroll for three runs in the fifth inning. Schroll had entered the game in the top of the fourth inning after Thiel left the game for a pinch-hitter. Schroll, after seven minor-league seasons, had begun the 1958 season with the Red Sox but had been sent back down to the minors in May.

The key hit in the fifth-inning rally was a two-out, two-run triple by Callison, driving in Thomas and Beard. Johnny came home on a single by Romano. The Indians bruised Schroll again two innings later. He surrendered two runs on back-to-back homers by Callison and Romano in the seventh inning before giving way to Jack Spring, who pitched scoreless ball in the final two innings for the Millers. Callison's 12th homer of the season gave him the league lead. Romano's two homers gave him 11 for the season.

The shutout was preserved in the final innings as shortstop Al Facchini started two double plays. Facchini had gotten his start on the sandlots of Northern California and represented San Francisco in the 1948 Hearst Sandlot Classic in New York before signing with the Boston Braves organization. The infielder, who spent two years in the military during the Korean War, was in his eighth minor-league season. On each of the double plays, he threw to second baseman Bobby Winkles, who relayed the ball to first baseman Joe Altobelli. Both Winkles and Altobelli became big-league managers. The defensive gem of the game was a diving catch by Indianapolis left fielder Eddie Phillips, a career minor leaguer who had had a cup of coffee (nine games) with the St. Louis Cardinals in 1953, appearing exclusively as a pinch-runner and scoring four runs.

The winning pitcher, Thomas, a Minneapolis native, allowed singles to Jose Valdivielso, John Lundquist, Spencer "Red" Robbins, and Ed Sadowski, struck out two, and walked not a player in getting his first win of the season, bringing his won-lost record to 1-4. Present at the game was Thomas's father, Carl Sr., who had pitched in the American Association for St. Paul and Louisville. His son's win was a fine Father's Day present. Young Carl wound up the 1958 season with a 9-9 record for Indianapolis. However, he did little to distinguish himself at the next level. He made it to the majors in 1960 with the Cleveland Indians and appeared in four games, all in relief. He pitched a total of 9⅔ innings and had a 1-0 record.

The shutout was the fourth suffered by manager Gene Mauch's Millers over a span of seven days. Mauch said, "We'll have a tough time staying in the first division on pitching and defense alone."[3] The team had an abysmal home record through June 15, going 14-20, seven of the losses by shutout, at Metropolitan Stadium. The Millers' road record was a stellar 23-8, and their overall record placed them third in the American Association, 4½ games behind the league-leading Denver Bears. Minneapolis ended the season in third place as Charleston led the standings. Indianapolis, with the split, finished the day in seventh place. The Indians finished the season in sixth place.

In the playoffs, the Millers excelled. They defeated Wichita in six games, then swept Denver for the league championship.

The batting heroes of the 8-0 Indianapolis win, Johnny Callison and John Romano, each found success at the major-league level, although not with the White Sox. Callison, who finished the 1958 American Association season with 29 homers and 93 runs batted in, was traded to the Philadelphia Phillies after spending parts of the 1958 and 1959 seasons with the White Sox. With Philadelphia for 10 years, he was named to All-Star teams in 1962, 1964, and 1965, and led the National League in doubles (1966) and triples (1962, 1965). From 1960 to 1968, he played for his Minneapolis manager, Gene Mauch. He finished his career with the New York Yankees and on May 8, 1972, homered off Bert Blyleven at Metropolitan Stadium, becoming one of 28 players to homer at Metropolitan Stadium in both the minor and major leagues.

Romano was another to homer in both the majors and minors at Metropolitan Stadium. After finishing the 1958 American Association season with 25 homers and 89 RBIs, he was called up to the White Sox, where he saw limited action. After the 1959 season, he was traded to the Cleveland Indians, where he broke out in 1961, having his best season. He batted .299 with 21 homers and 80 RBIs and was named to the All-Star team for the first time. His second All-Star Game appearance came the following season when he hit a career-high 25 homers. Of his 129 major-league homers, 11 came at Metropolitan Stadium, the first being off Jack Kralick on May 9, 1962.

And that brings us to the third player who homered on June 15 and came back to homer at Metropolitan Stadium in the big leagues – *246* times. Harmon Killebrew was far from washed up. At Chattanooga he turned things around, batting .308 with 17 homers in 86 games, and he spent the end of the season with the Senators. The next season, 1959, he slammed 42 homers for the Senators and was on the way to the Hall of Fame, where he was inducted in 1984. When he retired, Killebrew's 573 home runs were the most by a right-handed batter in American League history, topping the mark of 524 set by Jimmie Foxx who, in 1958, was the hitting instructor with the Minneapolis Millers. (Foxx had 534 career home runs but 10 were in the National League.)

SOURCES

In addition to Baseball-Reference.com and the sources shown in the Notes, the author used the following:

Briere, Tom. "Miller Drought Ends with 8-4 Victory after 8-0 Loss," *Minneapolis Morning Tribune*, June 16, 1958: 23.

Koelling, Lester. "Indians Trade Killebrew for Third New Player in a Week," *Indianapolis News*, June 16, 1958: 14.

"Thomas' Shutout Gives Indians Split," *Indianapolis Star*, June 16, 1958: 19.

NOTES

1   Sid Hartman, "Hartman's Roundup: Thomas' First Game Here Is Shut Out," *Minneapolis Morning Tribune*, June 16, 1958: 24.

2   *The Sporting News*, June 25, 1958: 36.

3   Bob Beebe, "Four Shutouts in Week Worry Mauch," *Minneapolis Star*, June 16, 1958: 9B.

BOTH TED WILLIAMS AND PUMPSIE GREEN STAR IN RED SOX-MILLERS EXHIBITION GAME

JUNE 16, 1958: MINNEAPOLIS MILLERS 14, BOSTON RED SOX 10

By Bill Nowlin

The Minneapolis Millers of the American Association were the Triple-A minor-league affiliate of the Boston Red Sox for two stretches, 1937-38 and 1958-60.[1] Ted Williams had won the Triple Crown for the Millers in 1938 and, as it happens, "The Kid" was with the Boston Red Sox from 1939 through 1960, including this game in 1958 when the Red Sox visited Bloomington for a midseason exhibition game.[2] When the Minnesota Twins became a major-league franchise in 1961, the Millers ceased operations.

In 1958 the Red Sox were nearing the end of a decade of mediocrity. They always had a couple of star players, Williams foremost among them, but after the 1950 season, they didn't contend for a pennant again until 1967. Only in 1951 did they finish less than a dozen games out of first place. The 1958 season was one of their better ones: They had a winning record at season's end (79-75, 13 games out of first place). The team had yet to field an African-American player. In 1959 Elijah "Pumpsie" Green became the first African American to play for the big-league Red Sox.

On June 15, the Sox had lost both halves of a Sunday home doubleheader to the Kansas City Athletics, 16-7 and 9-4. They were in second place, though, with a 30-28 record and were seven games behind the New York Yankees.[3]

Into the 1990s, the Red Sox typically played one in-season exhibition game each year against their top affiliate in the minors.[4]

They left Boston for Chicago to play the White Sox on Tuesday, June 17, playing the Millers on Monday night. It was a quick visit. Within an hour after the game, they were off to Chicago. But the game was a very eventful one, with 24 runs scored, a Millers win, and some memorable moments.

The game drew very well, bringing 18,368 fans to the ballpark. They didn't have to wait long for what many hoped most to see. Pitching for the Millers was left-hander Jack Spring. With one out, Pete Runnels singled. Ted Williams took his stance in the batter's box – facing the "Williams shift." Spring missed the plate three times in succession; with a 3-and-0 count, he put the next one over and Williams hit it well – a "cloud-scraping" blow over the "small regiment of kids waiting beyond the right field screen."[5] They played him too shallow, said the Associated Press feed. "Ted's smash dropped near an asphalt runway beyond the fence."[6] It was hit a roughly estimated 410 feet. The fence was at 355 feet, but it passed that and reached a light tower 55 feet beyond that.[7]

Ted Williams (right) played with the Minneapolis Millers in 1938 before going up to the Red Sox the following year. In 1958 he played for the Red Sox in an exhibition game against the Millers. Years later, Williams posed with Rod Carew, who was making a push to become the first player to hit .400 in a season since Williams had done so in 1941

METROPOLITAN STADIUM

Before the top of the first was done, the Red Sox had scored five runs off Spring. Dick Gernert singled and Gene Stephens drew a walk. Sammy White then doubled in one run, another scoring on a throwing error. Jimmy Piersall singled in the fifth run.

Millers manager Gene Mauch, a teammate of Ted's from 1956 and 1957, must have assumed this would be par for the course. Managing the Red Sox was Pinky Higgins.

Starting for the Red Sox was Bob "Riverboat" Smith. The southpaw worked the first six innings of the game, not allowing a run through the first four. Al Schroll had replaced Spring after a scoreless second. Neither team scored in the second, third, or fourth. In the bottom of the fifth, the Millers scored twice on Frank Kellert's single and a home run by Tommy Umphlett over the screen in left field. Schroll allowed only one hit in the four innings he pitched against the big leaguers.

And in the bottom of the sixth, Smith was banged around for six more runs, the biggest blow a two-out, first-pitch bases-clearing triple by Pumpsie Green, batting right-handed against Smith. It gave the Millers an 8-5 lead. Green's triple to center field was reported at 400 feet.[8]

With Tom Borland on the mound for the Millers, Boston responded with four runs in the top of the seventh, all thanks to a grand slam over the low right-field fence by first baseman Marty Keough, who had taken over for Dick Gernert. This gave Boston the lead, 9-8.

The lead didn't last long. Right-hander Willard Nixon pitched the seventh and eighth for the Red Sox, allowing six runs in the seventh to match the six-run sixth. A throw to Keough intended to nab Lu Clinton went astray and Clinton made it to third base on the error. With one out, both Kellett and Umphlett drew walks. Harry Malmberg singled to tie the game, 9-9. The pitcher, Borland, then singled, driving in two more. Eddie Sadowski singled for the 12th run, and Green (batting from the left side of the plate) singled for the 13th (and his fourth RBI). The 14th run scooted in on a fielder's choice grounder hit by Jose Valdivielso.

Now it was 14-9 in favor of the Millers.

Stephens singled and Nixon doubled in the top of the eighth, the Red Sox picking up their 10th but final run of the game.

Nixon held the Millers scoreless in the eighth but didn't have to pitch the ninth. With the 14-10 lead, the Millers had already won the game. Borland got the win; Nixon bore the loss. Despite the 24 runs, 24 hits, and six bases on balls, the game lasted 2:24.

For "the usually weak-hitting Millers," the 14 runs matched their high for the year.[9]

Neither Jackie Jensen nor Frank Malzone played in the game. Because neither liked to fly, they received dispensation to take the train from Boston to Chicago.[10] The *Boston Traveler* reported that Williams enjoyed catching up with old friends, residents of the area that he had not seen for years.[11]

SOURCES

In addition to the sources cited in the Notes, the author consulted Baseball-Reference.com.

NOTES

1. For a very detailed history of the Millers, see stewthornley.net/millers.html. Stew Thornley points out that the "1930s connection between the Red Sox and Millers was a looser affiliation than the one from 1958-60, when the Millers were a full-fledged farm team." Email to author on August 26, 2019.

2. Williams had played in the Millers' home ballparks: Nicollet Park in 1938, and in Metropolitan Stadium for this 1958 game.

3. The standings were tightly bunched. Eighth-place Baltimore was only four games behind the Red Sox, 11 GB.

4. In earlier times, it was not uncommon to play a number of exhibition games during the season. In 1934, for instance, the Red Sox played nine such games against various teams, one of which was the company team from Burnham & Morrill, the canner of B&M Baked Beans in Portland, Maine. During the 1990s, they played seven such games. The last "normal" in-season exhibition game was in 1999 against the Pawtucket Red Sox. All told, the Red Sox' record for in-season exhibition games is 142-86-9. The Red Sox had played spring-training exhibition games against the Millers as early as 1922 (four games, all played in Tennessee) and one in Alabama in 1927. The Millers won two of those five games. This 1958 game was the first Millers-Red Sox game since the 12-9 win for the Millers in 1927.

5. Associated Press, "Ted Homers but Millers Beat Red Sox," *Fergus Falls* (Minnesota) *Daily Journal*, June 17, 1958: 8.

6. "Ted Homers."

7. Roger Birtwell, "Pumpsie and Ted Both Star," *Boston Globe*, June 17, 1958: 25, 27.

8. Riger Birtwell, "Pumpsie Looks Good as Hitter," *Boston Globe*, June 18, 1958: 42.

9. The phrase and the most complete account of the game are thanks to Tom Briere, "Millers Beat Boston 14-10 as Ted Thrills 18,638," *Minneapolis Morning Tribune*, June 17, 1958: 12.

10. "Keough No Threat at First Base," *Boston Traveler*, June 17, 1958: 49.

11. "Keough No Threat."

SEPTEMBER 29, 1958: MILLERS WIN THEIR SECOND JUNIOR WORLD SERIES

MINNEAPOLIS MILLERS 7, MONTREAL ROYALS 1

By Rich Arpi

When the Shaughnessy playoffs began after the 1958 American Association season, the chances of the Minneapolis Millers were viewed only as fair. The Shaughnessy playoff system was named after International League President Frank Shaughnessy, who promoted the plan in the 1930s. It paired the first-place team with the fourth-place team and the second-place team with the third-place team in the first round of the postseason playoffs. The winners would meet for the league championship. The champion would then meet the champion of the International League in the Junior World Series. (It had originally been called the Little World Series.)

Between 1933 and 1957, the Millers made the postseason 15 times. In 1933 and 1934, the American Association had East and West Divisions and the Millers, as champions of the West Division, met the Columbus Red Birds, champions of the East Division, only to lose both times. Starting in 1936, when the Shaughnessy playoff system started, the Millers lost in the first round every year they made the playoffs except once.

The 1958 regular-season champions of the American Association were the Charleston (West Virginia) Senators, the top farm club of the Detroit Tigers. They finished with a record of 89-62, 7½ games ahead of the Wichita Braves, the top farm club of the Milwaukee Braves (83-71). The Millers (82-71), the top farm team of the Boston Red Sox, finished in third place, just a half-game behind Wichita. Finishing in fourth place were the Denver Bears, affiliated with the New York Yankees, 10 games back at 78-71. In the 22 years of the Shaughnessy playoff system in the American Association between 1936 and 1957, the team finishing in first place in the regular season had also won the playoff championship seven times; the team that finished second won the playoff championship six times; the team finishing third won seven times; and the fourth place team won only twice.[1]

Denver upset Charleston in seven games in their first-round series in 1958. The Millers faced the Wichita Braves, with the first three games in Wichita. Wichita won Games One (4-2) and Three (9-2). The Millers won Game Two, 5-4. Led by a home run from left fielder Art Schult and a four-hit shutout by Al Schroll, the Millers won Game Four at home, 2-0. This would be the first of 11 straight wins that would lead them to the Junior World Series title. The Millers disposed of the Braves with wins in Games Five (4-3) and Six (3-2). Strong pitching from Tom Borland and Tom Hurd won Game Five, and a complete game from Dean Stone won Game Six.

The American Association championship series opened at Metropolitan Stadium on September 18 with the Millers breezing by the Denver Bears, 10-1. Schroll pitched a complete game, allowing only four hits. The next game was won by the Millers, 4-1. Because of scheduling conflicts at Metropolitan Stadium, the next five games would be played at Denver. The Millers made quick work of the Bears, however, with wins on September 20 (14-13 in 11 innings) and 21 (6-4).

The Montreal Royals, managed by Clay Bryant, were the top farm club of the Los Angeles Dodgers in 1958. They finished first in the International League by 2½ games with a record of 90-63. They beat Columbus and Toronto to win the International League championship series. Montreal had a strong starting rotation with Tom Lasorda (18 wins), Rene Valdes (15 wins), Bill Harris (14 wins), and Bob Giallombardo (12 wins). The Millers would beat all four, in succession, during this series. Other notable Royals were infielders Jim Koranda, Sparky Anderson, Bobby Dolan, and Clyde

Parris and outfielders Solly Drake, Bob Lennon, and Tommy Davis.

The Junior World Series opened in Montreal on September 26. The series was played 44 times between 1904 and 1960, and the American Association had won it 26 times; the Association had won six of the last seven series played. Played only periodically before 1920 (1904, 1906, 1907, and 1917) it was an annual postseason series between 1920 and 1960 (except for 1935). The Millers in 1958 were playing in the series for the third time. Their first appearance was in 1932 when they fell to the Newark Bears. In Game Five of that series, an out call on a Newark batter in the top of the ninth inning with two out was reversed five times. The Newark batter was finally ruled safe, and Newark scored four runs to salt the game away. If the batter had been ruled out, the Millers could have won the game and taken a three-games-to-two lead in the series. As it was, the Millers lost the next game and the series, four games to two. In 1955 the Millers finished first in the regular season, swept Denver and Omaha in four games each, and beat Rochester in seven games to win their first Junior World Series. The last four games of that series were the last baseball games played at Nicollet Park.

In 1955 the Millers were still a farm club of the New York Giants, an affiliation that began in 1946. The move of the Giants to San Francisco in 1958 meant a transfer of their Triple-A farm club as well. In 1957 the San Francisco Seals of the Pacific Coast League, were the top farm club of the Boston Red Sox. In 1958 the Seals moved to Phoenix and became the Triple-A club of the Giants; Minneapolis, meanwhile, affiliated with the Red Sox.

Most of the 1958 Millers players were of major-league or marginally major-league caliber. Twenty-eight of the 34 players on the roster for all or part of the season spent or would spend at least a few months in the major leagues. The major-league careers of Paul Smith (1b), Frank Kellert (1b), Harry Malmberg (2b), Tom Umphlett (cf), Stu Locklin (of), Duane Wilson (p), Harry "Fritz" Dorish (p), Tom Hurd (p), and Bert Thiel (p) were behind them. In contrast, Jerry Zimmerman, Pumpsie Green, Lou Clinton, Schroll, Stone, and Bill Monbouquette would begin decent major-league careers in the following years. In addition, the major-league career of Art Schult was almost over (he would spend 1959 and 1960 with the Chicago Cubs) and the major-league playing career of Gene Mauch (1944-1957) was over; his career as a well-respected major league manager had not yet begun. He would sharpen his skills as a playing manager for the Millers in 1958. Often he would start the game at either second base or third base and then let Malmberg or Red Robbins finish the game.

The Millers dispatched the Royals 6-2 in Game One in Montreal before 8,791 fans, behind 7⅓ innings from Schroll and 1⅔ innings from Tom Hurd. The Millers also won Game Two, 7-2, before a crowd of 4,029, behind the pitching of Stone and Dorish. The Millers took a commanding lead in the series by edging the Royals 3-2 in Game Three before 5,882 fans. Bob Smith and Hurd did the pitching.[2]

The series switched to Metropolitan Stadium for Game Four and any subsequent games. Montreal took a 1-0 lead – its only lead of the series – in the second inning. The Millers struck back with five runs in the third inning, three scoring on a bases-loaded triple by right fielder Clinton. Schult followed with his seventh home run of the playoffs, after hitting 20 in the regular season. The Millers added two runs in the seventh inning on a triple by Borland and a home run by Clinton. Borland, with a sharp five-hitter, shut down the Royals 7-1 before 7,072 spectators.[3]

Borland said after the game, "I've pitched only one better game this year. That was a three-hit shutout against Indianapolis. I had really good control. I was a little shaky in the second inning when Montreal scored. But I tried to think this was just another game and settled down."[4]

Catcher Jerry Zimmerman added, "Borland's curve ball and fastball were great. I never caught 11 straight winners before." American Association President Ed Doherty revealed the key to the Millers championship when he said, "I've never seen a team have better pitching than the Millers had in the playoffs and Little World Series." Schroll won three playoff games, allowing only three runs (two earned) in 25⅓ innings. Stone and Smith each had a complete-game win, and clutch relief pitching from Hurd helped win several games. Each Miller collected about $1,500 for the playoff championship, with $740 coming from the Junior World Series games.[5]

In 1959 the Millers appeared in their fourth Junior World Series. They beat Omaha in six games and Fort Worth in seven games to win the American Association playoff championship, but fell to the Havana Sugar Kings in a hard-fought and tense seven-game series.

MEMORABLE GAMES AT MINNESOTA'S DIAMOND ON THE PRAIRIE

NOTES

1. League playoff totals derived from league results reported in Lloyd Johnson and Miles Wolff, eds., *The Encyclopedia of Minor League Baseball. Second Edition* (Durham, North Carolina: Baseball America, 1997).

2. The *Minneapolis Tribune*, September 9-29, 1958 was used for game accounts and attendance figures. Almost identical stories appeared in the *St. Paul Pioneer Press*.

3. Tom Briere, "Millers Crush Montreal 7-1, Win Little World Series," *Minneapolis Tribune*, September 30, 1958: S1.

4. Sid Hartman, "Borland: Second Best Game of the Year," *Minneapolis Tribune*, September 30, 1958: S1. The Zimmerman and Doherty quotes were also from Hartman.

5. "Millers Collect $1,500 Apiece," *Minneapolis Tribune*, September 30, 1958: S1.

ART SCHULT HITS FOR THE CYCLE IN WIN

APRIL 29, 1959: MINNEAPOLIS 9, HOUSTON 5

By Alan Cohen

"This could be Art's best year. I expect it to be. He does too."
    Minneapolis Millers' manager Gene Mauch[1]

The Buffs of Houston were visiting the Minneapolis Millers on April 29, and a slugfest materialized with Minneapolis prevailing, 9-5, behind the hitting of Art Schult and Lou Clinton and the pitching of Nels Chittum.

The Houston Buffs had joined the American Association at the beginning of the 1959 season, when the league expanded from eight to 10 teams and introduced divisional play. Prior to 1959 Houston had a team in the Texas League. The Buffs were not affiliated with a major-league team. Minneapolis was in the second year of its Triple-A affiliation with the Boston Red Sox, after being affiliated with the New York Giants from 1946 through 1957.

"I think I had a little wind with me, but I don't care how far over the fence they go just so I get four bases and the Millers get the runs."
    Art Schult[2]

The starting pitchers were Chittum for Minneapolis and Billy Joe Bowman for Houston.

Minneapolis scored four first-inning runs off Bowman. With one out, Shep Frazier walked and Chuck Tanner singled. That brought Schult to the plate. A Bowman fastball exploded off Schult's bat for a three-run homer. It was estimated that it landed 460 feet from home plate and rolled another 54 feet. His clout was followed by a somewhat more mundane homer by Lou Clinton that cleared the 405-foot sign in center field.

The sluggers of the Houston Buffs were quick to respond. In the top of the second inning, Ray Noble's solo homer, his seventh of the season, led off the inning. The 40-year-old catcher, whose career had begun with the New York Cubans in 1945, had played three seasons with the New York Giants. After Ev Joyner walked and Phil Jantze singled, Roy Smalley's three-run blast, his fourth, off a hanging curveball, tied the game at 4-4. For the balance of the game, Chittum abandoned the curve and stuck to his repertoire of sinkers and sliders.

In the third inning, Minneapolis threatened to break the deadlock, loading the bases with one out. At that point Houston manager Rube Walker changed pitchers, bringing on Lloyd Merritt to replace Bowman.

Gene Mauch was a player-manager for the Minneapolis Millers in 1958 and 1959.

MEMORABLE GAMES AT MINNESOTA'S DIAMOND ON THE PRAIRIE

Merritt struck out Ed Sadowski and Jim Mahoney and the game remained tied.

In the fourth inning, Merritt was lit up for three runs. Pumpsie Green singled and moved to second when Frazier grounded out. Tanner was then walked, bringing up Schult, who this time kept the ball in the ballpark, lashing a single over third baseman Phil Jantze's head into left field. The single gave the Millers a 5-4 lead. Tanner and Schult came home on a two-run triple by Clinton, and the score was 7-4. Minneapolis extended its lead with single runs in the seventh and eighth innings off Mel Wright, who had entered the game in the seventh inning after Merritt had left the game for a pinch-hitter. Schult tripled in the seventh inning and came home on a single by Ed Sadowski. The eighth-inning run was driven in by Schult, who completed his cycle with a resounding double off the 405-foot sign in center field, scoring Green, who had singled for his second hit of the game.

The announced "crowd" of 226 saw Houston score once in the ninth inning when Dick Cole drove in Smalley, but it was a case of too little, too late.

With the seven-hit complete-game win, Chittum improved his record for the young season to 2-0. Before the season he had been acquired from the St. Louis Cardinals organization in a trade for Dean Stone. Chittum was called up to the Red Sox at the beginning of August and went 3-0 in 21 relief appearances. He started the 1960 season with Boston and was sent back to the minors in early May after six appearances without a decision. Merritt was charged with the loss, his third with no wins. His only big-league experience was with St. Louis in 1957. He had appeared in 44 games with the Cardinals, going 1-2 with a 3.31 earned-run average.

The Millers, with the win, were 10-6, a half-game out of first place in the American Association's Eastern Division. The unaffiliated Buffs were in second place with an 8-8 record in the Western Division. At year's end, the Millers had a 95-67 record, placing second in the Eastern Division standings to the Louisville Colonels. In the playoffs, Minneapolis defeated Omaha in six games and went onto defeat Fort Worth in seven games for the league title. In the Junior World Series, the Millers lost to International League champion Havana in seven games.

The Houston Buffs did not fare as well, finishing in the Western Division basement with a league-worst 58-104 record. The following season, Houston became the Triple-A affiliate of the Chicago Cubs and finished with an 83-71 record, good for third place.

Prior to the game, the Millers gave a lifetime American Association pass to their team physician, Dr. Paul Pierson. The longevity of the pass in Minnesota was only through 1960, as with the expansion of the American League in 1961, the Twin Cities welcomed the Washington Senators moving to Metropolitan Stadium to become the Minnesota Twins.

The days of the American Association were numbered. The league shrank to six teams in 1961 when the Twins joined the American League, and in 1963, three remaining teams in the league were absorbed by the Pacific Coast League, one went into the International League, and the remaining two (Omaha and Louisville) went without Triple-A baseball.

Rube Walker, the Houston manager, was fired on June 21, with the team mired in the basement (29-41). His successor, Del Wilber, did not do any better (29-63). Walker resurfaced as a pitching coach at the major-league level and is most famous as the pitching coach of the 1969 New York Mets.

Gene Mauch went on to manage at the big-league level beginning in 1960 with the Philadelphia Phillies, taking over the team in midseason. After being fired by Philadelphia in 1968, he became the first manager of the expansion Montreal Expos in 1969. He moved on to the Twins in 1976, becoming only the second man to manage both the Minneapolis Millers and the Minnesota Twins. (Bill Rigney was the other.) Beginning in 1981, Mauch managed the California Angels, with whom he had his greatest success, winning the American League West in 1982 and 1986.

Schult, the hero of the game, brought his early-season average to .317 (.435 against Houston) with his four-hit performance. He simply owned Houston pitching early in the season. His homer on April 29 was his fourth of the season, all against Houston, and 11 of his 15 RBIs, including five on April 29, were against the Buffs. For the season, he batted .289 with 16 homers and 71 RBIs. Schult's homer was his 15th at Metropolitan Stadium. In all, during two seasons with the Millers, he had 19 homers at Metropolitan Stadium, breaking the record of 16 previously set by Willie Kirkland and tied by Bill Taylor. He had first played in Organized Baseball in 1948 at the age of 20 and, prior to 1959, he had played parts of three seasons in the big leagues with three different teams, getting into 110 games. On July 13, 1959, his contract was purchased by the Chicago Cubs and he made the quick trip from Minneapolis to Chicago. He was in 54 games with the Cubs in 1959 and 1960, retiring after the 1960 season.

On June 17, the Millers signed Roy Smalley, who had factored in four of Houston's runs on April 29. Smalley had last played in the majors in 1958. Smalley, who would play most of his games with Minneapolis at second base, was the brother-in-law of manager Mauch. Smalley had been released by Houston earlier in June in an economy move. With the Millers, Smalley hit 10 homers at Metropolitan Stadium between July 15 and the end of the season.

Lou Clinton, who shared the spotlight with a homer, triple, and three RBIs, made it to the Red Sox in 1960 after batting .251 with 20 homers and 77 RBIs in 1959. He played eight major-league seasons with five American League teams, batting .247 with 65 home runs in 691 games. Of those homers, 12 came at Metropolitan Stadium, the first being on August 17, 1962, off Jack Kralick in the first game of a doubleheader. Over three seasons with the Millers, Clinton had 16 homers at Metropolitan Stadium.

On July 21 and July 27, respectively, the Minneapolis keystone combination from the April 29 game, second baseman Pumpsie Green and shortstop Jim Mahoney, were called up to the Red Sox. When Green played his first big-league game on the evening of July 21, 1959, he became the first person of color to play for the Boston Red Sox.

SOURCES

In addition to Baseball-Reference.com and the sources mentioned in the Notes, the author used the following source:

Briere, Tom. "Schult's Bat Cuts Swath in Buff Hurling for 9-5 Miller Win," *Minneapolis Morning Tribune*, April 30, 1959: 21.

NOTES

1. Bob Beebe, "Mauch Sees Schult's Best Year," *Minneapolis Star*, April 30, 1959: 1D.
2. "Hits for Cycle: Schult Admits Wind Helped 514-Foot Blast," *Minneapolis Morning Tribune*, April 30, 1959: 23.

YAZ DEBUT DOESN'T COUNT; MILLERS STILL PREVAIL OVER OMAHA

SEPTEMBER 15-16, 1959: MINNEAPOLIS MILLERS 4, OMAHA CARDINALS 3
10 INNINGS (NULLIFIED GAME)
MINNEAPOLIS MILLERS 5, OMAHA CARDINALS 3 (7 INNINGS)
MINNEAPOLIS MILLERS 3, OMAHA CARDINALS 2 (12 INNINGS)

By Dave Mona

Well aware of Carl Yastrzemski's reputation as the best prospect in the Boston Red Sox minor-league system, Minneapolis Millers manager Gene Mauch couldn't wait to get the young second baseman into his lineup.

He should have.

The timing seemed perfect.

Mauch's Millers had finished their American Association season in second place in the Eastern Division with a 95-67 record. Minneapolis opened the playoffs against the Omaha Cardinals, who had finished first in the Western Division with an 83-78 record.

The series was tied at two victories apiece as the teams prepared for Game Five at Metropolitan Stadium in the best-of-seven series.

Lee Howell, a seldom-used outfielder with a .105 batting average in just 11 games, was called to report for military duty. With an open roster spot, the Millers quickly persuaded the Red Sox to send up Yastrzemski from the Raleigh Capitals, where he had just won the Class B Carolina League batting title with a .377 average.

Yastrzemski was a gifted athlete, as adept at basketball as he was at baseball. He graduated from Bridgehampton (New York) High School in 1957. While there he broke a basketball scoring mark previously held by Hall of Fame football player Jim Brown. It was his basketball prowess that earned him a scholarship to Notre Dame to study business.

After a standout season as a freshman infielder at Notre Dame, Yastrzemski signed with the Red Sox, who assigned him to Raleigh.

Although more than three years younger than the league average, his statistics were beyond impressive. Besides batting .377, he hit 15 home runs and drove in 100 runs. He walked 78 times while striking out just 49 times in 451 at-bats. His OPS (on-base percentage plus slugging percentage) was an astonishing 1.051. He also showed good speed, stealing 16 bases.

As impressive and comfortable as he was at the plate, Yastrzemski was still a work in progress in the field. He alternated between second base, where he made 32 errors, and shortstop, where he made 13, for a total of 45 errors in 116 games. His good speed and range, combined with a strong arm, stirred visions of a future outfielder.

Coming off victories in both the American Association playoffs and Junior World Series in 1958, expectations were high for the Millers in 1959.

Outfielder Chuck Tanner led the team with a .319 batting average, 12 homers, and 78 runs batted in. Center fielder Tom Umphlett hit .265 with 53 RBIs. Veteran Roy Smalley, manager Mauch's brother-in-law, played second, third, and shortstop and hit 15 home runs with 56 RBIs. Lou Clinton added 20 homers and 77 RBIs. Second baseman Pumpsie Green batted .320 through 98 games before being called up to Boston where he became the team's first Black player, 12 years after Jackie Robinson broke the color barrier with the Brooklyn Dodgers. The Red Sox became the final team in major-league baseball to integrate.

METROPOLITAN STADIUM

Tom Borland, with 14 wins, led the pitching staff, followed by Nelson Chittum with 11 and Ted Bowsfield and Earl Wilson with 10 each.

Heading into the fifth game of the playoff series, Mauch couldn't wait to insert Yastrzemski into his lineup at second base. As soon as Howell's military conflict became known, Millers business manager George Brophy notified the league of the team's intention to replace Howell with Yastrzemski. In a letter to both teams the league appeared to have certified Yastrzemski's spot on the roster. Howell, however, left a day early to visit his family, and the Millers in a wire to American Association President Ed Doherty updated him on the player movement and said they planned to use Yastrzemski that day.

Just to be safe, Mauch met with league Secretary Jim Burris before the game and asked if Yastrzemski could play. Burris said yes.

The two teams had a history of disputed plays during the season, and the Millers, leading 1-0 into the fifth, added another run on a close play at the plate.

Millers infielder Herbie Plews slid home on a close play at the plate and was called out by umpire Tom Bartos. After a conversation with first-base umpire Bill Kinnamon, Bartos changed his call to safe, saying that catcher Chris Cannizzaro didn't have control of the ball at the time of the tag.

Four Omaha errors accounted for the Millers' first three runs as Omaha starter Frank Barnes allowed just three hits over the first nine innings.

Millers starter Ted Wills struck out 11 in 5⅔ innings before leaving the game with a sore arm and his team ahead 2-0.

Omaha's Ben Mateosky tied the game with a two-run homer off Millers reliever Billy Muffett in the sixth. Omaha went ahead 3-2 in the next inning, but the Millers evened the score at 3-3 on an unearned run in the bottom of the seventh.

Yastrzemski, given an intentional walk earlier, led off the 10th with a solid single. Joe Macko bunted Yastrzemski to second, and Stu Locklin singled hard to right. Taking off on contact, Yastrzemski never slowed as he rounded third and slid safely home ahead of the sweep tag by catcher Nick Testa. Barnes had to be restrained from attacking the umpire, who again ruled in favor of the Millers, and it looked as if they had gone ahead in the series three games to two.

But not quite.

Omaha general manager Bill Bergesch, who watched the game from the press box, originally said he had no plans to protest the game, but he changed

In the 1959 season opener, Chuck Tanner homered in his first at-bat in a Minneapolis Millers' uniform. In the Millers' home opener that year, Tanner again homered in his first at-bat. Four years earlier, in his major-league debut, with the Milwaukee Braves, Tanner had homered in his first time up. Tanner had a .319 batting average with Minneapolis in 1959 and led the American Association in doubles. He later managed four teams in the majors. With the Chicago White Sox in 1972, he was named American League Manager of the Year. In 1979 he led the Pittsburgh Pirates to the world championship.

his mind. When questioned about his pregame conversation with Mauch, league Secretary Burris confirmed that he had told Mauch that Yastrzemski could play, but said he thought Mauch was talking about the original date, at the end of the week.

At that point, Bergesch contacted Doherty to file is protest.

Late in the night Doherty ruled in favor of Omaha. The results of the game were erased and a doubleheader was schedule for the next day. It would be without Yastrzemski, who would be eligible on the following day in case the Millers advanced to the finals against the Fort Worth Cats.

Before a minuscule announced crowd of 455, the Millers swept both games. They took the seven-inning opener, 5-3. First-baseman Joe Macko's first-inning home run gave the Millers a 2-1 lead.

With the score tied 3-3 in the bottom of the sixth, Clinton hit a two-run double off reliever Bob Darnell. Clinton, battling a late-season hitting slump, had been demoted to eighth in the Millers' batting order.

In the second game, Minneapolis jumped to a 2-0 lead in the first on a double by third baseman Red Robbins off Omaha lefty Tom Cheney.

A home run by Omaha first baseman Mateosky tied the score in the sixth. Millers starter Tracy Stallard allowed five hits and six walks while striking out 10 in 6⅔ innings.

Chet Nichols finished the seventh before giving way to Muffett, who had allowed three hits and one earned run in the protested game the day before.

Cheney had gone 6⅔ innings without allowing a hit. Muffett was also pitching well, and Mauch let him bat to lead off the 12th. A right-handed hitter, he lined Cheney's first pitch to him over the right-field fence for the series-winning run.

Muffett had pitched briefly at Omaha the year before and split the 1959 season between Phoenix and Minneapolis. He batted .207 with two home runs spread over seven seasons of Triple-A ball.

Asked by *Minneapolis Star* writer Bob Beebe about his heavy relief load over two days, Muffett said, "All I needed was enough work. I feel great right now."[1]

With Yastrzemski eligible two days later, the Millers went on to defeat Fort Worth for the American Association championship. They advanced to the Junior World Series, where they lost in seven games to the Havana Sugar Kings.

MILLER NOTES:

Omaha dropped out of the American Association after the 1959 season.

Under orders from Red Sox management Yastrzemski transitioned seamlessly from second base to left field in the 1960 season. He batted .339 with 7 home runs and 69 runs batted in. He joined the Red Sox the next spring and starred there for the next 23 years to pave the way for his election with 94.6 percent of the votes to the Hall of Fame in 1989.

Mauch began his 26-year major-league managerial career in 1960 with the Philadelphia Phillies.

Stallard also was promoted to the Red Sox in 1960. A year later he earned a spot in baseball history when he threw the pitch that Roger Maris hit for his record-breaking 61st home run.

NOTES

1 Bob Beebe, "Millers Face 'Tougher' Fort Worth, *Minneapolis Star*, September 17, 1959: 1D.

MILLERS WIN SECOND CONSECUTIVE AMERICAN ASSOCIATION CHAMPIONSHIP

SEPTEMBER 25, 1959: MINNEAPOLIS MILLERS 4, FORT WORTH CATS 2

By Brian M. Frank

In his first season managing the Minneapolis Millers, Gene Mauch led the team to the pinnacle of minor-league baseball. The Millers marched through the postseason in 1958, beating Wichita in six games, sweeping Denver for the American Association championship, and then sweeping Montreal in the Junior World Series. The encore would not be so easy. In 1959, after winning its first-round series against Omaha in six games, Minneapolis fell behind the Fort Worth Cats three games to two in the final series. But the Millers fought back to win Game Six, 6-3, behind a well-pitched game by lefty Ted Wills. An optimistic Mauch commented after the game, "The club right now has the perfect attitude for winning. ... The boys are just in the right state of mind."[1]

There were questions about whether Game Seven would be played as scheduled – on Friday, September 25 – after a drenching rain soaked the field after Game Six. The rain fell for nine hours overnight without a tarp covering the infield. International League President Frank Shaughnessy had informed the American Association that he would be unable to get the International League champion Havana Sugar Kings into the United States for a Sunday game if the Association's championship series went past Friday night.[2] Both the Millers and the Cats hoped to get Game Seven in on its scheduled day so the Junior World Series could start on Sunday, a day sure to draw a large crowd. In a futile attempt to get the field in playable condition, several hundred gallons of fuel oil were burned on the infield during the afternoon. However, the field remained soggy, with standing water in parts of the outfield.[3] "I've never seen a field in such poor shape," Mauch observed before the game.[4]

The Millers sent Tom Borland to the mound for the decisive game. Borland had taken the loss in Game Three, when he lasted just 4⅓ innings, allowing two runs on seven hits and one walk, while striking out seven. Fort Worth countered with Al Lary, who'd already had a dominant performance in the series, hurling a four-hit shutout in Game Four. However, the big right-hander was working on just two days' rest since that masterpiece.

The first run of the game came in the second inning. Millers cleanup hitter Joe Macko belted a solo home run, which was just fair and barely cleared the fence. It was the third home run in the series and fifth of the postseason for Macko, who played for Fort Worth in 1958 and for 104 games in 1959 before coming to the Millers in an early-August trade.

Fort Worth answered back in its next at-bat when Moe Thacker, who hit just .233 with eight home runs during the regular season, hit one over the left-field fence to tie the score.

An odd series of events in the Millers' half of the fourth inning proved to be the decisive factors in the ballgame. Stu Locklin led off the inning by drawing a walk. Macko bunted and was safe when Fort Worth third baseman Emil Syngel's throw to first was low. Red Robbins sacrificed both runners up a base. It appeared that Lary might escape the jam unscathed when he retired Ed Sadowski on a popup for the second out.

Johnny Goryl hit what appeared to be an inning-ending roller; however the ball hit a muddy spot, trickled past second baseman Jerry Kindall, and rolled into right field as two runs crossed the plate. "On a dry field I might have made the play," said Kindall. "I was playing it to bounce and it slithered right through. I overran it, and didn't have a chance to make a play. I really don't know how I could have fielded it on a wet ground."⁵ Mauch later commented, "Sure, it was lucky. But we'll take it. It's happened to us many times. It isn't how it happens – it's what is posted on the scoreboard that counts."⁶ The mud-aided single put the Millers in front 3-1.

Borland took full advantage of the runs. After surrendering a single in the fourth, he didn't allow another hit until the eighth, when Ed Phillips led off with a single. Pinch-hitter Ron Santo, a 19-year-old third baseman called up from Double-A for the playoffs, flied out for the second out. Thacker then singled, to put runners at first and second. Both advanced on a grounder to first by Jim Woods. With the tying runs in scoring position and two out, Borland got Ray Bellino to hit a hard grounder to Goryl at shortstop for the final out of the inning, and the Millers clung to their 3-1 lead.

Minneapolis added an insurance run in the eighth off reliever Joe Schaffernoth. Sadowski doubled to bring home Stu Locklin, who'd singled and gone to second on a sacrifice, to make the score 4-1.

Fort Worth cut into the lead in the ninth, when Kindall, a St. Paul native who starred at Washington High School and the University of Minnesota, led off the inning by driving a ball over the left-field wall for his third home run in three games. But Borland wasn't to be denied. He retired Bob Will on a groundball to third, got Ken Walters to fly out to right, and struck out Syngel to finish the game and send the defending champions back to the Junior World Series.

After celebrating on the field, the triumphant Millers headed to the locker room to continue their festivities. The joyous scene prompted trainer Tommy McKenna to say it was the wildest locker-room celebration he'd ever seen.⁷

Borland had thrown a complete game, allowing two runs on five hits and a walk, while striking out seven. "First time I've beaten them all season," the lanky left-hander exclaimed amid his celebrating teammates. "I've been hit pretty hard by them before, but I knew I had good stuff tonight as soon as I warmed up."⁸

"I had the best stuff I've had in two years," Borland declared. "Never won a ballgame I enjoyed winning more."⁹ This was quite a statement coming from the pitcher who'd closed out the Millers' four-game sweep of the Montreal Royals in the 1958 Junior World Series by throwing a complete game. "A magnificent job, absolutely magnificent," Mauch gushed over his pitcher's performance. "Look at the pressure he was under on every pitch. He actually seemed to get stronger as the game went along."¹⁰

In two years at the helm, Mauch had won two American Association championships and was leading his team into a second straight Junior World Series, where they hoped to repeat. "This year's team gave me a little more satisfaction in winning the playoffs than last year's," Mauch said. "We had our backs to the wall when we came back and won this one. Of course the latest one is the best one anyways."¹¹

SOURCES

In addition to the sources cited in the Notes, the author consulted Baseball-Reference.com and Retrosheet.org.

NOTES

1   Bob Beebe, "Playoff at Stake; Attitude 'Perfect' – Mauch," *Minneapolis Star*, September 25, 1959: 13B.

2   John Morrison, "Millers Win Final Game," *Fort Worth Star-Telegram*, September 26, 1959: 12.

3   Morrison: 11.

4   Morrison: 12.

5   "Borland Savors His First Win Over Cats." *Minneapolis Tribune*, September 26, 1959: S1.

6   "Borland Savors His First Win Over Cats."

7   "Borland Savors His First Win Over Cats."

8   "Borland Savors His First Win Over Cats."

9   Bob Beebe, "Doherty Hails Millers, Eyes 6th Straight AA Series Win," *Minneapolis Star*, September 26, 1959: 11A.

10 "Borland Savors His First Win Over Cats."

11 Jim Byrne, "Mauch, Spirit Hailed in Millers' Surge," *Minneapolis Star*, September 26, 1959, 11A.

THE LAST MINOR-LEAGUE POSTSEASON GAME AT METROPOLITAN STADIUM

SEPTEMBER 28, 1959: MINNEAPOLIS MILLERS 6, HAVANA SUGAR KINGS 5 (SECOND GAME OF JUNIOR WORLD SERIES)

By Alan Cohen

Ed Sadowski, one of three baseball-playing brothers, homered off lefty Luis Arroyo to win the second game of the 1959 Junior World Series for the Minneapolis Millers, 6-5, as the Millers came back from a 5-2 deficit with four runs on three homers in the last two innings.

The starting pitchers were Ted Wills (9-10) for Minneapolis and Mike Cuellar (10-11) for Havana. Only 1,062 fans braved the cold late-September weather to cheer on their team.

The Havana players had all they could due to avoid freezing in the cold North. They had a fire going in a wastebasket in the dugout, and, between at-bats, they would guzzle down hot coffee. The visitors took an early 2-0 lead in the second inning. Dan Morejon's walk was followed by singles by Ray Shearer and Rogelio Alvarez, and the Sugar Kings had their first run. With runners on first and third with one out, Enrique Izquierdo hit an apparent double-play grounder, but Roy Smalley mishandled the ball and Shearer came across with the second run of the inning.

The Millers quickly tied the score on a two-run homer by Smalley following a double by Spencer "Red" Robbins. The second Miller fielding mishap of the day helped Havana regain the lead in the top of the fourth inning. Alvarez walked and advanced to third when a pickoff attempt by Wills went past first baseman Haywood Sullivan. Alvarez was doubled home by Leo Cardenas.

Havana extended its lead to 4-2 in the seventh inning. Izquierdo singled with one out. Minneapolis tried for a force play on Cuellar's bunt, but the throw was late, and the Sugar Kings had runners on first and second. After Yo-Yo Davalillo was retired, Elio Chacon's broken-bat single (the bat splintered into five pieces) scored Izquierdo. Further damage was avoided when Minneapolis center fielder Tom Umphlett made a sliding catch to rob Tony Gonzalez of a hit.

In the bottom of the seventh inning, Minneapolis manager Gene Mauch inserted himself into the lineup as a pinch-hitter for Wills. Wills had allowed only six hits, but his mates' errors did him in. Only two of the four runs he allowed were earned. Mauch grounded out, and Minneapolis was unable to score in the seventh.

A member of the Havana team that played Minneapolis in the 1959 Junior World Series, Leo Cardenas became a steady shortstop for the Minnesota Twins 10 years later.

MEMORABLE GAMES AT MINNESOTA'S DIAMOND ON THE PRAIRIE

When the Millers were in Havana for the 1959 Junior World Series, manager Gene Mauch (second from left) and others met Fidel Castro (to Mauch's left).

Murray Wall took over the mound duties in the top of the eighth inning and gave up Havana's final tally. Morejon doubled and was singled home by Cardenas after errors by Haywood Sullivan and Wall prolonged the inning. The errors were the third and fourth of the game by the Millers, and two of Havana's five runs were unearned.

Cuellar was cruising along and had allowed only five hits in the first seven innings. But he tired in the bottom of the eighth, and the Millers retied the game with three runs. After Johnny Goryl's leadoff single, Lou Clinton homered for the Millers' second circuit clout of the game to bring the Millers within a run of the Sugar Kings. After Umphlett flied out, manager Preston Gomez of Havana changed pitchers, bringing in his relief ace, Luis Arroyo, whose arsenal of pitches featured a screwball, and whose earned-run average was a mind-blowing 1.15. Arroyo retired the first batter he faced, Joe Macko, on a popup for the second out of the inning.

"I shouldn't have risked the fast ball so much with the wind blowing like that to left."[1]

- Luis Arroyo

Arroyo faced Robbins and chose not to use his screwball. Robbins deposited a fastball over the left-field fence and the score was tied. After Wall pitched a scoreless top of the ninth, Ed Sadowski led off the bottom of the ninth for the Millers and, with the count 2-and-2, found a fastball to his liking. He hit a long fly ball that hugged the foul line and, despite an unfavorable right-to-left wind, landed fair in the left-field seats. The game was over. To make sure he didn't miss home plate, Sadowski did the unconventional and slid across the plate. Sadowski explained the decision to slide by saying, "I didn't want to take any chances. I lost a homer once before when I didn't touch home plate because guys congratulating me bumped me away."[2]

Murray Wall was credited with the win. He pitched in parts of four big-league seasons, mostly with the Red Sox, going 13-14 in 91 games. Earlier in 1959, he was with the Red Sox and was traded to Washington. After appearing in one game with the Senators, he was returned to the Red Sox, as the player for whom he had been traded reported to Boston with a sore arm. The Red Sox sent him to Minneapolis at the end of July when they called up Earl Wilson. Wall never returned to the big leagues.

Luis Arroyo took the loss. He had first pitched in the minor leagues in 1948 and first pitched in the big leagues in 1955 with the Cardinals, going 11-8 and being named to the All-Star team. By 1959 he was in the Cincinnati organization. He was with the Reds during the 1959 season but was sent to Havana in July. During the 1960 season, he was traded to the New York Yankees, where he shined as a reliever. His 1961 season was exceptional. He went 15-5 with a league-leading 29 saves (credited retroactively when saves became an official statistic in 1969), was named to the All-Star team, and finished sixth in the Most Valuable Player balloting. He was credited with the win in the third game of the 1961 World Series, pitching the final two innings as the Yankees, on Roger Maris's homer, broke a 2-2 tie and went up two games to one over the Cincinnati Reds in the Series.

Three of the Minneapolis players who homered played in the big leagues. Smalley, by the time he played for Minneapolis in 1959, had played 11 seasons in the majors, and his big-league career was over. He last played with the Philadelphia Phillies, his final game being on April 21, 1958.

Over three seasons with the Millers, Lou Clinton had 16 homers at Metropolitan Stadium. He made it to the Boston Red Sox in 1960 and played eight major-league seasons, batting .247 with 65 home runs in 691 games. Of those homers, 12 came at Metropolitan Stadium.

Spencer "Red" Robbins was a career minor leaguer who spent 14 years in the minors, making 11 stops. He finished up at Charlotte, North Carolina, in 1962. Ed Sadowski, who seemed to have more foul-ball homers than fair balls over the fence in 1959, made it to the majors with the Red Sox in 1960. In parts of five big-league seasons, including three with the expansion Los Angeles Angels, he batted .261.

Each of the managers in the game managed in the majors. Mauch went on to manage at the big-league level beginning in 1960 with the Philadelphia Phillies, taking over the team two games into the season. After being fired by Philadelphia in 1968, he became the first manager of the expansion Montreal Expos in 1969. He moved on to the Twins in 1976, becoming only the second man to manage both the Minneapolis Millers and the Minnesota Twins. (Bill Rigney was the other.) Beginning in 1981, he managed the California Angels, with whom he had his greatest success, winning the American League West in 1982 and 1986.

Preston Gomez, whose major-league playing career consisted of eight games with the 1944 Washington Senators, had some success as a minor-league manager before becoming a big-league coach and manager. After managing in the Junior World Series in 1959, he took over as manager of Spokane in 1960 and guided the Dodgers' affiliate to the Pacific Coast League championship. He was the first manager of the expansion San Diego Padres in 1969. In three full seasons, the team went 176-309, finishing last in the National League West each season. He was fired 11 games into the 1972 season. He also managed the Houston Astros and Chicago Cubs.

The Minneapolis-Havana series was even up at one game apiece. Winter-like weather forced the postponement of the third game in Minneapolis, and the remainder of the series was moved to Havana. The last five games of the Series were played there. The Sugar Kings, with Fidel Castro looking on, won the series in seven games.

The Sugar Kings were not long for Havana. Castro had come to power in 1959, and it was said that there were more automatic rifles than bats in the ballpark during the 1959 Junior World Series games. In 1960 the Sugar Kings were moved to Jersey City. Precipitating the move was an explosion at a nearby ammunition dump on June 26 that delayed play for 90 minutes.[3] Shortly thereafter, the team relocated and became the Jersey City Jerseys.

SOURCES

In addition to the sources listed in the Notes, the author used Baseball-Reference.com and the following:

Briere, Tom. "Millers Win, 6-5, Tie Havana Series," *Minneapolis Morning Tribune*, September 29, 1959: S-1.

Hall, Halsey. "Puzzled Arroyo Seeks Chance," *Minneapolis Star*, September 29, 1959: 13B.

NOTES

1. Bob Beebe, "Junior Series Moved to Havana Because of Weather," *Minneapolis Star*, September 29, 1959: 11B.
2. "Chilled Cubans Thaw on Java," *The Sporting News*, October 7, 1959: 30.
3. "Munitions Dump Explodes, Delaying Havana Twin-Bill," *The Sporting News*, July 6, 1960: 30.

MILLERS PLATE 10 IN SECOND GAME OF DOUBLEHEADER, FINALLY SOLVE COLONELS

MAY 8, 1960: MINNEAPOLIS MILLERS 10, LOUISVILLE COLONELS 2

By Mike Lynch

If there was ever a game where one team had an advantage over the other, it would have been the May 8, 1960, contest between the hometown Minneapolis Millers and the visiting Louisville Colonels at Metropolitan Stadium. The Colonels went into the doubleheader with the Millers at 12-7 and were only a half-game behind the first-place Houston Buffs in the American Association standings. Five of Louisville's wins had come against Minneapolis, which had yet to beat the Colonels. At 8-11, Minneapolis was tied with Indianapolis, and both were only a game better than the last-place Charleston Senators.

The Millers, Triple-A affiliate of the Boston Red Sox, had a habit of shooting themselves in the foot whenever they played the Colonels, the Milwaukee Braves' Triple-A affiliate, committing 15 errors in four games, and they did it again in the first game of the doubleheader when they made five more miscues in a 7-4 loss. Making matters worse was that they blew a late 4-1 lead by allowing three runs in the eighth inning and three more in the ninth. The latter trio came after third baseman Marlan Coughtry dropped a perfect throw by center fielder Dave Mann that would have gunned down the runner and given the Colonels a runner at second with two outs.

Instead, Tracy Stallard intentionally walked Joe Morgan to load the bases and set up a force, but Earl Hersh singled over the drawn-in infield to score two, and Morgan scored the third run of the inning on Hawk Taylor's sacrifice fly. The Millers' highlight came in the bottom of the seventh when Mann doubled and was sacrificed to third by Chuck Schilling, and Carl Yastrzemski was intentionally passed. With Stu Locklin at the plate, Mann, a journeyman speedster, took off for home and Yastrzemski lit out for second. While the Colonels focused on Mann, Yastrzemski continued to third and got credit for two stolen bases on the play.[1]

In addition to sloppy play, the Millers' offense had stalled and their four runs in the first game gave them only six in three games heading into the second game of their doubleheader with Louisville.

Starting for the Millers was 24-year-old, 6-foot-6 prospect Don Schwall, a former basketball star at the University of Oklahoma whom the Red Sox lured away from Oklahoma with a $65,000 bonus in 1957.[2] Schwall followed a 7-5 rookie season with Waterloo of the Class D Midwest League in 1958 with a breakout campaign in which he went 23-6 with a 3.36 earned-run average in 30 games with Alpine of the Class D Sophomore League in 1959. Promoted to Minneapolis in 1960, the righty fireballer was 1-2 going into his fourth start of the season.

Louisville sent right-hander Don Nottebart to the mound to face Schwall. Like Schwall, Nottebart was a 24-year-old former high-school star, but he signed with the Braves right out of high school and had been pitching professionally since he was 18. The Massachusetts native, who grew up idolizing Braves legend Warren Spahn and fancied himself a right-handed version of his idol, had all the makings of a star.[3] After a rocky start following his high-school graduation in 1954, Nottebart fashioned three straight 18-win seasons from 1955 to 1957, moving his way up each year from Class D Wellsville to Class B Evansville to Double-A Atlanta.

After a dismal 1958 with Triple-A Wichita of the American Association, Nottebart enjoyed his fourth 18-win season in five years, going 18-11 for Louisville in 1959. Having won three of his first four decisions in 1960, Nottebart went into his May 8 start against the Millers boasting a minor-league record of 87-52.

Little did he know he would run into an unexpected buzz saw that sent him back to the dugout not long after he left it. Mann started the onslaught with a checked-swing blooper that dropped safely inside the right-field line, and he sped around the bases for a leadoff triple. Schilling sent Mann home with a sacrifice fly to left to stake the Millers to a 1-0 lead, then Yastrzemski walked and went to second on a single by Locklin.

Bob Lawrence singled Yastrzemski home with the Millers' second run and Walter Brady followed with a hit to center that plated Locklin and sent Nottebart to the showers. Louisville skipper Ben Geraghty turned to bespectacled right-hander Howie Koplitz, a Wisconsin native who signed with the Detroit Tigers out of high school in 1956 and was in his first season with the Colonels. Koplitz's day was even shorter than Nottebart's, and he left the game after walking Coughtry and Jim Mahoney, forcing in Lawrence with the fourth tally of the frame.

That brought Frederico "Chi-Chi" Olivo into the fray. Olivo had spent much of his 20s playing in his native Dominican Republic and in Puerto Rico before signing with the Braves in 1955 at the age of 27. Olivo kicked around the minors and found some success with Class A Jacksonville in 1957, going 16-12, and pitching to a 15-11 record and a 2.64 ERA in 1958. Olivo began the 1960 season with Double-A Austin of the Texas League and went 2-1 in eight games before moving up to Louisville.

Olivo had already come through in his first appearance for the Colonels when he tossed two scoreless innings in the first game of the doubleheader to earn the win. Nevertheless, not only did he fail to stop the first-inning bleeding, he contributed to it. Schwall dropped a squeeze bunt in front of the mound and Olivo's errant throw got past catcher Bob Uecker for a two-run error that also sent Mahoney to third and Schwall to second.[4]

Mann tallied his second hit of the inning and plated Mahoney and Schwall to extend the Millers' lead to 8-0, then Mann stole second and scored the ninth run of the inning on Yastrzemski's single to center. The Colonels finally got out of the inning, but the hole they dug was too deep to escape from. Of course, that didn't stop the Millers from lending a hand by committing more errors.

In the top of the fifth, Mahoney booted Amado Samuel's grounder, and Locklin dropped Taylor's fly to right for a two-base error that put Colonels on second and third. Mahoney made his second error of

Carl Yastrzemski debuted for the Minneapolis Millers in 1959 although his official record doesn't note this because it was only in the postseason. He played the entire 1960 season with Minneapolis before going up to the Red Sox to succeed Ted Williams in left field. Williams had also played his last season in the minors, in 1938, with the Millers.

the inning when he threw wildly to first after corralling Howie Bedell's grounder and Samuel scored to give Louisville its first run of the game. Mahoney then started a 6-4-3 double play, but Taylor crossed the plate to make the score 9-2.[5]

The Millers scored their 10th run of the game in the sixth, only the second time in the season they had reached double digits, thanks in part to the Colonels' comedy of errors.[6] Yastrzemski's second hit of the game, two fielder's-choice outs, an error, a walk, and a wild pitch increased Minneapolis's lead to 10-2. Schwall completed the seven-inning game without allowing a run in the top of the seventh and evened his record at 2-2 with the victory.[7]

SOURCES

In addition to the sources cited in the Notes, the author accessed Retrosheet.org, Baseball-Reference.com, and SABR.org.

NOTES

1 Dave Mann began his professional career in 1952 at 19 and played for four different franchises before joining the Boston Red Sox' Triple-A team in 1960. He was coming off seasons in 1958 and '59 in which he stole 66 and 65 bases, respectively, and he finished the 1960 season with 50. The May 9, 1960, *Minneapolis Star* (Page 33) and *Louisville Courier-Journal* (Page 19), and the May 18, 1960, edition of *The Sporting News* (Page 30) either reported or listed in their box scores that Yastrzemski had two stolen bases on the double steal. The *Minneapolis Tribune* (Page 25) listed in its box score that he had one.

2 Curt Smith, Don Schwall biography at SABR's BioProject, sabr.org/bioproj/person/don-schwall.

3 Bob Wolf, "Admiration for Spahn Drew Nottebart Into Braves' Chain," *The Sporting News,* December 4, 1957: 20.

MEMORABLE GAMES AT MINNESOTA'S DIAMOND ON THE PRAIRIE

4 The *Louisville Courier-Journal* reported that Olivo's throw got past catcher Hawk Taylor, but Taylor didn't enter the game until he pinch-hit for Olivo in the fifth inning.

5 With nine more errors in the doubleheader, the Millers ran their total to 24 miscues in their first six games against Louisville.

6 Minneapolis beat Dallas-Fort Worth 10-0 on April 23.

7 Minor league doubleheaders at the time typically featured a nine-inning game and a seven-inning game, but not always in that order and some went a full nine innings and beyond. For instance, Charleston and Buffalo met for a doubleheader the same day Minneapolis played Louisville and the first game went 10 innings before Charleston scored the winning run. Regardless of extra innings, the teams played all nine innings in the second game as well.

LAST MILLERS GAME AT MET STADIUM

SEPTEMBER 8, 1960: ST. PAUL SAINTS 7, MINNEAPOLIS MILLERS 0 (GAME 2)

By Joe O'Connell

On a cool 1960 September evening in Bloomington, Minnesota, one of the greatest rivalries in minor-league baseball came to an end.

But nobody knew.

When the St. Paul Saints visited Metropolitan Stadium to play the Minneapolis Millers on September 8, little did anyone know that it would be the last game ever between the two teams and the last American Association game to be played there.

For the record, Saints starter Jim Golden, pitching in the evening game of a doubleheader, won his 20th game of the season, allowing only four hits and three walks in a 7-0 Saints victory.

The Saints finished the season with an 83-71 record and lost four games to two to Louisville in the post-season playoffs.

The Millers finished the season by winning one of three games at Houston and finishing with a fifth-place record of 82-72.

But the real end of the season occurred at a meeting of major-league owners on October 26, at which they allowed the Washington Senators to move to Minnesota for the 1961 season.

While that was great news for fans who had tried for the previous decade to lure major-league baseball to the Twin Cities, it marked the end of the line for both the Millers and the Saints and, with it, a storied rivalry.

The two teams were separated by the Mississippi River and the great loyalty of their fans ... nearly equaled by dislike for one another.

Nicollet Park, just off the busy intersection of Lake Street and Nicollet Avenue in south Minneapolis, and Lexington Park, the Saints home at Lexington and University Avenues, were separated by just several miles and a 30-minute streetcar ride.

A sign of the pride and competition between the cities was that the streetcar journeyed over the Lake

Jim Golden

Street Bridge unless you were from St. Paul, in which case the ride took you over the river on the Marshall Avenue Bridge. It was actually the same bridge ... only the names were changed to preserve the rivalry.

Tom Mee, the public-relations director for both the St. Paul Saints and the Minnesota Twins, frequently referred to the rivalry as "probably the shortest road trip in professional baseball."

Both cities built new ballparks in the mid-1950s, motivated by the need to modernize and the fact that

MEMORABLE GAMES AT MINNESOTA'S DIAMOND ON THE PRAIRIE

neither city would ever get major-league baseball without a modern ballpark.

Meanwhile, the leaders of the Minneapolis effort purchased farmland in Bloomington, just off Cedar Avenue and what was to become Interstate 494. Metropolitan Stadium opened in 1956 with a seating capacity of 18,200, but with the possibility of adding enough seating to more than double its capacity. Eventually the ballpark had more than 45,000 seats, allowing it to host professional football on a field that ran north to south between the third-base line and the right-field bleachers. The Millers drew an impressive crowd of 18,366 for their inaugural game against Wichita.

For St. Paul that new ballpark turned out to be Midway Stadium, located on Snelling Avenue, south of the Minnesota State Fair Grounds. It opened in 1957 with a seating capacity of 10,250 and an Opening Day crowd of 10,169.

The distance between the two new ballparks was 10.7 miles.

In a competition that ran from 1902 to 1960, the Saints held a 679-626 advantage over the Millers.

As the highest level of minor-league baseball, both the Millers and the Saints featured an array of promising rookies and longtime veterans either on the last legs of their career as players or on the start of careers as managers or coaches

The outfield trio of Willie Mays, Ted Williams, and Carl Yastrzemski led a list of Millers who eventually were elected into the Baseball Hall of Fame. Other Millers Hall of Famers were Roger Bresnahan, Jimmy Collins, Rube Waddell, Red Faber, Bill McKechnie, Zack Wheat, George Kelly, Billy Herman, Ray Dandridge, Hoyt Wilhelm, Monte Irvin, Orlando Cepeda, Dave Bancroft, and Jimmie Foxx.

Likewise, St. Paul had its share of future Hall of Famers, led by Duke Snider and Roy Campanella. That list also has Charles Comiskey, Miller Huggins, Bill McKechnie, Leo Durocher, Lefty Gomez, Dick Williams, and Walter Alston.

The fact that McKechnie appears on both lists was not unusual. In fact, it was relatively common for players to move from one team to another, as was the case with first baseman Gail Harris, the former Millers slugger who was to play a key role in the final-game victory as a member of the Saints.

One of the highlights of the rivalry was the "split doubleheader," in which where the teams would play an afternoon game in one park and an evening game in the other.

It was common for a brushback pitch in game one to be followed by a brawl in the second game. It was a classic case of neighbors not getting along well.

That final game at Met Stadium was part of a split doubleheader, but both games were at the Millers' home field. The time between games allowed the home team to clear the ballpark and charge a separate admission to the season-ender.

For the host Millers, the 1960 season had been less than fulfilling. While the team performed well on the field, fans were not excited. The thrill of the new ballpark had diminished, and fans still resented the move of the New York Giants to San Francisco despite some flirtation with the Twin Cities.

Millers fans seemed less enchanted with being a Boston Red Sox farm club than a Giants Triple-A franchise, and the lack of enthusiasm was reflected in attendance.

Millers general manager George Brophy, in a midyear dispute over the local media's fixation on dwindling crowds, had taken to not announcing daily attendance figures. Only after the final game did he reveal that annual attendance had dropped from 160,167 in 1959 to 115,702 in 1960. Major-league teams considering a move to the relatively virginal Midwest were unlikely to be impressed with an average attendance of 1,500 per game.

Each team had a personal interest in the final series. For the Saints it was a chance for Golden to win 20 games. For the Millers the question was whether Yastrzemski, successfully making the transition from second base to left field, could win the American Association batting title in a close race with Denver's Bobo Osborne.

In addition, Yastrzemski was heading into the doubleheader with a 30-game hitting streak, the league's longest of the season.

The baseball teams had substantial competition as the season neared its end. Harper Lee's *To Kill a Mockingbird* was the number-one best seller, a new dance called the Twist was taking over dance floors, and nightly television reports from the Rome Olympics introduced Americans to a new sports hero, Wilma Rudolph.

The teams agreed on a shortened seven-inning first game, which the Millers won on a four-hit shutout behind 6-foot-6 right-hander Don Schwall, who was slotted into the parent Boston Red Sox pitching rotation in 1961, where he responded with a 15-7 won-lost record and a 3.22 earned-run average.

Crafty veteran Art Fowler of the Saints, 38 years old and 13 years removed from a stint as a Miller, held the Millers to just two hits in a losing effort. Fowler was to return to Met Stadium in 1969 as a pitching coach under new Twins manager Billy Martin.

Yastrzemski went 0-for-2 in the first game to end his hitting streak and followed that with an 0-for-4 performance in the night game.

The Saints pounded Millers pitching for 13 hits en route to a 7-0 victory in the nightcap. First baseman Harris, a stalwart of Millers lineups in the mid-1950s, went 2-for-4 with two home runs and two runs batted in. Center fielder Carl Warwick went 3-for-5 with two singles and a double, while Johnny Goryl, another former Miller, and a future Twins infielder, coach, and manager, chipped in with a single and a run scored.

Just three days earlier Golden had gone the distance in winning his 19th game.

"We were expected to finish what we started," Golden recalled years later in an interview with the author. "We didn't pay much attention to pitch counts. We did chart each game as to where pitches were hit and off of what kind of pitch."

Golden also recalled another unusual aspect of the intercity series.

"We never went to the visitors clubhouse at Met Stadium," he said. "We'd get together and dress at our home clubhouse at Midway Stadium. Then we'd take a bus to Metropolitan Stadium. After the game we would return to Midway to shower and change back into our street clothes."

MILLER NOTES:

Yastrzemski finished second in the American Association batting race at .339 vs. Denver's Osborne's .342. Yastrzemski became Boston's starting left fielder in 1961. He starred there for the next 23 years and was elected to the Hall of Fame in 1989.

With the Twins moving to Met Stadium in 1961, Boston moved its Triple-A affiliate to Seattle, and the parent Dodgers moved the Saints to Omaha.

The Twins, in their first year in the majors, drew 1,256,723 fans, third best in the American League.

Golden, promoted to the Los Angeles Dodgers in 1960, appeared in one game that year and compiled a 9-13 major-league record over the next four years with the Dodgers and Houston, pitching mostly in relief.

SOURCES

Conversations with Tom Mee.

Author interview with Jim Golden, March 2020.

TWINS LOSE FIRST HOME OPENER

APRIL 21, 1961: WASHINGTON SENATORS 5, MINNESOTA TWINS 3

By Dave Lande

In their first home opener, before 24,606 fans at yet-to-be-completed Metropolitan Stadium, the Minnesota Twins played from behind the entire game before tying it, 3-3, in the bottom of the eighth inning and then losing it when the expansion Washington Senators scored two runs in the top of the ninth inning.

Both starters, Joe McClain for the Senators and Camilo Pascual for the Twins, gave up three earned runs before each was removed for a reliever in the ninth. The Twins' Ray Moore gave up two runs in the top of the ninth, and the Senators' Dave Sisler kept the Twins scoreless in the bottom of the ninth for his first save of the year.[1]

McClain's control was flawless as he had yet to walk a batter in 17⅓ innings to start the season.[2] The same could not be said of Pascual, who walked three batters. "I had no sharpness," the Cuban said. Pitching coach Eddie Lopat observed: "It was the first time he'd pitched in eight days. That's too much rest for Camilo. You saw the real Pascual in the last three innings he pitched. He suddenly found his groove."[3]

The Senators opened the scoring in the top of the first inning with two runs. Marty Keough led off with a single and took third on a single by Danny O'Connell. Gene Woodling hit into a double play, scoring Keough from third. The next batter, Dale Long, homered to

The Twins' first game in Minnesota

deep left-center field. (Long had set a major-league record in 1956 when he hit a home run in eight consecutive games as a member of the Pittsburgh Pirates.)

Both teams scored in the fourth inning. The Senators' Billy Klaus walked to lead off and went to second on a single by Willie Tasby. After Coot Veal popped out, Pete Daley singled to left to score Klaus from second, making the score 3-0.

The Twins narrowed the gap by scoring two runs in the bottom of the inning. The first batter, Lenny Green, was hit by a pitch and Don Mincher homered to deep center field, making the score 3-2. Mincher and McClain, both rookies, were teammates in 1960 at Charleston, the top farm team of the previous Senators (now the Twins). In December 1960 McClain was drafted from Charleston by the new Senators as the fifth pick in the 1960 premium expansion (minor-league) draft.[4]

There was no more scoring until the bottom of the eighth, when the Twins tied the game on Green's two-out homer to deep right field.

Moore replaced Pascual to start the ninth and walked Billy Klaus. After Tasby popped out, Veal singled, moving Klaus to second. Daley then singled to left field, scoring Klaus and moving Veal to third. Veal scored on a squeeze-play bunt by McClain. "Don't tell me I'm not a great bunter," McClain said after the game. "That pitch was coming straight for my eyes. The bunt was on, all right, but I wasn't thinking much about the squeeze when I saw that thing heading for me. I just put the bat up there in self-defense."[5]

The Twins put two runners on base in the bottom of the ninth off McClain. Bob Allison got aboard when Senators second baseman Danny O'Connell dropped his pop fly, and, after Jim Lemon struck out, went to third on Battey's single to right. Sisler replaced McClain and walked pinch-hitter Elmer Valo, loading the bases with one out.

But Sisler got the next two batters, both pinch-hitters. Hal Naragon popped out to short and Pete Whisenant struck out on three pitches to end the game. Naragon said, "I tried to hold back on the pitch that I popped up on. It was a fastball, high and inside. A bad pitch to swing at."[6] Whisenant added, "The fastball I went for with two strikes was six inches outside. But I'm up there to hit, and I didn't dare to take a pitch that close with the bases full."[7]

Twins slugger and icon Harmon Killebrew was unable to play; he was still recovering from a pulled leg muscle suffered the previous week.[8] After taking batting practice before the game, Killebrew agreed with Twins trainer Doc Lentz and manager Cookie Lavagetto that it would be better for him to sit out the game.[9]

Given that this was the first home game ever for the Minnesota Twins, it was a day of firsts for the team that played in Washington as the Senators before moving to Minnesota after the 1960 season. A few of the firsts that day include:

1. First batter – Marty Keough, Senators
2. First Twins batter – Zoilo Versalles
3. First pitcher and first Twins pitcher – Camilo Pascual
4. First hit – Marty Keough, Senators, single in first inning
5. First Twins hit – Reno Bertoia, single in third inning
6. First home run – Dale Long, Senators, first inning
7. First Twins home run – Don Mincher, fourth inning

In addition to Twins owner Calvin Griffith, notables in attendance at the game included Commissioner Ford Frick, American League President Joe Cronin, former American League President Will Harridge, and Minnesota Governor Elmer L. Andersen. Governor Andersen threw out the ceremonial first pitch of the game to manager Lavagetto, who then gave the ball to Andersen as a souvenir.[10]

Also in attendance at the game in the bleachers was 65-year-old farmer Paul Gerhardt, who, with his father, tilled the land on which much of Metropolitan Stadium was built. "That's where the melons used to be and sometimes the sweet corn," Gerhardt said, pointing to home plate.[11]

About 2,200 tickets bought for the game went unused.[12] Parking conditions were muddy as the lot had yet to be blacktopped.[13]

SOURCES

Retrosheet.org

Baseball-reference.com

retrosheet.org/boxesetc/1961/B04210MIN1961.htm

baseball-reference.com/boxes/MIN/MIN196104210.shtml

MEMORABLE GAMES AT MINNESOTA'S DIAMOND ON THE PRAIRIE

NOTES

1. Retroactively awarded. Saves were not an official statistic until 1969.
2. Bob Beebe, "McClain's Control 'Secret to Success,'" *Minneapolis Star*, April 22, 1961: 12A.
3. Beebe.
4. Baseball-reference.com, baseball-reference.com/players/m/mcclajo01.shtml.
5. Jim Klobuchar, "Nats Laud McClain, But He's Not So Sure," *Minneapolis Tribune*, April 22, 1961: 11.
6. Dwayne Netland, "'We Had Chances,' Says Cookie; Twins Praise McClain's Hurling," *Minneapolis Tribune*, April 22, 1961: 11.
7. Netland.
8. "Killebrew Not Ready Today," *Minneapolis Tribune*, April 22, 1961: 12.
9. Charles Johnson, "Lowdown on Sports," *Minneapolis Star*, April 22, 1961: 12.
10. "Twins Sing 'Elmer's Tune' and 'Official' Fans," *Minneapolis Tribune*, April 22, 1961: 11, 12.
11. Frank Wright, "Twins Slam That Ball Where His Corn, Melons Used to Grow," *Minneapolis Tribune*, April 22, 1961: 1.
12. "24,606 View Home Opener," *Minneapolis Tribune*, April 22, 1961: 12.
13. "Cal Hails Play, Disappointed at Attendance," *Minneapolis Tribune*, April 22, 1961: 11.

ORIOLES' JIM GENTILE BLASTS TWO GRAND SLAMS ON CONSECUTIVE PITCHES

MAY 9, 1961: BALTIMORE ORIOLES 13, MINNESOTA TWINS 5

By Mike Huber

On Tuesday, May 9, 1961, before a crowd of 4,514 fans at Minnesota's Metropolitan Stadium, the Baltimore Orioles played an afternoon game against the Twins. Baltimore's record was 12-10, while Minnesota's was 11-11. This game was Baltimore's first in Minnesota, as the Twins franchise moved from Washington after the 1960 season.[1] If any of the fans showed up in the third inning, they had already missed witnessing history being made, as Baltimore slugger Jim Gentile hit two bases loaded home runs in consecutive at-bats, in the first and second innings, to tie a major league record. Not only were they on consecutive at-bats, they were on consecutive pitches!

In the top of the first, Twins hurler Pedro Ramos walked right fielder Whitey Herzog, gave up a double to center fielder Jackie Brandt, and then walked third baseman Brooks Robinson. That set the stage for first baseman Jim Gentile. After the game, Diamond Jim described his at-bats. "In the first inning, Pedro Ramos ... had two strikes on me and he threw me a pitch that was up around my chin and not quite as fast as I expected…. At the last minute I lashed out to upper-cut the ball, and even though Ramos had made me hit the pitch he hoped I would hit, the ball sailed over the fence in centerfield."[2] Officials estimate the shot to have traveled at least 430 feet.[3]

Ramos gave his version: "I am in trouble, so I try to pitch inside. But I make it too good. I look up, and the ball, she is over the center-field fence."[4] So, four batters into the game provided Baltimore with a 4-0 lead. Ramos retired the next three Orioles to end the inning. The Twins has one base runner on a leadoff single by shortstop Zolio Versalles in their half of the first but did not score.

In the second frame, after an out by second baseman Marv Breeding, Orioles pitcher Chuck Estrada singled to right field. Paul Giel was brought in from the bullpen to relieve Ramos. He proceeded to walk Herzog, as the top of the order was up again. Brandt reached on an error by Giel, allowing Estrada to score and both Herzog and Brandt moved up a base. Robinson again drew a few pass, and Gentile strode to the plate. In his words, "In the second inning, Paul Giel threw me another pitch that was good. I don't know whether it was a screwball or a slider, but I know it fooled me for an instant. As it broke away from me, I swung and I wasn't trying to hit it out…. I was really surprised when I got my bat around enough to pull it over the right field wall."[5]

Al Costello, a writer for the *Baltimore Sun,* described the blast with: "This time Gentile hit the first pitch to right field, over the 360 mark by a goodly 30 or 40 feet, two-thirds of the way up into the bleachers."[6] The same quartet[7] scored as in the first inning. Jim stated, "[Manager Paul] Richards normally didn't say anything, but when I came back to the dugout after the second one, he looked at me and said, 'Son, I don't think that's ever been done.'"

Gentile had become the fourth ballplayer to hit two grand slam home runs in the same game and the first to hit them on consecutive at-bats. The eight runs plated by Gentile established a new record for the most runs driven in by a batter in two consecutive innings.[8] Before the Twins had retired five batters, they were down 9-0.

The Twins mounted a small comeback in the bottom of the fourth inning. First baseman Don Mincher walked to lead off for the Minnesotans. After pinch-hitter Elmer Valo flied out to right, right fielder Bob Allison homered, a mammoth blast to left field. Second baseman Billy Gardner grounded to short and then Hal Naragon, who had pinch-hit for

MEMORABLE GAMES AT MINNESOTA'S DIAMOND ON THE PRAIRIE

Pedro Ramos and Paul Giel both gave up grand slams to Jim Gentile on May 9, 1961.

Giel in the second, launched a deep home run over the fence in right-center field. Versalles singled and Twins centerfielder Lenny Green doubled to center. Estrada struck out left fielder Dan Dobbek to end the inning, but Minnesota had notched three runs on the board.

Bill Pleis came on as the fourth Minnesota pitcher in the top of the fifth (Don Lee had pitched two scoreless innings after Giel). Pleis walked the first man he faced, catcher Gus Triandos. Shortstop Ron Hansen followed with a home run, deep down the left field line. That made the score 11-3, in favor of the Orioles. It stayed that way until the top of the eighth inning, when Earl Robinson pinch-hit for Herzog. He singled up the middle and Brandt followed with a double to left field, advancing Robinson to third. Brooks Robinson sent a fly ball to center field which Dobbek caught, and Earl Robinson scored on the sacrifice fly. Brandt scampered to third on Brooks Robinson's sacrifice and he came home on Gentile's sacrifice fly, a pop fly to left that was fielded by the shortstop Versalles. Baltimore 13, Minnesota 3.

In the bottom of the ninth, Paul Richards swapped out five players in a merry-go-round that filled the score card. Earl Robinson stayed in the game, playing right field. Jim Busby went to center, batting in Gentile's place. Walt Dropo came on play first, batting in the pitcher's spot. Gordon Jones came in from the bullpen to pitch, and he would bat in the fifth spot, where Dick Williams was. Russ Snyder went to play left replacing Williams, batting in Brandt's position. After this was settled, Allison led off for the Twins and parked the ball far beyond the left-center fence for his second home run and third run batted in of the game. Harmon Killebrew added a solo home run for the home team in the bottom of the ninth, and that was all the scoring.

Gentile finished with nine RBIs as the Orioles beat the Twins 13-5. Home runs accounted for fifteen of the game's eighteen runs. The first five batters in Baltimore's lineup accounted for eight of their eleven hits. The Twins used six pitchers "in an attempt to halt Baltimore's batting rampage."[9] Orioles pitcher Wes Stock was Chuck Estrada's roommate in 1961. After the game, Stock said, "I told Gentile, 'I could win 20 games if you hit two grand slams a game for me.' But he never did. I hope Estrada sends Gentile a case of beer every year on the anniversary of that game to thank him.'"[10]

"I was the most surprised man in the world when I was told I had set three major league records when I hit those home runs in the first two innings,"[11] wrote

Diamond Jim, in an article he penned in the *Baltimore Sun*. The nine runs driven in by Jim Gentile set a new Oriole high for one game. The previous club record of seven RBIs had been jointly held by Gentile and Triandos.[12] Through the first 22 games of the 1961 season, Gentile was in the zone, batting .338 and slugging .738 with an OPS of 1.215.

Norman Boyles, a Greensboro, NC, mathematician, calculated the odds of hitting two grand slam home runs in a player's first two times at bat to be 6,581,192-to-1.[13] A week before Gentile's accomplishment, Chuck Weatherspoon of the Class B Wilson Tobs had turned the trick. According to the *Baltimore Sun*, "After that feat, Boyles put his mathematics to work and thus had the figures at hand when Gentile connected."[14]

The Baltimore Orioles hit a total of five grand slam home runs in 1961. Each one was off of Jim Gentile's bat, including the two on May 9.[15] This established an American League record which stood until 1987.[16]

ACKNOWLEDGEMENTS

The author thanks Rachel Hamelers, science librarian and reference services manager at Trexler Library, Muhlenberg College, and Bill Stetka, director of Orioles Alumni, for their assistance with obtaining sources.

SOURCES

"The Odds Agin' Him," *Baltimore Sun*, May 10, 1961.

Costello, Al, "Gentile Leads Loop in RBIs," *Baltimore Sun*, May 10, 1961.

Gentile, Jim, "Unawed By Swat Records," *Baltimore Sun*, May 10, 1961.

"Gentile Hits Four-Run Homers Two Innings in a Row as Orioles Crush Twins," *New York Times*, May 10, 1961.

Olderman, Murray, "Hot Tempered Oriole," *The Saturday Evening Post*, August 26, 1961.

"Two Grand Slams in One Game," baseball-almanac.com/feats/feats11.shtml

"The Ballplayers – Jim Gentile," baseballlibrary.com/ballplayers/player.php?name=Jim_Gentile_1934

"May 9, 1961 Baltimore Orioles at Minnesota Twins Box Score and Play by Play," http://baseball-reference.com/boxes/MIN/MIN196105090.shtml

"Top 40 Orioles of All Time: #36, Jim Gentile – Camden Chat," camdenchat.com/2014/1/8/5286404/orioles-top-40-greatest-jim-gentile

"Classic Minnesota Twins!: Twins Killers: Diamond Jim Gentile's Two Grandslams At The Met, May 9, 1961," classicminnesotatwins.blogspot.com/2014/05/twins-killers-diamond-jim-gentiles-two.html

"Doug Wilson's baseball bookshelf: Diamond Jim Gentile: A Baseball Player Who Knew How to Wait," dougwilsonbaseball.blogspot.com/2014/11/diamond-jim-gentile-baseball-player-who.html

"Retrosheet Boxscore: Baltimore Orioles 13, Minnesota Twins 5," retrosheet.org/boxesetc/1961/B05090MIN1961.htm

"Jim Gentile Becomes the First Major League Baseball Player to Hit a Grand Slam in Back to Back Innings," todayifoundout.com/index.php/2012/05/jim-gentile-becomes-the-first-major-league-baseball-player-to-hit-a-grand-slam-in-back-to-back-innings/

NOTES

1. "Classic Minnesota Twins!: Twins Killers: Diamond Jim Gentile's Two Grandslams At The Met, May 9, 1961," http://classicminnesotatwins.blogspot.com/2014/05/twins-killers-diamond-jim-gentiles-two.html
2. Jim Gentile, "Unawed By Swat Records," *Baltimore Sun*, May 10, 1961.
3. Al Costello, "Gentile Leads Loop in RBIs," *Baltimore Sun*, May 10, 1961.
4. Murray Olderman, "Hot Tempered Oriole," *The Saturday Evening Post*, August 26, 1961.
5. Gentile.
6. Costello.
7. "Classic Minnesota Twins!: Twins Killers: Diamond Jim Gentile's Two Grandslams At The Met, May 9, 1961," http://classicminnesotatwins.blogspot.com/2014/05/twins-killers-diamond-jim-gentiles-two.html
8. "Gentile Hits Four-Run Homers Two Innings in a Row as Orioles Crush Twins," *New York Times*, May 10, 1961.
9. "Gentile Hits Four-Run Homers Two Innings In A Row as Orioles Crush Twins."
10. "Doug Wilson's baseball bookshelf: Diamond Jim Gentile: A Baseball Player Who Knew How to Wait," http://dougwilsonbaseball.blogspot.com/2014/11/diamond-jim-gentile-baseball-player-who.html
11. Gentile.
12. Costello.
13. "The Odds Agin' Him," *Baltimore Sun*, May 10, 1961.
14. "The Odds Agin' Him."
15. "Top 40 Orioles of All Time: #36, Jim Gentile – Camden Chat," http://camdenchat.com/2014/1/8/5286404/orioles-top-40-greatest-jim-gentile
16. "The Ballplayers – Jim Gentile," http://baseballlibrary.com/ballplayers/player.php?name=Jim_Gentile_1934

JULIO BECQUER HITS FIRST PINCH-HIT AND WALK-OFF HOME RUN IN MINNESOTA TWINS HISTORY

JUNE 20, 1961: MINNESOTA TWINS 5, BALTIMORE ORIOLES 4

By Bruce Harris

The 1961 American League baseball season ushered in change. The Washington Senators moved to Minnesota, becoming the Twins. It was the inaugural season for two new expansion teams, the Los Angeles Angels and the new Washington Senators. Julio Becquer also experienced change as the season got underway. Beginning in 1955, Becquer had played for the Senators. However, on December 14, 1960, the Angels made Becquer the 55th overall pick in the 1960 expansion draft, paying $75,000 for the first baseman. It proved to be a poor investment. Becquer had only eight official at-bats with the Angels. He walked once, had no hits, and struck out five times. On May 10, 1961, Los Angeles placed Becquer on waivers. The Philadelphia Phillies purchased him and immediately sent Becquer to the Buffalo Bisons, their affiliate in the Triple-A International League. Becquer did not fare much better in Buffalo. He was hitting .150 when his old team (the Washington Senators), now called the Minnesota Twins, purchased him for about $10,000.[1] The date was June 2, 1961. The next day, Becquer was in a Twins uniform.

The Twins had a three-game losing streak (they were 24-39) as they prepared to host the 32-32 Baltimore Orioles in Metropolitan Stadium for a three-game series and the start of a 10-game homestand. A total of 17,851 paid to see lefty Jack Kralick oppose Baltimore's veteran right-hander Hal Brown.

In the first inning, Kralick retired the Orioles in order, but Brown immediately ran into trouble. Billy Martin led off the Twins half of the first with a single. One out later, Harmon Killebrew hit Brown's first pitch 400 feet over the left-center-field fence for his 17th home run of the year.[2] The Orioles got a run back in the third inning. Earl Robinson started things off with a double inside third base. With two outs, Brooks Robinson drove him in with a single to center field.

With the Twins leading 2-1, Brown began the bottom of the third by walking Jim Lemon. Bob Allison followed with a single, putting runners on the corners with no outs. Brown nearly worked his way out of trouble. He retired Dan Dobbek and Earl Battey. But Jose Valdivielso blooped a single over

Cookie Lavagetto was the first manager of the Minnesota Twins. Although the Twins won this June 20, 1961 game, Lavagetto was fired as manager after only two more games.

first, scoring Lemon. The Twins had a 3-1 lead after four innings.

The Orioles threatened in the top of the fifth inning but failed to score. With one out, Earl Robinson bunted his way on. Jerry Adair walked. After a double steal, Dave Philley pinch-hit for Brown. Kralick struck him out on a slow curve before retiring Brooks Robinson on a fly out to center.

The score remained 3-1 until the eighth inning. Jack Fisher had replaced Brown for the Orioles. He surrendered a one-out single to Allison, a shot that went off Brooks Robinson's glove. The hit proved costly. With two outs, Battey's run-scoring double off Earl Robinson's glove in deep right-center gave the Twins a 4-1 lead entering the ninth inning.

Three outs away and Kralick pitching well, it appeared as though the three-game losing streak would come to an end. Through eight innings, Kralick had allowed only four hits. But back-to-back singles by Jim Gentile and Gus Triandos opened the ninth. Minnesota manager Cookie Lavagetto went to the mound to speak to Kralick, but the lefty remained in the game. After the mound visit, Ron Hansen lined out to center. Then Earl Robinson, who entered the game hitting .140, got his third hit of the night, a three-run, 390-foot game-tying home run to right field. It was Robinson's first major-league home run[3] and tied the score. Adair singled, and that was all for Kralick. Chuck Stobbs relieved him. He struck out Fisher (trying to bunt), but Brooks Robinson singled, sending Adair to third. Stobbs got out of trouble, inducing Dick Williams to pop out to the catcher.

With the score tied, 4-4, the stage was set. Becquer pinch-hit for Stobbs to open the bottom of the ninth inning. He sent a Fisher curveball 370 feet over the right-center-field screen. It was both the first pinch-hit home run and the first walk-off home run in Twins history. After the game, the jubilant Becquer said, "I go up to hit, not to walk. There is no pressure, because I can usually get a piece of the ball. Tonight I happened to get a bigger piece than usual."[4]

Losing pitcher Fisher fell to 2-8. He said, "I've faced Julio many times in the last few seasons. I think this was only the second or third hit he's gotten off me."[5] It was the third time the Twins had beaten Fisher in 1961.

Chuck Stobbs picked up his first win of the season (against two losses). Kralick pitched solid baseball for eight innings. According to the Orioles' Triandos, Kralick had "great stuff" but "might have tired a little in the ninth."[6] Kralick disagreed. "I felt strong," he said. "They just started to drop the hits in there. The pitch I threw to Earl Robinson was outside, and he hit it out of the park."[7]

Two weeks later, Becquer provided another big moment for Twins fans. In the first game of a Fourth of July doubleheader, the Twins trailed 4-2 in the bottom of the ninth. After two singles and a walk, they had the bases loaded with two outs. Becquer was summoned to pinch-hit for Bill Tuttle, and he electrified the crowd with a walk-off homer into the right-field seats.

Looking back on his career decades later, Becquer said, "I was a fairly good hitter, but I had no power.[8] I could hit the ball out once in a while but I was a spray hitter. I was somewhat a small guy for first base; I wasn't the standard first baseman. I was a great fielder which helped me a lot. I developed a good reputation as a pinch-hitter and that helped me stay in the big leagues."[9]

After the 1961 season Becquer thought he was through playing major-league baseball. He spent time in the minors and played ball in Mexico. In 1963 he discovered he was one week short of qualifying for a pension. Twins owner Calvin Griffith placed Becquer on the big-league roster.[10] On September 18, he appeared for the last time, running for Battey in the eighth inning.

SOURCES

In addition to the sources cited in the Notes, I consulted the Baseball-Reference.com, Retrosheet.org, Newspapers.com, and the following:

Beebe, Bob. "'Dr.' Becquer's Serum Saves 'Snake Bit' Twins," *Minneapolis Star*, June 21, 1961: 1F.

Briere, Tom. "Becquer Blast Propels Twins by Orioles 5-4," *Minneapolis Morning Tribune*, June 21, 1961: 21.

Elliot, Jim. "Birds Lose to Twins on Becquer's Homer in 9th, 5-4," *Baltimore Sun*, June 21, 1961: 19.

Swol, John. "Julio Becquer, a Member of 1961 Minnesota Twins Team, Passes Away," twinstrivia.com/2020/11/06/julio-becquer-a-member-of-1961-minnesota-twins-team-passes-away/.

baseball-reference.com/boxes/MIN/MIN196106200.shtml

retrosheet.org/boxesetc/1961/B06200MIN1961.htm

NOTES

1. Some reports say the Twins paid Buffalo $20,000 for Becquer. See Sid Hartman (Hartman's Roundup), "Mele Corrected Becquer's Style," *Minneapolis Morning Tribune*, July 5, 1961: 20.

2. Killebrew finished the 1961 season with 46 home runs.

3. Earl Robinson finished the season with eight home runs. He hit 12 home runs during his four-year major-league career.

4. Dwayne Netland, "Becquer Scored on Rebound," *Minneapolis Morning Tribune*, June 21, 1961: 21.

MEMORABLE GAMES AT MINNESOTA'S DIAMOND ON THE PRAIRIE

5 Netland.

6 Netland.

7 Netland.

8 Becquer hit five home runs in 1961. He hit 12 home runs during his seven-year big-league career.

9 Nick Diunte, "How Julio Becquer Linked the Cuban Legacy of the Washington Senators and Minnesota Twins Franchises," November 3, 2020. forbes.com/sites/nickdiunte/2020/11/03/how-julio-becquer-linked-the-cuban-legacy-of-the-washington-senators-and-minnesota-twins-franchises/?fbclid=IwAR2GKdvkMirEDv_oA6qGkB-oVS7SnWQm3_xitwZ89UYcqbLM903r4lmSe3QI&sh=9a71933458e8.

10 Diunte.

BECQUER'S SUDDEN JULY FOURTH SHOT

JULY 4, 1961, GAME 1: MINNESOTA TWINS 6, CHICAGO WHITE SOX 4

By Gene Gomes

Roman candles and bottle rockets lit up the evening sky on the Fourth of July in the Twin Cities. In the afternoon the Minnesota Twins produced baseball fireworks in the first game of a doubleheader at Metropolitan Stadium against the Chicago White Sox. It was the summer of 1961, and fans were coming out in strong numbers to support their new baseball team.

During the first game of the series, the night before, a big crowd of 30,392 had to wait out a 48-minute seventh-inning rain delay. They were rewarded as the Twins prevailed, 7-6. Minnesota was 31-46 after winning five of its last eight. Chicago had lost five of six after winning 12 in a row. The White Sox were in fifth place at 39-39, 7½ games ahead of the Twins. White Sox manager Al Lopez was not pleased afterward, saying, "Both teams played lousy ball tonight."[1]

White Sox pitcher Billy Pierce came into Tuesday's game with a 4-6 won-lost record. To date, the longtime White Sox left-hander's career record was 183-149 with seven All-Star selections. Twins manager Sam Mele chose rookie right-hander Bert Cueto as his starter. Cueto was 0-3 but had pitched well in his major-league debut against the White Sox, on June 18, allowing three runs in eight-plus innings.

Chicago scored first, in the third inning on a walk to J.C. Martin, his steal of second, and Luis Aparicio's single. Pierce blanked the Twins in their half of the third, and Floyd Robinson led off the fourth with a single. Two outs later Jim Landis walked, and Cueto was lifted with a 3-and-2 count on Martin because of a finger blister. Martin singled to center on rookie reliever Bill Pleis's first pitch for two runs and a 3-0 Chicago lead.

In the fifth inning the Twins broke the shutout. Bill Tuttle delivered his first homer of the year, over the right-field fence. In the top of the sixth, Chicago answered with a run on a bases-loaded sacrifice fly by pinch-hitter Al Smith. That made it 4-1.

After Pleis retired the White Sox in the seventh, Jim Lemon led off the home half by hitting one over the right-field screen for his eighth home run. Neither team scored in the eighth inning and it remained 4-2. Pleis had pitched well enough for four innings to keep Minnesota within reach. Mele brought in veteran Chuck Stobbs to pitch the ninth. The 32-year-old left-hander retired Landis, Sammy Esposito, and Bob Roselli in order.

The Twins had collected only six hits off Pierce through eight innings. Harmon Killebrew led off the ninth and flied out to center fielder Landis in front of the wall. After Bob Allison singled, Lopez replaced Pierce with right-hander Russ Kemmerer to face Lemon. Lemon flied out to right field. With two outs, catcher Earl Battey kept the ninth going with a single to left, his second hit of the game. Lopez made another move and brought in Frank Baumann to retire left-handed hitter Lenny Green and stop the rally. But Baumann walked Green and the bases were loaded. The fans got excited and hoped for a hit that could tie the game.

Lopez stepped out of the dugout again, and the fans were standing and making noise over the manager's plight. He called for the veteran right-hander Warren Hacker. Hacker was used strictly in relief by Lopez, having posted four saves thus far.[2] His job was to retire Bill Tuttle and finish this win.

Mele decided to make a move in this spot and told pinch-hitter Julio Becquer to get ready.

Once Hacker was summoned to come in and pitch, Mele informed umpire Hank Soar that Becquer was to bat for Tuttle. The matchup would now be lefty versus righty, and Becquer had been in this role before.

Becquer was hitting only .233 overall but was 2-for-3 in his last three pinch-hit attempts. His custom was to go up to the plate swinging, and Hacker delivered the first pitch. It was right in there and Becquer made full contact and sent the ball deep to right-center field. When the ball sailed over the fence at the 365-foot sign, the Twins had a thrilling two-out pinch-hit walk-off grand slam to win the game. Becquer trotted around the bases to loud cheers and full-throated roars. He was slapped on the back by third-base coach Clyde McCullough as he went by, and followed Allison, Battey, and Green across home plate. With the 6-4 victory the Twins had swiped a game the White Sox thought they had in the win column.

After the game Mele was asked why the part-time first baseman Becquer didn't play regularly. He explained: "He's more effective as a pinch-hitter. Julio tends to swing at bad balls occasionally. Over a period of time this would catch up with him. But in a situation like today, where the pitcher has to get the ball near the plate, Becquer is tough."[3] This was the third pinch-hit homer of the season for the 29-year old. He was a sizzling 8-for-14 (.571) with nine runs batted in in a pinch. As a regular in the lineup, he was 3-for-20 (.150).

Ron Henry roomed with Becquer on the road. He said that Becquer "is a fellow deadly serious about pinch-hitting successfully."[4] Becquer had a habit of arriving early every day and said, "I must be ready at all times. It's hard to keep your timing when you don't play every day, so I come out early every day to take batting practice."[5]

Because of the late game Monday night, several players came in too late to take batting practice. Becquer was able to get in even more time in the batting cage. "Becquer talks about pinch-hitting a lot," Henry said. "We really agree on swinging at that first pitch if it's anywhere near over. Becquer can hit any pitch, and the pitchers see him only one time a game or less. It's hard to pitch to him. And they can't afford to throw a bad pitch and get behind him."[6]

Becquer's grand slam was unusual in that each run scored was charged to a different pitcher. The losing pitcher was Frank Baumann. Lopez felt that the key play of the game was the walk issued to Lenny Green by Baumann. "We took Baumann out after that," Lopez said. "And why not? A man doesn't deserve to stay in after walking a man in that situation."[7]

The winning pitcher was Stobbs, who said, "Sure picked up an easy victory after pitching only the ninth inning. But I've lost my share of the same type in a hurry."[8] The win for Stobbs was the last of his career and 1961 was his last season. He compiled a 107-130 career mark, with 89 of the losses for poor Washington Senators teams.

Julio Becquer was born in Havana in 1931. He was signed in 1952 and went to a Senators farm team in Drummondville, Quebec. He competed in parts of five seasons for Washington before being claimed by the expansion Los Angeles Angels in December 1960. Becquer struck out in five of his first six at-bats for manager Bill Rigney and was sold to the Phillies organization in May 1961. He was assigned to Buffalo and played 19 games for the Bisons. before the Twins purchased his contract. "I was resigned to spending the season in the International League until the Twins bought me," Becquer said.[9]

After 1961 Becquer's future with the Twins looked uncertain. He joined the Mexican League and in 1963 got a call from Twins owner Calvin Griffith, who told him he needed some more time playing to earn his pension. He said Griffith told him, "I want you to fly here right away, and I want to reinstate you on the club until you qualify."[10]

Becquer was signed, and in September appeared in one game as a pinch-runner for the Twins. He scored a run and he scored his pension as well. Becquer left baseball after a few more years in Mexico. He worked in sales in Minnesota for 30 years before retiring. He spoke at an event in 2016 and said, "I've always been grateful to Calvin Griffith."[11]

SOURCES

Newspapers

- Chicago Tribune

Online sources

- baseball-reference.com
- newspapers.com
- Nowlin, Bill. "Chuck Stobbs," SABR Baseball Biography Project, sabr.org/bioproj/person/d5feb98d, accessed March 24, 2020.

NOTES

1. Dwayne Netland, "Batting Hero Allison Almost Goat in Field," *Minneapolis Tribune*, July 4, 1961: 13.
2. Saves were compiled only unofficially from 1960 to 1968. The four saves by Hacker were credited retroactively after saves became an official rule in 1969.
3. Dwayne Netland, "'Becquer More Valuable on Bench,' Says Twin Pilot," *Minneapolis Tribune*, July 5, 1961: 20.
4. Max Nichols, "Extra Drill Helps Becquer in Pinch," *Minneapolis Star*, July 5, 1961: 49.
5. Nichols.
6. Nichols.
7. Dwayne Netland, "'Becquer More Valuable on Bench,' Says Twin Pilot."

8   Sid Hartman, "Mele Corrected Becquer's Style," *Minneapolis Tribune,* July 5, 1961: 20.

9   Netland, "Becquer Scored on Rebound," *Minneapolis Tribune,* June 21, 1961: 21.

10 Matt Welch, "The Cuban Senators," ESPN.com-Page2, accessed March 10, 2020.

11 Remarks at the Society for American Baseball Research Halsey Hall Chapter meeting in Minneapolis on April 9, 2016.

THE FIRST INSIDE-THE-PARK HOME RUN IN TWINS HISTORY

JULY 4, 1961 – GAME 2: MINNESOTA TWINS 4, CHICAGO WHITE SOX 2

By Gene Gomes

Sports columnist Charles Johnson wrote of the 1961 Twins team: "Actually it's strange that a team which hasn't played .500 ball at home can keep the spectators excited, enthused and applauding."[1] It was more than just the fact that it was the first year of major-league baseball in Minnesota. It was the kind of competitive play they offered that pleased the fans. Long home runs, close games, and comeback wins were marks of this team from the start.

Most of the home-run power was produced by Harmon Killebrew. Year after year he thrilled fans with dozens of long balls. From 1959 to 1972 Killebrew averaged 37.8 home runs per year. His 573 major-league home runs ranked fifth most in baseball history at the time of his retirement. But in the second game of a July 4 doubleheader in 1961, he accomplished something for the first and only time in his major-league career.

The Chicago White Sox visited Metropolitan Stadium the first week of July. They were rudely greeted by the Twins in the first two games of the series, losing 7-6 Monday night and 6-4 in Tuesday's first game. White Sox manager Al Lopez chose veteran pitcher Cal McLish to start the second game of the day. McLish had come to Chicago in a trade with Cincinnati in December and was 4-7 with a 4.31 earned-run average. He was needed to turn around the recent course of games for the White Sox, who had lost six of their last seven.

Minnesota took the first game of the day in exhilarating fashion with a ninth-inning rally, and manager Sam Mele was hoping for a sweep with the 26-year-old left-hander Jack Kralick taking the mound for the Twins. Kralick came in with a 7-5 record, having pitched into the seventh inning in 14 of his 16 starts. Kralick was in the regular rotation this season after splitting time between starting and relieving in 1960. His batterymate was Earl Battey, who also caught the first game.

Neither McLish nor Kralick was known as an overpowering pitcher. The tall and lanky Kralick used control and a slow curve to keep hitters off balance, while McLish had the advantage of experience. Both pitchers were on their game this day, and a duel was developing through the early innings. The White Sox had some early chances, "but the hit they needed could not be supplied as the middle of the batting order was made to look feeble in the clutch of Kralick's slick knuckle ball."[2]

The day was warm, but the bats were not. Through seven innings the game was scoreless, each pitcher having given up only five hits. McLish had not permitted a Twins baserunner past second, and Kralick stranded six runners. In the eighth, the White Sox had another chance. With one out, Floyd Robinson stroked his third single and Jim Landis walked. But Minnie Miñoso and Roy Sievers were set down by Kralick, leaving runners on second and third.

In the home half of the eighth, outfielder Lenny Green led off with a single. Bill Tuttle followed with a sacrifice, and that brought up Kralick. Mele didn't lift him for a pinch-hitter. Perhaps he was saving that move for later. Kralick indeed had a hit in each of his last five starts and had won three of four decisions in those games. Either way, Mele's hunch paid off when Kralick coaxed a 3-and-1 count off McLish and then rapped the next pitch to center field for a single. When Green rounded third and scored, the Twins had the lead over the White Sox, 1-0. Things continued to fall apart for Chicago when Zoilo Versalles laid down a bunt toward third, and it rolled dead for a hit. McLish induced Billy Martin to ground one to shortstop Luis Aparicio. Instead of a double play, Aparicio rushed to get the speedy Versalles at second, bobbled it, and had to settle for the out at first.

There were two out with Kralick on third and Versalles on second. McLish hadn't yielded many hard-hit balls and faced Killebrew with first base open. He had pitched him carefully in his last start against Minnesota, retiring him once and walking him twice. Killebrew was red-hot coming into this series, hitting .360 (second in the league) with 24 home runs (tied for third). He had just been named to the American League All-Star team and was pleased, saying, "It's always an honor to be chosen. It means you're having a pretty good year."[3]

The fans were keyed up to see Killebrew at the plate. He had not hit safely thus far in this series, going 0-for-11. When McLish tried to pump one past him, Killebrew took his long stride and swung. Next came the stunning, crackling sound of the bat meeting the ball, and a cannon shot to center field. As the line drive soared toward the fence, Landis retreated at full speed and leaped. He crashed into the fence as the ball struck it near the top and bounded away. Shaken, Landis could not gather himself and get the ball in. Killebrew hustled around the bases and crossed the plate with an inside-the-park home run.

Killebrew had given the Twins a 4-0 lead in the most unlikely fashion. This was the only inside-the-park homer he ever hit in the majors. After the game Killebrew said, "I honestly thought it would go out of the park."[4]

With a comfortable four-run lead, Mele sent his ace back to the mound for the ninth. The fans were still savoring the three-run homer. The White Sox' Al Smith led off with a grounder to third and beat it out for a single. On the play, Jose Valdivielso threw past first for an error. Sherm Lollar singled to left, advancing Smith to third. Sammy Esposito continued his hitless day, taking a called third strike. Bob Roselli pinch-hit for McLish and grounded out to third for the second out as Smith scored.

Aparicio kept hopes alive by hitting a soft bouncer past the pitcher. Kralick needed just one more out. Floyd Robinson followed with his fourth hit, to right field. This drove in Lollar, and Aparicio scooted to third. It was 4-2 with runners on first and third. Kralick was showing fatigue, but Mele chose to leave him in to pitch to Cam Carreon, batting for the injured Jim Landis. An extra-base hit would have tied the game and Carreon got good wood on it, sending it to deep center. Bill Tuttle was there, however, and he grabbed it to end the game. The frustrated White Sox couldn't pull it out, and the Twins held on.

Jack Kralick notched his eighth win and sixth complete game. Of his single that broke the tie in the eighth, he said, "I've always been able to hit a little, but I'm not one who could do .300 regularly. Yes, I was tired in the ninth, but I was happy to see Killebrew give me a cushion with his inside-the-park home run after my single."[5] On his trouble fielding Aparicio's groundball in the ninth, he remarked, "When that happens, I just make myself forget it. I go for the next play and bear down."[6] Kralick finished 1961 with a 13-11 record. The Twins were 18-14 in games he started.

Minnesota outhomered Chicago 7-0 in the series. The White Sox finished a respectable fourth at the end of the season but were held back by a losing record on the road. Cal McLish logged a 10-13 mark in 1961, his only year with the White Sox. He was bothered all year with a double hernia but after treatment went on to pitch for the Phillies until 1964.

The Twins wrapped up their first season in Minnesota in seventh place with a 70-90 mark. They were more successful at the gate: They ranked third in the American League in attendance, behind New York and Detroit.

Killebrew's was the first inside-the-park homer in Twins history, and the only one hit by a Twins player in 1961. Twenty were hit in the major leagues that season, and the only other one at Metropolitan Stadium was by Nellie Fox on September 6.[7] Through 2019, there have been 53 inside-the-park home runs hit in Twins games. Of the total, 12 were hit at Metropolitan Stadium, 19 at the Hubert H. Humphrey Metrodome, and 3 at Target Field.[8]

Killebrew crashed 29 round-trippers at home in 1961, still a franchise record as of 2019. He holds the all-time career record for Metropolitan Stadium home runs with 246, including two as a member of the Kansas City Royals in 1975. Killebrew racked up 46 total in 1961, matching Jim Gentile, but that number trailed those of Roger Maris (61) and Mickey Mantle (54). The mild-mannered Killebrew led the American League in home runs six times, on the way to becoming arguably the most beloved player in Minnesota Twins history.

SOURCES

Online sources

- newspapers.com
- baseball-reference.com
- Skelton, David E. "Jack Kralick," sabr.org/bioproj/person/cefb31eb
- Wancho, Joseph. "Cal McLish," sabr.org/bioproj/person/a0ea7e9e

- Wancho, Joseph. "Harmon Killebrew," sabr.org/bioproj/person/55c51444

NOTES

1. Charles Johnson, "Win or Lose, Twins Thrill," *Minneapolis Star*, July 5, 1961: 49.
2. Richard Dozer, "Sox Prove Dud: Twins Win 6-4, 4-2," *Chicago Tribune*, July 5, 1961: 46.
3. "Killebrew Happy About Selection," *Minneapolis Tribune*, July 4, 1961: 13.
4. Dwayne Netland, "'Becquer More Valuable on Bench,' Says Twin Pilot," *Minneapolis Tribune*, July 5, 1961: 20.
5. Johnson.
6. Max Nichols, "Extra Drill Helps Becquer in a Pinch," *Minneapolis Star*, July 5, 1961: 49.
7. Team Batting Event Finder, bbref.com/pi/shareit/OjUEj (baseball-reference.com Play Index), accessed April 2, 2020.
8. John Swol, "Twins Inside-the-Park Home Runs Are a Rarity," posted on twinstrivia.com. (twinstrivia.com/2016/06/15/twins-inside-the-park-home-runs-are-a-rarity/), on June 15, 2016; and baseball-reference.com, Players/Finders and Advanced Stats/Home Run Logs, accessed April 2, 2020.

ALLISON AND KILLEBREW HIT FIRST-INNING GRAND SLAMS AS TWINS ROUT INDIANS

JULY 18, 1962: MINNESOTA TWINS 14, CLEVELAND INDIANS 3

By Paul Hofmann

The Wednesday afternoon game between the Cleveland Indians and Minnesota Twins produced a modern-era major-league first when the Twins' Bob Allison and Harmon Killebrew blasted first-inning grand slams in the 14-3 blowout victory.[1] The same team hitting two grand slams in one inning has been matched only four times since Allison and Killebrew accomplished the rare feat.[2]

The Indians and Twins were both contending for the American League pennant. The third-place Indians, losers of 7 or their last 8 games, were clinging to third place with a record of 48-41, 4½ games behind the first-place New York Yankees. The fourth-place Twins were only a game behind Cleveland with a record of 48-43.

Right-handed swingman Barry Latman took the mound for the Indians. The 6-foot-3-inch Latman was making his ninth start of the season and had a record of 4-5 with a 3.52 earned-run average. He was opposed by former Indian Dick Stigman. The Twins' left-hander, who appeared in 25 games in relief, was making his first start of the season and entered the game with a record of 3-2 and a 3.09 ERA. The start was particularly special for Stigman: His father, John Stigman, was in attendance. It was the first time his father was seeing him pitch in the majors.[3]

A crowd of 15,829 turned out at Metroplitan Stadium despite the threat of showers. The temperature approached 80 degrees as Stigman started the game by striking out the first three Indians batters, Willie Tasby, Tito Francona, and Chuck Essegian. Latman would not be as fortunate.

The Twins quickly got things going in the bottom half of the inning when center fielder Bill Tuttle drew a leadoff walk. Vic Power followed with a single to left and both advanced on Latman's errant pickoff throw to first base. Tuttle scored when Rich Rollins sliced a single to short right, Power advancing to third. Killebrew walked to load the bases. Allison, the Twins right fielder, cleared the bases with a home run to left field. It was Allison's 11th home run of the season and the fifth grand slam of his career. Catcher Earl Battey pulled his sixth home run of the year into the left-field stands to make the score 6-0, and Latman was chased before he retired a single batter.

Indians manager Mel McGaha called on right-hander Jim Perry in an attempt to restore order and get out of the first inning. Bernie Allen greeted Perry with a single to left, then Zoilo Versalles flied out to right for the first out of the inning. Allen went to second when Stigman grounded out to Bubba Phillips at third. It appeared that Perry and the Indians would be able to get out of the inning when Tuttle drew his

Harmon Killebrew (on deck) and Bob Allison (at bat) first played together in the majors with the Washington Senators. After the Senators moved to Minnesota, they were a powerful duo in the early years of the Twins.

second walk of the inning and Power singled to right to drive in Allen, increasing the Twins advantage to 7-0. Rollins walked on four pitches and the bases were loaded again. Killebrew hit the Twins' third home run of the inning when he "lambasted his third career grand slam to the fifth row from the top of the leftfield bleachers."[4] The inning came to a merciful end when Allison popped out to shortstop Woodie Held in short left field.

The Twins sent 14 batters to the plate and scored 11 runs on seven hits and four walks in the historic inning. The 11-run inning was a Twins record and nearly a franchise record: The Washington Senators scored 12 runs in the eighth inning of a 19-4 victory over the St. Louis Browns on July 10, 1926.[5]

Staked to an 11-run lead, Stigman cruised through the next four innings, giving up three harmless singles. Meanwhile, the Twins added another run in the bottom of third when Killebrew smacked his second home run of the game. It was Killebrew's 24th homer of the season. The red-hot Killebrew, in the midst of what would be an 11-game hitting streak, was 12-for-26 (.462) with 7 home runs and 22 runs batted in over his last seven games.[6]

The Indians got on the board in the top of the sixth. With one out, Francona was hit by a pitch. After a fly out to left by Essegian, catcher Johnny Romano hit a two-run homer to make the score 12-2.

The Twins added two runs in the bottom of the seventh. Battey led off with a single to center and moved to third when Allen also singled to center. Versalles, the only Twin who didn't get a hit in the game, grounded to Held at short, Battey holding at third and Allen moving to second. The right-handed-batting Stigman drove in Battey with a sacrifice fly to right, which also advanced Allen to third. Allen scored the Twins' 14th and final run of the game when Tuttle doubled to left.

Perry, scheduled to lead off the eighth inning for the Indians, was lifted in favor of pinch-hitter Gene Green. The right-handed journeyman outfielder-catcher rounded out the scoring with the Indians' second home run. Stigman retired the next three batters to end the eighth.

Right-hander Bob Hartman pitched a 1-2-3 eighth for Cleveland. It was the last major-league appearance of his career before he was sent down to Triple-A Salt Lake City when the Indians recalled 19-year-old Sam McDowell.[7] Stigman pitched a scoreless ninth to wrap up the Twins' 14-3 victory. The time of the game was a surprising 2 hours and 18 minutes, given the marathon first inning.

After the game, reporters asked Allison and Killebrew – both of whom had started the 1962 season very slowly – about their historic grand slams. Allison said he was "just looking for a good pitch to hit," adding, "The pitcher Barry Latman got behind on me and then threw a good fastball and I got hold of it."[8] Killebrew said, "I didn't think we'd get the bases loaded again. I was just trying to hit the ball somewhere. I didn't want to make the last out."[9]

The grand slams by Allison and Killebrew overshadowed Stigman's effort on the mound. The hurler from tiny Nimrod, Minnesota, went the distance, giving up three runs (all earned) on six hits and a walk. He struck out 11 and moved his record to 4-2. Commenting about how tired he felt, Stigman said, "In about the sixth inning, I was pretty tired, then I got my second wind. Right now, though, my eyes feel as if they're in the back of my head. I'm not used to going nine innings."[10]

Stigman's effort prompted reporters to ask manager Sam Mele if he would remain in the starting rotation, to which the Twins skipper responded, "You're darned tootin' Stigman's going to be moved into the starting rotation."[11] Mele cited three reasons why Stigman deserved the opportunity. "First, he pitched a whale of a ballgame. Second, he might be a run-producing pitcher. And, third he got a hit and drove in a run."[12]

Stigman remained in the Twins' starting rotation for the remainder of the season. In his 14 remaining starts he went 8-3 and finished the year with a record of 12-5. The Twins went 42-28 the remainder of the season, but were unable to run down the pennant-winning New York Yankees. The Twins finished in second place with a record of 91-71, five games behind New York. The Indians never regained their early-season form and finished in sixth place with a record of 80-82, 16 games off the pace.

SOURCES

In addition to the sources cited in the Notes, the author consulted Baseball-Reference.com and Retrosheet.org.

baseball-reference.com/boxes/MIN/MIN196207180.shtml

retrosheet.org/boxesetc/1962/07181962.htm

NOTES

1   Contrary to the game account in the *St. Paul Pioneer Press* on July 19, 1962, this was not the first time in major-league history that two players from the same team hit a grand slam in the same inning. On August 16, 1890, Chicago Colts veteran third baseman Tom Burns and rookie catcher Malachi Kittridge each hit a grand slam in the bottom of the fifth inning in an 18-5 victory over the Pittsburgh Alleghenys.

2. The four other times the same team has hit two grand slams in one inning during the modern era: Houston (Denis Menke, Jim Wynn) vs. New York, July 30, 1969, ninth inning Milwaukee (Cecil Cooper, Don Money) vs. Boston, April 12, 1980, second inning. Baltimore (Larry Sheets, Duffy Dyer) vs. Texas, August 6, 1986, fourth inning. St. Louis (Fernando Tatis, 2) vs Los Angeles, April 23, 1999, third inning. Tatis is the only player in major-league history (as of 2019) to hit two grand slams in one inning.

3. "Stigman's Starter Role Set – Mele," *St. Paul Pioneer Press,* July 19, 1963: 17.

4. "Twins' KO Punch Floors Indians," *St. Paul Pioneer Press,* July 19, 1962: 17.

5. "Killer, Allison Silence Critics," *St. Paul Dispatch,* July 19, 1962: 22.

6. Arno Goethel, "Killebrew, Allison Set Record for Grand Slams; Twins Win, 14-3: Stigman Goes Route in Win," *St. Paul Pioneer Press,* July 19, 1963: 17.

7. Steven Schmitt, Bob Hartman, SABR BioProject.

8. "Killer, Allison Silence Critics."

9. "Killer, Allison Silence Critics."

10. "Stigman's Starter Role Set – Mele."

11. "Stigman's Starter Role Set – Mele."

12. "Stigman's Starter Role Set – Mele."

JACK KRALICK ALMOST PERFECT IN FIRST NO-HIT GAME FOR TWINS

AUGUST 26, 1962: MINNESOTA TWINS 1, KANSAS CITY ATHLETICS 0

By Tim Otto

Although the 1961 Twins had finished their inaugural season in Minnesota with a won-lost record of 70-90, seventh in the American League, Twins owner Calvin Griffith was optimistic heading into the 1962 season. "We're bound to show youthful improvement. Established American League performers Pascual, Ramos, Kralick, Battey, Killebrew and Allison haven't reached their peaks yet. They'll get better and we'll rise to the first division with their improvement."[1]

Jack Kralick had become a regular member of the Twins' starting rotation in his sophomore season, posting a won-lost record of 13-11 and an earned-run average of 3.61 in 1961. He gave credit to pitching coach Eddie Lopat. "I learned a lot of pitching theory from Lopat."[2] Griffith rewarded Kralick's progress with a salary increase to $12,500 before the start of spring training. "I went in expecting a battle for the money I wanted," Kralick said. "He named the exact figure I had in mind and I was signed in three minutes."[3] Griffith said, "With better defense and better luck, he's a potential 20-game winner."[4]

A better infield defense appeared possible as the season began. Rookie Rich Rollins had won the third-base job, allowing Harmon Killebrew to move to left field. Another rookie, Bernie Allen, was now the starting second baseman. Improvement from shortstop Zoilo Versalles, in his second full season, could be expected. On April 2 the Twins obtained first basemen Vic Power and left-handed pitcher Dick Stigman from the Indians in exchange for starting pitcher Pedro Ramos. "Power should be a steadying influence on the kids," said Twins manager Sam Mele. "They won't have to worry about making perfect throws. If it's within Power's reach, he'll come up with the ball."[5]

After losing six of their first eight games, the Twins showed the improvement their owner had predicted. Minnesota won 34 of it next 53 games and was alone in first place on June 14, a half-game ahead of the defending World Series champion New York Yankees. Although the Twins dropped out of first place after losing the next three games at Kansas City, Minnesota was never more than two games out of first place until the Yankees swept a three-games series at Metropolitan Stadium on July 6, 7, and 8.

Kralick, however, was not having the success Griffith had predicted for him. Through the end of July, he had only one complete game in 24 starts. His record stood at 6-8, and his ERA had ballooned to 4.55. But from August 3 through 21, Kralick posted a 3-0 record in five starts, with two complete games and a 3.00 ERA. What was the reason for his turnaround? Kralick explained, "I've got my curve ball

Jack Kralick and Earl Battey celebrate Kralick's no-hitter.

again. When my curve was hanging, I had to depend on my slider and they were long-balling me."[6]

Kralick's next start was at home against Kansas City on Sunday, August 26. After splitting the first two games of the weekend series, the Twins were tied for second with the Angels, four games behind the first-place Yankees. The Athletics, although ninth in the standings, were leading the American League in batting average.[7] Kralick had last faced the A's on August 8 in Kansas City. The A's George Alusik hit a two-run homer off him in a seven inning, no-decision effort that the Twins lost in the bottom of the ninth, 4-3.

A crowd of 23,224 was settling into their seats as Kralick faced the first Kansas City batter, Bobby Del Greco. A 15 mile-per-hour wind blowing in from center held up Del Greco's drive to left for the first out. "It would have been out of there except for the wind," Kralick said after the game.[8] The next two batters were retired on routine plays. In the bottom of the first, Power hit a one-out single and advanced to second on left fielder Manny Jimenez's error. A's starting pitcher Bill Fischer retired Rollins on a grounder to third and Killebrew on a called third strike to leave Power stranded at second base.

A similar pattern played out over the next three innings. Kralick retired the A's in order in the second on a strikeout and two groundballs hit back to him. One-out singles by Battey and Allen were wasted when Versalles hit into a double play to end the Twins half of the inning. In the third the A's again were retired in order on two groundouts and a strikeout. Kralick started the bottom of the third inning by reaching on an infield single. One out later Power's single to left put runners on first and second, but neither advanced on Rollins's fly out to center. Killebrew ended the inning by lining out to left.

In the top of the fourth, the A's Ed Charles hit a drive to deep right-center. Bob Allison leaped at the fence to rob Charles of a home run.[9] The next batter, Jerry Lumpe, grounded to Power, with Kralick covering first base, to end the inning, as the A's again went down in order. With two outs in the bottom of the inning, Allen and Versalles singled but were left on base when Kralick grounded out to second.

The fifth and sixth innings saw each team retired in order. After the A's half of the seventh, Kralick had retired all 21 batters he had faced. "I first noticed that I had a no-hitter going in the fifth inning," Kralick said after the game. "I wasn't even thinking about a perfect game until the seventh or eighth, when I couldn't remember pitching from a stretch."[10]

The Athletics' Fischer had allowed seven singles over the first six innings but had given up no walks or runs. The Twins finally scored in the bottom of the seventh. After Allen's leadoff single, Versalles bunted in front of the plate. Catcher Billy Bryan's throw to second was late, and both runners were safe. Kralick's sacrifice bunt moved both runners into scoring position, and Lenny Green's fly out to center was deep enough to score Allen.

With the Twins now leading by a score of 1-0, Kralick ended the A's half of the eighth inning by retiring Manny Jimenez on a groundball fielded by Power, who flipped to Kralick covering the base for the 24th out in a row. The Twins made three routine outs in the bottom of the eighth, and the score remained 1-0 heading into the final inning.

Kralick took the mound in the ninth three outs away from a perfect game. Wayne Causey, leading off for the A's, grounded to Allen for the first out. Alusik, who had homered off Kralick on August 8, pinch-hit for the A's eighth-place hitter, Bryan. The first pitch to the right-handed batter was a strike on the inside corner. The next pitch was close to the plate, but inside for a ball. Another ball followed, a little farther inside. Alusik hit the next pitch on the ground past third base, but foul, to even the count at two balls and two strikes. The count went to 3-and-2 when Kralick's next pitch was just outside at the letters. Alusik then fouled a fastball back to the screen. Another fastball missed high and outside, and the A's had their first baserunner of the game.

Dick Howser ran for Alusik, and Billy Consolo batted for Fischer. After a called strike on a fastball, Kralick's next pitch was high for a ball. Battey's attempted pickoff throw to first got away from Power, but Howser couldn't advance when Power quickly retrieved the ball. Consolo then hit a foul popup that was caught by Power near the Twins dugout. After a ball high and outside, Del Greco hit a popup in almost the exact place that Consolo had. When Power caught the ball, the Twins dugout emptied, as the team celebrated the first no-hit game at Metropolitan Stadium and the first by a Twins pitcher.

Kralick complimented his batterymate after the game: "Battey caught a whale of a game. He realized in the first inning that my curve wasn't breaking well, so he called for a lot of sliders and fastballs with an occasional changeup." Commenting on his ninth-inning battle with Alusik, Kralick said, "I didn't want to give him anything too good to hit. He hit one pretty good off me in Kansas City."[11] Asked whether he was disappointed about not pitching a perfect game, Kralick replied, "I suppose it's a little nicer to have a perfect game, but it really makes no difference to me."[12]

SOURCES

The author accessed Baseball-Reference.com and Retrosheet.org. for box scores/play-by-play information, player, team, and season pages, pitching and batting game logs, and other data:

baseball-reference.com/boxes/MIN/MIN196208260.shtml

retrosheet.org/boxesetc/1962/B08260MIN1962.htm

Broadcast of ninth inning of Kansas City at Minnesota game, August 26, 1962, WCCO Radio.

NOTES

1. Tom Briere, "Kids Expected to Soup Up Twin Motors for Fast Rise," *The Sporting News*, February 28, 1962: 25.
2. Tom Briere, "Kralick Fattens Up in Pocketbook and Weight Department," *The Sporting News*, January 17, 1962: 19.
3. Tom Briere, "Kralick Fattens Up in Pocketbook and Weight Department."
4. Tom Briere, "Kralick Fattens Up in Pocketbook and Weight Department."
5. Arno Goethel, "Power Slated to Aid Kids on Twins' Infield," *The Sporting News*, April 11, 1962: 37.
6. Arno Goethel, "Nifty Lefties Fuel Twins' Flag Rocket," *The Sporting News*, September 1, 1962: 28.
7. "American League Club Statistics," *The Sporting News*, September 1, 1962: 22.
8. Arno Goethel, "Hitless Gem Caps Kralick's Alger Climb," *The Sporting News*, September 8, 1962: 5.
9. Goethel, "Hitless Gem Caps Kralick's Alger Climb."
10. Goethel, "Hitless Gem Caps Kralick's Alger Climb."
11. Goethel, "Hitless Gem Caps Kralick's Alger Climb."
12. Associated Press, "Twins' Kralick Pitches Majors' 5th No-Hitter," *Cleveland Plain Dealer*, August 27, 1962: 31.

PASCUAL REACHES 20-WIN GOAL IN SEASON FINALE

SEPTEMBER 30, 1962: MINNESOTA TWINS 1, BALTIMORE ORIOLES 0

By Richard Cuicchi

Camilo Pascual had good reason to be anxious about his start for the Minnesota Twins against the Baltimore Orioles on the final day of the 1962 season. In his ninth major-league season, it was the closest he had come to winning 20 games in a season. With 19 wins under his belt for the first time in his career, he had failed in his previous two outings to attain his long-awaited personal goal, a 20th win that would elevate him to the class of elite American League pitchers.

A young upstart pitcher from Baltimore did his best to spoil the day for the Twins hurler. Pascual wound up having to pitch one of his best games of the season to get the win and reach the prestigious milestone.

The Twins also had reason to celebrate the end of the season, since the franchise posted its first winning season since 1952, when it was in Washington. Now in 1962, in their second season in Minnesota, the Twins were optimistic about the future as they finished in second place, five games behind the New York Yankees.

Pascual had won number 19 on September 16 in a complete game against Cleveland. With three potential starts left in the season, it seemed likely that he would get at least one more win. However, Baltimore stopped him on September 21 and Cleveland defeated him four days later. Pascual had never lost more than two games in a row during the season. Yet he put pressure on himself to get his 20th victory in his final start. In his era of the majors, 20 wins earned a measure of credibility for pitchers. In Pascual's case, the milestone would put him in the conversation with Whitey Ford, Frank Lary, Jim Bunning, and Early Wynn for ranking as the top hurler in the league.

Pascual's opponent on the mound that day was 21-year-old rookie John Miller, a late-season call-up from Triple-A Rochester. In his major-league debut, on September 22, Miller had picked up a win by pitching three shutout innings in middle relief. Manager Billy Hitchcock wanted to get a longer look at Miller to determine whether his young newcomer would fit into the big-league rotation the next season along with Baltimore's early-20s pitching corps that included Chuck Estrada, Milt Pappas, Jack Fisher, and Steve Barber.

The contest at Metropolitan Stadium was played under the threat of rain, although 11,550 fans still attended a meaningless game in the standings. The Twins trailed only the Yankees in attendance and had drawn over 175,000 more spectators than in their inaugural season.

Harmon Killebrew, the American League home-run and RBI leader, got the Twins on the board in

Camilo Pascual

MEMORABLE GAMES AT MINNESOTA'S DIAMOND ON THE PRAIRIE

Battey and Camilo Pascual, the battery for the Twins' final game of 1962

the first inning. He singled in Lenny Green, who had walked, stolen second, and taken third on catcher Andy Etchebarren's throwing error. It turned out to be the only run of the game, which settled in as a pitcher's duel.

Miller was magnificent in his control throughout his seven innings; he gave up only one other hit, a third-inning single by Pascual, while walking only two. In the eighth inning Dick Hall relieved Miller, who had been lifted for a pinch-hitter. After the first inning, no other Twins runner reached second base.

On the other side of the ledger, Pascual was equally as effective. He gave up his first hit with two outs in the fifth inning and yielded only two other singles the rest of the game. The three hits were the fewest he allowed all season in a starting assignment. He walked only one and struck out seven. The game was his best outing of the season.

Pascual struck out Pete Ward for the last out of the game. In one of his earlier attempts for 20 wins, against the Orioles on September 21, it was Ward who helped spoil his bid with an RBI-single late in the game.

Miller would continue to impress Orioles coaches in the following Florida Instructional League season. Manager Dee Phillips bragged about his young pitcher: "He's a lot of pitcher. The more we see of Miller, the better we like him." Pitching instructor Harry Breechen said, "That boy is good. He opened our eyes when he pitched 10 innings for the parent Baltimore team last September and gave up only two hits."[1] However, Miller's career never fully matched the expectations set for him. He pitched parts of three additional seasons with the Orioles, while his only full season in 1966 included a 4-8 record and 4.74 ERA in 23 games. He was out of baseball by age 27.

Pascual celebrated after the game, saying, "This is wonderful. The game I wanted most and I got it with my best pitching job of the season." He added, "I felt a lot of pressure out there in the eighth and ninth innings. But I kept telling myself to relax. I didn't want to tighten up in that situation. Walking off that mound after the ninth was one of the happiest experiences I've ever had."[2]

During the game, Twins manager Sam Mele had to balance personal goals of Pascual and rookie third baseman Rich Rollins, who was on the verge of hitting .300 in his first full major-league season. Mele said, "If Rich had gotten a hit in his first or second time at bat, I'd have taken him out, because he'd have his .300 average. But I wanted him in the lineup to help Pascual." He added, "I'm sorry Rollins didn't make it. He deserved it after the great season he had."[3] Rollins wound up going 0-for-3, settling for a .298 average.

Killebrew had a career-best 48 home runs and 126 RBIs, which both led the American League. He would surpass both of those numbers in 1969 (49 home runs and 140 RBIs) when he was voted the AL Most Valuable Player.

Pascual finished with a 20-11 record and a 3.32 earned-run average. He led the American League in complete games (18), shutouts (5, tied with Jim Kaat and Dick Donovan), and strikeouts (206). He became the eighth American League pitcher to record back-to-back 200-strikeout seasons, joining some of baseball's greatest pitchers: Rube Waddell, Walter Johnson, Ed Walsh, Bob Feller, Hal Newhouser, Herb Score, and Jim Bunning.[4]

The 1962 major-league season was Pascual's first playing for a winning team. He made his major-league debut in 1954 as a 20-year-old from Cuba and posted a losing record in his first five seasons with the hapless Washington Senators. But in 1959 he won 17 games and led the league in complete games and shutouts. He improved in 1963 with 21 wins and a 2.46 ERA. Pascual was noted for his sharp-breaking curve that was often compared to Sandy Koufax's, considered one of the best in history.

The 1962 Twins accomplished a 21-game improvement in wins over their first season in Minnesota. Their 91 victories were the most for the franchise since 1945. They won their first pennant three years later, in 1965, but lost to Los Angeles in seven games of the World Series.

METROPOLITAN STADIUM

SOURCES

In addition to the sources cited in the Notes, the author consulted Baseball-Reference.com and the following:

Hatter, Lou. "Orioles End Season, Lose to Twins, 1 to 0," *Baltimore Sun*, October 1, 1962: 17.

Kritzer, Cy. "Pascual, Donovan Lead A. L. Slab Stars," *The Sporting News*, November 3, 1962: 25.

Pietrusza, David, Matthew Silverman, and Michael Gershman. *Baseball: The Biographical Encyclopedia* (New York: Total Sports Illustrated, 2000): 869.

NOTES

1. Fred Lieb, "Mound Flash Miller Wears Comer Label," *The Sporting News*, November 3, 1962: 27.

2. Dwayne Netland, "Pascual: Game I Most Wanted," *Minneapolis Star Tribune*, October 1, 1962: 26.

3. Netland.

4. Keith Sutton, "Pascual 8th A.L. Hurler to Fan 200 in Successive Seasons," *The Sporting News*, October 20, 1962: 16.

NEW TWINS RELIEVER SAVES THE DAY AIDED BY MELE'S MARAUDERS

MAY 26, 1963: MINNESOTA TWINS 5, CHICAGO WHITE SOX 2

By Sarah Johnson

In early-season coverage of their third year in Minnesota, local newspapers often highlighted Twins or Met Stadium happenings that reminded readers how young the new franchise still was. Case in point: a late May Sunday-afternoon game against the Chicago White Sox that saw the Twins win their seventh in a row, the team's longest winning streak since they moved to the North Star state.[1] It featured a pair of pitchers new to Minnesota aided by three home runs from a group one newspaper writer called "Mele's Marauders,"[2] an ode to Twins manager Sam Mele, bringing the Twins a 5-2 victory on May 26, 1963.

Bill Dailey

In 1963 the Twins played in the 10-team American League and, after a slow start to the season, they entered the late May series with the White Sox having won six of nine games on their last road trip. Their record prior to the May 26 game stood at 19-21, while the White Sox were at 24-17. Both the White Sox and Twins would finish the season behind the American League champion New York Yankees, with Chicago ending up in second place at 94-68 (10½ games back) and Minnesota finishing third at 91-70 (13 games back).

The Twins were looking to sweep the White Sox in the third game of the weekend series on a cloudy spring day with the temperature in the low 60s.[3] (Sunday, May 26, was not the day before Memorial Day; the holiday was then celebrated on May 30 before being moved to the last Monday of May by the Uniform Monday Holiday Act of 1968.) Right-hander Jim Perry, acquired earlier in May from the Cleveland Indians for left-hander Jack Kralick, was making his second home start for the Twins. After the early-season trade for Perry, the *Minneapolis Tribune* reported on Mele's satisfaction with the deal: "Mele immediately placed Perry in his regular starting rotation with right handed Camilo Pascual and left handed and Dick Stigman. 'It balances our staff,' said Mele, 'particularly in our park, and against right-handed power clubs like Boston at Fenway Park.'"[4] Perry was opposed by right-hander John Buzhardt, who had shut out Minnesota in April at White Sox Park for his first win of the season.

The game started inauspiciously for the Twins when, with two out in the top of the first, White Sox third baseman Pete Ward, right fielder Floyd Robinson and first baseman Joe Cunningham hit back-to-back-to-back singles, putting Chicago ahead 1-0. Despite this early lead, the White Sox had only one extra base hit in the game (a fifth-inning double by second baseman Nellie Fox, scoring center fielder Jim Landis for their second and last run) and went 1-for-7 with runners in scoring position.

The Twins tied the score in the bottom of the second on a solo home run by shortstop Zoilo Versalles. Minnesota led the American League with 225 home runs in 1963, including right-handed slugger Harmon Killebrew's team-leading 45. In his column "The Sporting Thing," *St. Paul Dispatch* writer George Edmond commented, "The Twins are blessed with long-ball hitters, which should make them ideally suited for their home park, where the home runs come somewhat more easily than in most of the parks they play on the road."[5]

After giving up only one run through five innings, Buzhardt ran into trouble in the bottom of the sixth when Twins first baseman Vic Power hit a one-out double to right field. The next batter, Killebrew, gave the Twins a lead they would not relinquish, hitting a two-run homer into the left-center-field bleachers to put Minnesota up 3-2. "That's the thing about Killebrew that kills you," claimed Joe Cunningham, the White Sox first baseman. "He's so strong he can hit any pitch out of any park."[6] "It wasn't a bad pitch," said Killebrew. "A slider low and away. I had to go out after it."[7]

In the pre-designated-hitter era, with the pitcher due to lead off the seventh inning, White Sox manager Al Lopez sent up pinch-hitter Charlie Maxwell. That move was unsuccessful as Perry pitched a scoreless top of the seventh and, when Minnesota added a run in the bottom of the seventh off White Sox knuckleballer Hoyt Wilhelm, the Twins pitcher started the top of the eighth with a two-run lead. Perry struggled, giving up singles to Robinson and Cunningham, and the Twins manager brought in reliever Bill Dailey. After beginning with a 3-and-0 count on the first batter he faced, left fielder Dave Nicholson, the side-arming right-hander recovered to strike out Nicholson looking and got the next batter, shortstop Ron Hansen, to ground into an inning-ending double play.

The White Sox skipper was impressed by the work of Dailey, according to Glenn Redmann of the *St. Paul Dispatch*: "'I never saw the guy as fast as he was today,' said Chicago manager Al Lopez. 'If he continues to throw like that, you guys have got yourselves one heckuva relief pitcher.'"[8] After Twins catcher Earl Battey hit a solo home run in the bottom of the eighth, Dailey retired the White Sox in order in the top of the ninth. The Twins reliever, also acquired earlier in the season from Cleveland, helped Perry win his third game of the season.

"He saved it for me," Perry said of Dailey after the game.[9] Saves were not an official statistic at the time, although they were reported unofficially in *The Sporting News*. In the early 1960s, the formula for the new stat called for a relief pitcher to be awarded a save if he faced the potential tying or winning run or if he came into the final inning and pitched perfectly with a two-run lead. Under this definition, Dailey was awarded 13 saves in 1963 (including this game) but was retroactively credited with 21 under less stringent rules after the save became an official statistic in 1969. Dailey ended the year with a 1.99 earned-run average and 72 strikeouts in 108⅔ innings – such a solid season in relief that Met Stadium organist Willie Peterson bestowed upon him his own entrance song, "Won't You Come Home, Bill Dailey?" to the tune of the song "Won't You Come Home, Bill Bailey?"

The game was not without controversy as reported by Richard Dozer in his game story for the *Chicago Tribune*: "Although no errors were charged in today's misadventure, there were a pair of costly misjudged fly balls by Sox outfielders, who joined the growing list of defensemen around the league who are unhappy about the poor background in Metropolitan Stadium. They claim the low seating arrangement and white-shirted spectators make it difficult to follow the ball."[10]

This had been a point of contention since the Twins' inaugural season, with the White Sox commenting on it in 1961 as well when left fielder Minnie Miñoso misplayed Twins second baseman Billy Gardner's ball to left field that went for a game-winning double in May. Miñoso "said he lost the ball in the shadows and background and didn't see it again until it was on top of him. 'I want to play safe but I could not see the ball after it go over the shortstop's head,' Minnie complained. 'It is very bad.'"[11] Even the home team had the same issue, with Harmon Killebrew saying later in 1963 that "the lights and shadows from the (Metropolitan) Stadium background during a day game make it hard to pick up the flight of a ball. And it isn't much easier at night."[12]

The game started at 1:30 P.M. and was played in a crisp 2 hours 15 minutes. The attendance was 19,553, and the Twins drew 1,406,652 to Met Stadium in 1963 (highest in the American League), proving that the support for this new franchise in Minnesota was very strong.

MEMORABLE GAMES AT MINNESOTA'S DIAMOND ON THE PRAIRIE

SOURCES

baseball-reference.com/boxes/MIN/MIN196305260.shtml

retrosheet.org/boxesetc/1963/B05260MIN1963.htm

NOTES

1 "Twins Streak Threatens Race," *St. Paul Dispatch,* May 27, 1963: 27.
2 Arno Goethel, "Killer, Zoilo, Battey Homer as Twins Win," *St. Paul Pioneer Press*, May 27, 1963: 20.
3 Weather Report, *Minneapolis Star Tribune*, May 26, 1963: 11B.
4 Tom Briere, "Perry Welcomes Twin Starting Job on 'Club That Wants Me,'" *Minneapolis Tribune*, May 3, 1963: 21.
5 George Edmond, "The Sporting Thing," *St. Paul Dispatch,* May 24, 1963: 30.
6 Dwayne Netland, "Dailey Secret? Throw Hard and Keep it Low," *Minneapolis Tribune,* May 27, 1963: 24.
7 Tom Briere, "Twins Bomb Chisox 5-2 for Seventh Win in Row," *Minneapolis Tribune*, May 27, 1963: 21.
8 Glenn Redmann, "Joining Twins Was Greatest Break – Dailey," *St. Paul Dispatch*, May 27, 1963: 27.
9 Netland.
10 Richard Dozer, "Twins Hit 3, Gain Seventh in a Row," *Chicago Tribune*, May 27, 1963: Section 3, 1.
11 Jim Klobuchar, "Stadium 'Sunfield' Rapped by Minoso," *Minneapolis Tribune*, May 2, 1961: 19.
12 Bill Hengen, "Roaming Around," *Minneapolis Star*, July 15, 1963:11B.

CHICAGO'S LANDIS AND ROBINSON HIT BACK-TO-BACK HOMERS IN NINTH AS WILHELM SHUTS DOWN TWINS IN RELIEF

AUGUST 31, 1963: CHICAGO WHITE SOX 2, MINNESOTA TWINS 0

By Mike Huber

The last Saturday in August of 1963 brought an afternoon match at the Met between the Minnesota Twins and the visiting Chicago White Sox. An announced crowd of 23,415 came out to the ballpark for this, the second of a three-game series. Minnesota, at 75-58, had won three in a row and six of its last seven games. The second-place Twins had been hammering opposing pitching, hitting home runs in each of their previous 10 games; in fact, they had crushed 24 home runs in that span, including a season-high and team record eight round-trippers against the Washington Senators on August 29.[1] In 133 games so far in the season, the Twins had scored 642 runs, highest in either league. In 12 games against the White Sox prior to this one, the Twins had hit 16 home runs off Chicago pitching.

Chicago, at 75-59, was a half-game behind the Twins, and its chances (as well as the Twins' chances) of catching the first-place New York Yankees were

Harmon Killebrew at bat in a 1963 game against the Chicago White Sox

slim. The White Sox had clubbed only six home runs in their last 10 games. However, they had won five of their last six contests, and both teams sought to continue their winning ways.

Minnesota manager Sam Mele called on left-hander Dick Stigman for the mound duties. He was in his second year with the Twins. Although he had won his previous start, against the Washington Senators, Stigman's record was 13-13, with a 3.25 earned-run average. He was opposed by Chicago's Joe Horlen. Horlen was in his second full big-league season. He had split time as a starter and a reliever for manager Al Lopez. Horlen, sporting a 3.70 ERA, had also won his previous start (against the Cleveland Indians), notching his seventh victory against five defeats.

After Stigman retired the White Sox in order in the top of the first, the Twins threatened in the bottom half. With one down, Rich Rollins and Jimmie Hall singled, but Horlen struck out Harmon Killebrew and got Don Mincher to fly out to center to end the inning.

Two innings later, the Twins put two more runners on base. Stigman led off with a single up the middle. Hall singled after two fly outs, and Killebrew again left two runners on base when he grounded a ball to short for a force out of Hall at second base.

In the sixth, Minnesota again created an opportunity. Hall doubled to left with one out, bringing Killebrew into the batter's box with a runner in scoring position for the third time. Killebrew checked his swing but "smashed the ball back at Horlen, who knocked it down with his bare hand."[2] The pitcher then picked it up and tossed to first in time to get Killebrew for the second out. Mincher grounded out to second for the third out.

In the seventh, Horlen stopped another ball with his bare hand. With one out, Earl Battey lined a ball that deflected off Horlen to Chicago shortstop Ron Hansen, who threw to first in time to get Battey. Back in the dugout after he had retired Zoilo Versalles for the third out, Horlen told manager Lopez that he had injured the index finger on his pitching hand and "couldn't grip the ball properly."[3] He had yielded six hits (five singles) in seven innings of work, with only Hall's double since the third inning. This meant Lopez had to make a call to the bullpen.

Hoyt Wilhelm entered the game to pitch the eighth inning. The 41-year-old Wilhelm was in his first season with Chicago. He had been traded from Baltimore with Dave Nicholson, Pete Ward, and Hansen to the White Sox in exchange for Luis Aparicio and Al Smith on January 14, 1963. He faced Stigman to lead off the bottom of the eighth for Minnesota. Stigman, batting right-handed, grounded out to short. Wilhelm then struck out Bernie Allen and Rollins.

For the Twins, Stigman was better than Horlen, allowing only one hit (a second-inning single by Jim Lemon) and one walk (to Jim Landis in the fourth) through the first six innings. Nicholson singled in the seventh and Nellie Fox singled in the eighth, but Chicago could not mount any threat in either inning and both men were left on base. Stigman had surrendered only three hits, all singles. Although Stigman had allowed one walk, no White Sox runner had even reached second base. The pitchers' duel now entered the ninth inning with the game still scoreless. That changed in a hurry.

On back-to-back pitches, the White Sox won the game with the long ball. Landis, coming into the game batting .234, led off the ninth inning and sent a Stigman fastball deep into the left-center-field seats. It was his 12th home run of the season. On the next pitch, Floyd Robinson pulled the ball into the right-field stands; it was his ninth of the year and the 26th homer allowed by Stigman. This must have rattled Stigman. Although he retired Nicholson on a line out and struck out Lemon, he walked Ward, prompting skipper Mele to make the call to the bullpen. Bill Dailey entered the game, making his 53rd appearance of the year. Dailey quickly retired Hansen, who lined out to shortstop Versalles for the third out.

Wilhelm made quick work of the Twins batters in the final frame. Hall, Killebrew, and Mincher were three-up and three-down, as Chicago won the 2-hour, 15-minute game. Robert Markus, beat writer for the *Chicago Tribune*, summed up the action, writing, "Joe Horlen and Hoyt Wilhelm turned the Minnesota Twins' heavy artillery into pop guns and the White Sox let loose two long-range missiles of their own"[4] as Chicago bested Minnesota, 2-0. The White Sox had beaten the Twins with their own brand of baseball, the home run.

Landis's homer to left field was measured at 386 feet. Robinson's shot to right field was charted at 352 feet.[5] After the game, Lopez told reporters, "I do know Landis always hits well at the Met."[6] Landis added, "This ain't no bad little ball park to hit in."[7] His average against Minnesota at Metropolitan Stadium through six games in 1963 was .269 (7-for-26), more than 30 points above his overall average. The next day he went 2-for-5 with another home run.

Minnesota's 10-game home run streak was halted. As a team, the Twins belted 225 home runs in 1963, led by Killebrew's league-best 45. They set a franchise record that stood for 56 seasons. That mark was demolished in 2019, when the Minnesota sluggers hit 307 home runs as a team, establishing a new major-league record. The White Sox hit only 114 home runs as a team in 1963. Landis and Robinson each contributed 13, accounting for about a quarter of the team total.

Both starters pitched well enough to win. There were only nine runners left on base in the entire game (four for Chicago and five for Minnesota). Rookie Jimmie Hall collected three of Minnesota's hits off Horlen, raising his batting average to .272, but he was stranded on the bases every time.

Wilhelm earned his third win of the 1963 campaign. The knuckleball-throwing right-hander was used primarily as a reliever by Chicago, and this was his 43rd relief appearance of the season. Wilhelm had made two starts for the White Sox before this game, on July 7 (against the Boston Red Sox) and on August 23 (against the New York Yankees). The future Hall of Famer made his final career start on September 7, 1963, a week after this game. It was against the Twins at White Sox Park. He pitched eight innings and allowed one earned run on six hits and two walks. He did not earn a decision, as the game went into extra innings, with Minnesota winning 4-2.

Chicago's win put the team back into second place in the American League standings; that's where they would finish the year, while Minnesota settled for third place. It was only the second win of the season for the White Sox at Metropolitan Stadium.

SOURCES

In addition to the sources mentioned in the Notes, the author consulted baseball-reference.com, retrosheet.org and sabr.org.

baseball-reference.com/boxes/MIN/MIN196308310.shtml

retrosheet.org/boxesetc/1963/B08310MIN1963.htm

NOTES

1 As of the end of the 2019 season, this single-game record still stood. Further, the Twins hit eight homers in a game *twice* in 2019.

2 Robert Markus, "Landis and Robinson Jolt Twins, 2-0," *Chicago Tribune*, September 1, 1963: 49-50.

3 Robert Markus, "Landis and Robinson Jolt Twins, 2-0."

4 Robert Markus, "Landis and Robinson Jolt Twins, 2-0."

5 These measurements come from Markus's article in the *Chicago Tribune*.

6 Tom Briere, "Chisox Nudge Twins on Homers in Ninth," *Minneapolis Tribune*, September 1, 1963: 15, 17.

7 Tom Briere, "Chisox Nudge Twins on Homers in Ninth."

TWINS RALLY FROM 7-1 DEFICIT

MAY 9, 1964: MINNESOTA TWINS 10, KANSAS CITY ATHLETICS 8

by Rich Arpi

The Minnesota Twins rallied from a 7-1 deficit with three runs in the sixth inning and four runs in the seventh to top the Kansas City Athletics 10-8 in this Saturday afternoon game. The Twins outhit the A's 14 to 5 and outhomered them 4 to 3. Twins pitchers struck out 12 batters but 10 walks and five timely hits by the A's led to eight runs and a daunting early lead. Each team used four pitchers, with four effective relief innings from Twins left-hander Gerry Arrigo highlighting the win. Arrigo had started the previous game for the Twins on Friday night but was knocked out after 1⅓ innings after giving up five runs on three hits in what turned into a 6-5 loss for the Twins.

Lee Stange started the game for the Twins and Orlando Peña for the A's. A solo home run by Rich Rollins in the first inning (his fourth) gave the Twins an early lead. It should have been 2-0 but Zoilo Versalles, who led off the frame with a single, was picked off first base by Peña.[1] The A's struck back in the third inning with four runs while collecting only two hits. Wayne Causey led off with a home run (his first), then two walks, a fielder's choice, and a three-run homer by Manny Jimenez (his third) knocked out Stange.[2] Jim Roland entered the game and threw 10 consecutive balls. Bill Fischer was quickly summoned into the game and despite a 2-and-0 count on pitcher Peña, struck him out on four pitches.[3]

Ed Charles grounds out to shortstop Zoilo Versalles as Wayne Causey advances to third on May 9, 1964.

In the fourth inning Fischer walked leadoff batter Causey, retired two batters, then surrendered a single to Jim Gentile and a home run to Rocky Colavito (his league-leading ninth), giving the A's a 7-1 lead. Fischer walked another batter before retiring the side. In the bottom of the fourth, the Twins crawled a bit closer with solo home runs from Jimmie Hall (his eighth) and Bob Allison (his seventh).

Fischer retired the A's one-two-three in the fifth inning, and Arrigo relieved him at the start of the sixth. Arrigo struck out the side in that inning and recorded another strikeout in both the seventh and eighth innings. He walked pinch-hitter George Alusik in the eighth inning, but a 4-6-3 double play meant he faced the minimum of nine batters in three innings.

Don Mincher's third home run of the season, after singles by Tony Oliva and Allison, knocked Peña out in the sixth inning and brought the Twins to within one run at 7-6. Mincher, at first base, and Allison, in left field, were in the starting lineup because Twins manager Sam Mele had decided to give Harmon Killebrew a day off to nurse his .167 batting average.[4]

Jack Aker got the Twins out after replacing Peña in the sixth inning, but in the seventh he walked Versalles and the Athletics' Causey booted Oliva's groundball that looked like a sure double play. Versalles took third base on the error and Oliva went to second base. Jimmie Hall was intentionally walked to load the bases. On 1-and-2 pitch, Bob Allison lined a double into the left-field corner, scoring three runs and giving the Twins a 9-7 lead.[5] Earl Battey singled in Allison, Joe Grzenda replaced Aker and after he got Vic Power to fly out, Earl Battey singled in Allison, giving the Twins their 10th run.

In the ninth inning Arrigo walked Ed Charles with one out. Jim Gentile then struck out for the second out, but Colavito scored Charles with a double. Manny Jimenez struck out to end the game. Arrigo gave up only one hit in four innings and collected his second win of the season, both against Kansas City. He struck out seven and walked two. On May 2 in Kansas City, Arrigo was the winning pitcher in a 7-3 Twins win in 11 innings. Arrigo finished the season with a record of 7-4 in 41 games, 12 of which were starts. He had 96 strikeouts in 105⅓ innings with an earned-run average of 3.84. After the season, after four years with the Twins, Arrigo was traded to the Cincinnati Reds for Cesar Tovar.

Asked about the difference between his Saturday performance and his start on Friday, when he was knocked out in the second inning, Arrigo said after the

FAN IN THE STANDS

In the 1960s and 1970s listeners knew baseball was on the way when the song "It's a Beautiful Day for a Ballgame" was played on WCCO Radio. The song signaled the beginning of the pregame show, *Fan in the Stands*. Randy Merriman, out at the Met well before the game started, picked a few fans to interview for the show. The fans then reached into a "batter's box," a small box from which they could pull a card at random; the card contained the name of one of the players from the roster of the Twins or the visiting team. If that player hit the first home run in the game, the fan would win a prize.

I picked ALOU to hit the FIRST homerun in Metropolitan Stadium on 5/5/71. If I win, I will receive an RCA Transistor Radio courtesy of Midwest Federal and the RCA and Whirlpool dealers. I understand that my player must hit the FIRST homerun in the game to win a radio for me.
P.S. HE DID IT! PLEASE SEND MY RADIO!
NAME_____
ADDRESS_____
CITY_____

I picked Clarke to hit the FIRST homerun in Metropolitan Stadium on 5/9/72. If I win, I will receive an RCA Transistor Radio courtesy of Midwest Federal and the RCA and Whirlpool dealers. I understand that my player must hit the FIRST homerun in the game to win a radio for me.
P.S. HE DID IT! PLEASE SEND MY RADIO!
NAME_____
ADDRESS_____
CITY_____

Collection of Stew Thornley

game that as a relief pitcher he did not have time to get jittery. Manager Mele commented, "We figure it is just as well not to let him know when he is going to start. Maybe that'll help with our pitching staff. Something has to. I've taken more walks than Harry Truman."[6]

Despite the win, Twins outfielder Bob Allison expressed underlying uneasiness. "There are a few things we're going to have to get straightened out on this team," he said. "We're playing some pretty miserable baseball. We've got the personnel to be a contender and a pennant winner. We sure haven't looked it, even winning like we did today."[7]

The win evened the Twins' record at 11-11, three games in back of the league-leading Chicago White Sox. (The deficit was reduced to 2½ games after the White Sox lost at Los Angeles at night.) It dropped the A's to 8-12. The season record between Kansas City and the Twins was evened at three games each, with Minnesota outscoring Kansas City 43-37 and hitting 20 home runs to the A's 13. The four homers in this game gave the Twins a total of 40 in 22 games.[8] They would hit 221 home runs in 1964, just short of their club record 225 homers hit the year before. Those 225 home runs would last as the club record until the 2019 squad blasted its way to a major-league record of 307.

The Twins finished the 1964 season with a record of 79-83, tied for sixth place with the Cleveland Indians. The A's, despite the worst record in the American League, 57-105, were very competitive against the Twins in 1964. The teams were 8-8 in their 16 games. Tony Oliva gave the A's plenty of trouble, batting .457 in 18 games with seven homers and 18 runs batted in.[9]

The *St. Paul Pioneer Press*, the *Minneapolis Tribune*, and Retrosheet all listed the paid attendance as 9,219. The *Tribune* mentioned that the actual crowd was much larger, and a bit more raucous than that, as 10,629 children were admitted free after a youth baseball clinic in the morning. That added up to 19,848. Arno Goethel, in his game account in the *Pioneer Press*, mentioned the attendance as 18,646, a discrepancy of 1,202 that may never be resolved.

NOTES

1   Arno Goethel, "Power-Hitting Twins Rally to Win," *St. Paul Pioneer Press*, May 10, 1964: 4, 1.

2   Retrosheet was consulted for exact play-by-play results. See retrosheet.org/games/regular season/1964/Minnesota Twins/game log/May 9. Both the *St. Paul Pioneer Press* and the *Minneapolis Tribune* listed the to-date season home run totals for each player who hit a home run.

3   Goethel.

4   Tom Briere, "Twins Wipe Out 7-1 Deficit, Triumph 10-8," *Minneapolis Tribune*, May 10, 1964: Sports 1-2.

5   Briere.

6   "Arrigo Turnabout: No Nervousness," *Minneapolis Tribune*, May 10, 1964: S7. The allusion to Truman was a reference to the former president's habit of taking walks for exercise.

7   Jim Klobuchar, "Mr. Finley, It looks Like They're all Going to Score," *Minneapolis Tribune*, May 10, 1964: S1.

8   Briere.

9   1965 Minnesota Twins Media Guide, 16.

CLINTON'S THROW TO RETIRE BATTEY AT FIRST HELPS ANGELS SHUT OUT TWINS

JULY 17, 1964: LOS ANGELES ANGELS 1, MINNESOTA TWINS 0

By Ralph Caola

Twins manager Sam Mele was not happy. His team had lost four of its last five games. The night before, fielding lapses, particularly a botched rundown, turned a 2-2 game into a 7-2 defeat at the hands of the last-place Washington Senators.

So before the game on July 17, 1964, Mele held a drill to work on the Twins' defensive problems. For an hour and a half, in 94-degree heat, the team practiced rundowns, cutoff plays, and pitchers covering first base.[1]

"We learned this last spring, but maybe we've forgotten it," Mele said. "We'll do some brushing up on things. This has got to stop."[2]

The Twins entered the game in fourth place with a record of 47-41. The Angels were in sixth place at 43-47. But the teams were headed in opposite directions. While the Twins were skidding, the Angels had won five of six.

The starting pitchers were Fred Newman (7-3) for the Angels and Dick Stigman (5-7) for the Twins. The two had butted heads five days before in Los Angeles, when Newman bested Stigman, 2-1. This game would be another pitchers' duel.

In the first inning, Stigman gave up a leadoff double to Bob Perry and walked Jim Fregosi, but escaped by getting Joe Adcock to hit into an inning-ending double play. Newman retired the Twins in order in their half.

One of the reasons the Angels won the 2-1 game in Los Angeles was a solo homer by Felix Torres. With two outs in the second, Torres repeated the feat, giving the Angels a 1-0 lead. Bobby Knoop followed with a single before Newman flied out to right to end the inning. In the bottom half, Bob Allison hit a one-out single for the Twins, but was erased when Rich Rollins bounced into a 6-4-3 double play.

The Angels got their third extra-base hit in as many innings when Willie Smith doubled to left with one out in the third. But he was stranded when Stigman retired the next two Angels.

Stigman got himself into trouble again in the fourth when he walked Lou Clinton and, two outs later, walked Knoop. Again he used the opposing pitcher to get out of the inning by striking out Newman.

Stigman pitched four more innings without allowing a hit. Al Worthington relieved him in the ninth and gave up a harmless single.

Earl Battey

MEMORABLE GAMES AT MINNESOTA'S DIAMOND ON THE PRAIRIE

In the bottom of the fourth, Tony Oliva and Jimmie Hall hit one-out singles. But Newman snuffed the rally when Harmon Killebrew and Allison struck out looking. After the game, Mele criticized his All-Stars saying, "That was our chance for a big inning. You don't have a big inning by taking called third strikes."[3]

In the fifth the Twins had a would-be rally ruined by an unusual play. With one out, Earl Battey sliced a one-hopper to Angels right fielder Clinton, who threw out Battey before he reached first.

The *Minneapolis Tribune* reported that Battey "jogged toward first" and that the Twins lost a baserunner "for lack of hustle." But Mele disagreed. "Battey didn't loaf," said Mele. "He ran as hard as he could. He just can't move very fast."[4] That year, the 6-foot-1 Battey reported to spring training weighing 260 pounds.[5]

The Twins had their best chance to score in the seventh. Allison led off with a single and took second when left fielder Willie Smith bobbled the ball.[6] Rollins sacrificed Allison to third. But Allison had to hold when Battey grounded out with the infield in, and Jim Snyder flied out to end the threat.

Mele was asked why, with a right-hander on the mound, he didn't have left-handed-hitting Don Mincher pinch-hit for the right-handed-hitting Snyder. He replied simply, "I felt Snyder would come through with a hit." Snyder's batting average was .193, Mincher's, .290. Snyder would play his last major-league game less than three weeks later.

Bob Lee replaced Newman and pitched the eighth and ninth. Lee threw nothing but fastballs,[7] disposed of all six Twins he faced, three on strikeouts, and secured the 1-0 victory.

Newman got the win and Stigman, the loss, in the 2-hour, 28-minute contest. Stigman won only one more game in 1964, finishing with 6 wins and 15 losses, the worst record of his career. On the other hand, Newman went on to have his best season, with 13 wins, 10 losses, and a 2.75 earned-run average. In 1966 Newman became plagued by arm problems. Both pitchers finished their major-league careers in 1967.

The offensive hero of the game was, of course, Felix Torres. In 1955 the Puerto Rico-born Torres was signed as an amateur free agent by the Cincinnati Reds. That year in Class D ball, he smacked 57 extra-base hits in just 108 games. Torres then left professional baseball for almost four years because of the racism he experienced while playing in the Georgia State League and South Atlantic League.[8]

He returned to the minor leagues in 1960 and the next year in Triple A hit 24 homers with 97 RBIs. In 1962, at the age of 30, Torres got his chance in the majors when he was drafted by the expansion Angels. He played with the Angels through 1964, his last season in the majors. He retired with a career batting average of .254 and 17 home runs in 1,191 at-bats.

The Twins had now lost five of six games. They continued what was to become a nightmare streak by losing their next six, for a total of eight straight. After grabbing a win, they proceeded to lose seven of their next nine, giving them 18 losses in 22 games and dropping them into sixth place with a record of 50-55.

The win was the Angels' third straight and they went on to win another three in a row. After a loss, they won six of their next eight, raised their record to 53-50, and moved into fourth place.

In 1964 Oliva led the American League in hits, doubles, runs scored, total bases, and batting average and was named the AL Rookie of the Year. Killebrew led in home runs and Allison was third in OPS.[9] Consequently, the Twins led the AL with 4.52 runs scored per game. Since they allowed 4.16 runs per game, Bill James's Pythagorean Formula[10] predicts that they should have won 88 games. So their actual total of 79 wins had to be considered disappointing.

In 1965 the Twins scored more runs (4.78 per game) and allowed fewer (3.70 per game), and outperformed their Pythagorean expectation. This time the formula predicted the Twins would win 101 games and they exceeded that by one game. The 102 wins were a 23-game improvement and the Twins won the pennant by seven games.

In some ways the Angels and Twins played the 1964 season as mirror images of each other. The Twins finished first in the AL in runs scored, the Angels, last. Coming into the July 17 game, the Twins had lost four of their last five games, the Angels had won four of their last five (and five of six). The Twins entered the game with a record of 47-41. Two days before, the Angels' record had been 41-47.

When the Angels first rose to a .500 winning percentage, their record was 47-47. When the Twins first sank to .500 their record was 47-47. In the first half of the season, the Twins were 44-37, the Angels, 37-44. In the second half, the Angels went 45-36, the Twins, 35-46. Finally, the teams missed by one game of having mirror-image final records. The Angels finished 82-80, the Twins, 79-83.

SOURCES

In addition to the sources cited in the Notes, the author relied on Baseball-Reference.com.

Retrosheet box score: retrosheet.org/boxesetc/1964/B07170MIN1964.htm

NOTES

1. "2nd-Division Teams Killing Twins Hopes," *St. Cloud* (Minnesota) *Times,* July 17, 1964: 9.
2. Lew Ferguson, "Now Defense Proves Costly to TC Hopes," *St. Cloud Times,* July 17, 1964: 10.
3. Dwayne Netland, "Stigman Mustn't Get Discouraged," *Minneapolis Tribune,* July 18, 1964: 13.
4. Tom Briere, "Angels Edge Stigman on Torres' Blast," *Minneapolis Tribune,* July 18, 1964: 12.
5. Jack Herrman, "Earl Battey," sabr.org/bioproj/person/df593af3. Accessed April 21, 2020.
6. Briere.
7. Briere.
8. baseball-reference.com/bullpen/Felix_Torres. Accessed April 23, 2020.
9. OPS is the abbreviation for the sum of a player's on-base and slugging averages. It correlates well with more complex methods that evaluate the runs for which a batter is responsible.
10. m.mlb.com/glossary/advanced-stats/pythagorean-winning-percentage. (I used two as an exponent.) Accessed April, 25, 2020.

TWINS WIN IN EXTRA INNINGS ON OPENING DAY

APRIL 12, 1965: MINNESOTA TWINS 5, NEW YORK YANKEES 4 (11 INNINGS)

By Steve West

A cold, wet winter is normally brightened by the approach of Opening Day, but in 1965 Opening Day was the last thing on most people's minds in Minnesota. A very cold winter was followed by deep snow in the northern part of the state during March, and when rain came in early April, the snow melted, causing a rapid rise in the Minnesota and Mississippi Rivers.[1] By Opening Day, Monday, April 12, Minnesota was suffering through what as of 2019 was still the worst flooding on record, with numerous areas across the state dealing with more than 20 feet of water. (Chaska, just southwest of the Twin Cities, reported a high of 34.5 feet.)

The previous day, President Lyndon B. Johnson had declared a "major disaster" in 39 counties across the state. The Minnesota National Guard had been mobilized and was working side-by-side with thousands of people to sandbag towns along the rivers, desperately trying to save lives and property. The eventual toll would include several deaths and more than $200 million in property damage, plus many thousands of people displaced from their homes.

The first pitch of the 1965 season.

METROPOLITAN STADIUM

On Sunday night, the Minnesota Twins held their annual "welcome home" baseball dinner, with several players unable to make it because of flooding near their homes in Burnsville, on the south side of the Minnesota River. On Monday the high water made it impossible for those players – including starting pitcher Jim Kaat – to make it from their homes to Metropolitan Stadium. Kaat later said, "I left for the park in Minnesota, but there was a huge backup. I got out of my car and a guy told me that the bridge was closed because of a big rain storm, and the river was flooded and no one could get over the bridge. And I said, 'I'm supposed to pitch today.'"[2] Kaat called a former teammate, Paul Giel, who was the sports director at local radio station WCCO. Giel arranged to pick up the players in a helicopter – two at a time – and carry them to the parking lot outside the ballpark.[3]

Once the players and a crowd of just 15,388 made it to the game, they sat in cold and windy conditions, with a temperature of 44 degrees at first pitch. The stadium was undergoing expansion, with the National Football League Vikings building a $1.2 million double-deck grandstand in left field, meaning that section of the park was closed to spectators.[4] The grounds crew had worked miracles to get the field ready for play, removing 40 inches of snow and ice from the field in the week prior to the game.[5] The weather was bad enough that the Twins announced the cancellation of Tuesday's game before Monday's game began (with the visiting New York Yankees complaining that they did that only because they would get a much bigger gate during the summer).

The Yankees came in as defending American League champions, having won the flag five years in a row, and were favorites for another pennant, although they were aging and going through several personnel changes. After the Yankees lost the World Series in 1964 to the St. Louis Cardinals, they had fired manager Yogi Berra and surprisingly appointed former Cardinals manager Johnny Keane to take his place. Mickey Mantle was also making the full-time move from center to left field to try to give some rest to his aching legs.

The Twins were picked to finish in the first division, although they were not considered serious contenders for the pennant. A couple of years with 91 wins had been followed by a slump to 79 wins and sixth place in 1964, and there were questions about whether they could bounce back. Even manager Sam Mele wasn't sure: "I think the Twins have to be better but I can't say how much."[6]

Mickey Mantle at bat for the Yankees in the first game of the 1965 season.

MEMORABLE GAMES AT MINNESOTA'S DIAMOND ON THE PRAIRIE

When the game began, Yankees starter Jim Bouton walked a couple of Twins batters in the bottom of the first, allowing one to score on a groundout. Then an error by new Yankees center fielder Tom Tresh gave the Twins a 2-0 lead in the second. That was the first of many errors this cold day, as the Yankees ended with five and the Twins with three. Meanwhile Kaat retired the first 10 batters he faced, and helped his own cause with a two-run single in the fourth. He gave up a solo home run to Elston Howard in the fifth inning (caught by one of the construction workers in the bleachers), and two more runs on a groundout and sacrifice fly in the seventh, but went to the ninth with a 4-3 lead.

Twins third baseman Rich Rollins had to leave the game early after wrenching his knee, and was replaced by Cesar Tovar, who was making his major-league debut. With two out in the ninth, Tovar dropped a Joe Pepitone pop fly, allowing Art Lopez (also making his debut, pinch-running for Mantle, who had singled to center) to score from second (he had advanced on a groundout) and tie the game. The game went into extra innings. Jerry Fosnow took over pitching duties for the Twins, after Don Mincher had pinch-hit for Kaat in the bottom of the ninth. Pedro Ramos entered the game to pitch for the Yankees in the bottom of the 10th.

Lopez returned the error in the bottom of the 11th, losing a fly ball in the wind in left field that let Twins leadoff hitter Bob Allison go all the way to third. The Yankees intentionally walked the next two hitters, and then secured two outs on a pop fly and strikeout. Next, Tovar came to bat. He made amends for his earlier error, stroking a single to center – the umpire ruled that a diving Tresh trapped the ball, although many thought it was caught[7] – to bring home the winning run and send the small crowd home happy. "I had to get a base hit," said Tovar. "You could never find a better spot to make up for an error."[8]

So the season was off to a winning start for the Twins, and for Jim Kaat the day ended with another helicopter ride, returning him and the other players across the rising floodwaters to their homes that evening.

NOTES

1. Jeff Boyne, "Mississippi River Flood of 1965," crh.noaa.gov/arx/?n=flood1965.
2. Richie Decker, "Jim Kaat and the 1965 Opener," http://twinsdaily.com/blog/253/entry-1044-jim-kaat-and-the-1965-opener-players-arriving-by-helicopter.
3. Max Nichols, "Marooned By Flood, Three Twins Reach Game in Helicopter," *The Sporting News*, April 24, 1965: 22.
4. "Stadium Expansion OKed," *Fergus Falls* (Minnesota) *Journal*, December 16, 1964: 8.
5. Dick Gordon, "Twins' Field Crew Chases Away Winter," *The Sporting News*, April 24, 1965: 19.
6. Jack Hand, "Managers See 6-Team NL Race, 3-Team AL Chase," *Clearfield* (Pennsylvania) *Progress*, April 12, 1965: 10.
7. Tom Yuzer, "Twins' Opener an Exciting One," *Fergus Falls* (Minnesota) *Daily Journal*, April 13, 1965: 12.
8. "Tovar Sheds Goat's Horns With Winning Smash in 11th," *The Sporting News*, May 1, 1965: 18.

KILLEBREW BELTS TWO HOMERS, INCLUDING GAME-WINNER IN EIGHTH

MAY 12, 1965: MINNESOTA TWINS 4, LOS ANGELES ANGELS 3

By Gregory H. Wolf

When the Minnesota Twins headed to Metropolitan Stadium to play the Los Angeles Angels on Wednesday, May 12, 1965, they had reason to be excited. The previous night, in the first contest of a three-game set with the visitors from Southern California, the Twins won in exciting fashion. With one out in the bottom of the ninth inning and the score tied 2-2, slugging first baseman Harmon Killebrew sent a bullet back to the mound that ricocheted off the leg of Angels starter Dean Chance and back toward home plate. His walk-off hit drove in Tony Oliva and gave the Twins their fourth consecutive win. More importantly, manager Sam Mele's squad improved its record to 15-7, one game in front of the Chicago White Sox and 1½ games ahead of the Angels.

Despite the loss, the Los Angeles Angels (the club officially changed its name to the California Angels on September 2, 1965, in anticipation of its move into the newly-constructed Anaheim Stadium) had been playing their best ball of the season. After a slow start, they had won 11 of 15 games for skipper Bill Rigney, who had guided the club since its admission to the AL during the expansion year of 1961.

A sparse crowd of 10,711 showed up on a beautiful, 64-degree evening at Metropolitan Stadium, located in Bloomington, about 11 miles due south of downtown Minneapolis. The Twins' faithful were treated to another exciting come-from-behind victory. It was an anxious time for Twins fans in another respect, too. The *Minneapolis Tribune* reported about trade rumors involving the popular Bob Allison and Don Mincher to the Boston Red Sox for Carl Yastrzemski and Chuck Schilling.[1]

The game got under way when Jim "Mudcat" Grant took the mound. The hard-throwing 29-year-old right-hander had thrived since the Twins acquired him from the Cleveland Indians the previous season at the trading deadline, winning 14 of 23 decisions, including a clean 3-0 slate in 1965. The Angels' light-hitting right fielder and former Rookie of the Year Award winner (1958), Albie Pearson, put Los Angeles on the board first against Grant with a home run in the first inning. Grant struggled with the gopher ball in 1965, surrendering a league-high 34; however, he still managed to lead the circuit in wins (21) and shutouts (6). The Angels increased their lead to 2-0 in the third inning on Jose Cardenal's sacrifice fly which scored Bobby Knoop, who had doubled and stolen third.

Al Worthington

MEMORABLE GAMES AT MINNESOTA'S DIAMOND ON THE PRAIRIE

The Twins' home-run-bashing offense (they led the American League with 221 round-trippers in 1964) did not intimidate the Angels' 20-year-old rookie southpaw, Rudy May, making just his fifth career start. A hard thrower who suffered from control problems, May had whiffed 10 in his major-league debut just about three weeks earlier and sported an impressive 2-1 record and a 1.73 earned-run average (ERA). He retired the first seven batters he faced before yielding a walk and two singles, including one off the bat of second baseman Jerry Kindall that drove in catcher Jerry Zimmerman for the Twins' first run.

The Angels maintained a 2-1 lead until the sixth inning, when first baseman Joe Adcock lined a two-out single to left field, scoring Cardenal. Still an offensive threat despite his bum knees, the 37-year-old Adcock had led the Angels in round-trippers with the 21 the previous year (even though he played home games in a pitcher's paradise, Dodger Stadium) and became just the 23rd big leaguer to hit 300 home runs. Killebrew blasted a home run, his fourth of the season, in the bottom of the sixth to pull Minnesota back to within one. The "Killer's" smash was music to the Twins' ears. The 28-year-old slugger had clouted 48, 45, and 49 home runs in the three prior seasons to lead the AL in that department each year. However, he had an unexpected power outage to start the 1965 season, going homerless in his first 12 games. "When Harmon Killebrew's bulging forearms snapped his bat through the strike zone and made full contact," wrote the *Star-Tribune* years later, "there was nothing else like it in baseball."[2] Standing just 5-feet-11, Killebrew generated his power from a short, compact swing.

The Twins entered the bottom of the eighth inning trailing 3-2. Pinch-hitter Frank Kostro drew a one-out walk from reliever Bob Lee, who had taken over from May to start the seventh. Lee was no slouch; as a rookie in 1964, the hard-throwing righty posted a 1.51 ERA in 137 innings. He went on to earn a berth on the American League All-Star team in 1965, and posted similar numbers (1.92 ERA in 131 innings).

Lee registered the second out by striking out Oliva, who had led the league in batting average as a rookie the previous season with a .323 average but had been mired in a slump thus far in 1965, entering the game batting only .267. Next up was Killebrew, who lived for these situations. The stocky Idahoan with a rapidly-receding hairline launched an estimated 450-foot blast that cleared the center-field fence and gave the Twins the lead, 4-3. "That was no pop-gun Harmon Killebrew used on the Angels," wrote Dick Couch of the Associated Press.[3]

Righty Al "Red" Worthington, a 36-year-old journeyman, relieved Grant to start the eighth inning and held the Angels scoreless in the final two frames to pick up the victory. The game, which was finished in 2 hours and 15 minutes, was typical for the mid-1960s – good pitching and low scoring. Each team managed just seven hits, three of which were home runs. There were no double plays and no errors.

The Twins are "going like gangbusters," wrote George C. Langford of United Press International.[4] Minnesota won its fifth consecutive game, but the club's lead in the standings shrank by a half-game in light of the Chicago White Sox's doubleheader sweep of the Kansas City Athletics.

SOURCES

In addition to the sources cited in the Notes, the author also consulted BaseballReference.com, Retrosheet.org, and SABR.org.

NOTES

1. AP, "Twins Trade Is Denied By Boston," *Minneapolis Tribune*, May 12, 1965: 19.
2. La Velle E. Neal, III, "Killebrew was 'Paul Bunyan with a uniform on,'" (Minneapolis) *Star Tribune*, May 18, 2011, startribune.com/sports/twins/122004519.html.
3. Dick Couch, Associated Press, "Killebrew Swings Hot Bat for Twins," *The Daily Reporter* (Dover, Ohio), May 13, 1965: 19.
4. George C. Langford, United Press International, "Killebrew's Muscle Returns to Form; Bosox Keep Yanks Sinking," *Daily Register* (Harrisburg, Illinois), May 13, 1965: 14.

TEBBETTS'S TECHNICALITY TURNS TIDE FROM TWINS TO TRIBE AFTER KAAT'S WARDROBE MALFUNCTION

JUNE 9, 1965: CLEVELAND INDIANS 2, MINNESOTA TWINS 1

By Nathan Bierma

A good manager, like a good magician, always has a trick up his sleeve. But a true tactician has a trick up someone else's sleeve. That's how Cleveland skipper Birdie Tebbetts overcame the overpowering Jim Kaat and the first-place Twins on a night in June 1965 at Metropolitan Stadium, invoking an obscure rule about jersey sleeves to rattle Kaat just in time for the Indians to pull out a comeback win.

The Twins (32-16), off to their best start since they moved to Bloomington five years earlier, entered the game with a 2½-game lead over the White Sox and a six-game lead over third-place Cleveland (25-21), in pursuit of the franchise's first pennant since 1933. The Indians, winners of four of their last five games, had also started off on the right foot, following four seasons of bouncing back and forth between fifth- and sixth-place finishes.

The teams had split the first two games of a four-game series when Kaat took the mound. Before the bizarre and contentious events of the ninth inning, the contest was merely a methodical pitchers' duel. Kaat picked the Cleveland lineup apart, retiring nine of his first 11 batters, eight of them on groundouts. Max Alvis drew a one-out walk in the second, and pitcher Ralph Terry drew a one-out pass in the third. Not until Vic Davalillo led off the fifth inning with an infield single could Cleveland come up with a hit off Kaat. The lanky lefty responded by striking out the next two batters, then getting Terry to ground out to second.

Terry, meanwhile, cruised just as steadily as Kaat. Acquired before the season in a trade with the Yankees, where he won two world championships,[1] the veteran scattered three hits over his first six innings. Seeking his 100th career win, Terry didn't give up a walk the entire night.

After six innings the game was scoreless and the hitters hapless. Only three Indians and four Twins had reached base, and none caused either starter to sweat. The hurlers suffered minor hiccups in the seventh, when Davallio struck again for Cleveland with a two-out single and then stole second. But Kaat got Pedro Gonzalez to ground out to strand the runner. In the bottom half of the inning, Bob Allison cracked a two-out double to left, only to see catcher Earl Battey fly out to center.

The Indians went quietly once more in the eighth. Then, with the game still scoreless, the Twins made

Jim Kaat, Earl Battey, and Vic Power were Gold Glove recipients for the Twins in the 1960s. However, on June 9, 1965, Kaat was undone for sartorial reasons.

their bid to avoid extra innings. Jerry Kindall led off with a double to the left-field corner. Kaat laid down a bunt, which catcher Joe Azcue fielded but threw wildly to first, leaving runners at the corners. The next batter, Zoilo Versalles, lifted a fly ball to center, and Kindall tagged up to give the Twins a long-awaited 1-0 lead.

After Terry retired the next two batters, it looked as though his only major mistake, the Kindall double, would be enough to lose the game. That eighth-inning sacrifice fly, the *Akron Beacon Journal* wrote, "loomed large as the 'winning' run for the Twins."[2] After all, "Kaat had three-hitted the Indians through the eight frames and needed only to hold them scoreless in the ninth for [a] shutout."[3]

The inning started according to plan, with Kaat fanning Chuck Hinton for the first out. But when Rocky Colavito worked the count to 2-and-1, Tebbetts emerged from the dugout to make his move.[4]

Tebbetts approached home-plate umpire Bill Haller and complained that Kaat had a hole in the sleeve of the undershirt below his jersey on his throwing arm, and that it was an illegal distraction to his hitters. Rule 1.11(c) required sleeves to be of the same length and not "ragged, frayed, or slit."[5]

Haller went out to the mound, confirmed the sartorial sin, and sent Kaat to the dugout for attention from Twins trainer George "Doc" Lentz. Lentz cut off the sleeve of the undershirt above the hole to remove it. Then, to comply with the rulebook, Lentz amputated a portion of the other sleeve so it would be the same length.[6]

Kaat was in the clear, but he could be forgiven if the unusual interruption had disrupted his rhythm. He was given a couple of warm-up pitches to adjust to the alteration, then had to finish the at-bat of Colavito. He walked Rocky on two straight pitches.

You might say the Indians had literally spotted an opening. The sleeve flap seemed to make the ace flappable.

With a runner on, up came Alvis, who had grounded out his last time up. Credit Kaat's shorn sleeves or just a crazy coincidence, but this time Alvis fared better.

"After a ball and a called strike on Alvis, Kaat came in with one a little too fat – and Alvis parked it deep in the left stands," lamented the *Minneapolis Star*.[7] The Indians took the lead.

Kaat retired Davalillo on a popup, but when he surrendered a single to Gonzalez, Minnesota manager Sam Mele pulled his starter and called for reliever Al Worthington to get the third out. After another single, Worthington finally did. After keeping Cleveland off the scoreboard – and, for the most part, off the basepaths – for 25 outs, the Twins would now have to come from behind.

His managing shenanigans having paid off in spades, Tebbetts brought in reliever Gary Bell to sew things up in the bottom of the ninth. After retiring Harmon Killebrew, Bell saw Jimmie Hall reach on a grounder misplayed by Chico Salmon.[8] Allison, one of the few Twins with a hit in the game, came to the plate representing the winning run. But Bell struck him out, and then got Battey to ground out to third to close out the most unlikely of wins.

"Tebbetts applied psychology at exactly the right minute to upset Kaat," wrote the *Akron Beacon Journal*, "thus proving to his tremendous satisfaction that managers indeed are necessary."[9]

Reporters asked Tebbetts afterward how long he had known about the hole in Kaat's sleeve. "From the first inning," Tebbetts said. Then, perhaps with a wink, he added, "[O]f course I really didn't see it until Colavito was at bat in the ninth inning."[10]

They asked Tebbetts if he credited his visit to the umpire with turning the tide in the ninth.

"No, I'd say you don't find many sluggers at Colavito's level willing to draw a walk in a ninth-inning situation as he did," Tebbetts demurred.

Mele was less amused.

"I called Tebbetts a lot of good names when he was standing at home plate," said Mele, a former Red Sox teammate and longtime friend of Tebbetts, about his off-color reaction to the ninth-inning intrusion. "He probably is the only manager who would do something like that – wait nine innings to call it. I won't forget it, and I don't think our players will either."[11]

"Can a friendship that increased through 18 years of baseball suddenly collapse over a hole in a sweatshirt?" asked the *Minneapolis Star*.[12] Mele pointed out that Tebbetts had spoken with an umpire about a hole in Kaat's sleeve in a meeting between the same two teams back on April 28. That time, Tebbetts said the sleeve was fine and the game should continue.[13] In a presumably unrelated detail, Tebbetts's team was ahead by three runs.

Still, Mele had to credit his friend with doing whatever it took to give his team a much-needed edge, and seemed to water down his sour grapes with some grudging affirmation. Had he been faced with the same opportunity, Mele admitted, "I might have done the same thing myself."[14]

METROPOLITAN STADIUM

SOURCES

In addition to the sources cited in the Notes, the author accessed Retrosheet.org, Baseball-Reference.com, SABR.org, and *The Sporting News* archive via Paper of Record.

NOTES

1. In addition to the 1961 and 1962 championship teams Terry was a part of, he pitched in three games with the Yankees in 1956, although he did not appear in the World Series. Terry is remembered for finishing two World Series. One was in 1960 when he gave up a home run to Bill Mazeroski that gave the Pittsburgh Pirates the championship. Two years later Terry pitched a four-hitter in a 1-0 win over the San Francisco Giants in Game 7 of the World Series.
2. Jim Schlemmer, Tebbetts Finds a 'Hole' in Minnesota Armor," *Akron Beacon Journal,* June 10, 1965: 36.
3. Schlemmer.
4. Schlemmer.
5. Max Nichols, "'Friend' Tebbetts Angers Mele in Sleeve Incidents," *Minneapolis Star,* June 10, 1965: 47.
6. Nichols.
7. Nichols.
8. Schlemmer. The play was scored as a hit.
9. Schlemmer.
10. Schlemmer.
11. Nichols.
12. Nichols.
13. Nichols.
14. Nichols.

HARMON KILLEBREW CLOUTS WALKOFF HOME RUN TO BEAT YANKEES

JULY 11, 1965: MINNESOTA TWINS 6, NEW YORK YANKEES 5

By Gregory H. Wolf

Harmon Killebrew clouted 573 home runs in his 22-year big-league career, but few were more dramatic than his walk-off, two-run smash with two outs in the ninth inning to give the Minnesota Twins an exciting victory over the New York Yankees, 6-5, on Sunday, July 11, 1965, at Metropolitan Stadium. "The scene could have been set in Hollywood," wrote Fred Down of United Press International. "[Killebrew's home run] was the most devastating blow struck against the Yankees all season."[1]

Heading into the game, the last before the three-day All-Star break, the Twins were hitting on all cylinders. Sitting atop the American League standings (52-29) by four games over the Cleveland Indians and 4½ games over the Baltimore Orioles, the Twins had played mediocre ball in June (16-13) and had slipped briefly out of first place. But manager Sam Mele's resilient club responded by reeling off nine consecutive victories in July before losing to the Yankees in the second game of a doubleheader, on July 10. One concern to the club was the loss of slugging left fielder and inspirational leader Bob Allison, who had fractured his wrist when he was hit by a pitch from Jerry Stephenson of the Boston Red Sox on July 6, and was expected to miss three weeks.

Winners of the last five AL pennants, the New York Yankees were trudging through a season their fans had not seen in two generations. Manager Johnny Keane, the former St. Louis Cardinals skipper whom the Yankees had hired after their seven-game loss to the Redbirds in the World Series the previous year, inherited an aged squad. In sixth place (41-45), New York was en route to its first losing season since 1925.

Both teams received good news prior to the game. The AL announced that Killebrew would start at first base in place of the injured Moose Skowron of the Chicago White Sox in the All-Star Game, to be played at Metropolitan Stadium in two days. Meanwhile, the Yankees' gregarious 24-year-old star, Joe Pepitone, was added to the AL roster.[2]

On a beautiful, 74-degree summer afternoon, 35,263 fans packed the Met expecting to see a well-pitched game featuring two of the brightest young southpaws in the league. Minnesota's 26-year-old Jim Kaat had established himself as one of the best young hurlers in the AL, as well as the premier fielding pitcher in baseball. He had led the team with 17 wins the previous season; his 42 starts would pace the league in 1965. New York's hard-throwing 24-year-old Al Downing had struck out a league-leading 217 in 1964 and was set to replace Whitey Ford as the

Sam Mele

club's left-handed ace. He was also the first African American pitcher to start consistently for the Yankees.

The Yankees came out swinging in the first inning. Four of the first five batters managed a hit but produced just one (unearned) run. After leadoff batter Bobby Richardson was erased on a 5-4-3 double play, Mickey Mantle and Elston Howard singled. Mantle, who had been out of the lineup since June 22 because of a leg injury, raced toward home on Hector Lopez's single to right field. Tony Oliva's throw was in time, but Mantle scored when Twins backstop Earl Battey misplayed the ball at the plate for an error.

Shortstop Zoilo Versalles put the Twins on the board in the third inning when he belted his 10th home run of the season, a solo shot with two outs, to tie the game at 1-1. Oliva and Killebrew led off the fourth inning with consecutive singles. Oliva, who had been on a tear in his previous 14 games, batting .375 (21-for-56), scampered home on Jimmie Hall's sacrifice fly; Battey drove in Killebrew on a line-drive single to left field to give the Twins a 3-1 lead. "This club is a bunch of fighters," Bob Allison told Minneapolis sportswriter Max Nichols about his club's relentless attack.[3]

Kaat encountered problems in the fifth inning when he yielded a one-out single to Phil Linz and walked Mantle. He had the Commerce Comet picked off at first base, but his errant throw to Killebrew enabled both runners to move into scoring position. Both scored on Howard's long double to center field as the Yankees tied the game at 3-3, and sent Kaat to the showers. With the run, Mantle became the 34th major leaguer to score 1,500 runs. In the bottom half of the frame, the Twins took a one-run lead on Rich Rollins's double, which scored Versalles.

Coming on in relief of righty Al Worthington with one out and two on in the seventh, Twins southpaw Bill Pleis fielded Pepitone's grounder and threw to first for the second out. Playing the odds, he intentionally walked Clete Boyer to load the bases and faced rookie left-handed center fielder Roger Repoz. The plan backfired as Pleis uncorked a wild pitch, enabling Howard to score as the Yankees tied the game yet again, 4-4.

The stage was set for an exciting, controversial ninth inning. Jerry Fosnow, the Twins' fifth pitcher of the day, surrendered a leadoff single to Howard. Pepitone hit what appeared to be an inning-ending double-play grounder, but third baseman Rollins muffed the ball. After Howard moved to third on a line out to right field by Boyer, Pleis fielded Repoz's grounder down the first-base line. As he applied the tag to Repoz, he dropped the ball; Howard romped home.

At first, home-plate umpire Ed Hurley ruled Repoz out on interference, and skipper Johnny Keane burst onto the field. After a heated exchange with Keane, Hurley consulted first-base umpire Red Flaherty, and reversed his call. Fosnow was charged with an error (the Twins' fourth of the game), the run counted, and the Yankees led, 5-4. Now it was Mele's turn to storm onto the field. With AL President Joe Cronin in attendance, Hurley stood by his call. Mele announced that the Twins would play the game under protest.

The Yankees brought in righty Pete Mikkelsen, the game's 10th pitcher, to face the top of the Twins' order, stacked with right-handers. With two outs and Rollins on first via a walk, Mikkelsen faced Killebrew. According to Joesph Durso of the *New York Times*, Killebrew fouled off two pitches with a 3-and-2 count, before he "ripped a fastball" that traveled an estimated 360 feet into the left-field bleachers, giving the Twins a dramatic 6-5 win.[4]

"The New York Yankees wear the scars today to prove that Harmon Killebrew belongs among the stars," wrote Fred Down.[5] The "Killer's" 16th home run made a winner out of Fosnow and saddled Mikkelsen with the loss. He finished with three hits in four at-bats, scored twice, knocked in two runs, and walked once; coincidentally, that was the same batting line for Elston Howard, who had integrated the New York Yankees in 1955.

Twins skipper Mele maintained a level head in spite of the thrilling victory. Told that his club was in its best position since 1933, when the Washington Senators (the team relocated to Minnesota for the 1961 season) won the pennant, Mele responded cautiously, "It's a long season and it's going to be a struggle. There are a lot of good teams."[6] Mele reminded the reporter that the Twins lost 18 of 22 games shortly after the All-Star Game the previous summer to fall out of contention by late July.

SOURCES

In addition to the sources cited in the Notes, the author also consulted BaseballReference.com, Retrosheet.org, SABR.org, and *The Sporting News*.

NOTES

1. Fred Down (United Press International), "Killebrew Convinces Yanks," *Cumberland* (Maryland) *Evening Times*, July 12, 1965: 10.
2. Associated Press, "Pepitone an All-Star; Killebrew Will Start," *New York Times*, July 12, 1965: 32.
3. *The Sporting News*, August 21, 1965: 13.
4. Joseph Durso, "Twins Beat Yanks, 6-5, on Killebrew's Homer in 9th," *New York Times*, July 12, 1965: 32.
5. Down.
6. Associated Press, "Twins Open Up 5-Game Lead," *Kansas City Star*, July 12, 1965: 13.

SENIOR CIRCUIT TAKES CHARGE IN MINNESOTA'S FIRST ALL-STAR GAME

JULY 13, 1965: NATIONAL LEAGUE 6, AMERICAN LEAGUE 5

By Greg Erion

Several themes were evident for All-Star Games played in the 1960s. First was the National League's crushing superiority during the midsummer classics. Of the 13 games played (two games were played from 1960 through 1962) the National League took 11; the American League won only once (the second game in 1962 was a tie).

Toward the end of the decade another development, the overwhelming dominance of pitching, manifested itself. Successive scores of 2-1, 2-1, and 1-0 from 1966 through 1968 reflected regular-season play where the equilibrium between hitting and pitching had gone out of balance.[1]

Another factor, born of expansion, was that new facilities and venues influenced the selection of where games took place. While venerated ballparks such as Fenway Park and Wrigley Field hosted contests, baseball's hierarchy determined it prudent to showcase recently built stadiums, too. New facilities for the expansion Houston Astros, New York Mets, Los Angeles Angels, and Washington Senators were the site of All-Star contests.[2] Older franchises with new stadiums were chosen as well: San Francisco's Candlestick Park in 1961 and Busch Stadium in 1966. A true anomaly took place in 1965 when the Minnesota Twins' Metropolitan Stadium became the site for the 36th contest. Neither the franchise nor the ballpark was new.

Metropolitan Stadium ("The Met") was nine years old, originally built for the minor-league Minneapolis Millers of the American Association. The Minnesota Twins franchise had shifted from Washington after the 1960 season, after being in the nation's capital since 1901. That Minneapolis was a new location for the majors helped lure the All-Star Game to the Twin Cities. Twins president Calvin Griffith's determination to make sure his club was duly recognized ensured that the game would take place in Minnesota. He had campaigned for Minnesota to host the game almost as soon as his team moved west. According to *The Sporting News*, Griffith was almost successful in 1963, when at the last moment Cleveland gained selection.[3] Undeterred, Griffith continued his quest and because of that persistence he gained approval for the game to take place in Minnesota in 1965.

Griffith had several tasks before him. The seating capacity of the Met was substandard. Construction of double-deck bleachers down the left-field line increased the capacity from 40,000 to 45,000.[4] The Minnesota Vikings of the NFL paid the bill and received terms for lower rent in return.[5] The seats would be completed mere days before the All-Star Game.[6] Griffith also undertook another enterprise, working with Twin City officials and business interests to ensure that visiting baseball fans and officials would get a favorable impression of the Twin Cities. This endeavor took on a life of its own, requiring a great deal of effort in the area of public relations.

The team itself unexpectedly boosted local interest in the All-Star Game. Pegged by many to finish fifth in 1965, the Twins got off to a quick start and by the end of April they and the Cleveland Indians were tied for first.[7] Starting pitcher Jim "Mudcat" Grant and veteran relievers Johnny Klippstein and Al Worthington, acquired at midseason the previous year, bolstered the staff. Future Hall of Famer Harmon Killebrew and the 1964 batting champion, Tony Oliva, led a potent offense. (Oliva would repeat in 1965.) Two off-field acquisitions also proved key to the team's success. Johnny Sain, perhaps the best pitching coach in the game, joined the club, as did Billy Martin. Martin's fiery style contributed toward a more aggressive baserunning game. Manager Sam Mele ably molded the players into a cohesive unit that played to its full potential.

On July 5, after being near the top of the standings all season, the Twins climbed back into first place and held the lead from then on. The following Sunday, July 11, Minnesota faced the New York Yankees, their last game before the All-Star break. The Yankees were in sixth place, 13½ games out, but their reputation (they had won the pennant the five previous seasons) was such that many felt they still had the ability to charge back into contention. Playing at the Met, where Griffith's project to add bleacher seats had been completed just two days before, Minnesota went into the bottom of the ninth down 5-4. With a runner on, two outs, and two strikes on Killebrew, he blasted a game-winning home run into the left-field seats. The blow proved fatal to New York, and confirmed the Twins as the team to beat. Two days later the 36th All-Star Game took place.

Griffith not only got the bleachers completed on time, his efforts to engage Minnesotans in the process of welcoming baseball to the state also came to fruition. Governor Karl Rolvaag and fellow citizens went out of their way to make visitors to the state feel welcomed. Local businessmen donated golf shirts, dinnerware and briefcases to guests and newsmen. Women received Betty Crocker cookbooks.[8] A smorgasbord was scheduled at the Met on the day of the game featuring over 120 local delicacies, including mooseburgers and roast pheasant.[9] Griffith had the pool at baseball's lodging headquarters stocked with fish and made sure visiting officials were provided with poles to catch them.[10]

Fans began gathering outside the stadium the night before the game hoping to obtain standing-room tickets, which would go on sale noon. Their wait included weathering a passing rainstorm that gradually gave way to morning clouds, which cleared just before game time.[11] Griffith's efforts to generate enthusiasm worked; an over-capacity crowd of 46,709 fans showed up to watch the game.

An underlying drama of the game was that after 35 contests (including the 1961 tie) each league had won 17 games. This development would have been largely unimagined after the 1949 All-Star Game, at which point the American League held a 12-4 advantage over the senior circuit. The tide began to turn in 1950 when the Cardinals' Red Schoendienst hit a 14th-inning home run for a 4-3 come-from-behind National League victory. The momentum carried forward as the National League proceeded to win 12 of the next 18 contests.

Of key importance in this surge of victories was the National League's early embrace of black playes. Aaron, Banks, Campanella, Clemente, Marichal, Mays, Newcombe, Robinson (Frank and Jackie), and others more than outnumbered their American League counterparts, who for much of the 1950s largely consisted of Larry Doby and Minnie Minoso, only gradually increasing as the 1960s began.[12] This imbalance of black talent at the All-Star Game in favor of the National League would prove telling in the game at Minnesota.

Managers for each league did not come to their selection through the traditional process, that of having led the previous year's World Series representatives. Johnny Keane, manager of the World Series champion St. Louis Cardinals, had resigned after winning the Series. The Yankees at season's end had fired his counterpart, Yogi Berra. In their place, Philadelphia's Gene Mauch and White Sox skipper Al Lopez, who had guided their teams to second-place finishes in 1964, led the squads.

Twins fans not only boasted of their first-place club but also crowed that Minnesota had more players on the squad than any other American League team as Lopez added Jim Grant, Jimmie Hall, Harmon Killebrew, Tony Oliva, and Zoilo Versalles to the roster. Twins catcher Earl Battey started at catcher; he was selected by a poll of players, managers, and coaches for that honor. Minnesota's Mele and coach Hal Naragon were members of the coaching staff. Twins reliever Bill Pleis was called on to throw batting practice on a field where the infield foul lines were colored red, white, and blue, and then white to the fences. Bases were red, white, and blue and the fungo-hitting circles contained red, white, and blue stars.[13]

Charley Johnson, sports editor of the *Minnesota Star and Tribune,* threw out the first pitch. He was a significant force in drumming up support to build Metropolitan Stadium and then later succeed in bringing major-league baseball to Minnesota. Johnson and the rest of the folks at the game did not have to wait long for the fireworks to begin.

A major attraction of the game for Minnesotans besides having a chance to see their local favorites play was the opportunity to view the National League stars, none of whom shined brighter than San Francisco Giant Willie Mays. Mays had played for the Millers in 1951. He was hitting a torrid .477 when called up to the Giants, much to the unhappiness of resident fans.

MEMORABLE GAMES AT MINNESOTA'S DIAMOND ON THE PRAIRIE

The outcry at his being taken from the Millers was so great that Giants owner Horace Stoneham found it necessary to buy ads in Minneapolis newspapers apologizing for taking the gifted outfielder from their midst.[14]

Mays, as usual, was having a great season. Leading the majors in home runs with 23 and batting at .339, he had just passed Stan Musial in career home runs with his 476th, placing him sixth on the all-time list. In the last game before the All-Star break, however, he and catcher Pat Corrales of the Phillies had collided in a bone-jarring play at the plate, and both players had to be removed from the game. There was legitimate concern that Mays might not be able to play.[15]

Mays did indeed play, and batting leadoff, promptly reminded Minnesotans why Stoneham had brought him to the majors 14 years earlier. On the second pitch of the game from Orioles starter Milt Pappas, Mays ripped a 415-foot home run into the left-field pavilion.[16] Musial was dinged once again; Mays's homer was his 21st hit in All-Star Game competition, breaking a tie with the St. Louis Cardinals great.

Mays's homer was just the initial blow. With two outs and Pittsburgh's Willie Stargell on first, the Braves' Joe Torre launched a home run, barely fair, into the left-field pavilion to make the score 3-0 against a stunned American League. Pappas gave way in the second to Minnesota's Grant, who at 9-2 was in the midst of his best season. Grant was as unsuccessful at holding the National League at bay as Pappas. Willie Stargell came to bat with a runner on third and homered into the right-field bullpen, making the score 5-0.

Meanwhile, the almost effortless pitching of San Francisco's Juan Marichal shut down the American League through the first three innings. He faced the minimum nine batters; Cleveland's Vic Davalillo's single in the third was erased when Battey grounded into a double play. Marichal, having pitched the maximum three innings allowed in the All-Star Game, gave way to Cincinnati's Jim Maloney to start the bottom of the fourth.

Maloney gave up one run that inning and was on the verge of getting through the fifth when disaster struck. With two outs, he walked Hall. Detroit's Dick McAuliffe homered over the center-field fence. Mays injured his hip when he slammed into the fence in an unsuccessful attempt to catch McAuliffe's drive but stayed in the game, a key development as it turned out. Brooks Robinson beat out an infield hit, which brought Killebrew to the plate. Having thrilled Twins fans with his game-winning homer over the Yankees two days before, he brought them out of their seats again, connecting off Maloney for a game-tying homer into the left-field pavilion. Maloney departed after allowing five runs in 1⅔ innings. It proved the only All-Star Game appearance of his career.

The game remained tied until the top of the seventh. Once again Mays proved to be the catalyst. Leading off, he drew a walk off Cleveland's Sam McDowell and advanced to third on Hank Aaron's single. Cubs third baseman Ron Santo came to bat and chopped the ball up the middle. Shortstop Versalles corralled the high chopper but there was no chance to get Mays at home or Santo at first. It proved to be the game-winning hit. (Santo had joked just the day before, "As a .258 hitter, I felt I was pretty much on the squad on a rain check."[17]) Mays's 17th run, the most in All-Star Game competition, merely extended a record he already held.[18]

There would be one more moment of drama. Versalles walked with two outs in the bottom of the eighth and moved to third on a single by Tigers catcher Bill Freehan, who took second on Mays's throw to third. Hall came to bat, Twins fans willing him to win the game. He flied to deep center, where Mays would normally have caught the ball with little effort, except that on contact Mays appeared to misjudge the ball. Recovering, he leaped to make a backhand catch, ending the inning. After the game he said, "I slipped as I started to go back. I was scared to death."[19]

Tony Oliva doubled to lead off the ninth, giving Twins fans hope for a rally, but Bob Gibson finished off the inning, getting the last two outs on strikeouts.

Sandy Koufax, who was pitching when Santo drove in the deciding run, got the win. Marichal edged out Mays for the Most Valuable Player of the game with his three innings of shutout ball, but the big news was that the National League had edged ahead of the American League in wins for the first time since the games began in 1933. As of 2014, their lead remains intact.

Killebrew's home run represented a consolation prize of sorts for Twins fans; however, an even greater reward awaited them on September 26, when the Twins beat the Washington Senators, 2-1, to clinch the pennant.

The All-Star Game represented Minnesota's ability to support major-league baseball; the Twins' triumph represented their ability to play better than anyone else did in the American League that year. Twenty years later the All-Star Game took place at the Metrodome, and in 2014, the 85th summer classic (including two ties) took place at Target Field. Minnesota subsequently won two pennants and two World Series championships after their encounter with the Dodgers. While these contests generated tremendous excitement, they could not recapture the first-time thrill of watching baseball's finest in July 1965 or the continuing pleasure of the locals achieving an unexpected pennant.

NOTES

1. Which it was. After the 1968 season, which saw a combined major-league batting average of .237, the pitching mound was lowered and the strike zone reduced in size, restoring a semblance of offense to the game.
2. Washington hosted the All-Star Game twice in the 1960s – first in 1963 and then in 1969, the latter driven in part by the celebration of professional baseball's centennial.
3. "Minnesota Has Reason to Be Proud," *The Sporting News*, July 17, 1965: 14.
4. Minnesota.twins.mlb.com/min/ballpark/min_ballpark_metropolitan_stadium.jsp
5. Jim Thielman, *Cool of the Evening, The 1965 Minnesota Twins* (Minneapolis: Karl House Publishers, 2005), 73.
6. "Twin Bleachers Completion Now Scheduled for July 9," *The Sporting News*, July 17, 1965: 20.
7. "Yanks, Phils Picked By Writers, Fans," *The Sporting News*, April 17, 1965: 1.
8. "Twin Cities Twinkles," *The Sporting News*, July 24, 1965: 8.
9. "Hungry for Mooseburger? It Was on All-Star Menu," *The Sporting News*, July 24, 1965: 5.
10. Thielman: 207.
11. "Twin Cities Twinkles:" 8; "Juan 'n' Willie Set N.L. Stars Winking," *The Sporting News*, July 24, 1965: 5.
12. The Boston Red Sox and Detroit Tigers did not even integrate their teams until the late 1950s and even then only with marginal utility players.
13. "Twin Cities Twinkles:" 6.
14. The ad appeared in the *Minneapolis Tribune*, May 27, 1951: E1.
15. James Hirsch, *Willie Mays: The Life, The Legend* (New York: Scribner, 2010), 430-431.
16. "Juan 'n' Willie." In a move designed to give Mays and Hank Aaron more at-bats, Mauch unconventionally placed them first and second in the batting order.
17. "Twin Cities Twinkles:" 8.
18. "Juan 'n' Willie."
19. "Juan 'n' Willie."

TWINS TAKE GAME ONE OF WORLD SERIES IN KOUFAX'S ABSENCE

OCTOBER 6, 1965: MINNESOTA TWINS 8, LOS ANGELES DODGERS 2

By Norm King

Game One of the 1965 World Series between the Los Angeles Dodgers and the Minnesota Twins was as noteworthy for who didn't play as it was for who did.

New York Yankee pinstripes were nowhere to be found in the fall classic for the first time in six years. The Bombers finished sixth in 1965 with a 77-85 record, the first time since 1925 that they had finished below .500. This season marked the end of a dynasty that had accounted for 29 American League pennants and 20 World Series titles since 1921.

Also missing from Game One was Dodgers ace Sandy Koufax, who led the National League with a 26-8 record and a 2.04 earned-run average. Game One fell on October 6, the same date as Yom Kippur, the Day of Atonement in the Jewish calendar. Jewish law forbids anyone working on that day, and Koufax, as a Jewish player, refused to pitch.

"It was a reflexive decision to do what was right in deference to his own family, in deference to his own tradition and in deference to recognition that, as a public figure, setting an example mattered," said Jane Leavy, author of a biography on Koufax.[1]

Fortunately for the Dodgers, pitching was the team's strength; they led the National League in team earned-run average (ERA), 2.81; complete games, 58; and shutouts, 17. Therefore, Dodgers manager Walter Alston had no qualms about starting the team's second best pitcher, Don Drysdale, in the first game. Drysdale's 23-12 record and 2.77 ERA would have made him a staff ace on any team that did not have a Koufax in the rotation. He was also in a groove, having pitched complete-game shutouts in his last two starts of the season.

The Twins countered with their best pitcher, Jim "Mudcat" Grant, who led the American League in wins with 21 (the only 20-win season of his career) and shutouts, with six.

Naturally, with this being the first game of the Series and a battle looming between two 20-game winners, everyone expected a pitching duel; but in the grand tradition of great expectations gone awry everywhere, this game had 20 hits, a bat-around inning, a rare hitting feat from an unlikely source, a heroic stroke from Zorro, and, possibly, one manager wishing his pitcher would change religions.

Anyone who has watched National Football League films of Minnesota Vikings playoff games in the 1970s may be excused in thinking that the Dodgers and Twins played in a blizzard. Such was not the case in Game One, as the temperature reached 68 degrees that afternoon (yes, afternoon). The pitchers copycatted

Versalles and Mele

each other in the first two innings; both retired the side in order in the first, while striking out the lead-off hitter (Grant struck out Dodgers shortstop Maury Wills while Drysdale returned the favor with Twins shortstop Zoilo Versalles). In the second, both pitchers gave up solo home runs. Dodgers right fielder Ron Fairly smacked one to deep right field off Grant, while Twins first baseman Don Mincher tied the game in the bottom of the inning.

Grant retired the side in order in the top of the third and then the Twins reached down inside themselves for their inner disc jockey because the hits just kept on coming during their turn at bat. The team's number-eight hitter, second baseman Frank Quilici, started the fun with a double. Grant reached on an error while trying to sacrifice Quilici to third (second baseman Jim Lefebvre dropped Drysdale's throw to first), and with two on, Versalles, nicknamed Zorro, swung his rapier-like bat and belted a three-run homer to left field. Another double followed, this time by left fielder Sandy Valdespino, before Tony Oliva grounded out. Drysdale then loaded the bases by giving up a single to third baseman Harmon Killebrew and walking Mincher (with a strikeout of center fielder Jimmie Hall sandwiched in between). Catcher Earl Battey singled to score Valdespino and Killebrew. Coming up for the second time in the inning, Quilici, who hit only .208 during the regular season, performed the rare feat of getting two hits in one frame during the World Series. His single scored Mincher, making the score 7-1.

After Quilici's hit, manager Alston came to the mound to take Drysdale out of the game. As he was leaving, Drysdale is reported to have said, "I bet right now you wish I was Jewish, too."[2]

The six-run, six-hit inning buried the Dodgers. Versalles drove Grant in with the Twins' eighth run in the sixth, and Wills' bunt single scored second baseman Lefebvre with a too-little, too-late run in the ninth. The 8-2 final allowed the Twins to take a 1-0 lead in the Series.

Even though he pitched a complete game and scattered ten hits – nine of them singles – Grant wasn't happy with his performance. He even went over to the box where U.S. Senator Hubert Humphrey of Minnesota was sitting, and told the senator that he (Grant) was not pitching well because he didn't have his curveball. Humphrey told him to stick with the fastball.

"I didn't have as good a fastball [today] as I had during the season," Grant said after the game. "Most of the game I had control trouble. I was 2-and-2 and 3-and-2 on most of the hitters."[3]

Alston, of course, put on as positive a spin on the loss as he could. "We got 10 hits, they got 10 hits, but theirs came in a bunch and scored runs. Ours didn't," he said.[4] He also pointed out that the Dodgers lost the first game of the 1959 World Series to the White Sox, 11-0, and came back to win the championship.

SOURCES

In addition to the sources cited in the Notes, the author also consulted Retrosheet.org and Baseball-Reference.com.

NOTES

1. "Q & A" with Jane Leavy: Author Speaks on How Koufax Overcame Bias, Pain," SI.com, posted September 3, 2002.
2. Jeff Merron wrote Drysdale's remark in ESPN.com. That quote appears in other articles as well.
3. Lew Ferguson, "Twins 'Have to Keep Going'" *Oneonta* (New York) *Star*, October 7, 1965.
4. Bob Myers, "Dodgers Haven't Given Up Hope," *Oneonta* (New York) *Star*, October 7, 1965.

TWINS BEAT DODGERS AT THEIR OWN GAME TO TAKE COMMANDING SERIES LEAD

OCTOBER 7, 1965: MINNESOTA TWINS 5, LOS ANGELES DODGERS 1

By Norm King

National League President Warren Giles would have been excused if he had thought that somebody in his office screwed up and sent the 1962 New York Mets to play Game Two of the World Series against the Minnesota Twins instead of the National League champion Los Angeles Dodgers. By committing three errors and allowing poor relief pitching to let a winnable game get away from them, the Dodgers looked more like those Mets, who lost 120 games, than the team that won 97.

The weather was cool and wet – the high reached only 58 and it drizzled throughout the game. Despite the conditions, fans expected a pitcher's duel between Dodgers ace Sandy Koufax and 18-game winner Jim Kaat. And for the first 4½ innings, that's exactly what they got. Then came the top of the fifth and a play that changed the course of the game.

The Dodgers' Ron Fairly led off the frame with a single to right. Jim Lefebvre followed with a liner to left that was drifting away from left fielder Bob Allison and looked like a sure double. But Allison ran a long way to the foul line and made a spectacular diving catch that left the Dodgers with one out and a runner on first instead of two runners in scoring position with nobody out. Good thing, too, because Wes Parker then grounded a single into right field that would probably have scored two runs. Instead, Kaat got the next two batters on foul pop-ups and the game remained scoreless.

"I don't know when I've seen a catch like that," said Twins manager Sam Mele. "It was a tremendous catch. It could have meant something big for the Dodgers if the ball had dropped in there."[1]

The game then proceeded from Allison's sublime to Dodger third baseman Jim Gilliam's ridiculous.

Anyone who ever did something because it seemed like a good idea at the time, only to regret it afterward, would know how Gilliam felt after the sixth. Gilliam started the 1965 season as a Dodger coach, but then went back on the active roster in May. He may have wished he was back in the coaching ranks after Zoilo Versalles's grounder bounced off him for a two-base error to lead off the inning. After center fielder Joe Nossek sacrificed Versalles to third, the Twins shortstop scored on Tony Oliva's double to give Minnesota a 1-0 lead. Harmon Killebrew's single then drove in Oliva, and the Twins led 2-0.

It was still anybody's game in the top of the seventh, when Fairly and Lefebvre singled to open the inning. After the runners advanced on a sacrifice by Parker, catcher John Roseboro singled to score Fairly; Lefebvre and Roseboro moved up on the throw to the plate. Dodgers manager Walter Alston then made a move that said a lot about his team's lack of scoring punch. Koufax was the next scheduled batter, and

Bob Allison robs Jim Lefebvre in the second game of the 1965 World Series.

Alston made the standard move by pinch-hitting for him because his team was behind in the late innings. The Twins were probably surprised when Don Drysdale, the loser of Game One, came out of the dugout swinging a bat. On the surface it seemed a bizarre move, but Drysdale was, in fact, an excellent hitting pitcher. His .300 batting average was the highest on the team that season. Drysdale also hit seven homers, an astounding total for a pitcher, in just 130 at-bats. By comparison, Lefebvre and left fielder Lou Johnson tied for the team lead in home runs with 12. The gamble didn't pay off, however, as mighty Drysdale struck out. Maury Willsfollowed and flied to center to end the threat.

Reliever Ron Perranoski replaced Koufax on the mound in the bottom of the seventh and started off well enough by getting the first two batters out. Leadoff hitter Versalles then tripled to right and while he was on third, he began dancing up and down the line in the tradition of Jackie Robinson. This rattled Perranoski, who threw a wild pitch with Joe Nossek at the plate, allowing Versalles to score. Nossek reached first on another error by poor Gilliam, but was stranded.

The Twins put the game away in the eighth. Killebrew walked and advanced to third on an Allison double. Killebrew was tagged out at the plate on a fielder's choice by first baseman Don Mincher. Allison advanced to third and Mincher to second on a balk by Perranoski. The Dodgers walked number-eight hitter Frank Quilici to load the bases and bring Kaat to the plate, and while Kaat was no Drysdale at the plate, his numbers weren't that bad (.247 average, one home run). His single brought two runners home and put the game away. Los Angeles threatened in the ninth with two runners on and one out, but didn't score.

The Dodgers were 7-5 favorites going into the Series and there had been some talk of a sweep. That talk continued, except that now the wags were speculating on the possibility of the Twins getting the brooms out. Suffice it to say that the Twins surprised everyone by beating both Drysdale and Koufax.

However, Alston knew from experience that being down 2-0 doesn't mean the Series is over. In 1955 his Brooklyn Dodgers were in this situation and won it all. The following year they were up 2-zip on the Yankees and lost. He was also the manager of a veteran team whose players knew what it took to get the ring.

As for Gilliam, it was simply one of those days. He had committed only one error in his previous 108 World Series chances, and didn't make any miscues the rest of this Series.

Now it was on to Los Angeles for Game Three.

SOURCES

In addition to the source cited in the Notes, the author also consulted: wunderground.com and the *Winona* (Minnesota) *Daily News.*

NOTES

1. Lew Ferguson, "Allison's Roll-Over Catch Snuffs Dodgers," *San Bernardino* (California) *Sun.* October 8, 1965.

MUDCAT TIES THE SERIES WITH PITCHING, HITTING IN GAME SIX

OCTOBER 13, 1965: MINNESOTA TWINS 5, LOS ANGELES DODGERS 1

By Norm King

It sounds like a corny Hollywood movie. The home team has its back against the wall. It calls on its best pitcher, who bravely goes to the mound despite being sick. He not only wins the game, but hits a home run to boot. And if that's not enough cornball for you, a friend had asked the pitcher to win a game for the man's wife, who recently died in an automobile accident.

Welcome to Game Six of the 1965 World Series, where everything described above really happened. The Minnesota Twins had their backs against the wall, having dropped three straight to the Dodgers in Los Angeles after winning the first two games in Minneapolis. Twins manager Sam Mele gave the ball to Jim "Mudcat" Grant, who had a 1-1 record in the Series and who only had two days' rest after giving up five runs (four earned) in five-plus innings in a 7-2 Twins loss. The pressure on Grant was compounded by the fact that he had a bad cold and sore knees.

"My head feels like a balloon, my cold's no better and my knees are bothering me," said Grant. "Otherwise, I'm all right."[1]

Claude Osteen started Game Six for the Dodgers. Osteen was the Twins' nemesis, having accumulated a 5-0 won-lost record against them when he pitched for the Washington Senators, plus a 4-0 shutout win in Game Three of this World Series.

So far, this had been a homer's Series, with each team winning in its home park. After taking the first two games at Metropolitan Stadium, the Twins lost all three games in Los Angeles, were shut out twice, and were outscored 18-2.

"In losing the three games in LA, the all-round play of the Twins was like that of disorganized sandlotters," wrote sportswriter George Raubacher. "Little Leaguers generally function better than did the Twins in three reverses away from home."[2]

Ouch.

Perhaps that critique didn't motivate Grant, but the need to win certainly did, and his pitching showed it, as he was almost perfect through four innings. Dodgers catcher John Roseboro reached safely in the third on an error by third baseman Harmon Killebrew, but was thrown out trying to steal second on a "strike 'em out, throw 'em out" double play with second baseman Dick Tracewski at the plate. Osteen started off well enough, giving up three hits and two walks through the first three frames, but keeping the Dodgers off the scoreboard. That all changed in the fourth.

Mudcat Grant

Twins catcher Earl Battey led off the inning with a groundball to second base but Tracewski, playing in place of the injured Jim Lefebvre, booted the ball and Battey was safe. Left fielder Bob Allison, who was 1-for-10 at this point in the Series, sent Osteen's third pitch on a long ride into the lower left-field pavilion, giving the Twins a 2-0 lead.

Grant gave up his first hit in the fifth, a harmless single by Dodgers right fielder Ron Fairly. Grant experienced his only tough spot of the game in the next inning. Tracewski singled and then, after Willie Crawford struck out while pinch-hitting for Osteen, moved to second on a base hit by shortstop Maury Wills. With two on and one out, Grant induced third baseman Junior Gilliam to pop to short and got center fielder Willie Davis to fly to center.

When managers make the standard move in a game, such as removing a pitcher for a pinch-hitter or walking the number-eight hitter to get to the pitcher's spot in the batting order, they know that sometimes these moves won't work. It's when both moves backfire in the same inning that the gray hair comes in. Dodgers manager Walter Alston would have bought a truckload of "Just For Men" if it had existed back then after the Twins' half of the sixth because his moves failed spectacularly.

Howie Reed replaced Osteen on the mound and, with one out, walked Allison, who then stole second while first baseman Don Mincher struck out looking. Alston then ordered Reed to walk second baseman Frank Quilici, who was hitting .188 for the Series, to get to Grant, who hit .155 during the season with no home runs. The same move blew up in the Twins' face in Game Five, when Dodgers pitcher Sandy Koufax got a single to drive in a run; and on this day Grant got a hit, too, except in this case it was a three-run homer to left-center, making the score 5-0.

It's a tradition in baseball that any pitcher who hits a home run can suddenly talk about hitting as if he's Ted Williams.

"I said to myself, 'He's going to throw me a curve. He can't afford to give me a fastball in a situation like this,'" said Grant. "Sure enough, he threw the curve. I knew it was gone the moment I hit it."[3]

The Dodgers didn't mount any further threats. Fairly belted a solo home run to right-center leading off the seventh, but otherwise Grant breezed through the rest of the game. He pitched masterfully, allowing only six hits and striking out five while not walking anyone. He stayed ahead of the hitters the whole game – of the 33 batters he faced, he threw first-pitch strikes to 28.

The fact that it was a win-or-go-home situation no doubt motivated Grant, but he had a deeper, more personal incentive as well. Before the game, he received a telegram from a friend that said: "Win the next one for Scotty. . . . Your friend, Howdy Doody."[4] Grant explained to a reporter that "Howdy Doody" was a friend of his in Kansas City and that Scotty, the friend's wife, had died in a car accident a week and a half before, and that they were married for less than a year.

"I thought about her when I went out to the mound," said Grant. "I'm glad I made my friend a little happier."[5]

On to Game Seven.

SOURCES

In addition to the sources cited in the Notes, the author also consulted *Sports Illustrated*.

NOTES

1. Associated Press, "Minnesota's Hopes Ride on Tired, Sick Pitcher," *Ellensburg* (Washington) *Daily Record*, October 13, 1965.
2. George Raubacher (Associated Press), "Twins Alive by Coming Alive," *Janesville* (Wisconsin) *Daily Gazette*, October 14, 1965.
3. Joe Reichler (Associated Press), "Twins Hero Inspired by Letter," *San Bernardino* (California) *Daily Sun*, October 14, 1965.
4. Reichler.
5. Reichler.

KOUFAX HAS NOTHING TO ATONE FOR IN GAME SEVEN MASTERPIECE

OCTOBER 14, 1965: MINNESOTA TWINS 5, LOS ANGELES DODGERS 1

By Norm King

Unfortunately for the Minnesota Twins, there were no Jewish holidays that would prevent Sandy Koufax from pitching for the Los Angeles Dodgers in Game Seven of the 1965 World Series. As a result, he came. He pitched. He shut the Twins out, 2-0. That's really all you need to know.

Actually, there's a little bit more to Game Seven than that. Dodgers manager Walter Alston elected to start Koufax on two days' rest, rather than Don Drysdale, who hadn't pitched in four days. Alston made it clear during a pregame meeting that Drysdale would take over if Koufax faltered.

Jim Kaat started for the Twins, also on two days' rest, and Twins manager Sam Mele was similarly not afraid to change pitchers at the first sign of trouble. He ended up using five pitchers in the game, all of whom shut the Dodgers out after Kaat gave up two runs in the fourth.

"You hate to lose but we didn't disgrace ourselves," said Mele. "We were beaten by the best pitcher that there is anywhere."[1]

Oddly enough, Koufax didn't breeze through the early innings. Some luck, plus good defense, kept the Twins off the scoreboard until he found his rhythm in the middle frames. He walked right fielder Tony Oliva and third baseman Harmon Killebrew back-to-back in the first inning with two out, prompting Alston to get Drysdale up in the bullpen. But Koufax struck out catcher Earl Battey to escape any damage. In the third, Drysdale began warming again after shortstop Zoilo Versalles singled with one out. Versalles stole second, but had to return to first when center fielder Joe Nossek was called out for batter interference. Koufax then struck out Oliva for the third out.

Lou Johnson opened the fourth with a home run to deep left, giving the Dodgers a 1-0 lead. Ron Fairly followed that with a double and scored on a single by first baseman Wes Parker. That was the end of the season for Kaat, who was replaced on the mound by Al Worthington.

The Twins' most serious threat came in the fifth. With one out, second baseman Frank Quilici doubled to left. Koufax walked the next batter, Rich Rollins, who was pinch-hitting for Worthington. Versalles was up next and he hit a scorcher toward third base that could have scored one, possibly two runs. However, third baseman Jim Gilliam made an outstanding backhanded stab and touched the bag for the force on Quilici. Nossek then grounded into a force play at second and the inning, and the Twins, were done.

"I didn't even have time to think about (the play)," said Gilliam. "It was about a foot from the bag and as I grabbed it, I slipped to one knee. But I saw the runner and knew I had time so I got up and stepped on the bag."[2]

"Gilliam's play could have been the turning point," said Mele. "Rollins has a chance to score from first, depending on what happens in the left-field corner. It was a great play, no doubt about it."[3]

Minnesota went three-up-three-down in the sixth, seventh, and eighth. Killebrew got a base hit with one out in the ninth, but – stop me if you've heard this one – Koufax struck out the next two batters to win the game with a flourish.

The game capped a remarkable World Series for Koufax, who was chosen Series Most Valuable Player for the second time (he also earned the honor in 1963 when the Dodgers swept the New York Yankees). He went 2-1 and gave up only one earned run in 24 innings pitched (a 0.38 earned-run average [ERA]), struck out 29, and threw two shutouts. He even had a hit and a run batted in.

While Koufax deserved the award, he wasn't the only suitable candidate. Ron Fairly had 11 hits in the Series, for a .379 batting average, with two home runs, three doubles, and a 1.069 OPS (on-base percentage plus slugging average). Maury Wills also had 11 hits, for a .367 average. If they had an unsung-hero award, Lou Johnson would have won easily. Johnson was a 31-year-old career minor leaguer with only 96 games of major-league experience prior to the 1965 season. After playing for six different organizations in such far-flung outposts as St. Jean, Quebec, and Ponca City, Oklahoma, he got his big break in 1965 when regular left fielder Tommy Davis broke his ankle on May 1. Johnson proved to be a sparkplug for the Dodgers, helped carry them to the pennant, and batted .296 with two home runs in the fall classic, one of which was the Series-winning hit.

Associated Press sportswriter Joe Reichler summed up the reasons for the Dodgers' victory quite succinctly: "In the final essence, it was Dodger pitching with the shutouts and the ability of Los Angeles' supposedly weak hitters to all but match the Twins in home run power that swung the balance to the Dodgers."[4]

As for Mele, if he didn't have enough on his plate during the Series, his wife, Connie, was several days overdue with the couple's fifth child. In fact, Sam was told during Game Five that she had gone into labor, but that turned out to be a false alarm. Connie gave birth to their fifth child, Scott, four days after the Series ended.

SOURCES

In addition to the sources cited in the Notes, the author also consulted game coverage in the *Milwaukee Journal*.

NOTES

1   William Leggett, "The Final Strength Was Sandy," *Sports Illustrated*, October 25, 1965.

2   Jack Hand, "Shutout Sandy Stymies Twins to Give Dodgers World Series," *San Bernardino* (California) *Daily Sun*, October 15, 1965.

3   Hand.

4   Joe Reichler, "Koufax Dominant Figure of World Series Champions," *Janesville* (Wisconsin) *Daily Gazette*, October 15, 1965.

DEAN CHANCE, JACKIE WARNER, AND BASERUNNING BLUNDERS DOOM THE TWINS

APRIL 26, 1966: CALIFORNIA ANGELS 3, MINNESOTA TWINS 2

By Thomas E. Merrick

April 1966 was a great time to be a Minnesota Twin. The Twins were the reigning American League champions – a title reserved for the New York Yankees in 14 of the previous 16 years. Only the seventh-game brilliance of Sandy Koufax had prevented the Twins from being fitted for World Series rings.[1] Minnesota was loaded with stars like 1965 Most Valuable Player Zoilo Versalles, two-time batting champion Tony Oliva, *The Sporting News's* American League Pitcher of the Year Mudcat Grant, slugger Harmon Killebrew, and pitchers Camilo Pascual and Jim Kaat. Relief pitching and basestealing were becoming part of baseball's winning formula, and Minnesota could boast of those, too. The Twins were picked, along with Detroit and Baltimore, to finish at the top of the standings again in 1966.[2]

On April 16 the Twins were facing the California Angels in the fifth game of their six-game season-opening homestand at Metropolitan Stadium. Minnesota had beaten Kansas City three straight times to open the season, but the Angels proved to be a tougher test, roughing up the Twins, 9-4, in the first of their scheduled three games. On this Saturday afternoon, Grant, winner of the season opener, opposed Dean Chance.

Grant made quick work of California in the first, getting three straight outs. The Twins had a scoring opportunity in their half of the inning but gave it away. With one out, Sandy Valdespino beat out a bunt, and went to third when Oliva lined a single to left.[3] But Valdespino committed the first of three costly Twins baserunning mistakes when he was picked off third base by Angels catcher Bob Rodgers for the second out. Oliva stole second base, keeping the flickering threat alive, but Don Mincher struck out.

Neither team scored in the second, but the Twins grabbed the lead in the third inning. With one out, Versalles's speed earned him an infield single,[4] and he took second on a groundout. That brought up Oliva with two outs. Chance threw a first-pitch strike, "jammed him three times, then came in low and away."[5] Oliva hit the 3-and-1 pitch over the fence – his fourth consecutive game with a home run[6] – putting Minnesota ahead 2-0. After the game, Chance called Oliva – who collected three hits, and hit the ball hard in each of his four at-bats – the best player in the American League[7] and asked plaintively, "How do you pitch that Oliva?"[8]

The fourth inning was uneventful, but in the fifth, Minnesota's Bernie Allen joined Valdespino in infamy. Allen drew a leadoff walk and was sacrificed to second, only to be picked off when Chance whirled and threw to shortstop Jim Fregosi, who was between Allen and second base. Allen broke toward third, but Fregosi threw to third baseman Paul Schaal, who returned the ball to Fregosi to apply the tag on Allen.[9] A Versalles groundout ended a once-promising inning. Twins manager Sam Mele was later asked how both Allen and Valdespino could have been picked off. His reply was a terse, "They fell fast asleep."[10]

The Angels' sixth inning began with a groundout. Grant had now retired the first 16 California batters. According to Fregosi, Grant had never looked better against the Angels: "He's throwing faster than ever and his slider was great."[11] Angels manager Bill Rigney agreed, saying he had never seen Grant throw faster.[12]

But Grant's stroll through the Angels' lineup was about to end. He walked Schaal, giving California its first baserunner. Chance pushed a bunt toward third in an attempt to sacrifice Schaal to second, but Killebrew was late to the ball, allowing Chance to reach base with California's first hit. Few players would be less likely to end a no-hitter than Chance. His career batting average was a microscopic .066. His next hit – his only other hit of 1966 – came in August!

The Angels rally continued with Jose Cardenal beating out a dribbler to the left of the mound, which filled the bases with one out. Bobby Knoop's fly ball was caught for the second out, but Schaal tagged up and scored. Cardenal was forced at second to end the inning, but Minnesota now led 2-1 after six.

To begin the Angels' seventh, Norm Siebern lined a single, and 18-year-old Willie Montanez ran for him. Rodgers lined out, bringing rookie Jackie Warner to the plate. Grant had fanned Warner in his first two at-bats, but this time, Grant fell behind, two balls and no strikes. He fired a fastball over the plate, and Warner hit it into the left-field seats 391 feet away, putting California ahead for good, 3-2.[13] Warner was the hero for the second time in his first four major-league games – he had hit a ninth-inning home run to beat the White Sox two days earlier. "I can't say enough about young Warner," proclaimed Chance. "He's doing it all."[14]

The Twins put together one more charge in the eighth. Russ Nixon, batting for Grant, doubled. Rookie Ted Uhlaender, "the Baylor speedster,"[15] ran for Nixon. When Versalles hit a grounder to shortstop, Uhlaender raced for third.[16] Fregosi made a high throw to Schaal "and it was going to be two on and no outs," except Uhlaender slid past the bag.[17] He dived back, but was tagged out by Schaal – at least according to the umpire.[18] Third-base coach Billy Martin vehemently disagreed. As the *Minneapolis Tribune* put it, "Martin raged, while Uhlaender burned, but the umpire's decision stood."[19] Tempers eventually cooled, and when they did, Valdespino flied to center for the second out. Oliva lined a ball that "nearly tore off Bobby Knoop's hand,"[20] but it was caught for the third out. Even after the game, Martin conceded nothing on the Uhlaender call: "Schaal hasn't tagged him yet! Uhlaender had no business going in the first place, but he was safe anyhow."[21]

Al Worthington pitched the ninth inning for the Twins, and faced just three batters despite giving up a leadoff triple to Tom Satriano. Jackie Hernandez ran for the plodding Satriano, but after Rodgers struck out, Hernandez "got crossed up with third-base coach Del Rice."[22] Hernandez mistakenly thought a squeeze play was on,[23] and broke for home while Warner was batting. He was easily tagged out by Twins catcher Jerry Zimmerman after a brief rundown in a play scored 2-5-2.[24] Warner struck out for the third time, ending the inning.

The Twins' ninth inning was easy for Chance. Mincher grounded out, Killebrew took a called third strike, and Jimmie Hall popped to second, closing out Minnesota's second consecutive loss to California. Chance had his first win of the season; Grant his first loss.

Grant did not take defeat lightly. He spent over an hour on the field after the game trying to forget the loss.[25] He did not blame the sloppy baserunning or Killebrew's failure to field Chance's bunt. Instead, he took full responsibility. "I should never let a rookie beat me," lamented Grant, "I struck [Warner] out earlier on fastballs, but I shouldn't have thrown him the fastball for the home run."[26]

Grant lost despite pitching well; Chance claimed a win even though, as Rigney recognized, he was not at his best.[27] Chance gave up seven hits and two walks, "But he fought all the way," said Rigney. "That's what makes him great. He never quits."[28]

The hitting stars, Oliva and Warner, traveled far different paths after this game. In 1966 Oliva hit .307, second only to Frank Robinson's .316, led the league with 191 hits – 25 were home runs – and took home a Gold Glove for his defense. In 1971 he won his third batting title, and over his 15-year career, all with the Twins, he hit .304. In addition to three batting crowns, Oliva led the AL in hits five times and in doubles four times. Injuries eventually diminished his skills and shortened his career, but he is one of the Twins' greatest players.

Incredibly, Warner beat the Twins again on April 23 when his two-out, two-run homer in the bottom of the eighth vaulted the Angels over the Twins, 4-3.[29] In

Dean Chance, Mudcat Grant, and Dave Boswell. Chance and Grant dueled at Met Stadium in an April 1966 game with Chance winning. The following year they were teammates.

MEMORABLE GAMES AT MINNESOTA'S DIAMOND ON THE PRAIRIE

his five games against Minnesota that April, Warner delivered 9 hits in 19 at-bats, including two doubles, a triple, and his two game-winning home runs. But American League pitchers made adjustments, and Warner did not. He was soon relegated to pinch-hitting and pinch-running duty, and by late July – hitting just .213 and striking out in 42 percent of his plate appearances – he was sent to the Pacific Coast League. He never returned to the major leagues.

NOTES

1. On just two days' rest, the Dodgers' Koufax beat the Twins 2-0 in the deciding game.
2. Joe King, "Tight Races Seen; Court Case Threat," *The Sporting News,* April 16, 1966: 7. The publication was picking the Baltimore Orioles to finish ahead of the Twins "by a slim edge."
3. Tom Briere, "Twins Stopped 3-2 by Chance, Angels," *Minneapolis Tribune,* April 17, 1966: 1S.
4. Briere.
5. John Hall, "Warner Wins Another for Angels," *Los Angeles Times,* April 17, 1966: D1, D2.
6. Hall.
7. Sid Hartman, "Hartman's Roundup," *Minneapolis Tribune,* April 17, 1966: 3S.
8. Briere.
9. retrosheet.org/boxesetc/1966/B04160MIN1966.htm.
10. Ira Berkow, "Creeak – Twins Unhinge on Basepaths," *Minneapolis Tribune,* April 17, 1966: 1S.
11. Hall.
12. Hartman.
13. Hartman.
14. Hartman.
15. Briere.
16. Hall.
17. Hall.
18. Hall.
19. Briere.
20. Hall.
21. Berkow.
22. Hall.
23. Hall.
24. Berkow. See, retrosheet.org/boxesetc/1966/B04160MIN1966.htm.
25. Hartman.
26. Hartman.
27. Hall.
28. Hall.
29. retrosheet.org/boxesetc/1966/B04230CAL1966.htm.

TWINS COME FROM BEHIND TO DEFEAT A'S 9-4 BEHIND FIVE HOME RUNS IN THE SEVENTH

JUNE 9, 1966: MINNESOTA TWINS 9, KANSAS CITY ATHLETICS 4

By Bob Webster

The Minnesota Twins belted five home runs in the bottom of the seventh inning to erase a 4-3 deficit and take the rubber game of a three-game series with the Kansas City Athletics, 9-4, before a crowd of 9,621 at Metropolitan Stadium. It was the first time an American League team hit five home runs in one inning, although the feat had been matched three times in the National League before this game and twice more since (as of 2020).

Camilo Pascual took the mound for the Twins on this 67-degree Thursday evening, but he did not last long. To the delight of the official scorer, who always liked the game to start out with a clean base hit, Bert Campaneris singled to left to lead off the game. Joe Nossek singled to right and Campaneris advanced to third. Mike Hershberger tapped one back to Pascual and Campaneris, caught off third, realizing he was not going to beat Pascual's throw to third, broke for the plate and was gunned down, pitcher-to-third-to-catcher. Danny Cater walked to load the bases. Ken Harrelson struck out looking for the second out of the inning but Larry Stahl tripled to left, clearing the bases. That was it for Pascual, who was replaced by Dwight Siebler. Dick Green singled in Stahl to make the score 4-0 before Siebler got Phil Roof to fly out to left for the third out.

Harrelson was not happy with the third strike called by home-plate umpire Red Flaherty. Harrelson kept barking at Flaherty from the dugout long enough that he became the first Athletics player to be thrown out of a game in the season. "That was the worst pitch I ever saw," Harrelson said. "That is the first time I've ever been thrown out of a game. I had my say – from the dugout. He didn't like it."[1]

Through the first four innings, Athletics' starting pitcher, Catfish Hunter, held the Twins scoreless on three singles and two walks, being helped by three double plays. In the bottom of the fifth, the Twins got a run against Hunter. After Jimmie Hall and Earl Battey grounded out, Bernie Allen singled to center. Bob Allison pinch-hit for Siebler and doubled Allen home to make the score 4-1. Zoilo Versalles fouled out to the catcher, ending the inning and stranding Allison on second base.

The Twins cut the lead to 4-3 in the sixth when Don Mincher singled to center with two out and Harmon Killebrew drove a fly into the left-field seats off Hunter, for his 10th home run of the season.

Twins reliever Pete Cimino retired the A's in the top half of the seventh and that's when the fun began.

Battey walked to lead off the Twins' seventh. One out later, Rich Rollins, pinch-hitting for Cimino, homered to deep left, scoring Battey in front of him to give the Twins a 5-4 lead. Versalles followed with a homer to left to make the score 6-4. A's manager Al

Calvin Griffith

MEMORABLE GAMES AT MINNESOTA'S DIAMOND ON THE PRAIRIE

MILLERS AND SAINTS MEET AGAIN

Angelo Giuliani, a longtime scout and director of Twins' clinics, was one of the players in the Saints-Millers Old-Timers' Game at Met Stadium in 1967.

A crowd of 34,000 came to the Met on September 1, 1967, to see the Twins open a three-game series with the Detroit Tigers. The Twins and Tigers were among four teams bunched within 1½ games of one another at the top of the American League standings. Beyond the lure of a torrid pennant race, early arrivals got to watch an Old Timer's Game between former stars of the Minneapolis Millers and St. Paul Saints. The Minneapolis players included Joe Hauser, who had hit 69 home runs for the Millers in 1933, and Ray Dandridge, who was the league's Most Valuable Player in 1950. St. Paul had Eric Tipton, a popular standout in the 1940s, and Angelo Giuliani, who grew up in St. Paul and played with both the Millers and Saints. Tipton was part of a three-run rally for the Saints in the first inning against Jess Petty and Rosy Ryan, who were considered graybeards when they pitched for Minneapolis in the 1930s. The Millers got their only run in the second as Frank Trechock doubled home Babe Barna, who had started the inning with a walk. Saints pitcher Dick Lanahan said he walked Barna "because his bay window kept me from seeing the plate." The pitchers rode in from the bullpen in a 1917 Model-T Ford touring car. After the Saints' 3-1 win, the Twins beat the Tigers 5-4 to retain sole possession of second place, a half-game behind first-place Boston.

Dark took the ball from Hunter and brought in Paul Lindblad. Sandy Valdespino grounded out to short for Lindblad's first and only out. The next batter, Tony Oliva, hit the Twins' third homer of the inning, over the right-field fence. Mincher followed with a blast to right field for the fourth home run of the inning. Pitcher John Wyatt replaced Lindblad, and Killebrew sent one over the left-field fence for back-to-back-to-back homers and his second home run in two innings. It was the fifth home run of the inning for the Twins and gave them a 9-4 lead. The next batter, Jimmie Hall, hit one high off the right-field wall for a double, just missing a home run by a few feet. Battey followed with a groundball to A's first baseman Ron Stone, who booted it for an error. Allen grounded out to end the inning. The five homers added up to 1,895 feet in total distance. Rollins's blast was measured at 368 feet by the Metropolitan Stadium equipment, followed by Versalles's at 370 feet, Oliva's at 401 feet, Mincher's at 376 and Killebrew's at 380 feet. If you add Hall's 380-foot double, the six blasted the ball 2,275 feet that inning.[2]

Hall thought he might have helped set a record of six home runs in an inning if it weren't for the public-address announcer, Bob Casey. "Yes, I knew about the record," Hall said. "The announcer told everyone that we had tied the record when I was standing in the batter's box. Sure it upset me a little. I know if I was the pitcher and I knew it was close to a record, I'd be bearing down that much more."[3]

"I think it's bush," said Hall. "When a pitcher hears that announcement, you know he's going to make sure you don't set a major-league record off him."[4]

Al Worthington came in to pitch the eighth and ninth innings, walking Hershberger to lead off the eighth and then retiring the next six batters to pick up the save.

The Twins are the only American League team as of 2020 to hit five home runs in an inning. Until 2017 the A's and the Cincinnati Reds were the only teams to give up five home runs in an inning. The Reds gave up five homers to the New York Giants in the fourth inning of their game on June 6, 1939. The Philadelphia Phillies hit five homers against the Reds in the fourth inning on June 2, 1949. On August 23, 1961, the San Francisco Giants hit five home runs against the Reds in the ninth inning. On April 22, 2006, It was the Milwaukee Brewers' turn to hit five home runs against the Reds, in the fourth inning.

METROPOLITAN STADIUM

Finally a different team was victimized when the Brewers gave up five home runs to the Washington Nationals in the third inning on July 27, 2017.

For the Twins pitchers, Pascual was chased after giving up four runs, all earned, on three hits in two-thirds of an inning. Siebler held the A's bats silent for 4⅓ innings, surrendering no runs on three hits. Cimino pitched the sixth and seventh innings, giving up one hit, while striking out two to earn the victory and even his record for the season at 1-1. Worthington pitched the final two innings and picked up his second save of the season.[5]

For the Athletics, Hunter lasted 6⅓ innings, giving up six runs on nine hits, three of which were home runs, and took the loss to drop to 4-5 for the season. Lindblad faced three batters – one groundout and two home runs – before giving the ball to John Wyatt. Wyatt gave up a homer, but in 1⅓ innings struck out three Twins batters.

Twins manager Sam Mele had a nice problem to deal with as the squad hit the road after this game to take on the White Sox in Chicago. Mincher had been on quite a streak of late. Including this game, in which he singled and hit one of the seventh-inning home runs, he had nine hits, including three home runs and three doubles, in 23 at-bats in six games. For four years, Mincher had been on the bench waiting for the opportunity to play regularly. He started the streak hitting just .194 but raised his batting average to .229.

Killebrew had also been hot. In his last 10 games he connected for seven homers and had 12 runs batted in. With Mincher at first, Killebrew played mostly at third, leaving Rollins with limited playing time and being relegated to pinch-hitting. Rollins was making the most of those opportunities, producing a two-run single and a sacrifice fly in his previous two pinch-hits, before hitting the two-run homer against the Athletics.

Mele wanted all three batters in the lineup, so he decided to start playing Mincher at first, Rollins at third, and Killebrew in left, to the dismay of Twins President Calvin Griffith, who contended that Killebrew didn't belong in left field.[6]

With the win, the Twins improved their record to 23-26, in sixth place in the single-division, 10-team league, nine games behind the first-place Orioles (34-19), while the Athletics fell to 19-30, in ninth place 13 games out.

SOURCES

Retrosheet.org

Baseball-reference.com

retrosheet.org/boxesetc/1961/B04210MIN1961.htm

baseball-reference.com/boxes/MIN/MIN196606090.shtml

NOTES

1 Sid Boardman, "Harmon Leads in Silent Way," *Kansas City Times*, June 10, 1966: 18.

2 "Hall Felt He Was on Spot," *Minneapolis Star:* June 10, 1966: 27.

3 Boardman.

4 "Hall Felt He Was on Spot."

5 Retroactively awarded. Saves were not an official statistic until 1969.

6 Max Nichols, "Mincher's Bat Exploding for Twins," *Minneapolis Star*, June 10, 1966: 27.

JIM KAAT OUTDUELS EARL WILSON FOR 25TH WIN

SEPTEMBER 25, 1966: MINNESOTA TWINS 1, DETROIT TIGERS 0

by Steve Ginader

On September 27, 1966, Jim Kaat was honored in front of 300 businessmen at the Minneapolis Chamber of Commerce by receiving the Chamber's highest award for achievement. This distinguished group was hoping it would be a prelude to a bigger accolade, baseball's Cy Young Award. Two days earlier, Kaat's 25th win had tied Sandy Koufax for the major-league lead. If assigned two more starts as he requested, Kaat could end the season with 27. Since 1925, only nine pitchers had achieved 27 or more wins in a season,[1] and Kaat aspired to join their ranks and position himself for this prestigious award. "I threw only 94 pitches in this game," said Kaat. "I think I would have more of a chance of getting hurt with too much rest."[2] His manager, Sam Mele, wasn't so sure. "I don't want to take a chance of Kaat hurting his arm," said Mele. "Kaat has had a great season. I don't want anything to happen to him because of getting too anxious."[3]

It was a sunny Sunday afternoon in Bloomington, Minnesota, when Kaat took the mound for the Twins in Metropolitan Stadium, facing Earl Wilson and the Tigers. With one week left in the regular season, the Baltimore Orioles had already clinched the American League pennant, and the Twins and Tigers were fighting for second place. With a win, the Twins would pull within one game of the Tigers.

For the first three innings, both pitchers were in command. Kaat had not given up a hit and the Twins only had two, a double by Earl Battey in the second and a single by Zoilo Versalles in the third. Both runners were left stranded. In the fourth, the Tigers got their first hit, a single by Don Wert, to lead off the inning. Wert was quickly erased as the next batter, Jake Wood, grounded into a shortstop-to-second-to-first double play. In the fifth, the Tigers failed again to get a runner past second base. After Willie Horton hit a one-out single, Mickey Stanley hit into the second 6-4-3 double play of the game. After the Tigers were retired in the sixth, Kaat had pitched through the order twice, facing the minimum 18 batters. Both hits were erased on double plays, and Dick McAuliffe was caught stealing after his one-out walk in the third.

Meanwhile, the Twins had their best scoring opportunity in the fifth. Ted Uhlaender led off the inning with a double and stole third as Versalles struck out. With one out Kaat bunted back to the pitcher, but Uhlaender was unable to score. Cesar Tovar ended the threat by flying out to center field, stranding Uhlaender at third. In the sixth inning, the Twins went quietly as the first two batters grounded out to first and Harmon Killebrew struck out.

Minnesota's best-hit balls of the day were all flagged down by Stanley in center. He made three Gold Glove-worthy catches in the game. The first

Jim Kaat received The Sporting News *award for American League Pitcher of the Year after winning 25 games in 1966. American League president Joe Cronin made the presentation prior to a 1967 game at Met Stadium and also presented the Manager of the Year award for 1966 to Baltimore's Hank Bauer.*

was on a fly ball hit by Tony Oliva to lead off the fourth, and the other two were on long fly balls in the seventh. Don Mincher led off that inning with a fly ball to deep right-center that sent Stanley on the run. He caught up to the ball and snagged it right before crashing through the swinging bullpen gate, saving a sure double or triple. After a one-out single by Battey, Stanley continued his outstanding glove work with another great catch on Uhlaender's fly to center. Versalles popped up to shortstop and the inning ended with no runs crossing the plate.

Kaat faced his toughest trouble in the eighth inning, when Horton stroked his second single of the game. Stanley pushed a bunt to first baseman Mincher, and Tovar, the second baseman, took the throw for the out, with Horton going to second. The next batter, Bill Freehan, hit a grounder into the shortstop hole that Versalles fielded. Knowing he could not throw Freehan out at first, Versalles threw to Killebrew at third, hoping to catch Horton trying for third. Killebrew caught the ball and in "a slow man's race"[4] chased Horton back to second. As the two lumbering men raced back to second, Killebrew caught Horton and tagged him just before he reached the bag. Kaat then struck out McAuliffe, his eighth strikeout of the day, to end the inning.

After two more scoreless half-innings, the stage was set for the bottom of the ninth. Oliva was due to lead off. "I told Sandy Valdespino to take the bats from the rack to the clubhouse," said Oliva with a big smile on his face.[5] In his three previous at bats, Wilson had retired Oliva on fastballs. After running the count to 2-and-2, Oliva belted a poorly placed fastball 390 feet over the right-field fence, giving the Twins the victory. "I wanted the ball high and tight and I threw it down the pipe," said Wilson, feeling the pain of his 11th defeat.[6] The home run was Oliva's 25th of the season, and it sealed Kaat's 25th win. The Twins played in Metropolitan Stadium from 1961 to 1981, and this game was the only 1-0 game won on a walk-off home run.

Mele had a change of heart and assigned Kaat two more starts, one at home against the Cleveland Indians and the other against the pennant-winning Orioles in Baltimore on the final day of the season. The other starters were shuffled around his schedule in order to give the team the best chance to finish in second. Kaat lost both games, ending his season with a 25-13 record. The starters who worked around Kaat's schedule, Mudcat Grant, Jim Perry, and Jim Merritt, won their games to propel the team to second place, one game in front of the Tigers.

The Cy Young Award was instituted in 1956 by Commissioner Ford Frick to honor the best pitcher in the major leagues. When Frick retired in 1967, the rules changed and each league presented an award. Kaat fell short of receiving the award in the final year of the single best pitcher; Koufax was the unanimous choice. With Kaat's stellar record, one could speculate that a year later the outcome might have been different. Despite his disappointing finish, Kaat still led the American League in victories and complete games. Although he had a long and successful career, one could argue that the 1966 season was his most successful and rewarding.

SOURCES

baseball-reference.com/boxes/MIN/MIN196609250.shtml

retrosheet.org/boxesetc/1966/B09250MIN1966.htm

NOTES

1. The pitchers who had won at least 27 games since 1925 to this point were Lefty Grove (who did it twice), Dizzy Dean (twice), Hal Newhouser, Robin Roberts, Don Newcombe, Dizzy Trout, Bob Feller, Bucky Walters, and George Uhle. Koufax joined this group on the final day of the 1966 season.

2. Max Nichols, "Mele Says 'No' on Two More Starts for Kaat," *Minneapolis Star*, September 26, 1966: 9B.

3. Nichols.

4. Tom Briere, "Kaat Wins No. 25 on Oliva Belt," *Minneapolis Tribune*, September 26, 1966: 31.

5. Briere.

6. Briere.

KILLEBREW BLASTS TWO TAPE-MEASURE HOME RUNS ON CONSECUTIVE DAYS

JUNE 3 AND 4, 1967: MINNESOTA TWINS 8, CALIFORNIA ANGELS 6; MINNESOTA TWINS 8, CALIFORNIA ANGELS 7

By Thomas J. Brown Jr.

The California Angels were trying to get out of the cellar. The team arrived in the Twin Cities and broke a four-game losing streak with a win on Friday, June 2, in the series opener. The Twins were trying to stay relevant in the American League pennant race. After Friday night's loss, they were 21-23.

Dave Boswell started for the Twins in the second game of the series. He had lost his last two starts and was trying to turn things around. Boswell walked two batters in the first but managed to get out of trouble. He retired the side in order in the second.

The Angels broke through off Boswell in the third. Paul Schaal doubled with two outs and came home on Jim Fregosi's single, giving California a 1-0 lead.

George Brunet was on the mound for the Angels. After winning his first start, on April 11, Brunet failed to win again in his next 10 starts. He entered the game with a 1-8 won-lost record. Brunet kept the Twins from scoring through the first two innings although they had runners in scoring position in both frames.

That changed in the third. After Rod Carew led off with a walk, Rich Rollins doubled. Both runners came home on Bob Allison's double to put the Twins up 2-1.

Brunet struggled again in the fourth, walking the leadoff batter. Two consecutive singles plated another Twins run and finished Brunet, who would end up with his ninth loss. "Nothing is working out," he grumbled.[1] "At home my wife lost the keys to the car and our cat had six kittens. We haven't even been able to give them away."[2]

Lew Burdette relieved Brunet and hit Rollins, the first batter he faced. Harmon Killebrew stepped up to the plate and "sent a three-run rocket into outer space."[3] Killebrew's home run landed in the second deck.

When the homer was listed at 430 feet, the Twins brass protested. Officials insisted that the ball had gone over 500 feet. Tom Briere of the *Minneapolis Star Tribune* wrote: "Considering the second deck is at least 70 feet above ground level, Killebrew's three-run blast was a 500-footer plus."[4] The spot was marked in orange to show where the homer was hit.

It was the first time a ball was hit there since the upper deck had been added to Metropolitan Stadium in 1965. Before this home run, the longest homer on record at the ballpark was Killebrew's 475-foot smash high into the batter's background in center field in 1961.

Killebrew said, "I think that it was a fastball that I hit. This one felt good but then the one that I hit in Detroit carried over the roof in center field." Burdette, when asked about the hit, said, "Heck, I've thrown longer ones than that."[5] Killebrew's home run put the Twins ahead 6-1.

The Twins' Boswell found trouble again in the sixth inning when his control left him. Don Mincher led off

Killebrew crushes a Lew Burdette pitch and sends it into the upper deck in left field on June 3, 1967.

with a double to left field. Jimmie Hall walked. Rick Reichardt lifted one into the left-field bleachers for his fifth home run of the season. The Twins' lead had been cut to two runs.

Twins manager Sam Mele replaced Boswell with left-hander Jim Ollom. The first batter he faced, left-hander Tom Satriano, sliced a home run into the left-field seats, narrowing the Twins lead to one run, 6-5.

After Ollom gave up a single to Bobby Knoop, Mele called in Jim Perry, who gave up singles to Bubba Morton and Schaal. Knoop tried to score from second on Schaal's single but was nailed at home by right fielder Sandy Valdespino. Fregosi walked. With the bases loaded, Mincher popped out to end the inning.

Bill Kelso pitched two scoreless innings for the Angels before being replaced by Minnie Rojas in the eighth. The Twins added two runs off Rojas, who walked Cesar Tovar and gave up a single to Carew to start the frame. Rollins' sacrifice moved the runners up.

Rojas intentionally walked Killebrew to load the bases. Then he walked Allison, bringing home the seventh Twins run. Pete Cimino was called in to stop the bleeding. After striking out Valdespino, he hit Zoilo Versalles to send Carew across the plate, giving the Twins a three-run lead at 8-5.

The Twins brought in Ron Kline to clean things up in the ninth. Before he could retire the side, the Angels made it 8-6 on doubles by Satriano and Mincher. When Kline got pinch-hitter Orlando McFarlane to ground out, he earned his first save of the season.

The win pushed the Twins closer to .500 and Killebrew's home run had the team fired up. "We're going to start rolling now. I can feel it. You're going to see us pitching some shutouts," hurler Dean Chance said after the game.[6]

The next day, a Sunday, 35,033 fans showed up at Metropolitan Stadium to celebrate Bat Day. Many of them were still talking about Killebrew's blast the day before; the place had been clearly marked in orange by the club. "It was the longest one that I've ever seen hit," Mele said.[7]

Jim Merritt started for the Twins. Merritt was coming off two shutouts and looking to earn his fourth win of the season. He retired the side in order in the first but California ended his 21-inning scoreless streak in the second.

Mincher led off with a double. Reichardt followed with his sixth homer of the year, a blast into the left-field pavilion, for a 2-0 lead.

Tony Oliva made an over-the-shoulder catch when the next batter, Bubba Morton, hit a shot into deep right field. His catch likely prevented another run from scoring. Oliva had just returned to the lineup after having stitches removed. "My finger is still sore, but I'm swinging good," he said. "I'm feeling better and moving better in the outfield."[8]

The Angels sent right-hander Jack Sanford to the mound. The 12-year veteran entered the game with a 3-2 record and a 3.26 earned-run average. Sanford retired the side in the first with the help of a pickoff of Carew at first.

As Killebrew led off the Twins half of the second, "it was announced that belated computations and estimations placed the length of Saturday's swat at 520 feet," the estimated distance it would have traveled unimpeded. The public-address announcer told the crowd that the seat where his ball hit would be removed to mark the spot.[9]

After hearing that bit of news, Killebrew stepped to the plate and hit Sanford's first pitch off the front of the second deck in left field. The home run was measured at 434 feet.

Killebrew said later that he hit a curveball. Asked to compare the home run to Saturday's, he said the same thing he said the previous day: "It's hard to compare home runs. I know I'm making pretty good contact. Same stance, same swing, same bat – 33 ounces, 35 inches."[10]

The home run raised his total to 12 for the year. It also brought Killebrew's RBI total for the year to 36. It was the most he had at this point in a season since 1959, when he had 40 RBIs on June 4. "I guess that maybe it's the hot weather. The heat helps you get loose," he said when asked about the fact that he ended up with five hits in the series against the Angels.[11]

The Angels took the run back in the third. Jose Cardenal and Fregosi singled. Cardenal scored from third when Killebrew couldn't handle a line drive by Mincher.

The Twins grabbed the lead when they scored four runs off Sanford in the fourth. Singles by Carew, Killebrew, and Oliva brought in a run. Versalles followed with his second home run of the season, putting the Twins ahead 5-3.

Versalles had been struggling at the plate, going 7-for-36 since May 26. "I changed my stance and spread out a little. When I spread out, I hit the long ball, and that's what I'm going to do from now on."[12]

The Twins added to their lead in the fifth. After Merritt led off with a double, Bill Kelso replaced Sanford. Tovar hit a sharp groundball that bounced off first baseman Mincher's glove. Tovar ended up at first and Merritt reached third. Carew's fly ball scored Merritt.

A single by Rollins and an intentional walk to Killebrew loaded the bases. Oliva's sacrifice fly brought Tovar home and the Twins were ahead 7-3.

MEMORABLE GAMES AT MINNESOTA'S DIAMOND ON THE PRAIRIE

The Angels tied the game in the seventh. Buck Rodgers, leading off, hit his first home run of the season. With one out, Johnny Werhas batted for Kelso and hit another one over the fence. It was also his first home run of the season.

Mele went to his bullpen for right-hander Al Worthington, who proceeded to give up a double to Cardenal and singles to Schaal and Fregosi. Fregosi's single plated two more Angels runs before Worthington was replaced by Jim Roland, who retired the side.

The game remained tied through regulation although the Angels had a chance to take the lead on a pair of walks in the top of the ninth. But Roland got Mincher to fly out and Reichardt to ground out on a comebacker.

After Perry retired the Angels in order in the 10th, Rollins opened the Twins half of the frame with a single to left field. It was his seventh hit of the series. Rollins said he was feeling better at the plate because he stopped swinging for the long ball. "I feel better now than I have for some time. I'm relaxed and feel strong."[13]

Ted Uhlaender ran for Rollins. Rojas walked Killebrew to put the winning run on second. Oliva then hit a grounder to second. Knoop hesitated as he looked to see if he could get Uhlaender out at third. By the time that he tossed the ball to second base, he had lost his opportunity for a double play.

Angels manager Bill Rigney met with Rojas and after a brief meeting, it was decided to pitch to Allison, who had been hitless all afternoon.

Third-base coach Billy Martin immediately gave Allison the bunt sign since he was the Twins best bunter. "I was not surprised at all to see the squeeze sign," Allison said later.[14] On Rojas's first pitch, Allison bunted just to the right of the mound. First baseman Mincher barehanded the ball and threw home. But his throw was wild and the fleet Uhlaender scored with a head-first slide. Allison was credited with single and his game-winning run batted in was his 31st RBI of the season. "Allison has always bunted real well, and he did the job for us again as he has so many times this season to win games," said Mele.[15]

The loss sent the Angels home with a second consecutive 1-6 road trip. "I'm afraid to answer the phone, Rigney said after the game. "It might be the ultimatum call."[16]

Bat Day was clearly a success as the team gave out 13,200 Little League bats to fans. The Twins and Angels knocked out 24 hits all over Metropolitan Stadium. "But the shortest hit of them all," wrote Tom Briere, "Allison's 30-foot bunt, enabled the Twins to take the series and level at .500 in the standings."[17]

Mele was pleased with his team. "We're up to a .500 record. That's the best position we've been in this year," he said. "If we can get over .500, I think we'll go. We've been playing our best baseball of the year the last two weeks."[18]

SOURCES

In addition to the sources cited in the Notes, I used the Baseball-Reference.com, and Retrosheet.org websites for box-score, player, team, and season pages, pitching and batting game logs, and other pertinent material.

baseball-reference.com/boxes/MIN/MIN196706030.shtml

retrosheet.org/boxesetc/1967/B06030MIN1967.htm

baseball-reference.com/boxes/MIN/MIN196706040.shtml

retrosheet.org/boxesetc/1967/B06040MIN1967.htm

NOTES

1. John Hall, "Brunet Takes Loss, 9th in Row," *Los Angeles Times*, June 4, 1967: 44.
2. John Hall, "Angels Lose but Fans Don't Lose Faith, Greet Team," *Los Angeles Times*, June 5, 1967: 41.
3. Hall, "Angels Lose."
4. Tom Briere, "Killebrew Blast Aids Twins, 8-6," *Minneapolis Tribune*, June 4, 1967: 53.
5. Briere, "Killebrew Blast."
6. Max Nichols, "Twins, Met Enter New Homer Era," *Minneapolis Star*. June 5, 1967: 36.
7. Hall, "Angels Lose."
8. Bill Hengen, "Twins Provide Example of Team Victory," *Minneapolis Star*, June 5, 1967: 37.
9. Tom Briere, "Announcer Tells of Harmon's Feat, Then … Kerpow," *Minneapolis Tribune*, June 5, 1967: 29.
10. Briere, "Announcer Tells."
11. Sid Hartman, "Hartman's Roundup," *Minneapolis Tribune*, June 5, 1967: 28.
12. Hartman.
13. Hartman.
14. Tom Briere, "Twins Squeeze by Angels, 8-7," *Minneapolis Tribune*, June 5, 1967: 27.
15. Hartman.
16. Hall, "Angels Lose."
17. Briere, "Twins Squeeze by Angels."
18. Nichols.

DEAN CHANCE IS PERFECT FOR FIVE INNINGS

AUGUST 6, 1967: MINNESOTA TWINS 5, BOSTON RED SOX 0 (5 INNINGS)

By Stew Thornley

The conclusion of a three-game series in Minnesota the first weekend in 1967 featured two teams fighting for the top spot in the American League and two of the top pitchers in baseball.

The Minnesota Twins, second-place finishers in 1966, had to go through a managerial change in June to climb into the race. The Boston Red Sox, who finished ninth the year before, were the surprise team in the American League, becoming a contender and, after a good month of July, the only team behind the first-place Chicago White Sox.

The Twins took the first two games of the August series against the Red Sox and had ace Dean Chance, who had a won-lost record of 13-8, going against 15-4 Jim Lonborg, who was on a one-day pass from Army Reserve duties in Georgia. The Twins weren't as fortunate with their stars and military commitment; second baseman Rod Carew, on his way to being the American League Rookie of the Year, had left the day before for two weeks of summer camp for the Marines.

Rain was forecast as Minnesota went for the sweep, an achievement that would put the Twins into second place by a percentage point over the Red Sox. Roy Campanella was on hand to present catching gear to Little Leaguers in a pregame ceremony, and then Chance and Lonborg took command.

The pair retired 18 of 19 hitters through the first three innings, Tony Oliva being the only baserunner with a two-out double in the bottom of the first.

The bottom two batters in the Red Sox batting order came closest to getting to Chance. Elston Howard hit a liner to right that initially looked like a hit, but Oliva was able to get to it. Lonborg followed and sent a fastball right down the middle to the warning track in left, where Bob Allison corralled it to finish the third. After the game, Chance told reporters, "I didn't know [Lonborg] was that good a hitter." A Boston writer responded, "He isn't."[1]

As the Red Sox were about to start the top of the fourth, the rain reached the point that the umpires called time. Play resumed after 25 minutes. Mike Andrews put down a bunt, perhaps trying to challenge Chance on the wet turf, but the pitcher stayed on his feet as he pounced on it and threw to first. Dalton Jones grounded out, and Carl Yastrzemski worked Chance to a full count (the only time Chance went to three balls on a batter in the game), fouled off a pitch, and then struck out.

Chance had handled the delay without a problem, but the extended time on the bench appeared to bother Lonborg, who walked Cesar Tovar on four pitches in the Twins' fourth. Tovar stole second as Tony Oliva

Dean Chance

struck out. Harmon Killebrew lined a single to left. Tovar held up in case the ball was caught and then, respecting Yastrzemski's arm, retreated to second. Allison hit a longer liner, this one over Yaz's head to the base of the left-field fence, scoring Tovar. Boston pulled the infield in, and Rich Rollins got one past Jones at third, bringing in Killebrew. The Twins did no more damage – Ted Uhlaender lined out to Andrews at second and Jerry Zimmerman flied to Tony Conigliaro in right – but they had the runs they needed, and the quick conclusion of the inning turned out to be more important.

Chance put down Conigliaro, Norm Siebern, and Rico Petrocelli, who hit a grounder up the middle but was thrown out by a half-step by shortstop Zoilo Versalles.

The game was now official, a good thing for the Twins because it didn't last much longer. Chance looked at a third strike to start the bottom of the fifth, and Versalles fouled off a pitch from Lonborg. Plate umpire Jim Odom then threw his hands in the air for the second time in the game, suspending play as the windswept rain was too much.

A letup in the downpour prompted the grounds crew to begin removing the tarpaulin only 10 minutes later, but they quickly put it back on as the rain fell heavily again. After a 57-minute delay, the game was called, not long before the sun peeked between clouds again. However, the field conditions, with sizable puddles in the outfield, meant the game went into the books at that time as a 2-0 win for the Twins and a perfect game for Dean Chance.

"It was a cheapie," Chance said of the perfect game. "I'm glad it was called because we won. I had good stuff, particularly my curveball, but who can honestly tell whether you've got no-hit stuff or not? I doubt that I could have pitched a no-hitter."[2]

Chance said he had pitched 18 no-hitters in high school, four of them perfect.[3] He had pitched two one-hitters in the major leagues, both at Met Stadium. (In 1962, while pitching for the Los Angeles Angels, he gave up only an eight-inning infield single to Versalles, and earlier in 1967 he allowed only a fourth-inning single to Danny Cater of the Kansas City Athletics.)

Less than three weeks later, Chance pitched a nine-inning no-hitter as Minnesota beat Cleveland, 2-1.

For Lonborg, the loss in the game was his third of the season against the Twins, leaving him with a career record of 0-6 versus Minnesota. However, he beat the Twins, and Chance, on the final day of the 1967 season, a win that gave the Red Sox the pennant by one game over the Twins and Tigers.

Although Chance said he was happy with a rain-shortened win and didn't think he could have gone all the way with a perfect game, Boston manager Dick Williams said, "Maybe it was only a five-inning no-hitter, but the way he was pitching it could've easily been nine."[4]

SOURCES

Author's scorebook and memories from the game.

In an August 17, 2004, interview with the author, Chance remembered his five-inning perfect game against Boston but not some of the details. He was especially surprised to hear that Elston Howard, traded earlier in the season from the Yankees to the Red Sox, had come the closest to getting a hit. He always thought Howard had spent his entire career with the Yankees. "Elston Howard?" he said. "Man, I would have lost money on that bet."

NOTES

1 Glenn Redmann, "Chance Happy Game Called: Nobody'll Remember How Long It Took," *St. Paul Pioneer Press*, August 7, 1967, 15.

2 Tom Briere, "Chance's Win Perfect (*)," *Minneapolis Tribune*, August 7, 1967, 31.

3 Briere.

4 Redmann.

RELIEVER'S 10 SHUTOUT INNINGS HELP SENATORS OUTLAST TWINS

AUGUST 9, 1967: WASHINGTON SENATORS 9, MINNESOTA TWINS 7 (20 INNINGS)

By Andrew Sharp

The slow climb of Gil Hodges' Washington Senators teams had brought the 1967 squad to heights unknown: a 55-55 record after shutting out the Twins in Minnesota on August 7. None of the previous expansion Nats had reached .500 so far into the season.

A month earlier, on July 8, Washington's record stood at 34-47, but winning 21 of 29 had pulled the team to break-even. The Twins cut the party short the next night, scoring a run in the eighth to beat the Nats, 3-2. Veteran Al Worthington, 38, relieved Jim Merritt and pitched two innings for the win. The two teams — the original and expansion Senators — matched up again on Wednesday evening, August 9, at Metropolitan Stadium. A crowd of nearly 17,000 came to see Twins right-hander Dave Boswell oppose Joe Coleman, a 20-year-old right-hander.

Shoddy fielding put Coleman in a hole in the first inning, even as he struck out the side. With runners on the corners, catcher Paul Casanova let a pitch get by him, then threw wildly to third. Two runners scored on the play. Another unearned run scored in the second when Senators third baseman Ken McMullen made an error on a ground ball by Rich Rollins.

Down 3-0, Hodges pinch-hit for Coleman in the top of the third. Reliever Bob Priddy yielded a run in two innings before Casey Cox gave up three more in his two innings. Surprisingly, the power-laden Twins scored six of their seven runs on singles, walks, and Washington misplays. The exception was Bob Allison's triple after Harmon Killebrew's third-inning double.

The Nats found themselves down 7-0 when they came to bat in the seventh. A hit batsman and a single by Casanova after a force out put runners on first and second. Both runners advanced on a slow grounder to third. With two down, shortstop Tim Cullen singled to center, scoring Washington's first two runs. Twins manager Cal Ermer summoned Mudcat Grant in relief.

A 21-game winner in 1965, the soon to be 32-year-old Grant had been so ineffective earlier in the year that he was dropped from the rotation. This game did nothing to restore Ermer's confidence in him. Pinch-hitter Mike Epstein greeted Grant with a single to left. Ed Stroud's single to center scored Cullen with the third run. McMullen's single to left scored Epstein with the fourth. Stroud beat a throw to third, with McMullen moving to second. Having seen enough, Ermer brought in Ron Kline. Kline had spent the previous four seasons as Washington's most effective reliever before being traded to the Twins in December 1966. Perhaps Washington slugger Frank

Cal Ermer took over as manager during the 1967 season and nearly got the Twins to the World Series.

MEMORABLE GAMES AT MINNESOTA'S DIAMOND ON THE PRAIRIE

Howard had an idea of what Kline would throw. In any case, Hondo was ready for it. A three-run homer to deep center, his 29th, tied the game. The blast was estimated at 435 feet.[1]

"When you blow a seven-run lead with two out, something's wrong," Ermer said after the game.[2]

Howard's blast set the stage for career performances by two relief pitchers, lefty Darold Knowles for the Senators and Worthington for the Twins.

Dick Lines, the fourth Washington pitcher, set down the Twins in order in the seventh. Kline started the eighth with a strikeout, but Casanova singled and Bernie Allen walked. The Twins had sent Allen to Washington as part of the trade for Kline. Ermer brought in Worthington, who retired the next two batters to end the threat.

Although Worthington began his career in July 1953 with back-to-back shutouts, he had been primarily a reliever since '55. He last started a game in 1959. Little did he know that tonight would be his longest outing ever out of the bullpen.

Knowles, who relieved Lines in the eighth, was in for an even longer night. Already used mostly to close games, he had never pitched more than six innings since coming up with the Orioles in 1964. Although he would be used as an emergency starter with Oakland for two weeks in August 1973 — he even threw a complete-game shutout — this outing would remain the longest of his career.

Worthington worked out of a jam in the ninth. A leadoff walk and a one-out single put runners on the corners. But the veteran right-hander induced an infield foul popout and got the third out on a fly ball. He then retired 17 batters in a row before Howard led off the 15th with a single.

Knowles retired 10 in a row before back-to-back walks — one of them to Worthington, the last time he ever reached base — in the 11th. Knowles ended that threat by getting Tony Oliva on a foul pop to the catcher. After Killebrew singled leading off the 12th, Knowles retired 11 in a row through the 16th.

"I really didn't get tired," Knowles told reporters. "It was a cool night, and in about five or six of those innings, they went out 1-2-3. ... I never was worried, but I did pitch carefully to Killebrew and Oliva. I never challenged them."[3] No doubt it helped that Killebrew was removed for a pinch-runner in the 12th.

Ted Uhlaender singled to lead off the bottom of the 16th. After a force-out grounder, 36-year-old rookie catcher Hank Izquierdo[4] made his major-league debut, pinch-hitting for Worthington. The rookie, too, grounded into a force out. A fly ball ended the inning. Worthington departed after 8⅔ innings, having faced 30 batters, yielded two hits, and fanned eight. One of his two walks was intentional.

Lefty Jim Roland took over for Worthington in the 17th and retired the Nats 1-2-3 for three innings. Knowles, meanwhile, gave up a two-out single in the bottom of the inning before striking out his 10th batter, the last of the 34 he faced over 10 innings. He yielded three hits and walked two.

Righty Dave Baldwin, a 29-year-old rookie who had taken the loss the previous night, took the mound for Washington in the 18th. Baldwin would later earn a doctorate and become a college professor (and a SABR member), but for now he was a pitcher who threw mostly side-arm and underhanded with an occasional overhand curve. Rich Rollins had hit one of those curves for a game-winning homer the night before.[5] Baldwin stayed away from that pitch this night, or as midnight passed, this morning. He retired the Twins in order in the 18th, but gave up a pair of two-out singles in the 19th before retiring the side on a popout to second.

Leading off the 20th, a weary McMullen hoped for the best. He had fouled out to first in the 17th when he was late on a Roland fastball. "We were all getting tired, that's for sure," McMullen said after the game. "I know my bat was getting heavier and heavier every time I went up."[6] That likely worked to his advantage as Roland tried to fool him with a changeup. The Nats third baseman hit it out the park for his 14th homer.

"Roland had them eating out of his hand until that changeup," Ermer said.[7]

Howard followed McMullen's homer with a double and was bunted to third. A sacrifice fly brought him in with an insurance run.

Baldwin gave up a leadoff single in the bottom of the 20th but a strikeout and a fly out left the Twins' hopes up to pitcher Jim Kaat as a pinch-hitter, the 21th player Ermer would use. (Hodges used 19.) Kaat flied out to right to end the game and give Baldwin his first major-league victory.

"You would have thought we had won the pennant," Baldwin said of the back-slapping and cheering in the Senators' dugout and clubhouse."[8]

"I can't remember a bigger victory," Howard said. "If this game was any indication, we'll go all the way," an exuberant Cullen predicted, as Washington had climbed to within 6½ games of first place.[9]

The 20-inning marathon — 5 hours and 40 minutes, ending at 1:29 A.M. — would have been the longest night game in history up to then had the Nats not beaten Chicago in 22 innings on June 12.[10] But Hodges knew this victory was more important: "It was a great comeback in a game which meant a lot, too. It's more important than that 22-inning one."[11] A loss would have put his Nats two games under .500, instead of back at the break-even mark.

By splitting the next four games, the Nats made it to the morning of August 14 as a .500 ballclub, at 58-58. But the World Series tickets some starry-eyed fans had begun to inquire about[12] never needed to be printed. Washington won just 18 of its last 45 games to finish at 76-85, tied for sixth place with Baltimore. Still, this was the best finish yet for the expansion Washington franchise, six wins better than expected based on the team's run differential.

The Twins came close to winning the pennant, finishing a game behind Boston. As meaningful as this game was for the Senators, it came to mean even more for Minnesota.

SOURCES

baseball-reference.com/boxes/MIN/MIN196708090.shtml

retrosheet.org/boxesetc/1967/B08090MIN1967.htm

NOTES

1. Associated Press, "Nats Top Twins in 20th Inning," *Boston Globe*, August 10, 1967: 41.
2. Lew Ferguson (Associated Press), "Senators Stop Twins, 9-7, in 20-Inning Marathon," *Daily Journal* (Fergus Falls, Minnesota), August 10, 1967: 10.
3. Ferguson.
4. Izquierdo was a bullpen coach for the Cleveland Indians in 1962 after a decade in the minors before giving it another go as a player. He appeared in 15 more games for the Twins in 1967 after this one before returning to the minors. He later scouted for the Twins and Cubs.
5. George Minot Jr., "Nats Call 20-Inning Triumph Keystone to 1st Division Drive," *Washington Post*, August 11, 1967: D2.
6. Minot.
7. Ferguson.
8. Minot.
9. Minot.
10. The night-game mark was eclipsed when St. Louis beat New York, 4-3, in 25 innings on September 11, 1974.
11. Minot.
12. Minot.

THE GAME WITH ALMOST EVERYTHING

JUNE 18, 1968: MINNESOTA TWINS 9, WASHINGTON SENATORS 8

by Rich Arpi

This game had many ebbs and flows and featured almost every play you could imagine. Twins starter Jim Merritt had a no-hitter for 5⅔ innings, and then bullpen implosions by both teams led to four lead changes in the last two innings. Among the 26 hits in the game were four doubles, two triples, and three home runs; all the extra-base hits were by the Twins except for two home runs by the Senators in the eighth inning. There were pinch-hitters, pinch-runners, a stolen base, a sacrifice, two sacrifice flies, two intentional walks, a hit batter, and an error. In addition, the game featured three double plays, an ejection, two runners thrown out at the plate, and a walk-off victory. About the only plays missing, unnoticed at the time, were a caught stealing and a balk.

Twins starter Jim Merritt retired the side in order in the first, third, and fifth innings. He walked right fielder Cap Peterson with two out in the second inning and third baseman Ken McMullen and first baseman Mike Epstein with two out in the fourth inning but got the third out each time without further incident. In the sixth inning, with one out, he hit second baseman Bernie Allen with a pitch, retired Frank Howard on a foul pop, and then allowed his first hit, a single by Ken McMullen, with Allen scampering to third base. As in the second and fourth innings, Merritt got the third out without further trouble. Peterson led off the seventh inning with the Senators second hit, a single to right. Catcher Paul Casanova hit into a 6-4-3 double play (Jackie Hernandez-Frank Quilici-Harmon Killebrew). Merritt finished off the inning with a strikeout of shortstop Ron Hansen.[1] In the fourth inning, with Frank Howard at the plate, Senators first-base coach Nellie Fox was convinced that Jim Merritt was throwing a spitball. Fox argued quite vehemently with home-plate umpire Red Flaherty, with Senators manager Jim Lemon also getting involved. Flaherty had to calm the situation by tossing Fox from the game.[2]

Meanwhile, the Twins built a 4-0 lead against Senators starter Phil Ortega and relief pitchers Bruce Howard and Dick Bosman. Tony Oliva led off the second inning with a base on balls. Bob Allison followed with a single and catcher Bruce Look walked to load the bases. Hernandez lofted a short pop to right field, too shallow for the runners to advance. Quilici, however, hit a fly ball deep enough to Frank Howard in left field and Oliva scored from third base. In the third inning, singles by Cesar Tovar, Killebrew, and Oliva led to a second run and knocked out Ortega. Bruce Howard relieved. Killebrew scored the Twins' third run when Allison flied to Peterson in right. In the bottom of the fifth inning, Howard was replaced by Bosman, and the Twins greeted him with three consecutive hits. Singles by Ted Uhlaender and Killebrew put men on second and first and a ground-rule double by Oliva that bounced into the right-field seats scored Uhlaender and sent Killebrew to third base. After Allison popped out to shortstop, Bruce Look received an intentional walk to load the bases. Hernandez grounded to third, and McMullen threw Killebrew out at the plate. Quilici grounded out, McMullen to Epstein, to end the inning.

Merritt seemed to be breezing along when he retired pinch-hitter Ed Brinkman (batting for Bosman) and leadoff batter Sam Bowens to start the eighth inning. Nobody witnessing the game had any ideas how difficult it would be to get the next four outs. Allen started the Washington rally by recovering from a two-strike count and singling to right field. Howard's 23rd home run of the season, a 381-foot blast to left-center, followed. Some reports had the ball still rising as it left the ballpark.[3] The two runs batted in gave the Senators' left fielder 50 RBIs, increasing his American League lead in that category. Some fans started to chant, "Bring in Perranoski, bring in Perranoski." When McMullen walked, Twins manager Cal Ermer summoned lefty Ron Perranoski to face first baseman Mike Epstein, a left-handed hitter. Epstein walked on four pitches. Perranoski stayed in the game even though the next five Senators batters were right-handed hitters. Ermer explained his reasoning in the *Minneapolis Star:* "Washington had three left-handed hitters on the bench in Del Unser, Ed Stroud, and Bill Bryan. If I bring in the right-handed Al Worthington, Washington manager Jim Lemon will pinch-hit one or more of these lefties and they are all stronger batters than the men they would replace."[4] Leather-lunged fans chanted for Worthington as Perranoski gave up a single to Peterson, scoring McMullen and cutting the Twins' lead to 4-3. The chanting got even louder as the light-hitting Casanova lofted his first homer of the year to left field, 390 feet away, scoring three runs, giving the Senators a 6-4 lead. The next batter, Hansen, singled. Perranoski finished the inning, however, by getting Brinkman, batting for the second time in the inning, to fly to right.

Dave Baldwin replaced Dick Bosman for the Senators in the bottom of the eighth inning. Bosman had pitched three innings, allowing five hits and one run, and stood to be the winning pitcher if the Senators could hold the lead. Quicili lined to second for the first out. Rich Reese, batting for Perranoski, singled to center field. Cesar Tovar doubled to right and Uhlaender homered to right, knocking in three runs, giving the lead back to the Twins at 7-6. It was Uhlaender's third hit of the game. Baldwin's day was finished when he walked Harmon Killebrew. Dennis Higgins replaced Baldwin on the mound. Jim Holt ran for Killebrew. Oliva flied to left for the second out. Allison doubled to center, and Holt tried to score from first base. A strong throw from Bowens nailed Holt at the plate.

Al Worthington came in to start the ninth inning for the Twins. He walked the leadoff batter, Bowens, who went to second as Allen grounded out to Reese at first. Howard grounded sharply to shortstop Hernandez, who threw wild to first (his 16th error of the season). McMullen singled to left, scoring Bowens and tying the score at 7-7. Epstein singled to right, scoring pinch-runner Ed Stroud, giving the Senators an 8-7 lead. When Peterson continued the barrage with another single, Twins manager Ermer waved in Jim Perry, who had not pitched since June 2 because of a pulled groin muscle. The future American League Cy Young Award winner (1970) had been used mainly in long relief and as a spot starter since his acquisition from Cleveland in 1963. He faced Casanova, the Senators

Hubert Humphrey made frequent visits to Met Stadium when he was vice president. Here he chats with announcer Halsey Hall. Herb Carneal is calling the game in the background.

catcher, who had hit a three-run homer the inning before. On the second pitch, Casanova hit the ball sharply to Hernandez, who started an inning-ending double play.[5]

The bottom of the ninth began with the Twins trailing 8-7. Dennis Higgins was still on the mound for the Senators. Bowens moved to left field to replace Howard, and Stroud, who had run for Howard in the top of the inning, now patrolled center field. Look struck out to begin the inning. Rich Rollins, pinch-hitting for Jackie Hernandez, singled to right field. Quilici, in the lineup because Rod Carew was on Marine Reserve duty, strode to the plate as the only Twins position player without a hit in the game. Quilici took two strikes and then lined two foul balls into the stands.[6] Finally he got his bat squarely on the ball and hit a line drive into left field. Bowens slipped and the ball skidded by him and sped toward the fence. Rollins scored easily from first base to tie the game. Quilici ended up on third with a triple, his third in five days after having one in his career previously.[7] Rich Reese was intentionally walked. Cesar Tovar then hit a sharp liner at second baseman Bernie Allen. The ball bounced off Allen's chest, and he had no chance to get Quilici trying to score. As he threw out Tovar at first base, Quilici slid across the plate with the winning run. The Twins erupted from the dugout to swarm him at the plate.

Bill Boni of the *St. Paul Dispatch* claimed there was no possible play at the plate while Allen said he would have had Quilici at the plate if the ball hadn't hit off the heel of his glove and then his chest. Ermer said he was sure the play would have been an easy double play if the ball had been an inch or two higher.[8] Of Quilici's triple, Bowens said, "I got over in front of the ball and just before it got to me it skipped to my left. I tried to get back, that's when I slipped. By the time I was able to get up and retrieve the ball in front of the fence, it was too late to keep him from making it to third."[9]

Ermer was upbeat after the game despite the second-guessing on the timing of his pitching changes. "Who the hell says baseball's dull? I've seen a lot of good games," he exclaimed. "But that was something else. I'd have to say it was the most exciting baseball game I've ever seen."[10]

The win gave the Twins a record of 33-31 and left them in fourth place, nine games in back of the league-leading Detroit Tigers. It was the fifth straight win for the Twins and the seventh straight loss for the Senators, dropping them to 24-37, in last place 16½ games behind Detroit. The Twins finished the 1968 season in a disappointing seventh place with a record of 79-83. The Senators (65-96) finished in last place. The Twins would win 11 of 18 games against the Senators and six of nine games at home.[11]

AUTHOR'S NOTE

This was the first major-league game I attended where I remember any of the details. I had attended a Twins game five or six years before but was too young to appreciate what was really happening on the field. On this pleasantly warm Tuesday evening of June 18, 1968, I was still four months shy of my 12th birthday. I had avidly followed the Twins since the 1965 World Series and had viewed numerous games on television, but this game was special and left me with lasting memories. Among them were just the excitement of driving into the Metropolitan Stadium parking lot, noting that we parked near the Boston Red Sox sign attached to a light standard, walking up the ramps, and finding our seats a dozen or so rows above the walkway between home and third base. I remember the leather-lunged fans chanting for Perranoski and then for Worthington and noticed that many fans left after Harmon Killebrew's last at-bat. A dog-eared Twins yearbook, costing all of 75 cents, is my remaining souvenir from this game.

NOTES

1. The *Minneapolis Tribune*, June 19, 1968, contains play-by-play of the run-scoring plays, and Retrosheet was consulted to fill out the game's scoresheet. There were several discrepancies in putout and assist totals for some players between the *Tribune* and Retrosheet.

2. Retrosheet gave the specifics on this ejection. The Minneapolis and St. Paul newspapers mentioned only the ejection of Fox, and it is not known if the crowd in attendance was informed of the ejection. Undoubtedly a majority remained in the dark and wondered what the rhubarb was all about.

3. Dave Mona, "Twins Outrally Senators 9-8," *Minneapolis Tribune*, June 19, 1968: 29, 31.

4. "Baseball Not Exciting – Don't Ask Ermer," *Minneapolis Star*, June 19, 1968: 4D.

5. "Baseball Not Exciting." The author for years has remembered that Perry threw only one pitch and was the winning pitcher after getting a double-play ball in the top of the ninth inning. The *Minneapolis Star* the next day and thus more reliable, reported that Perry threw two pitches.

6. Glenn Redman, "Fans Have Picnic Second-Guessing Cal," *St. Paul Dispatch*, June 19, 1969: 49.

7. Sid Hartman column, *Minneapolis Tribune*, June 19, 1968: 30.

8. "Baseball Not Exciting – Don't Ask Ermer."

9. Glenn Redman, "Hopper Fools Bowens, Gives Quilici Triple," *St. Paul Pioneer Press*, June 19, 1968: C16.

10. Mona.

11. 1969 Minnesota Twins Media Guide: 48.

CÉSAR TOVAR PLAYS ALL NINE POSITIONS, LEADS TWINS TO VICTORY

SEPTEMBER 22, 1968: MINNESOTA TWINS 2, OAKLAND ATHLETICS 1

by Mike Huber

Since the beginning of professional baseball, players were assigned to and thus played a specific position. There have always been a few instances when players have switched (among the outfield or infield), but not until 1911 did fans see the true exception. The Philadelphia Phillies' Jimmy Walsh was the first major leaguer to play all nine positions, but he did it over the course of the entire season.[1] More than 50 years later, Oakland's Bert Campaneris became the first player to play all nine positions in the same game, accomplishing the feat on September 8, 1965, in a game against the California Angels. The A's were defeated by the Angels, 5-3, as Campaneris was 0-for-3 with a walk. Minnesota's César Tovar did them both one better, by playing all nine positions in a game in which his team earned the victory, against the Oakland Athletics.

It was the last home game of the 1968 season for the Twins. A modest crowd of 11,340 fans came through the turnstiles at Metropolitan Stadium for the Sunday afternoon affair. Minnesota had a record of 74-81 and after this game would be on the road for its final six contests, destined to finish the season without a winning record. It was time for a bit of celebration and fun. Tovar, finishing his third full season in the majors, was voted Most Valuable Twin for the second consecutive year by his teammates. He was going to play all nine positions for one inning each, beginning as a pitcher and moving through the field in order (catcher in the second inning, first base in the third, second base in the fourth, etc.). The Oakland A's were in sixth place (78-77), and this was their final road game before they wrapped up the season at home. Blue Moon Odom got the starting nod for the A's.

The only other player to man all nine positions, Campaneris, led off against Tovar and popped out to Twins third baseman Ron Clark in foul territory. Reggie Jackson struck out. Danny Cater walked, as Tovar had the fans cheering his "double and triple pumps."[2] This, however, resulted in a balk by Tovar, advancing Cater to second. When Sal Bando fouled out to first baseman Graig Nettles to end the inning, Tovar's work on the mound was done. It had taken him 19 pitches to retire the side.[3] None of the Oakland batters he faced had put the ball into play in fair territory. His one inning of scoreless pitching meant that his 0.00 career earned-run average is the lowest in Twins franchise history

In the bottom of the first, Tovar led off with a walk, becoming the first pitcher to bat in the leadoff spot for the Twins. After Clark was retired, Nettles was hit by a pitch. Bob Allison forced Nettles at second and Tovar went to third, but he was stranded when Rod Carew grounded out to first.

In the top of the second, the 5-foot, 9-inch Tovar semi-crouched behind the plate. According to

Cesar Tovar played all nine positions in the Twins' final home game in 1968.

Minneapolis's *Star Tribune*, "the shin guards were too long for his stubby legs."[4] Rookie southpaw Tom Hall had entered the game to pitch in relief of Tovar. Hall had split seven previous appearances as a starter and reliever, but it had been six days since he last pitched. When Odom struck out to end the inning, Tovar was credited with a putout behind the plate. Five Oakland batters had settled in the batter's box in the second and Tovar didn't let a single ball by him

In the third, Tovar took over at first base while Nettles moved to center field. Campaneris flied out to Nettles (in one of only two games he ever played in center). Next up was Jackson, who pulled a pitch that first baseman Tovar snared and, from his knees, threw to the pitcher Hall covering first in time to get Jackson.

The scoreless tie ended in the home half of the third. Tovar singled to center and stole second. Odom set down Clark and Nettles on strikes, but Allison drilled a triple to right, plating Tovar with the go-ahead run

In the next three innings, Tovar moved around the infield. The Oakland batters could not get anything going, and Tovar had only one chance, retiring Bando in the fourth while playing second base

In the bottom of the fifth, Tovar led off for the third time but grounded out, third to first. Clark reached on an error by second baseman Dick Green. With Nettles batting, Clark took off for second and catcher Jim Pagliaroni threw the ball into center field. Clark motored to third on the error and was given credit for a steal of second. Nettles walked and Allison hit a comebacker to Odom on the mound. Clark broke for home and Odom threw the ball to Bando at third who tagged out Clark. Carew sent a single to left, and Nettles scored the Twins' second run of the game.

Hall blanked the Athletics until the eighth inning. Only Jackson had notched a hit, a single in the sixth, but Hall then induced Cater to ground into a double play and the A's did not capitalize. With one out in the top of the eighth, Dave Duncan, pinch-hitting for Odom, singled to right. Allan Lewis entered as a pinch-runner. Campaneris singled to right as well, allowing Lewis to get to third base. With Jackson now at the plate, Campy stole second base. Jackson then hit a comebacker to the mound, but Hall couldn't make a clean play, and with the error, Oakland had loaded the bases with one out. Twins skipper Cal Ermer strode to the mound and motioned to the bullpen, bringing in Al Worthington to relieve Hall. The first batter he faced was Cater, who sent a sacrifice fly to center, driving in Lewis with an unearned run, preventing the shutout. Tovar made the catch in center and threw a perfect strike to third, preventing Campaneris from also tagging. Worthington then struck out Bando, preserving the Minnesota lead

In the ninth, with Tovar now in right field, the Athletics went three-up, three-down against Worthington. John Donaldson flied out to center, but Tovar let Allison make the catch. Tovar had starred in the 2-1 Minnesota win. At the plate, he was 1-for-3 with a walk. His stolen base in the third was his team-record 33rd successful swipe of the season. In addition to the assist he had in the third inning, Tovar made five putouts – one as a catcher, one as a second baseman, and three in the outfield.

Tovar's teammates also had fun changing positions, and those keeping a scorebook had to stay on their toes. Allison went from left to center, back to left, and then back to center. Clark, Carew, and Hernandez each played shortstop, in addition to Tovar. Jerry Zimmerman started as the catcher and remarked after the game that he "finally made it to the ninth spot in the batting order."[5]

After the game, the Twins organization presented Tovar with a color television set for his performance. Minnesota finished with a home record of 41-40. Although the fans enjoyed this final home game of the season, their annual attendance was just 1,143,257, their lowest in their first eight seasons in Minnesota.[6]

Tovar finished the 1968 season with a .272 batting average. Over his 12-year career, he played 943 games in the outfield and over 500 more as an infielder or designated hitter. This was the only game in his career in which he played as a pitcher, catcher, or first baseman.

Sparked by this victory, Minnesota went on to win its next three games, sweeping a series from the California Angels. Oakland and Minnesota closed the season with a three-game set played at the Oakland-Alameda County Coliseum. Oakland took two of the three games and still finished in sixth place, three games ahead of the Twins in the American League standings.

SOURCES

In addition to the sources mentioned in the Notes, the author consulted baseball-reference.com, mlb.com, retrosheet.org and sabr.org.

baseball-reference.com/boxes/MIN/MIN196809220.shtml

retrosheet.org/boxesetc/1968/B09220MIN1968.htm

METROPOLITAN STADIUM

NOTES

1. In his rookie season of 1910, Walsh played every position except pitcher, catcher, and first base. He ended his six-year career with only one appearance on the mound, pitching 2⅔ innings in an October 9, 1911, game against the Boston Rustlers, in which he allowed eight earned runs (for an ERA of 27.00). It was the last game of the season for the Phillies.

2. Dave Mona, "'Utility' Tovar, Twins Win 2-1," *Minneapolis Tribune*, September 23, 1968: 29.

3. Ron Bergman, "Athletics Lose, Launch Final Homestand Tonight," *Oakland Tribune*, September 23, 1968: 41.

4. Mona.

5. Mona.

6. Mona.

BILLY MARTIN'S HOME DEBUT

APRIL 18, 1969: MINNESOTA TWINS 6, CALIFORNIA ANGELS 0

By Dave Mona

Billy Martin preferred to make points with his fists, but the weapon of choice in his home opener as a major-league manager was The Blade.

Martin had prepped all his life to be a big-league manager. He'd been a major-league player and coach, a minor-league manager and a student ready to learn from an assortment of teachers.

Shortly after the end of the 1968 season, Twins owner Calvin Griffith fired manager Cal Ermer and made Martin the manager.

The waiting was over. This was 1969 and it was his year to put all that knowledge and aggression to work.

As a player, scout, coach, and manager in the Twins system, Martin had a deep knowledge of personnel.

And one of his favorites was Tom Hall, a 21-year-old left-handed pitcher whose weight was generously listed at 149 pounds. Martin had spent the 1968 season managing the Denver Bears, the Twins' Triple-A affiliate. The team finished with a 65-50 record under Martin after he took over from Johnny Goryl in May, and Hall was quickly establishing himself as a starter who could throw multiple pitches for strikes.

Nicknamed "The Blade" because of his razor-like physique, Hall was at his early-season best against the Angels.

As a former infielder, Martin was well aware of the Twins' weakness at shortstop. Incumbent Jackie Hernandez was made available to Kansas City in the expansion draft, and Martin helped engineer the trade of Jim Merritt, a left-handed starter, to Cincinnati for shortstop Leo Cardenas. In Martin's plans, Hall was ready to supplant Merritt in the Twins' starting rotation that included Jim Perry, Jim Kaat, Dean Chance, and Dave Boswell.

The Twins opened on the road, losing their first four games. They followed that with three victories on the West Coast, setting the stage for the home opener.

Martin looked on appreciatively from the home dugout as a crowd of 22,857 turned out for the opener. It was the third biggest home opener for the Twins since they moved to Minnesota in 1961.

Hall allowed just two hits in a 6-0 Twins victory while securing the first shutout of his 10-year major-league career. Over his first 21⅔ innings, he allowed just one earned run.

His complete game was the first for a Twins pitcher in 1969, although Kaat had pitched 11 innings in the Twins' 17-inning loss to Kansas City in the opening series.

The only hits allowed by Hall were a first-inning triple by Jim Fregosi and a seventh-inning single by Lou Johnson.

Cardenas, the player many of the fans had come to see, singled off shortstop Fregosi's glove in the fourth inning to score Harmon Killebrew from second with the first run of the game, and Frank Quilici singled in another run.

Four straight singles off knuckleball specialist Eddie Fisher raised the Twins' lead to 4-0 in the sixth with Bob Allison and George Mitterwald each driving home a run.

Martin's strategy was to use speed and surprise to spark the offense and rattle the opposing defense. No one expected that speed to come from slugger Killebrew, but no one was exempt from Martin's speed edict. Twice Killebrew reached second on throwing errors by California infielders after beating out infield singles, and he scored easily from second on Cardenas' single after Killebrew had walked to start the fourth and taken second on a groundout.

In the 1969 season, Killebrew recorded eight of his career 19 stolen bases, often as the caboose behind Rod Carew, Cesar Tovar, or both.

Rich Reese, as often happened during the year, replaced Killebrew as a pinch-runner at second and scored when Angels left fielder Rick Reichardt misplayed Tony Oliva's single in the eighth inning.

The hit was Oliva's second of the game and eighth in his last 12 at-bats. After going an uncharacteristic 0-for-10 in the second and third games of the season, Oliva went 15-for-38 to raise his batting average to .395, second only to catcher John Roseboro's .429.

Killebrew's two infield singles in three at-bats raised his batting average to .267. Carew was the only Twins starter held hitless in the game, but he was still .385 at the end of the game.

After the game Martin credited Carew, Cardenas, and Oliva with making hit-saving plays.

Hall's pitch count climbed in the sixth and seventh innings and Martin sent pitching coach Early Wynn to the mound, but Martin said he was not contemplating a change. "I know Hall from Denver last year, where I saw him pitch out of jam situations," Martin said. "That's what I like about him ... the ability to pitch through trouble,"

Meanwhile, in the Angels' clubhouse, manager Bill Rigney, after a closed-door session with his players, was less impressed with Hall than he was critical of his own team.

"We gave up. We went home," Rigney told *Los Angeles Times* beat writer Ross Newhan. "We were awful ... flat ... dead. ...

"I told them that they played like a bunch of old men. I told them that when they got behind they simply quit.

"Hell, that's the time when you've got to be a real player. We just packed our bags and went home."[1]

When asked about Hall's limiting his team to two hits, Rigney said, "Tom who? His name must be Mandrake. He's like a magician. My guys acted like they've never seen a curve before."[2]

Hall was selected in the third round by the Twins in the January 1966 draft. Because of his size he attracted little interest at either Riverside High or Riverside Community College in Southern California.

"The Twins," he said, "were the only team to talk to me. I was disappointed that the Dodgers didn't come around. They were my favorites."

While Hall's college credentials didn't attract wide interest, his curve and control impressed Twins scout Jess Flores, who pitched for the Angels when they played in the Pacific Coast League.[3]

Based upon urging from Flores, the Twins signed Hall and he moved quickly through the system, compiling a 31-13 record as he moved rapidly from Sarasota to Orlando, Wisconsin Rapids, Charlotte, and Denver.

Leo Cardenas, shown with 1969 teammate Frank Quilici, drove in the first run of the game in his first home game for the Twins.

Promoted to the Twins near the end of the 1968 season he won two of three decisions while compiling a 2.43 earned-run average.

"He's going to be a fine pitcher," Martin said.[4]

"Hell," Rigney joked, "he's a regular black Whitey Ford. He's going right into the Hall of Fame."[5]

TWINS TOPICS

Hall finished the 1969 season with an 8-7 record and a 3.33 ERA. The shutout was one of three in his 10-year major-league career in which he was 52-33.

Merritt, traded to the Reds to make room for Hall, went 17-9 in 1969 and became a 20-game winner the next year. He battled arm troubles for the final five years of his big-league career, in which his won-lost record was 7-24.

Cardenas played 160 games at short for Martin's 1969 Twins, hitting .280 with 10 home runs and 70 runs batted in.

Rigney's frustrations only intensified. The team's only manager since its 1961 inception, he was gone a month after the Twins series. His team was mired in a 10-game losing streak with a record of 11-28 when he was fired. Rigney had managed the Minneapolis Millers in 1954 and 1955 at Nicollet Park, their home before Met Stadium. When the popular Martin was fired at the end of the 1969 season, Rigney succeeded him. He won the American League West title in 1970, losing to the Baltimore Orioles for the AL pennant. He came back in 1971 and was fired in 1972 in favor of former Twins infielder Frank Quilici.

Willie Peterson, the Twins organist since they moved to Minnesota, died the day before the home opener after a long illness. For many years he was the answer to a popular trivia question: "Who was the only man to play for both the Minnesota Twins and the Minnesota Vikings?"[6]

(*Editor's Note:* Dave Mona, who wrote this story, was the *Minneapolis Tribune* beat reporter covering the Twins in 1969. His game account provided much of the material for this story.)

NOTES

1. Ross Newhan, "'We Quit,' Rigney Storms After Loss," *Los Angeles Times,* April 19, 1969: Part III, 2.
2. Newhan.
3. "Angels' Fregosi 'Dampens' Pitching Success of Hall," *Minneapolis Tribune,* April 19, 1969: 16.
4. Tom Briere, "Hall Puts Angels on Two-Hit 'Diet' for 6-0 Twins Win," *Minneapolis Tribune,* April 19, 1969: 15.
5. Sid Hartman column, *Minneapolis Tribune,* April 19, 1969: 16.
6. "Willard Peterson, Twins' Organist, Dies of Cancer," *Minneapolis Star,* April 19, 1969: 3A.

TOVAR AND CAREW STEAL HOME IN THE SAME INNING

MAY 18, 1969: DETROIT TIGERS 8, MINNESOTA TWINS 2

By Thomas J. Brown Jr.

The Minnesota Twins had grabbed first place in their division by the end of April 1969. They stayed atop the standings until May 15, when they lost to the Baltimore Orioles to fall behind the Oakland A's. The team returned to Metropolitan Stadium in hopes of reclaiming the top spot in the AL West.

The Detroit Tigers beat the Twins in the first game of a two-game series when Tigers ace Denny McLain shut them out, 6-0. Twins manager Billy Martin told reporters, "We're hurting ourselves by making too many physical and mental mistakes. Until we tighten up, we're in trouble."[1]

Despite their three consecutive losses, the Twins managed to remain just one game behind Oakland. The 20,778 fans who showed up for the Sunday afternoon game were hoping to see the team that had played so well in April when they went 13-7 and not the one that was struggling at the moment.

Martin started Dave Boswell. Boswell entered the game with a 4-3 record and had pitched well in his last start when he outdueled Orioles ace Mike Cuellar. (That was the last game the Twins won before going into their slide.)

Boswell struggled in the first inning. Mickey Stanley led off with a single and reached third when Al Kaline punched a single into the gap in right field. When Norm Cash hit a grounder in the gap between second and short, the only play was a force out at second as Stanley crossed the plate to give Detroit the lead.

Left-hander Mickey Lolich took the mound for the Tigers. Lolich had won his last game, 3-1 over the White Sox, striking out 10 batters. After Cesar Tovar led off with a double, Lolich struck out Rod Carew and then got the next two Twins to fly out and leave Tovar stranded.

Boswell appeared to get his rhythm going in the second when he got the first two batters to hit weak pop flies for easy outs. Singles by Bill Freehan and Lolich put runners at the corners, but Boswell got out of the inning by striking out Stanley.

Lolich gave up singles to the first two batters he faced in the second and then walked Rick Renick to load the bases with one out. But Boswell hit a groundball back to Lolich that led to an inning-ending double play.

Dick McAuliffe led off the Detroit third with a triple. It was his 57th triple with the Tigers. Kaline followed with a double to bring McAuliffe across the plate and make the score 2-0. Boswell limited the damage as he retired the next three batters to strand Kaline at third.

The Twins tied the score in their half of the inning. Tovar led off with a single. As he "danced off first base, drawing repeated throws from Lolich," the Tigers starter committed a balk with Carew at bat.[2]

Lolich then walked Carew. With Harmon Killebrew at bat, the two speed demons pulled off a double steal. But Lolich struck out Killebrew and got Tony Oliva on a popup, for two outs.

Cesar Tovar

MEMORABLE GAMES AT MINNESOTA'S DIAMOND ON THE PRAIRIE

"Tovar, in no mood to see the rally come to such an untimely end, caught Lolich in a double rocking motion," a Detroit sportswriter commented.[3] The speedy Tovar slowly stretched out his lead until he was almost halfway down the line when Lolich delivered. He easily beat the throw to the plate with a slide.

Carew stayed at second although he could have made it to third on Tovar's play to home. "[He] preferred to earn his stolen base," wrote Dave Mona of the *Minneapolis Tribune*.[4] Two pitches later, he took off for third and stole it easily when he beat Freehan's throw.

Lolich was clearly having trouble with the baserunners. With two outs, most fans expected Martin to play it safe and hope that Killebrew would hit Carew home. But Martin, "who thrives on the audacious, gave Carew the go sign" and Carew took off on the next pitch.[5] He easily made it home to tie the game, 2-2.

The five stolen bases by Tovar and Carew were a team record for stolen bases in a game. It was the fourth time Carew had stolen home in four tries and the third time he had accomplished the feat in 1969.

Lolich was asked after the game if he was embarrassed about the basestealing. "I was flattered," he said. "They were as much as telling me that they couldn't hit me so they'd have to score another way. Actually, it bolstered my confidence."[6]

Lolich said, "[N]obody likes to be run on." When Tovar came to bat in the fourth, Lolich hit him on the first pitch. "I didn't throw at Tovar when I hit him his next time up, although it may have looked that way. It was an inside pitch that just got away from me," Lolich said later.[7]

When Detroit came to bat in the fifth, Boswell sent Kaline sprawling in the dirt with an inside pitch. As Kaline picked himself up, Boswell was warned by the umpire and given a $50 fine. After the game Martin defended his pitcher. He said there was no reason "to throw at Kaline when the score was tied 2-2 and every baserunner was important."[8]

But the Twins didn't savor their baserunning glory for very long. After pitching two scoreless innings, Boswell again struggled in the sixth. When Lolich popped out to third for the second out with two Tigers onbase, it looked as though the Twins might get out of trouble.

But on Stanley's pop to short right field, Carew and Oliva collided as both tried to catch the ball. By the time the two players recovered, Stanley ended up on second and Freehan and Tommy Matchick had scored. Carew ended up with a sore back but remained in the game. Oliva left the game with a dislocated index finger.

Then McAuliffe singled and Stanley scored to give the Tigers a 5-2 lead. After Kaline walked, Martin replaced Boswell with Joe Grzenda. Grzenda walked Norm Cash to load the bases, then balked to bring home McAuliffe with the fourth Tigers run of the inning.

Martin went to the bullpen again. He brought in Ron Perranoski for his 18th appearance of the season. Perranoski struck out Gates Brown to end the inning.

Martin said later that he was worried about using Perranoski too frequently. He said he had been talking to Al Worthington, who had retired after the 1968 season, about returning to bolster the bullpen.

The Tigers got single runs in the seventh and eighth innings to make the final score 8-2. The Twins' problems were not only on the mound; Lolich also shut down their offense. After surrendering the two runs in the third, he held Minnesota hitless the rest of the game. The Twins got four men on base, three of them on walks and one hit batter. The last time came in the ninth when Lolich walked Renick. But the game ended when pinch-hitter Frank Quilici hit into a double play.

Martin told reporters that "the pitching hasn't been what we thought it would it be but we still have to admit that we're beating ourselves."[9] He expressed his frustration with his players, saying, "We're going to have to stop making the same old mistakes or else."[10]

Martin also stirred up an eruption in the front office when he criticized several personnel moves, particularly the decision to send relief pitcher Charlie Walters down to the Double-A Charlotte Hornets.

"I may be old-fashioned but I thought that when you went from the big leagues, you go to Triple A," Martin said. "How am I supposed to tell something like that to Walters?" Sherry Robertson, who ran the Twins farm system, termed Martin "totally out of line," adding, "I don't tell him how to manage his team. I don't need him to tell me how to run the department."[11]

As the feud played out in the press, the Twins won their next game, two days later, defeating Baltimore 3-2 in 13 innings, then lost three more games. They turned things around on May 24 when they won the first of four straight games. When the month ended, they had reclaimed first place in the division.

SOURCES

In addition to the sources cited in the Notes, I used the Baseball-Reference.com and Retrosheet.org websites for box-score, player, team, and season pages, pitching and batting game logs, and other pertinent material.

baseball-reference.com/boxes/MIN/MIN196905180.shtml

retrosheet.org/boxesetc/1969/B05180MIN1969.htm

NOTES

1. Dave Mona, "Careless Twins Lose to Detroit, Displease Martin," *Minneapolis Tribune*, May 19, 1969: 29.
2. George Cantor, "Doesn't Pay to Steal; Tigers 8, Twins 2," *Detroit Free Press*, May 19, 1969: 1D.
3. Cantor, "Doesn't Pay to Steal."
4. Mona, "Careless Twins."
5. Mona, "Careless Twins."
6. George Cantor, "Mick Flattered by Steals," *Detroit Free Press*, May 19, 1969: 5D.
7. Cantor, "Mick Flattered."
8. Mona, "Careless Twins."
9. "Lolich Mental Mistakes Keep Twins Skein Alive," *Winona* (Minnesota) *Daily News*, May 19, 1969: 13.
10. Mona, "Careless Twins."
11. Dave Mona, "Internal Combustion: Martin Blasts Farm Department," *Minneapolis Tribune*, May 19, 1969: 29.

EARLY FIREWORKS DOOM A'S IN BIG SERIES OPENER

JULY 4, 1969: MINNESOTA TWINS 10, OAKLAND ATHLETICS 4

by Steve Ginader

It was a hot, humid Independence Day in Bloomington, Minnesota. Early-morning thunderstorms were a concern but by game time the skies had cleared. The announced crowd of 30,654 was the largest yet recorded for a Fourth of July game in Minnesota. The Oakland Athletics and the Minnesota Twins, who were fighting for first place in the newly formed American League West Division, were facing off in the opening game of a big three-game series. A's owner Charles Finley was in attendance and in a pregame news conference predicted the A's to win the division "because I told [manager] Billy Martin of the Twins he's got some older fellows who are going to get tired in August. And we're going to win."[1]

Bob Miller was the starting pitcher for the Twins. Although originally signed by his hometown St. Louis Cardinals in 1957, he was now playing for his fourth team and had turned into a "whatever is needed utility pitcher."[2] Recently thrust into a starting role, Miller was making his third start of the year. At age 30 he was a veteran pitcher on an experienced squad coming off multiple top-three finishes in the last seven years, including a World Series appearance in 1965.

Catfish Hunter, who signed out of high school in 1964, was the starting pitcher for the A's. At age 23 he was in the early stages of a 15-year career that culminated with his induction into the Hall of Fame. In May 1968 Hunter had pitched a perfect game against the Twins. Harmon Killebrew struck out three times, twice on called third strikes. Afterward Killebrew said, "He was throwing better than I've ever seen him throw."[3] But in 1969 Hunter did not fare as well against the Twins. By Independence Day he had three starts against them, losing twice (with one no-decision) and five home runs surrendered.

After Miller retired the A's in order in the top of the first, the Twins wasted no time in solving Hunter in the bottom of the inning. Ted Uhlaender hit a leadoff double, and one out later Tony Oliva drove him home with a double off the right-field fence. Killebrew was next and he continued the early fireworks with a home run to left to bring in the second and third runs of the inning. The fans were just settling in and before they knew it, the Twins were ahead by three.

Miller's job in the top of the second was to hold the A's scoreless and preserve the three-run lead. He got off to a shaky start as Sal Bando led off with a single and after two wild pitches wound up at third base with no outs. After two groundouts and a fly out, Bando was stranded and the Twins still had their lead.

Leo Cardenas and Rod Carew

Minnesota Twins

METROPOLITAN STADIUM

Both teams went in order in their next at-bats, and then the Twins tacked on a fourth run in the third with back-to-back doubles by Oliva and Rod Carew. The onslaught continued in the bottom of the fourth when Leo Cardenas hit a towering home run to center field. Two outs later, Uhlaender singled and Carew cleared the bases with the Twins' third home run of the day. That was it for Hunter: manager Hank Bauer pulled him and brought in pitcher Jim Roland. The Twins added a run off Roland and the inning ended with the Twins up 8-0. Hunter's day ended early with a record of eight hits (four doubles, three home runs, and a single) and seven runs surrendered. "With Catfish Hunter, it's either short and sweet or long and loud." "They're either going to pop the ball into the stands or he's going to pitch a shutout," observed manager Hank Bauer. "You can't defense the long ball."[4]

The game settled down for the next two innings as Miller surrendered only two singles and the Twins could not muster any offense off Jim Nash, who replaced Roland. However, in the bottom of the seventh, Nash surrendered two runs. After Cardenas struck out to lead off the inning, Cesar Tovar hit a one-out single, stole second, and took third when a pickoff attempt went awry. After another strikeout, Uhlaender and Carew hit back-to-back doubles off Nash and the Twins scored their ninth and 10th runs.

Through eight innings, Miller had surrendered five hits and a walk but was the beneficiary of three double plays. The only remaining storyline was Miller's quest for his first complete game since 1963. It was a sultry day and the ballpark staff had already treated 10 people for heat exhaustion. Miller thought he might be the 11th. "I lost 100 pounds out there," he told reporters during his postgame interview.[5]

To lead off the ninth, Miller issued his second walk, to Ted Kubiak. After two fly-ball outs it was looking as though he would not only get the complete game, but also a shutout. "Of course, I was thinking of the shutout in the ninth inning. I've never had one," he said.[6] Bando stepped to the plate and stroked his second single of the game, advancing Kubiak to second. This brought manager Martin to the mound for a conversation with Miller. In very few words, Miller persuaded Martin to keep him in. Then Danny Cater hit a single to drive in Kubiak and Rick Monday hit a three-run homer to right center. Finally, Tom Reynolds grounded out to end the game. The shutout was lost but the Twins won the game and Miller achieved a complete-game victory.

The win pulled the Twins into a virtual tie for first. They would continue to expand the lead and win the West Division title by nine games over the second-place A's. The A's were still trying to prove themselves to their fans and owner. Of the lack of crowds in Oakland, Finley said, "Heck, I told [the players] we haven't proved anything yet. We've got to prove a winner before the people come out to see us in Oakland."[7] The A's did prove winners in the 1970s by winning five consecutive division championships, but for now the title remained in Minnesota. Despite Finley's prediction, the veteran players on the Twins were not ready to yield their crown to the young Oakland Athletics.

SOURCES

baseball-reference.com/boxes/MIN/MIN196907040.shtml

retrosheet.org/boxesetc/1969/B07040MIN1969.htm

NOTES

1. Tom Briere, "Finley: Owners Hurting Baseball," *Minneapolis Tribune*, July 5, 1969: 9.
2. Steve Treder, "Not Just Any Bob Miller," *Hardball Times*, September 6, 2005.
3. Ron Bergman, "Catfish Is Perfect," *Oakland Tribune*, May 9, 1968: 39.
4. Ron Bergman, "Twins Destroy the A's," *Oakland Tribune*, July 5, 1969: 9.
5. Dave Mona, "Twins Slug A's 10-4," *Minneapolis Tribune*, July 5, 1969: 9.
6. Mona.
7. Briere.

KILLEBREW DOES IT AGAIN: TWO-RUN GAME-WINNING HOMER; TWINS COME FROM BEHIND TO DEFEAT A'S 7-6

JULY 6, 1969: MINNESOTA TWINS 7, OAKLAND ATHLETICS 6

By Bob Webster

Harmon "Killer" Killebrew lived up to his name on this Fourth of July weekend. Going into a three-game series with the Oakland Athletics, the Minnesota Twins (43-34) were one game behind the A's (42-31). Prior to the Friday series opener, Killebrew's batting average was .273 with 19 home runs and 72 runs batted in. After Tony Oliva doubled in Ted Uhlaender in the first inning, Killebrew drove Oliva home with a two-run bomb over the left-field fence to give the Twins a 3-0 lead. Killebrew added a single in the sixth inning as the Twins tied the Athletics for first place in the American League West with the 10-4 victory.

Saturday, Killebrew was 3-for-4 with six runs batted in (RBIs), including home runs in the first and second innings, to help the Twins take a one-game lead over the Athletics by a score of 13-1.

Killebrew raised his batting average to .283, up by 10 points in the past two games, and was up to 22 home runs and 80 RBIs.

In the third and final game of the series, on Sunday, July 6, Blue Moon Odom took the mound for the Athletics. Odom, 11-3 with victories in his last four decisions, also sported an impressive 2.28 earned-run average. On the mound for the Twins was Dave Boswell, who was 10-8 for the season with a 3.09 ERA.

The Athletics jumped on Boswell early. In the top of the first, Ted Kubiak lined out to center fielder Cesar Tovar. Dick Green walked and with Reggie Jackson at the plate, a wild pitch by Boswell sent Green scampering into second. Jackson doubled high off the right-field wall with Green stopping at third. Green thought the ball was going to be caught, so he held up.[1] Sal Bando singled to left, driving in Green and Jackson for the first two runs of the game. Danny Cater grounded into a 6-4-3 double play to end the Athletics' half of the first.

Odom took the mound in the bottom of the first, feeling good about his team's two-run lead. Odom retired Uhlaender and Rod Carew on groundouts and Oliva on a line out to center.

Boswell surrendered a leadoff double to Rick Monday to start the second but struck out Joe Rudi, walked Dave Duncan, fanned Odom, and retired Kubiak on a grounder to first.

The hot-hitting Killebrew singled to start the bottom of the second, but Odom struck out Rich Reese and John Roseboro, then got Leo Cardenas to ground to second for an inning-ending force play.

The Twins threatened in the bottom of the third. Tovar doubled to lead off the inning. He held at second as Boswell reached on a ball hit to third base. Odom buckled down and struck out Uhlaender and Carew, then Oliva grounded out to second to end the inning. At the end of three, the Athletics held on to their two-run lead.

Boswell allowed another walk in the top of the fourth but got out of the inning.

Killebrew led off the bottom of the fourth with another hit, this time a single to right. Reese followed with a single, and, when Jackson misplayed the ball in right, Killebrew scored and Reese went to third. Roseboro singled in Reese to tie the game, 2-2. Roseboro was caught stealing, Cardenas popped out to first baseman Cater in foul territory, and Tovar flied out to center to end the inning.

Kubiak singled to begin the top half of the fifth for the Athletics. Green struck out and Jackson walked. Bando flied out to left with the runners holding. With two outs, Cater drove one 380 feet into the left-field seats for a three-run homer to give the Athletics a 5-2 lead.[2] With Boswell scheduled to lead off the bottom of the fifth, Twins manager Billy Martin wanted Boswell to finish the inning. After hitting Monday with a pitch, Boswell retired Joe Rudi on a groundout to second to retire the side.

In the bottom of the fifth, Charlie Manuel, pinch-hitting for Boswell, grounded out, first to pitcher. Uhlaender and Carew both grounded out to retire the side.

Joe Grzenda came in to pitch for the Twins and retired the side one-two-three on three grounders to make easy work of the Athletics in the top half of the sixth.

After a leadoff double by Oliva in the bottom of the sixth, Odom buckled down and retired Killebrew, Reese, and Roseboro, stranding Oliva at second.

The Athletics scored again in the top of the seventh. Green homered to left off Grzenda to lead off the inning. Grzenda then walked Jackson and Bando followed with a base hit to right, Jackson stopping at second. Cater grounded into a pitcher-to-short-to-first double play and Monday was out on a comebacker to first to end the inning with the Athletics now leading 6-2.

Odom hit Cardenas with his second pitch in the Twins' seventh. Before this hit-by-pitch, there had been a lot of words exchanged between dugouts about pitches that were too far inside to batters on both teams. Boswell hit Monday in the fifth, and Grzenda dusted off Jackson in the top of the seventh.[3] Cardenas walked slowly to first, carrying his bat most of the way. When he arrived at first, he said something to Odom, who said something back. With Tovar at the plate and Odom distracted, Cardenas took second on a wild pitch.[4] Tovar singled to center, scoring Cardenas. Graig Nettles, pinch-hitting for Grzenda, walked. Athletics manager Hank Bauer replaced Odom with the Athletics' top reliever, Rollie Fingers. Uhlaender, the first batter he faced, grounded out to short, with both runners advancing. Carew executed perfectly by hitting behind the runners as he grounded out to second, scoring Tovar with Nettles taking third. Oliva singled to right, Nettles scored, and the Athletics' lead was down to one run at 6-5. The hot-hitting Killebrew stepped to the plate. To the amazement of the 23,611 fans in the ballpark on this Sunday afternoon, Killebrew hammered another homer into a 15-MPH wind into the left-field seats 360 feet away to

Harmon Killebrew was named the Most Valuable Player in the American League in 1969. The following year he received his award from American League president Joe Cronin.

give the Twins a 7-6 lead.[5] Rich Reese grounded out to end the inning.

Ron Perranoski came in to pitch the final two innings as the Twins held on for the 7-6 win.

Killebrew started the three-game series with the Athletics with 19 home runs and 72 RBIs. At the end of the series, he had 23 home runs and 84 RBIs and was 8-for-12, raising his batting average from .273 to .289. "There are some stretches when you feel real comfortable at the plate and you feel you can hit anything the pitcher can throw," Killebrew said after the game. "Then there are times you can't seem to hit a pitch when it comes right up the middle. Right now I feel pretty comfortable out there."[6]

After the game Carew was leading the American League with a .357 batting average. Oliva was in third place, batting .328, and Cardenas was ninth at .294. Killebrew, with 82 RBIs, led second-place Boog Powell of the Orioles with 74 and the Athletics' Reggie Jackson with 66.

Killebrew's seventh-inning homer was the 16th time in the Twins' 46 victories in 1969 that he drove in the deciding run.[7]

SOURCES

retrosheet.org/boxesetc/1969/B07060MIN1969.htm

baseball-reference.com/boxes/MIN/MIN196907060.shtml

NOTES

1. "Bauer's Tactic Turns Sour – and A's Blow It," *San Francisco Examiner*, July 7, 1969: 57.
2. Dave Mona, "Killebrew Sinks A's," *Minneapolis Tribune*, July 7, 1969: 34.
3. "Bauer's Tactic Turns Sour – and A's Blow It."
4. Mona: 33.
5. Mona: 33.
6. Mona: 33.
7. Mona: 33.

METROPOLITAN STADIUM POSTPONEMENTS

Minneapolis Millers, 1956-1960
Minnesota Twins, 1961-1981
Postponed by rain unless otherwise indicated

MINNEAPOLIS MILLERS

1956
(13 postponements, 1 game shortened by rain, and 1 game shortened by curfew; 1 game not made up; 1 game rained out elsewhere made up in Minnesota)

Thursday, April 26, vs. Wichita, cold
Made up as part of doubleheader June 15

Friday, April 27, vs. Indianapolis, cold
Made up as part of doubleheader June 12

Thursday, May 10, vs. Charleston
Made up as part of doubleheader July 1

Sunday, May 13, vs. Louisville
Made up as part of doubleheader June 26

Thursday, May 24, vs. Omaha
Made up as part of doubleheader July 22

Monday, May 28, vs. St. Paul
Made up August 6

Thursday, June 14, vs. Indianapolis
Made up as part of doubleheader August 14

Saturday, June 16, vs. Wichita
Made up as part of doubleheader August 31

Monday, June 25, vs. Louisville
Made up as part of doubleheader July 31

Wednesday, July 18, vs. Denver
Made up as part of doubleheader July 19

Thursday, July 19, vs. Denver
(second game of doubleheader)
Made up as part of doubleheader July 20

Monday, July 30, vs. Louisville
Made up as part of doubleheader August 1

Thursday, August 2, vs. Louisville
Not made up

Other:

Thursday, June 19 – Game 1 of doubleheader
(scheduled for seven innings)
Millers beat Denver 4-2 in game stopped by rain
with one out in the last of the sixth

Friday, September 14 (playoffs)
Millers lost 1-0 to Indianapolis in a game called
by curfew after 8 innings
The game was delayed 3 times by rain totaling
2 hours 58 minutes in delays (final delay was 2:15).
It was called after 8 innings by a 12:50 A.M. curfew.

A game that was rained out in Charleston July 29
was made up as part of a doubleheader in Minnesota
August 3.

1957
(5 postponements and 1 tie game shortened by rain; 1 game called by rain elsewhere made up in Minnesota)

Saturday, May 25, vs. Indianapolis
Made up as part of doubleheader June 22

Sunday, June 16 (doubleheader), vs. Charleston
Makeup games scheduled as parts of doubleheaders
July 30 and August 16

Friday, June 21, vs. Indianapolis
Made up as part of a doubleheader August 26

Tuesday, June 25, vs. Denver
Made up as part of doubleheader June 27

Friday, August 30, vs. Omaha
Made up as part of doubleheader August 31

Other:

Thursday, August 1, vs. Wichita
Minneapolis scored in the last of the ninth to tie
the game, 2-2, and had a runner on third
with two out. Joey Jay was in the process of

MEMORABLE GAMES AT MINNESOTA'S DIAMOND ON THE PRAIRIE

intentionally walking Bill Taylor when the game was called because of rain. The game was replayed as part of a doubleheader August 22.

A tie game that was called by rain in Indianapolis on August 10 was made up as part of a doubleheader in Minnesota August 5.

1958

(4 postponements)

Thursday, June 24, vs. Charleston
Made up as part of doubleheader June 25

Friday, July 4, vs. St. Paul (morning game)
The afternoon game, in St. Paul, was played; the morning game was made up at night.

Monday, August 25, vs. Omaha
Made up as part of doubleheader August 26

Sunday, September 14, vs. Wichita (playoffs)
Made up September 15

1959

(10 postponements and 1 game shorted to allow visiting team to catch its plane)

Monday, May 4, vs. Charleston, rain and hail
Made up as part of doubleheader May 6

Tuesday, May 5, vs. Charleston
Made up as part of doubleheader August 18

Friday, May 22, vs. St. Paul
Made up July 20

Sunday, June 14, vs. Houston, wet grounds (seven-inning second game of doubleheader)
Made up as part of doubleheader August 6

Wednesday, June 17, vs. Dallas
Made up as part of doubleheader July 31

Thursday, June 30, vs. Indianapolis
Made up as part of doubleheader August 15

Sunday, August 16, vs. Indianapolis (seven-inning second game of doubleheader stopped by rain in the first inning)
Made up August 17

Thursday, September 1, vs. Denver
Made up as part of doubleheader September 2

Friday, September 18, vs. Fort Worth, rain and cold (playoffs)
The postponement of the second game of the playoffs forced a change in the schedule, which called for the Millers to host the first two games. However, Metropolitan Stadium wasn't available for a makeup on September 19 because of preparations for a National Football League exhibition game on September 20, so the series was shifted to Fort Worth for the next four games (the rained-out game being made up in Fort Worth).

Tuesday, September 28, vs. Havana, cold (Junior World Series)
The third game of the playoffs was called off because of cold weather. It was made up in Havana, where the remaining games of the series were played.

Other:

Monday, August 17, vs. Indianapolis, game called after seven innings to allow Indianapolis to catch its plane.

1960

(7 postponements)

Wednesday, April 27, vs. Charleston, cold
Made up June 27

Thursday, April 28, vs. Charleston, wet grounds
Made up as part of doubleheader August 17

Friday, May 6, vs. Louisville, cold
Made up as part of doubleheader July 31

Monday, May 9, vs. Indianapolis, cold
Made up as part of doubleheader May 11

Thursday, May 26, vs. Houston
Made up as part of doubleheader July 7

Sunday, August 28, vs. Houston, wet grounds (doubleheader)
Made up as part of doubleheader August 29 and on August 31

METROPOLITAN STADIUM

Wednesday, September 7, vs. St. Paul
Made up as part of doubleheader September 8

MINNESOTA TWINS

1961

(4 postponements, 1 tie game, and 1 game shortened by rain; 1 game not made up)

Saturday, May 6, vs. Boston
Made up as part of a doubleheader, Tuesday, June 27

Tuesday, September 12 (doubleheader), vs. Los Angeles
Rescheduled: one game as part of a doubleheader, Wednesday, September 13, and the other to be played on an open date on Thursday, September 14

Wednesday, September 13 (doubleheader), vs. Los Angeles
Made up as doubleheader on Thursday, September 14, still leaving one game that was never made up

Friday, September 22, vs. Washington
Made up as a doubleheader Saturday, September 23

Other:

Tuesday, September 5, vs. Chicago, tie 3-3 after 9 innings, called by fog
Tie game replayed as part of a doubleheader on Wednesday, September 6
The game was called at 11:50 P.M. after a 37-minute delay (had also been a 30-minute delay in the sixth inning). The umpires (John Rice was the crew chief) might have called the game earlier in the ninth, but Al Smith had homered to tie the game in the top of the inning, and the score would have reverted to the eighth, giving the Twins a 3-2 win, if the ninth weren't completed. The inning was played out even though the newspaper reported that the fog was so thick that outfielders wouldn't be able to see fly balls hit to them.

Saturday, September 30
Twins lost to Detroit 6-4 in a game called by rain in the top of the sixth

1962

(2 postponements, 1 tie game, and 1 game shortened by rain)

Friday, April 13, vs. Los Angeles (home opener), snow. (6 inches of snow had fallen on Thursday.)
Made up as part of a doubleheader Friday, June 22

Sunday, July 15 (second game of doubleheader), vs. Boston
Made up as part of a doubleheader Sunday, August 19

Other:

Wednesday, August 22, vs. Washington, tie 8-8 after 10 innings, called at 1:30 A.M. after third rain delay (this one a half-hour delay)
Replayed as part of a doubleheader Thursday, August 23

Friday, May 11
Twins lost to Kansas City 5-3 in a game called by rain in the last of the eighth

1963

(4 postponements)

Monday, April 29, vs. Baltimore
Made up as part of a doubleheader Friday, June 21

Thursday, May 2, vs. Boston
Made up Wednesday, July 10 (day after the All-Star Game, which had been scheduled as an open date)

Sunday, May 12 (second game of doubleheader), vs. Kansas City
Made up as part of a doubleheader Wednesday, June 12

Tuesday, July 16, vs. New York (rained out in the top of the second inning – game was scoreless)
Made up as night game as part of day-night doubleheader Saturday, September 14

1964

(4 postponements, 1 tie game, and 1 game shortened by rain)

MEMORABLE GAMES AT MINNESOTA'S DIAMOND ON THE PRAIRIE

Tuesday, April 21 (home opener), vs. Washington
Made up Wednesday, April 22

Wednesday, April 29, vs. Cleveland
Made up on Monday, June 22 (ended as tie and replayed as part of a doubleheader Wednesday, June 24)

Monday, May 11, vs. Chicago
Made up as part of doubleheader Friday, June 26

Monday night, September 7 (night game of day-night doubleheader), vs. New York
Made up Tuesday, September 8

Other:

Monday, June 22, vs. Cleveland, 8-8 tie after 10 innings
Replayed as part of a doubleheader Wednesday, June 24

Sunday, October 4
Twins lost to Los Angeles 3-0 in a game called by rain after six innings

1965

(5 postponements)

Tuesday, April 13, vs. New York, severe flood conditions causing traffic difficulties (postponement announced during game on April 12)
Made up as night game as part of a day-night doubleheader Saturday, July 10

Wednesday, April 14, vs. Detroit
Made up as part of a doubleheader Sunday, June 27

Sunday, May 23, vs. Kansas City
Made up as part of a doubleheader Thursday, July 15

Saturday, June 5, vs. Washington
Made up as part of a doubleheader Tuesday, August 3

Thursday, September 16, vs. Kansas City
Made up Monday, September 20

1966

(4 postponements)

Sunday, April 17, vs. California
Made up as part of a doubleheader Thursday, June 15

Tuesday, May 10, vs. New York (rained out in the last of the first – scoreless game)
Made up as part of a doubleheader Sunday, July 17

Wednesday, May 11, vs. New York
Made up as a night game of a day-night doubleheader Saturday, September 3

Saturday, August 13, vs. Kansas City
Made up as part of a doubleheader Sunday, August 14

1967

(6 postponements and 1 game shortened by rain)

Monday, April 17, vs. Cleveland
Made up as part of a doubleheader Tuesday, June 6

Thursday, April 20, vs. Baltimore
Made up as a night game of a day-night doubleheader Saturday, June 10

Saturday, June 10, vs. Baltimore
The scheduled day game was postponed although the night game, scheduled as a makeup game for the April 20 postponement, was played. The June 10 day game was made up as part of a single-admission doubleheader on Sunday, June 11.

Monday, May 1, vs. New York
Made up as night game of a morning-night doubleheader Tuesday, July 4

Wednesday, June 7, vs. Cleveland
Made up as part of a doubleheader Monday, September 4

Friday, June 30, vs. Washington (rained out in the bottom of the first with the Twins leading 1-0)
Made up as part of a doubleheader Sunday, July 2

Other:

METROPOLITAN STADIUM

Sunday, August 6
Twins beat Boston 2-0 in a game called by rain in the bottom of the fifth inning (perfect game by Dean Chance)

1968

(5 postponements and 2 games shortened by rain)

Tuesday, April 23, vs. Baltimore, snow and cold
Made up as part of a doubleheader Thursday, August 15

Wednesday, May 15, vs. Oakland
Made up Friday, September 20

Friday, May 17, vs. California (rained out in the bottom of the fourth – scoreless game)
Made up as part of a doubleheader Tuesday, July 23

Saturday, May 18, vs. California
Made up as part of a doubleheader Sunday, May 19

[The reason for the crisscross in makeup dates of the May 17 and May 18 games is that the plan for the May 17 rainout was to make it up when California came back to Minnesota in July; when the May 18 game was also postponed, a double header was scheduled for May 19]

Tuesday, September 17, vs. California
Made up as part of a doubleheader Wednesday, September 18

Other:

Tuesday, September 3
Twins lost 4-1 to Boston in a game called by rain after five innings

Saturday, September 21
Twins beat Oakland 2-1 in a game called by rain after 5½ innings

1969

(2 postponements)

Friday, May 16, vs. Detroit
Made up as part of a doubleheader, Tuesday, July 29

Tuesday, July 15, vs. Chicago, rain and drenched in field after the wind contributed to a rip in the tarpaulin
Made up as part of a doubleheader Wednesday, July 16

1970

(6 postponements and 1 game shortened by rain)

Sunday, April 12, vs. Oakland
Made up Monday, August 10

Monday, April 13, vs. Kansas City, snow
Made up Thursday, May 14

Tuesday, April 14, vs. Kansas City (game was postponed the day before because of a continued bad-weather forecast)
Made up Monday, September 28

Wednesday, May 27, vs. Milwaukee
Made up as part of a doubleheader Monday, September 7

Wednesday, September 9 (second game of double header), vs. Oakland
Made up as part of a doubleheader Thursday, September 10

Monday, September 14, vs. California (rained out in the top of the second with the Twins ahead 4-1)
Made up as part of a day-night doubleheader Tuesday, September 15 (the makeup game was the night game)
Note: A sacrifice fly and run batted in by Brant Alyea were erased because of the rain. It had given Alyea RBIs in 10 straight games. The next day Alyea walked twice and struck out and was removed for a pinch-runner in the sixth inning, stopping his RBI streak at 9 games.

Other:

Wednesday, April 22
Twins beat Chicago 3-1 in a game called by rain after five innings

1971

(5 postponements and 1 game shortened by rain;

MEMORABLE GAMES AT MINNESOTA'S DIAMOND ON THE PRAIRIE

2 games not made up)

Wednesday, April 21, vs. Kansas City, wet grounds
Made up as part of a doubleheader Sunday, July 11

Thursday, June 24, vs. Oakland (called after 2½ innings – game was scoreless)
Made up as part of a doubleheader Friday, September 3
Note: In the top of the third Oakland pitcher Chuck Dobson ripped the lower part of his pants (right leg) stealing second and was later thrown out at home. Dobson repaired the rip with white tape, but Minnesota manager Bill Rigney objected, requiring Dobson to go to the locker room to change pants. Dobson returned, yelled toward the Minnesota dugout, exchanging unfriendly words with Rigney, and started his warm-up pitches for the bottom of the third. After three warm-up pitches, time was called and the game eventually postponed. Dobson fired the ball on one hop into the Twins dugout, nearly hitting pitching coach Marv Grissom and almost setting off a fight.

Saturday, July 10, vs. Kansas City
Made up as part of a doubleheader Sunday, September 19

Thursday, July 29, vs. Washington
Not made up

Wednesday, September 22, vs. Milwaukee
Not made up

Other:

Friday, June 4
Twins lost to Cleveland 4-2 in a game called by rain and threatening tornadoes in the last of the sixth

Notable Delay
Tuesday, August 25, 1970, vs. Boston (delayed in bottom of the fourth for 42 minutes by a bomb threat)

1972

(5 postponements, 1 game shortened by rain, 1 suspended game)

First seven home games wiped out by strike (April 6, 8, 9 vs. California; April 10, 11, 12, 13 vs. Chicago)

Saturday, April 22, vs. Oakland, cold and wet grounds (home opener following strike)
Made up as part of a doubleheader Monday, September 11

Monday, May 29, vs. Kansas City
Made up as part of a doubleheader Thursday, June 29

Monday, June 19, vs. Cleveland
Made up as part of a doubleheader Tuesday, June 20

Friday, August 25, vs. Detroit
Rescheduled as part of a doubleheader Saturday, August 26

Saturday, August 26 (second game of doubleheader), vs. Detroit
Made up as part of a doubleheader Sunday, August 27

Other:

Suspended game: Friday, May 12, Twins and Milwaukee tied after 21 innings when the game was suspended by a 1:00 A.M. curfew; completed Saturday, May 13, with Milwaukee winning 4-3 in 22 innings

Tuesday, June 13
Twins beat Detroit 3-1 in a game called by rain after six innings

1973

(4 postponements and 1 game shortened by rain)

Sunday, April 15, vs. Oakland, rain, wind, and cold (called after Oakland first inning with Oakland ahead 1-0)
Made up as part of a doubleheader Tuesday, September 20

Tuesday, May 1, vs. Cleveland, cold and wet grounds
Made up as part of a doubleheader Thursday, July 12

METROPOLITAN STADIUM

Monday, May 7, vs. New York (rained out with two out in the top of the first – scoreless)
Made up as night game as part of a day-night doubleheader Saturday, July 7
Sunday, May 27, vs. Baltimore
Made up as part of a doubleheader, Tuesday, August 7

Other:

Saturday, May 26
Twins lost to Baltimore 7-2 in a game called by rain and wet grounds after seven innings

1974

(2 postponements, 1 tie game, and 1 game shortened by rain)

Friday, April 12, vs. Kansas City, rain and wet grounds
Made up as part of a doubleheader Saturday, September 14

Saturday, August 3, vs. Oakland
Made up as part of a doubleheader Monday, August 5

Other:

Thursday, April 11, vs. Chicago, tied 4-4 after 6 innings, called by rain and an unplayable field
Tie game replayed as part of a doubleheader Sunday, June 23

Friday, August 2
Twins lost to California 3-2 in a game called by rain and muddy grounds in the top of the seventh

1975

(5 postponements, 1 game shortened by rain, 1 suspended game started elsewhere completed in Minnesota, and 1 game postponed elsewhere replayed in Minnesota)

Thursday, April 17, vs. California
Made up as part of a doubleheader Tuesday, July 1

Wednesday, April 23, vs. Chicago, wet grounds
Made up as part of a doubleheader Saturday, August 2

Sunday, April 27 (doubleheader), vs. Texas
One made up as part of a doubleheader Friday, July 4
One made up as part of a doubleheader Tuesday, September 9

Tuesday, April 29, vs. Oakland, rain, cold, and wet grounds
Made up as part of a doubleheader Tuesday, June 17

Wednesday, April 30, vs. Oakland, wet grounds (light rain fell and the game was postponed at 6:00 P.M.; the rain had stopped by the scheduled start time although the grounds may have been unplayable)
Made up as part of a doubleheader Friday, September 12

Other:

Friday, August 1
Twins lost to Chicago 5-1 in a game called by rain in the last of the sixth

Saturday, July 12, to Saturday, July 19
Twins game in New York July 12 was suspended after 13½ innings and completed in Minnesota July 19 with New York winning 8-7 in 16 innings.

Twins game in New York that was postponed on Sunday, July 13, was made up as part of a double header in Minnesota on Sunday, July 20.

1976

(3 postponements and 1 game shortened by rain)

Sunday, May 2, vs. Milwaukee, snow
Made up as part of a doubleheader Tuesday, August 31

Tuesday, July 27, vs. Texas (called by rain in the top of the third – game was scoreless)
Made up as part of a doubleheader Wednesday, July 28
Note: The game was postponed at 10:15 P.M. At 10:00 Texas pitcher Bert Blyleven called the Minnesota dugout and, pretending to be an official of the Twins, said the game was being post

MEMORABLE GAMES AT MINNESOTA'S DIAMOND ON THE PRAIRIE

poned. The message was relayed to the locker room, and the players began undressing and showering before the game was finally called. (Blyleven later said it was the umpire in chief, Nestor Chylak, he impersonated when making the call to the dugout.)

Monday, September 13, vs. Oakland
Made up as part of a doubleheader Tuesday, September 14

Other:

Thursday, June 17
Twins beat Detroit 4-0 in a game called by rain after five innings
Note: Detroit scored four runs, capped by a two-run home run by Aurelio Rodriguez, to tie the game 4-4 in the top of the sixth. The game was called in the last of the sixth, before Minnesota could complete its at-bats, and the score reverted to the fifth inning, giving Dave Goltz a shutout.

1977

(2 postponements; 1 game not made up)

Thursday, September 1, vs. Oakland
Not made up

Friday, September 23, vs. Milwaukee
Made up as part of a doubleheader Sunday, September 25

1978

(7 postponements)

Tuesday, April 18, vs. Oakland, rain and wet grounds
Made up as part of a doubleheader Friday, August 11

Sunday, April 23, vs. California
Made up Thursday, June 22

Friday, May 12, vs. Boston
Made up as part of a doubleheader Monday, July 24

Friday, May 26, vs. Kansas City
Made up as part of a doubleheader Wednesday, August 16

Saturday, May 27, vs. Kansas City (called by rain with Minnesota leading 1-0 in the top of the third inning)
Made up as part of a doubleheader Friday, September 22

Thursday, June 15, vs. Cleveland
Made up as part of a doubleheader Sunday, September 3

Friday, June 30, vs. Chicago (called by rain in the top of the second inning – game was scoreless)
Made up as part of a doubleheader Sunday, July 2

1979

(6 postponements)

Friday, April 20, vs. Seattle, cold and wet grounds
Made up as part of a doubleheader Tuesday, July 3

Wednesday, May 9, vs. Toronto
Made up as part of a doubleheader Saturday, July 21

Tuesday, May 29, vs. Oakland
Made up as part of a doubleheader Friday, August 10

Saturday, June 16, vs. Baltimore
Made up as part of a doubleheader Monday, August 27

Sunday, August 26, vs. New York
Made up Thursday, September 20

Tuesday, August 28, vs. Baltimore
Made up as part of a doubleheader Wednesday, August 29

1980

(7 postponements with 1 game made up on the road and 1 rain-shortened game)

Sunday, June 1, vs. Baltimore (called by rain after four innings with Baltimore ahead 4-0)
Made up as part of a doubleheader Monday, July 21
Note: Baltimore's Rick Dempsey and Minnesota's John Castino were ejected in the second inning for fighting.

METROPOLITAN STADIUM

Wednesday, June 4, vs. Boston
Made up as part of a doubleheader Friday, July 25

Thursday, June 5, vs. Toronto
Made up as part of a doubleheader Sunday, June 8

Wednesday, June 18, vs. Detroit (called by rain with Minnesota ahead 1-0 in the top of the fourth)
Made up as part of a doubleheader Thursday, August 21
Note: Jerry Koosman of the Twins had retired the first 10 batters of the game when it was called.

Saturday, August 16, vs. California
Made up Monday, August 18

Thursday, September 11, vs. Milwaukee
Rescheduled as part of a doubleheader in Milwaukee Tuesday, September 16; the double header on the 16th was rained out, and the two games were made up as part of doubleheaders Wednesday and Thursday, September 17 and 18.

Saturday, September 20, vs. Chicago
Made up as part of a doubleheader Sunday, September 21

Other:

Wednesday, September 3, vs. Cleveland
Twins lost to Cleveland 7-1 in a game called by rain in the last of the seventh

1981

(0 postponements and 1 tie game)

18 home games canceled by strike

Other:

Wednesday, April 29, vs. Seattle, tied 7-7 in the last of the eighth, called by rain

Made up as part of a doubleheader Friday, August 14
Note: The Twins scored three runs in the last of the eighth to tie the game, 7-7, the tying run scoring on a run-scoring triple by Dave Engle. With the rain falling hard, third-base coach Billy Gardner waved Engle home on the hit, but Engle was thrown out at the plate. The game was then called.
(Tie game occurred during what became the season's first half because of the strike and was rescheduled and made up during what became the season's second half)

REESE PINCH-HIT SLAM ENDS MCNALLY'S STREAK

AUGUST 3, 1969: MINNESOTA TWINS 5, BALTIMORE ORIOLES 2

By Stew Thornley

Rich Reese had a .322 batting average in 1969 for the Minnesota Twins. He was platooned at first base with Harmon Killebrew, who usually moved to third when a left-hander was pitching. With most of his plate appearances (nearly 80 percent) against right-handers that season, Reese figured he wouldn't be in the lineup against Baltimore southpaw Dave McNally on Sunday, August 3. Thus, Reese enjoyed his Saturday night, extending it to 4:00 the next morning as he socialized with Boog Powell and Clay Dalrymple of the Orioles.[1]

The first weekend of August 1969 brought Baltimore to Minnesota for a preview of a likely postseason meeting. Both the Orioles and the Twins led their new divisions and were in line to play in the first league playoff game two months later.

Beyond the excitement of the series, attendance was boosted by the Twins' first annual Camp-in. The idea of Minnesota pitching coach Early Wynn, an avid camper, the event drew thousands of fans from as far away as Florida and California. A section of the Metropolitan Stadium parking lot was filled with campers and recreational vehicles, converted from everything from buses to hearses, and the site of movies, dances, and other entertainment.[2]

In addition, the weekend was to be capped by Dave McNally of the Orioles, who came into August with a record of 15 wins and no losses. Wins and losses by a pitcher are determined by more than just a mound performance, and McNally earned the nickname "McLucky" from his teammates for the times they bailed him out during the year. Seven times McNally had left a game trailing, but the Orioles came back each time to take him off the hook.

Still, McNally had been outstanding. In his previous outing that year in Minnesota, in May, he took a no-hitter into the ninth before Cesar Tovar broke it up. McNally finished with a one-hit shutout for his sixth win of the year. Nine wins later he was back and hoping to become the first American League pitcher to win 18 straight games and the first to win 16 in a row to start the season.

Baltimore and Minnesota split the first two games of the series, and attendance topped 40,000 for the rubber game on Sunday. McNally's pitching opponent was another left-hander, Jim Kaat, who gave up a leadoff single to Don Buford but retired the next three batters in the first. One was Frank Robinson, who looked at a third strike, argued with plate-umpire Frank Umont, and was thrown out of the game. The ejection also brought a quick exit for Orioles

The idea of Minnesota pitching coach Early Wynn, an avid camper, the event drew thousands of fans from as far away as Florida and California.

manager Earl Weaver when he came out to quarrel, the second straight day in which Weaver got run in the first inning.

In the bottom of the inning, the Twins threatened with two out when Harmon Killebrew doubled and Tony Oliva singled. Killebrew tried to score on the play but was gunned down by Baltimore centerfielder Paul Blair. It appeared they might have missed their best shot at McNally, who settled down and did not allow more than one baserunner in an inning over the next five.

Kaat was sharp, too, but Baltimore got to him in the fourth on singles by Merv Rettenmund (Frank Robinson's replacement in right field) and Powell to put runners at the corners with no out. Brooks Robinson grounded into a double play with Rettenmund scoring.

The run held up into the seventh. McNally retired Tony Oliva and Bob Allison on flies to Blair and was down to the bottom part of the order. Leo Cardenas singled off Robinson's glove at third, and Frank Quilici lifted a soft drive over shortstop Mark Belanger to put runners on first and second. Tom Tischinski was scheduled to hit. The third-string catcher was in the game as John Roseboro was getting a rest, and his backup, George Mitterwald, had recently left for two weeks in the Army Reserve.

Manager Billy Martin decided not to give Tischinski a chance at the plate, instead sending up Rick Renick, who drew a walk to load the bases, and Kaat was due up. Martin's choices for another pinch-hitter were all left-handed: Reese, Graig Nettles, and Charlie Manuel. He went with Reese.

The fans cheered expectantly as Reese approached the plate, more loudly when he looked at the first pitch for a ball, and, after a strike, even louder when McNally missed again. A walk would force in the tying run along with bringing leadoff hitter Cesar Tovar to the plate. Reese swung and missed at a pitch and then fouled one off.

The next pitch was inside. "McNally almost nicked me with the next pitch," Reese said after the game. "Actually, I tried to get hit because it would have forced the tying run home."[3]

With the count full, the runners were moving as McNally delivered a fastball on the outer part of the plate. Reese lifted it to left. Buford first started in, then went back as the ball carried, perhaps helped by the wind. It looked as though the drive could be off the fence; instead, it landed three rows into the bleachers for a grand slam. Met Stadium erupted. Some yelled, "15 and 1."[4]

Reese rounded first and didn't see a runner in front of him. At first he feared that in his excitement he had passed Renick before realizing that the runners were going on a 3-2 pitch.[5] When he crossed the plate, the Twins had a 4-1 lead.

Al Worthington relieved Kaat and gave up a homer to Blair to start the eighth. The Twins got the run back in the bottom of the inning on a one-out single by Oliva that scored Rod Carew. That was it for McNally, who walked off the mound to a loud ovation from the Minnesota fans.

When Worthington finished off the Orioles in the ninth, Kaat had his first win since July 17 and McNally his first loss since September 17, 1968.

For Reese, the pinch-hit grand slam was the first of three he hit in his career. He remembers them well, but, more than 45 years after his homer off McNally, some of the details got even better. Rather than recall that ball three almost hit him, as he was quoted in the newspaper, he said the pitch had nicked him. "Frank, that hit me," he said he told Umont, who, according to Reese, growled, "Get back in there." And as Reese finished his circuit, getting a grand slam rather than forcing home only one run by being hit by a pitch, he remembers Umont muttering to him, "You dumb son of a bitch."[6]

Whether the tale was embellished or not, it remains one of the top events in Minnesota Twins history.

SOURCES

In addition to those cited in the notes, the following sources were useful: Retrosheet.org, Baseball-reference.com, and the author's scorebook from the game.

NOTES

1. Author interview with Rich Reese, August 1, 2015.
2. Mike Ponsor, "Ol' Campground at the Ball Park Filling Up Fast," *Minneapolis Tribune*, August 2, 1969: 1.
3. Sid Hartman, "Martin's Strategy a Success," *Minneapolis Tribune*, August 4, 1969: 27.
4. At least one fan yelled "15 and 1," referring to what McNally's record would be if the Twins held the lead. It was the author of this article. Others may have shouted similar sentiments.
5. Dave Mona, "Reese's Homer Stops McNally," *Minneapolis Tribune*, August 4, 1969: 27. The newspaper story quotes Reese as saying, "I couldn't figure out what happened when I was rounding first." In the August 1, 2015 interview with the author, Reese related this with the implication that his confusion was in part because of the fogginess of the late night/early morning while out with Powell and Dalrymple. The reader may enjoy his latter-day recollections (the author certainly did) and come to his or her own conclusions about their veracity.
6. Author interview with Rich Reese, August 1, 2015.

PERRY'S 20TH VICTORY PUSHES TWINS NEARER PENNANT

SEPTEMBER 20, 1969: MINNESOTA TWINS 3, SEATTLE PILOTS 2

By Doug Skipper

Jim Perry set down the final 17 batters he faced to notch his 20th win of the 1969 season, a 3-2 decision over the Seattle Pilots before a Saturday afternoon crowd of 12,797 at Metropolitan Stadium. Perry surrendered just six hits and two walks and struck out eight on the way to his 12th complete-game victory of the season.

Right fielder Tony Oliva stroked a run-scoring double to the gap in left field to drive in second baseman Rod Carew with the winning run in the bottom of the ninth inning and secure the win for Perry, who improved to 20-6 with the win for the American League West-leading Twins.

Jim Perry was credited with his 20th win of the season when Tony Oliva drove in the winning run in the last of the ninth.

It took the 6-foot-4 right-hander a few innings to settle in. Perry surrendered singles to second baseman John Donaldson and right fielder Steve Whitaker leading off the first inning but struck out the next three hitters to end the threat. Perry fanned left fielder Danny Walton to record the 1,000th strikeout of his career,[1] caught center fielder Steve Hovley looking, and set first baseman Greg Goossen down swinging.

In the second inning, Perry walked Pilots catcher Jerry McNertney to start the frame and surrendered a two-run home run to third baseman John Kennedy. Trailing 2-0 with no one out, Perry walked shortstop Ron Clark, and Twins manager Billy Martin trotted out to the mound. "He told me that I wasn't throwing the way I was when I won the first 19," Perry told *Minneapolis Tribune* sportswriter Dave Mona. "But he told me to settle down because he knew I was going to win 20."[2]

Mona wrote, "Martin has said all year that one of Perry's greatest assets is that he listens to advice,"[3] and, after Martin's mound visit, Perry escaped further damage when he induced a force out and converted a comebacker into an inning-ending double play.[4]

He allowed only three more hits – a single by Whitaker in the third and singles by McNertney and Kennedy in the fourth. After that, he retired 17 straight batters.

While Perry was rounding into form in the early innings, Pilots right-hander Gene Brabender, at 6-feet-5½ a bit taller than Perry,[5] kept the Twins off the scoreboard for six innings.

Brabender retired the side in order in the first, stranded two runners after two-out singles by center fielder Cesar Tovar and catcher John Roseboro in the second, and marooned two more in the third after a bunt single by left fielder Ted Uhlaender and Carew's single to center.

Brabender managed to escape another jam in the fifth. With the Twins trailing 2-0, Uhlaender stroked a one-out single to left and Carew walked, but Seattle first baseman Greg Goosen snared Oliva's liner and doubled Carew off first to end the inning. Brabender walked third baseman Harmon Killebrew, who became the 1969 AL Most Valuable Player, to open the sixth inning, and one out later Tovar singled to left. But Brabender escaped again and still led 2-0 after stranding eight baserunners through six innings.

The Twins finally cashed in in the seventh. After Perry grounded out, Uhlaender scorched a triple into the right-field corner, his third hit of the day, and Carew drove him home with a single to right field. Oliva followed with a single to right, and with runners on first and third and one out, Pilots manager Joe Schultz summoned righty Diego Segui to the mound. Segui struck out Killebrew, but first baseman Rich Reese, "performing with the same calm that has characterized his performance all year, slapped a Segui pitch to left center to tie the game and moved Oliva to third," Mona recounted in the next day's *Minneapolis Tribune*.[6]

In Mona's words, Tovar then "laid down a perfect bunt toward third as Oliva raced for the plate," but Kennedy "fielded the ball on the dead run and underhanded a perfect throw to catcher Gerry McNertney an instant before Oliva reached the plate."[7]

Mona reported that "Tovar's bunt was ruled to have been so well placed that he was credited for the third hit of a perfect afternoon."[8] However, the scoring decision was later reversed; the hit was changed to a fielder's choice, and Tovar was credited with two hits instead of three, and the Twins for 12 instead of 13.[9]

After Perry set down the Pilots in order in the top of the eighth, Roseboro drew a walk when he was awarded an automatic ball four by second-base umpire Jake O'Donnell, who ruled that Segui had taken more than 20 seconds between pitches. Schultz objected when O'Donnell invoked the infrequently called rule, and was ejected by home-plate umpire Jerry Neudecker for arguing. The controversial call came to nothing however, when Herman Hill, running for Roseboro, was gunned down by McNertney when he tried to steal second.

At the time, Perry was at bat. Martin had let his starting pitcher hit for himself for the fourth time. "Martin, in a show of confidence, kept his bullpen inactive most of the game and let Perry hit for himself in the third, fifth, and seventh innings despite the deficit," Mona wrote.[10] After he struck out to end the eighth inning, Perry returned to the mound for the ninth, and was perfect for the fifth straight frame. He induced Hovley to ground out, struck out Goossen, and retired McNertney on a fly to left.

The Twins made sure that Perry would not be needed for another inning. With one out, Carew singled to left field. It was his third hit in the day, ending a 4-for-31 slump over his previous nine games.

"Carew, who studied video tapes of his batting style the last several days, apparently found the answer to his problems," Mona wrote. "He said he found that he had been hitting out of too much of a crouch and taking his eyes off the ball just before the swing."[11]

"The flaws were eliminated yesterday as he had three hits to raise his batting average four points to .334 and virtually cinch the American League batting title. He needs only 32 appearances in the final 11 games to qualify."[12]

"After [Carew] singled to left with one out in the ninth, Perry, sitting next to John Roseboro on the Twins bench, pointed at a hole in left-center and predicted that the game would end if Oliva could hit a ball in that direction," Mona wrote.[13]

Perry was prophetic. Oliva followed with his league-leading 38th two-bagger of the year, a liner over Clark's head at shortstop that darted through the gap between Walton in left and Hovley in center, and Carew scampered around the bases with the winning run.[14]

"I saw the ball go over the shortstop's head and I just knew it was through," Perry said. "I was pushing Rod around the bases."[15]

Mona wrote that "Carew, running at top speed, nearly ran into Perry who raised his arms as he led the Twins' cheering section from the dugout."[16]

With the win, Perry improved to 20-6, his final ledger for the season. He made three more starts without a decision. Segui was tagged with the loss to fall to 11-6. The setback was the 93rd for the Pilots in 152 games. The expansion franchise finished the season 64-98, in last place in the six-team American League West, and was moved to Milwaukee before the 1970 campaign.[17]

The Twins improved to 91-60 under Martin and moved closer to the first-ever AL West Division title.[18] After they lost the series finale to the Pilots the next day, the Twins clinched the division title with a win Monday in Kansas City.[19] They finished the season with a 97-65 record under the fiery Martin but were swept in three games in the first American League Championship Series by the Baltimore Orioles, despite fine pitching performances from Perry and Dave Boswell, who had secured his 20th win eight days after Perry.

In spite of the postseason loss, the 1969 season represented a remarkable turnaround for the Twins, who had finished seventh in the 10-team American League in 1968 with a 79-83 record under manager Cal Ermer.

Martin inserted Perry into the rotation and left him there for the entire season.[20] He called on Perry as a starter 36 times in 1969 (he also relieved 10 times), and the veteran right-hander rewarded his new manager's confidence when he posted a 20-6 record with a 2.82 earned-run average. He became the sixth pitcher to win 20 games for the Twins since the team moved to Minnesota in 1961.[21]

Perry, who spent four years with Cleveland and was Martin's teammate there as a rookie in 1959, was traded to Minnesota during the 1963 season.[22] He never started more than 25 games for Sam Mele (Minnesota's manager from 1961 to 1967) or for Ermer (who took over the Twins during the 1967 season). Perry started just 18 times in 1968, posting an 8-6 record and a 2.27 ERA in 139 innings.

"Perry just fell on evil ways with the Twins," former Cleveland general manager Frank "Trader" Lane told *Minneapolis Star* sportswriter Mike Lamey before Perry's start against Baltimore in the 1969 ALCS. "Sam Mele apparently wasn't high on him. He wasn't used for a while and lost his sharpness. But look at him now."[23]

Perry said he had prepared for his role in the rotation. "Two weeks before the season started this year, I went over to the Decathlon Club at 7 A.M. and worked out. I think that helped me to report in good shape." Mona suggested that reporting in good shape was "something that immediately distinguished him from his pitching teammates."[24]

Despite his preparation for the season, Perry had earned just two more wins than losses by the Fourth of July, when Minnesota started the day in second place in the AL West with a 43-34 record. The Twins earned an Independence Day victory to pull into a tie with division-leading Oakland behind Ray Miller, and moved into first place when Perry defeated the Athletics 13-1 on July 5. Minnesota cruised to the AL West flag by winning 54 of its final 85 games. Perry won 12 of his final 14 decisions, a key reason for Minnesota's mid-season turnaround.[25]

"Perry laughed when he was asked what he would have thought if someone had predicted he would win 20 games back on July 4 when he was 6-4. "I guess I would have said that man was a fool."[26]

After his 20th win, Perry told Mona that he would "like to think" that he would be considered a full-time member of the starting rotation when the Twins reported to Orlando, Florida, for spring training in February 1970.[27]

He was in the rotation, but it wasn't for Martin. A week after the season ended, Twins owner Calvin Griffith fired the fiery manager. While winning the AL West in his first season as a major-league manager, Martin battled with the Twins front office, publicly criticized the franchise's farm system, brawled with Boswell outside a bar in Detroit, and panned several of his players in conversations with the press.[28]

Twins fans were outraged and some staged protests,[29] but Griffith stuck by his decision, one that disappointed Carew and Perry. "He gave me a chance to pitch," Perry said. "I know some players didn't like the ways things were handled, but you can't satisfy 25 players."[30]

Having proved himself under Martin in 1969, Perry performed spectacularly in 1970 for new manager Bill Rigney. He led the league with 24 wins, earned the AL Cy Young Award, and pitched in the All-Star Game. He won 30 more games over the next two seasons before moving on to Detroit (where he was briefly reunited with Martin), Cleveland, and Oakland to close out his career. Perry finished with a lifetime record of 215-174 and a 3.45 ERA. He and his brother Gaylord Perry, a 1991 Baseball Hall of Fame inductee, combined to post 529 career victories, second most by any brother combination in major league history.[31]

SOURCES

In addition to the sources cited in the Notes, the author accessed Retrosheet.org, Baseball-Almanac.com, Baseball-Reference.com, SABR.org, FanGraphs.com, and *The Sporting News* archive via Paper of Record, as well as the following articles on the SABR BioProject website for background information:

Bjorkman, Peter C. "Tony Oliva," sabr.org/bioproj/person/tony-oliva/

Keenan Jimmy, and Frank Russo. "Billy Martin," sabr.org/bioproj/person/billy-martin/

Wancho, Joseph. "Jim Perry," sabr.org/?posts_per_page=10&s=jim+perry

Wancho, Joseph. "Rod Carew," sabr.org/bioproj/person/rod-carew/

NOTES

1. Dave Mona, "Perry Takes 20th; Twins Nip Seattle 3-2," *Minneapolis Tribune*, September 21, 1969: 1S; "Major Flashes, American League, Milestone for Perry," *The Sporting News*, October 4, 1969: 22.
2. Mona: 1S.
3. Mona: 1S.

METROPOLITAN STADIUM

4   According to baseball-reference.com, the Twins finished 1969 with 177 double plays, one short of league-leading Boston

5   According to baseball-reference.com, Perry was 6-feet-4.

6   Mona: 5S.

7   Mona: 5S.

8   Mona: 5S.

9   "A change in the scoring of Sunday's [*sic*] game has taken a base hit away from Tovar. The play called a fielder's choice instead on a play in which a man was thrown out at the plate …" "Twins," *Minneapolis Tribune*, September 23, 1969: 40.

10 Mona: 1, 5S.

11 Mona: 5S.

12 Mona: 5S. Carew finished the season with a .332 average and won the first of his seven AL batting titles.

13 Mona: 5S.

14 Oliva finished the season with 101 runs batted in and an AL-leading 39 doubles.

15 Mona: 5S.

16 Mona: 5S.

17 Pitcher Jim Bouton Manager Joe Schultz was a frequent target of Bouton's humorous diary entries, and several of the players in the September 20 game, including Brabender and Hovley, were portrayed. However, Bouton had been traded to the Houston Astros on August 24, and his late-season diary entries took aim at the Astros organization. Jim Bouton and Leonard Shecter, ed., *Ball Four, My Life and Hard Times Throwing the Knuckleball in the Big Leagues*, (New York: World Publishing Company, 1970).

18 The American and National Leagues had both added two teams and split into six-team East and West Divisions for the 1969 season. The Seattle Pilots and Kansas City Royals were the franchises added to the AL.

19 Mike Lamey, "'Bubbly' Iced, but untasted," *Minneapolis Star*, September 22, 1969: 1A. According to Lamey, Twins equipment manager Ray Crump hauled four cases of champagne that had been set aside but never used for a pennant-clinching ceremony in 1967, from storage, and brought the bubbly to Kansas City for the 1969 celebration.

20 Dave Mona, "July 4: When Flag-Waving Twins Ignited the Fireworks," *Minneapolis Tribune*, September 23, 1969: 39.

21 "Perry Becomes Sixth 20-Gamer for Twins," *Minneapolis Tribune*, September 21, 1969: 5S.

22 Mike Lamey, "Perry Investment Pays Off," *Minneapolis Star*, October 3, 1969: 9B. The Twins acquired Perry for pitcher Jack Kralick and an estimated $100,000 cash on May 2, 1963. Lane was Cleveland's general manager from 1958 to 1960 when Perry joined the club; Gabe Paul was the general manager who traded Perry to Minnesota.

23 Lamey, "Perry Investment Pays Off," *Minneapolis Star*, October 3, 1969: 9B.

24 Mona, "Perry Takes 20th; Twins Nip Seattle 3-2": 5S.

25 Mona, "July 4: When Flag-Waving Twins Ignited the Fireworks."

26 Mona, "Perry Takes 20th": 5S.

27 Mona, "Perry Takes 20th": 5S.

28 Mike Lamey, "Billy Martin Fired," *Minneapolis Star*, October 13, 1969: 1.

29 Max Nichols, "'Bring Martin Back,' Chant Furious Twins' Fans," *The Sporting News*, November 1, 1969: 15.

30 "Carew Hits Dismissal," *The Sporting News*, November 1, 1969: 15.

31 Joe and Phil Niekro won 539, 10 more than the Perry brothers. Greg and Mike Maddux are a distant third at 394.

KILLEBREW'S PERFECT DAY NOT ENOUGH TO BEAT PILOTS AND CLINCH DIVISION TITLE

SEPTEMBER 21, 1969: SEATTLE PILOTS 4, MINNESOTA TWINS 3

By Mike Lynch

The champagne was on ice while 15,443 waited to erupt after their Minnesota Twins defeated a Seattle Pilots team they had already beaten 11 times in 14 games, including eight of eight at Metropolitan Stadium. At 91-60 with an 11-game lead over the second-place Oakland A's, the Twins saw that the clinching of the first-ever American League West Division title was merely a formality.[1]

Seattle was an expansion team made up of castoffs led by manager Joe Shultz and made famous, or infamous, by pitcher Jim Bouton's seminal book Ball Four, which chronicled the former All-Star's time with a woeful Pilots team that finished their only season in Seattle in last place in the AL West at 64-98 and 33 games behind the Twins.[2]

The Pilots offense boasted former Twins first baseman Don Mincher, who helped Minnesota win a pennant in 1965. Mincher was pacing the Pilots with 23 homers and earned a spot on the AL All-Star team as a replacement for teammate Mike Hegan, who was battling a muscle pull. Third baseman Tommy Harper had a league-best 71 steals and a clear path to a stolen-base crown.[3]

Minnesota Twins

Met Stadium was used for football although as the Twins played at home September 21, 1969, the Minnesota Vikings were opening their regular season with a loss to the Giants in New York.

METROPOLITAN STADIUM

The Twins were well-rounded and led on offense by Harmon Killebrew, Rod Carew, Tony Oliva, and Rich Reese. Killebrew went into the game leading the league with 134 runs batted in and 136 walks, and his 44 homers were just behind sluggers Frank Howard and Reggie Jackson, who had 46 apiece. Carew was leading the AL in hitting at .334, Oliva's 185 hits and 38 doubles were both league bests, and Reese was hitting .321 with a .512 slugging percentage.

Minnesota manager Billy Martin sent Dean Chance to the mound to face career minor leaguer Bob Meyer. Chance had been one of the best pitchers in baseball from his first full season in 1962 to 1968, when he won 110 games and posted a 2.72 earned-run average, both of which were seventh best in all of baseball.[4] He was the AL's best pitcher in 1964 and easily won the Cy Young Award, and though limited by a frozen shoulder that kept him out of action in June and July, he was pitching to a 2.95 ERA in 14 starts heading into the September 21 contest.[5]

Meyer, a 30-year-old southpaw, was making only his fifth start of the season for Seattle after spending most of the year with the Iowa Oaks of the Triple-A American Association. Meyer was 8-11 with a 4.00 ERA in 27 games with the Oaks that capped off a nine-year minor-league career in which he went 62-80 with a 3.92 ERA in 225 games.[6] Despite a less than impressive résumé that included three losses in four starts since joining Seattle in late August, Meyer had a respectable 3.04 ERA.

Harper led off with a single to center, then stole second. Steve Whitaker flied to left but Danny Walton's bunt to third went for an infield single and the Pilots had runners on first and second (Harper didn't advance on the single) with Steve Hovley at the plate. Hovley was slugging only .379 with 3 homers and 18 RBIs in 80 games, so Harper and Walton took off on a double steal and made it safely, putting both in scoring position with only one out.[7] However, Hovley lined to shortstop Leo Cardenas, who snared the liner and stepped on second base for an inning-ending double play.

Meyer began the bottom of the first by getting Cesar Tovar on a grounder to short and striking out Carew, but made a mistake when he knocked Killebrew off the plate with a high and inside fastball. Meyer followed with a strike that Killebrew belted into the left-field seats to stake the Twins to a 1-0 lead. Oliva flied to right to end the inning.

Chance and Meyer traded goose eggs in the second and third innings. Chance fanned Mincher and got catcher Jerry McNertney to pop to short and John Donaldson to ground to third. Meyer struck out Bob Allison and got Rick Renick on a foul pop to first before George Mitterwald singled to left. McNertney picked off the Twins catcher and the game went to the third.

Chance had an easy time in the top of the third, retiring John Kennedy on a grounder to third, Meyer on a bouncer to first, and Harper on a fly to center. Meyer also retired the side in order on Cardenas's fly to center, Chance's strikeout, and Tovar's fly to right. The Pilots scored twice in the top of the fourth to go up 2-1. Walton followed Whitaker's strikeout with a walk and went to second on Hovley's single to right. Mincher walked to load the bases and Walton scored on McNertney's grounder to shortstop that forced Mincher at second. Donaldson singled up the middle to plate Hovley, then stole second, but Kennedy struck out looking to end the threat.

Minnesota tied the game in the bottom of the inning when Killebrew followed another Carew strikeout with his second homer of the game, a shot that cleared the left-field wall by 40 feet. Meyer kept the score at 2-2 by coaxing Oliva to ground to short and fanning Allison for the second time in as many at-bats.

Harper singled off Chance with one out in the fifth, but that was the righty's only blemish as Meyer popped to first, and Whitaker and Walton grounded to second and third, respectively. Meyer allowed another single to Mitterwald in the bottom of the inning, but Cardenas grounded to short and the Pilots turned an inning-ending double play.

Seattle took a 3-2 lead in the top of the sixth with help from the Twins. Hovley led off with a single to left and went to third on Mincher's single to right. McNertney grounded to third. Hovley took off for home and Renick fired to the plate. Hovley reversed course and Mitterwald tagged him out as he ran him back toward third, then tagged out Mincher, who was trying to advance on the play. Suddenly the Pilots had a runner on first with two outs and the light-hitting Donaldson at the plate.[8]

Donaldson bunted to third for a hit and McNertney scored when Renick threw past Killebrew at first for an error. Kennedy grounded to third to end the inning and the Twins wasted little time tying the game at 3-3 in their half.

Career pinch-hitter Frank Kostro led off the bottom of the sixth in place of Chance and struck out looking.[9] Meyer hit Tovar with a pitch and the Twins' center fielder took the game into his own hands by stealing second and third with Carew at the plate. Carew singled to right to drive Tovar home with the tying run and Killebrew recorded his third hit of the game, a single to left that sent Carew to second. Oliva struck out and McNertney gunned down Carew attempting to steal third on the third strike, and the game went to the seventh knotted at 3-3.

Lefty starter Jim Kaat took the mound for Minnesota for his seventh relief appearance of the season and retired the side in order, getting Greg Goossen, hitting for Meyer, on a fly to left, Harper on a lineout to first, and Whitaker on a grounder to second.[10] Bob Locker, acquired from the Chicago White Sox for pitcher Gary Bell on June 8, entered the game for the Pilots boasting a 2.19 ERA in 46 games since joining the team.

Locker retired pinch-hitter Ted Uhlaender, batting for Allison, on a grounder to second and Reese, hitting for Renick, on a grounder to first before surrendering Mitterwald's third single of the game with two outs. Cardenas fanned to end the bottom of the seventh.

In the top of the eighth, Reese went to first base, Killebrew moved to third, and Uhlaender took over in left. Kaat made quick work of Seattle, wrapping strikeouts of Walton and Mincher around a Hovley grounder to short.

The Twins had a chance to take the lead in the bottom of the eighth when Kaat led off with a single and went to third when Mincher made an error on Tovar's bunt. With runners at first and third and no outs, Schultz called on lanky southpaw John O'Donoghue. Carew grounded to second and was thrown out at first, but Tovar advanced to give Minnesota two runners in scoring position with one out. O'Donoghue walked Killebrew intentionally to load the bases and the move paid off when Oliva tapped back to the mound for an inning-ending double play, pitcher-to-catcher-to-first.

In the top of the ninth, Kaat quickly dispatched McNertney on a popup to first and Donaldson on a grounder to first that Reese fielded and threw to Kaat for the out. "But Seattle shortstop John Kennedy refused to follow the script and set upon a new personal frontier as a power hitter," wrote Dave Mona in the *Minneapolis Tribune*.[11]

Kennedy hit a fly ball that just cleared the left-field wall to give Seattle a 4-3 lead. It was his fourth and last homer of the season. Kaat fanned O'Donghue to end the inning, but the Missouri native evened his record at 2-2 when Uhlaender grounded back to him, Reese grounded to first, and Mitterwald flied to right to end the game.

SOURCES

In addition to the sources cited in the Notes, the author accessed Retrosheet.org, Baseball-Reference.com, and SABR.org.

NOTES

1. Prior to 1969, the American and National Leagues had no divisions and the teams that finished in first place in each league won the pennant and faced off in the World Series.

2. The Pilots moved to Milwaukee in 1970 and became the Brewers, but Bouton didn't go with them because he'd been traded to the Houston Astros on August 24, 1969, for pitchers Roric Harrison and Dooley Womack.

3. Harper easily led the American League in stolen bases with 73. Oakland's Bert Campaneris finished second with 62.

4. I used a minimum of 1,150 innings, which is slightly higher than the minimum of 1,134 for qualifiers (7 seasons x 162 games per season).

5. The Cy Young Award was still being given to only one pitcher in 1964 regardless of league, and Chance earned 17 votes, finishing ahead of Chicago Cubs pitcher Larry Jackson (2 votes), and Los Angeles Dodgers ace Sandy Koufax (1). Frozen shoulder, also known as adhesive capsulitis, is a "painful condition in which the shoulder becomes stiff and inflamed, and movement becomes limited." my.clevelandclinic.org/health/diseases/15359-frozen-shoulder.

6. Meyer had a brief stint with the Brewers after the Pilots moved to Milwaukee in 1970, but lasted only 10 games before calling it a career.

7. Seattle's success rate through Game 152 on September 20, 1969, was 74.7 percent on 160 steals in 214 attempts. They ended the season with 167 steals in 226 attempts and a 73.9 percent success rate.

8. Going into the game, Donaldson was hitting .237 and slugging .290, and the run he drove in in the fourth inning was only his 19th RBI in 317 at-bats.

9. Kostro's strikeout came in his last major-league at-bat. He played parts of seven seasons in the majors, appeared in 266 games, and 153 of those appearances came as a pinch-hitter. He had 192 plate appearances in 53 games as a third baseman.

10. Kaat had started 286 of his first 316 career appearances (90.5 percent) from 1959 to 1968, and 316 of 352 (89.8 percent) from 1959 to September 17, 1969, his last appearance before the September 21 game.

11. Dave Mona, "Seattle Rally Stalls Twins 4-3," *Minneapolis Tribune*, September 22, 1969: 37.

OCTOBER 6, 1969: TWINS PLAY FIRST PLAYOFF GAME IN METROPOLITAN STADIUM

BALTIMORE ORIOLES 11, MINNESOTA TWINS 2

By Thomas J. Brown Jr.

The Minnesota Twins returned home with their backs to the wall. They lost the first two games of the first American League Championship Series to the Baltimore Orioles. Both games had gone into extra innings.

The Twins had the lead in the first game until the ninth when the Orioles tied the score. Baltimore eventually won it on Paul Blair's single in the bottom of the 12th. The two teams battled to a scoreless tie through 10 innings in the second game before Baltimore scored the winning run in the 11th off Ron Perranoski, the loser of the first game.

Twins manager Billy Martin chose Bob Miller to start when the two teams took the field at Metropolitan Stadium. Miller had finished the season with a 5-5 record. He had been used as a starter and reliever all season.

Billy Martin's last game as manager of the Twins was the final game of the American League playoffs in 1969.

Many fans wondered why Martin was using righthander trailing two games to none "instead of the gutty competitor Jim Kaat."[1] Martin responded to his critics, saying, "I don't think that it reflects anything on any of our other pitchers. Let's just say that Miller is a low-ball pitcher and the Orioles are a good high-ball-hitting club."[2]

Prior to the 1969 season, Miller had contemplated retiring. "I talked to Billy. He told me to come on down to Orlando [the Twins' spring-training home]. That he was going to use me."[3] Miller responded with a fine season in the majors as Martin used him in crucial situations.

Miller started shakily. He surrendered consecutive singles to Don Buford and Blair in the first inning. He rebounded to get a force out and double play, preventing any Baltimore baserunners from crossing the plate.

The Twins gave their fans hope that they would make a comeback when they scored off Baltimore starter Jim Palmer in the bottom of the first. Palmer got the first two batters to ground out before giving up a double to Tony Oliva. Oliva reached third on a wild pitch and scored on Rich Reese's single to give the Twins a 1-0 lead.

When Miller took the mound in the second, he struggled again. Brooks Robinson led off with a double. Robinson reached third when Oliva slipped and then dropped Davey Johnson's pop fly.

Oliva was playing injured. He had hurt his throwing arm in the final play of second game as he tried to keep Boog Powell from scoring. Martin had considered keeping him out of the game but Oliva had insisted on playing.

"I couldn't throw the ball. I couldn't lift my arm high enough to swing the bat. I couldn't throw the ball two feet. But I insisted that Billy play me because this was such an important game," he said afterward.[4]

With runners on first and third, Elrod Hendricks doubled to center field. Hendricks reached third when Cesar Tovar tried to throw out Johnson at home. After Miller got the next two batters out on fly balls, Buford singled to score Hendricks, giving Baltimore a 3-1 lead.

Martin replaced Miller with Dick Woodson, who struck out Blair to end the inning. It was the only time all afternoon that Blair failed to connect for a hit.

As the Orioles took the field in the bottom half of the inning, Orioles manager Earl Weaver filed a protest with home-plate umpire Frank Umont. Weaver claimed the Twins were "cheating" by placing a man in the outfield scoreboard to call the pitches.[5]

"We had Curt Motton in our dugout with field glasses. Motton observed that there was a head bobbing out there [in a hole in the scoreboard]. The man had his arms up high when the pitch was a curveball and down low when it was a fastball," said Weaver.[6]

His protest was denied. Umont told Weaver that the man was working and could stay out there if he wanted. Weaver later noted that after the protest "the man in the scoreboard disappeared."[7]

The Twins were robbed of a scoring chance in the bottom of the third when Buford made a spectacular backhanded catch on Carew's drive to left. The play seemed to give Palmer and the Orioles a lift.

Baltimore built on its lead in the fourth. Light-hitting Mark Belanger led off with a triple. Woodson walked Buford. Blair then doubled and both baserunners scored. Frank Robinson walked, finishing Woodson. Tom Hall retired the next two batters but the Orioles now led by four runs, 5-1.

Blair had made some adjustments at the plate after struggling at the end of the season. Hitting coach Charlie Lau sat him down and reviewed films before the game. "They showed that I had been taking a lot longer stride recently. I just took a shorter stride and started hitting again," Blair said.[8]

A triple by Leo Cardenas in the Twins' fourth went for naught, but Minnesota notched its second tally in the bottom of the fifth. Harmon Killebrew doubled to center field with two outs. He came home when Reese hit his second single of the game.

Baltimore's advantage swelled to four runs in the sixth. Buford doubled off Al Worthington, the fourth Twins pitcher of the game. Buford moved to third on Blair's second single and scored when Frank Robinson followed with a single that made the score 6-2 and chased Worthington from the game.

Buford had also spent time with Lau watching game films and it was paying off. "The first two games they pitched me inside – jammed me with hard pitches," he said. "Basically what I did was move away from the plate more and concentrate so that those inside pitches looked like they were over the plate."[9]

After a single by Cardenas in the sixth, Palmer shut down the Twins for the next 2⅔ innings. Although it was not Palmer's best performance, he didn't need to worry. Every one of his teammates got in the act as the Orioles notched 18 hits with Blair and Buford accounting for half of them.

Blair led with the way with five hits, the fourth coming in the eighth when he homered off Dean Chance. Chance, a former 20-game winner, had been scratched from a starting role because of an injury. He pitched a faultless seventh before Blair homered behind a Buford single. The home run expanded the Orioles' lead to six runs at 8-2.

Martin sent Perranoski to the mound in the ninth after Chance gave a leadoff hit to Johnson. Perranoski was the seventh Twins pitcher. While the left-hander had been the anchor of the Twins bullpen that year, finishing with 31 saves and a 2.11 earned-run average, he had failed to shut down Baltimore in the previous two games.

Hendricks lined a pitch down the line past first that looked like an apparent double. Johnson scored. Oliva ran the ball down and threw it to Carew. His throw bounced past Carew and Reese, the first baseman, had to run out to right field to retrieve it. The error allowed Hendricks to circle the bases and score the Orioles' 10th run.

The fans at Metropolitan Stadium began booing. The Twins had not made any announcement about Oliva's injury so fans were frustrated with their team's play. Oliva expressed his disappointment with the fans, saying "This is the first time this happened to me. Why they do this to me? I play good all year – and then this."[10]

After surrendering a single to Belanger, Perranoski got the next two outs. Blair now strode to the plate and hit a line drive down the right-field line. Oliva seemed reluctant to catch the ball and Blair ended up on second with his second double and fifth hit of the game.

With the score now 11-2, the Twins were down to their final three outs. Palmer gave up a single to John Roseboro before striking out Cardenas. Pinch-hitter

Graig Nettles singled, giving fans one last bit of hope that their team might make a comeback.

But Palmer got the next two batters out. The win sent the Orioles to the World Series. Palmer, who earned the complete-game victory, said afterward, "I struggled and didn't have good rhythm. But after the fifth inning I got my rhythm and was able to pop the ball. The big lead didn't hurt me either."[11]

The Twins finished with 10 hits, three more than their total in the first two games. But "they played with the unaccustomed attitude of the underdog."[12] It was a disappointing finish to their season.

As the team looked forward to 1970, the biggest question was whether Martin would return as their manager. He had fought with management over his combative and outspoken managing style. When asked what the Twins needed next season, Martin said, "A new manager."[13]

SOURCES

In addition to the sources cited in the Notes, I used the Baseball-Reference.com and Retrosheet.org websites for box-score, player, team, and season pages, pitching and batting game logs, and other pertinent material.

baseball-reference.com/boxes/MIN/MIN196910060.shtml

retrosheet.org/boxesetc/1969/B10060MIN1969.htm

NOTES

1 Tom Briere, "Martin Stands Firm Against Second Guess," *Minneapolis Tribune*, October 7, 1969: 24.

2 Dave Mona, "Miller Pitches for Twins Life," *Minneapolis Tribune*, October 6, 1969: 36.

3 Mona, "Miller Pitches for Twins Life."

4 Sid Hartman column, *Minneapolis Tribune*, October 7, 1969: 24.

5 Tom Briere, "Twins Were Spying," *Minneapolis Tribune*, October 7, 1969: 24.

6 Briere, "Twins Were Spying."

7 Briere, "Twins Were Spying."

8 Jim Elliot, "Films Held Secret for Blair, Buford," *Baltimore Sun*, October 7, 1969: C1.

9 Elliot.

10 "Booing at Met Hurts Oliva," *Minneapolis Star*, October 7, 1969: 48.

11 Hartman.

12 Dave Mona, "Baltimore Blasts Twins Hopes 11-2," *Minneapolis Star Tribune*, October 7, 1969: 24.

13 Tom Briere, "Martin Stands Firm Against Second Guess," *Minneapolis Tribune,* October 7, 1969: 24.

EARL WILSON NEARLY ACHIEVES A "LITTLE LEAGUE HOME RUN" AFTER STRIKING OUT

APRIL 25, 1970: MINNESOTA TWINS 4, DETROIT TIGERS 3

By Chad Moody

A key cog in Detroit's starting rotation since the mid-1960s, Tigers pitcher Earl Wilson headed into the 1970 campaign having posted the fourth-most wins among all American League hurlers since 1962 – including a league-leading 22 victories in 1967. Additionally, the big right-hander could provide rare offensive punch from his position. Frequently used as a pinch-runner and pinch-hitter, Wilson ranks among the best-hitting pitchers of all time in tallying 35 home runs and 7.3 offensive wins above replacement during his career.[1] During a 2019 discussion with the slugging pitcher's former rotation mate, Denny McLain, sportscaster Bob Page said succinctly when reflecting on Wilson's success with the bat: "He was awesome!"[2] While facing the Minnesota Twins on the afternoon of April 25, 1970, however, it was Wilson's failure with the bat that set in motion one of the strangest plays in major-league history.

The American League East-leading Tigers, celebrating the anniversary of their 70th season as an American League team, brought an eight-game winning streak into Metropolitan Stadium to face the Twins, who themselves were only a half-game back in the AL West. Played in front of 11,095 spectators, the game featured a fine pitching matchup with Wilson squaring off against ace Minnesota left-hander Jim Kaat.

The contest got off to a slow start, with neither team able to cross home plate heading into the fourth inning. Wilson had allowed only one Twin to reach base. Kaat, on the other hand, had survived constant trouble by forcing Detroit into inning-ending double plays in each of the first three innings.

After Kaat was able to set the Tigers down in order to begin the fourth, Minnesota broke through against Wilson in the bottom of the inning with two solo home runs to nearly the same spot down the right-field line off the bats of Tony Oliva and Rich Reese.[3] Things settled down again in the fifth, with neither team mustering a serious scoring threat. Leading off the top of the sixth, Mickey Stanley got the Tigers on the scoreboard when he slugged one of Kaat's offerings into the left-field seats to cut Minnesota's lead to 2-1. Although Kaat allowed two more baserunners in the inning, he escaped without further damage. Wilson retired the side in order in the bottom of the inning to hold the Twins to their precarious one-run lead heading into the seventh.

The top of the seventh began uneventfully, with Kaat retiring the first two Tigers batters on groundouts. Wilson was the next to step into the batter's box. The hurler had doubled earlier in the game, but this time he swung and missed at strike three. With the inning seemingly over, Twins catcher Paul Ratliff innocuously rolled the ball back to the mound as he and his teammates exited the field. Even the television network broadcasting the game cut away to commercials, leaving viewers unaware of the chaos that was about to ensue.[4]

As it turned out, Ratliff did not cleanly catch strike three; he trapped the ball in the dirt, allowing the batter by rule to run for first base. "I didn't know you had to tag the runner in that case," admitted the Twins' rookie backstop.[5] Although first-base umpire Marty Springstead signaled the correct call, only Tigers third-base coach Grover Resinger apparently noticed. "Resinger saw Springstead give the safe sign," said third-base umpire Larry Napp. "He told Wilson to stay put and let the Twins get off the field. It was a smart play on his part."[6] Indeed, most of Minnesota's players were already in their dugout when Resinger vociferously instructed Wilson to run. The 6-foot-3,

216-pound pitcher was already past first base and advancing to second before Twins left fielder Brant Alyea alertly realized what was happening. Located near first base on his way in from the outfield, Alyea took action. "I saw him going to second so I tried to scoop up the ball and head him off at third," he said. "But when I went to scoop it up, I missed it."[7] This miscue allowed Wilson to chug around third base and head for home at the urging of a frantic Resinger. By this time, however, Alyea was able to backtrack to the loose ball and throw it to shortstop Leo Cardenas, who had converged upon home plate along with a "reception party" of Twins players.[8] Now caught in a pickle, the "exhausted, bewildered" Wilson attempted to retreat to third base but was tagged out by Alyea, who had taken the return throw from Cardenas.[9] "There were a lot of people standing around home plate – I saw one Twin player there but I thought he was a coach," said Wilson. "I was halfway home before I realized he wasn't and by then I was trapped."[10] Once the dust settled on the play, an error was charged to Ratliff and an improbable K767 (dropped third strike with the putout from the left fielder to the shortstop to the left fielder) was recorded in the scorebooks.

The weird play – called by Twins manager Bill Rigney "one of the daffiest" he had ever seen –resulted in some serious implications for the rest of the game.[11] Rigney protested the fact that Resinger had entered the field during the play without penalty to cheer Wilson on. "I wanted to find out what Resinger is doing on the field," the Twins manager said. "He was out on the mound. I wanted to know why Wilson wasn't out just because Resinger is interfering."[12] Home-plate umpire John Rice acknowledged that Resinger was indeed on the field – but not near the mound. "The rule says a coach cannot physically assist a player," Rice explained. "Resinger was not physically assisting Wilson."[13] Although Minnesota was unharmed on the scoreboard by the crazy play, "several minutes of explanations, discussions, and arguments" resulted in the ejection of Twins veteran reserve slugger Bob Allison.[14] Most importantly, however, Wilson – who had allowed only three hits in six innings – was also lost due to a pulled hamstring in his left leg that he suffered while rounding the bases.

Reliever Tom Timmerman replaced the injured Wilson in the bottom of the seventh and set down the Twins in order, while Kaat likewise shut down the Tigers 1-2-3 in the top of the eighth. Leading off the bottom of the eighth for the Twins, Ratliff doubled and Frank Quilici singled. This set the table for Kaat, who helped his own cause with a sacrifice fly to center, scoring Ratliff and providing Minnesota with a much-needed insurance run heading into the final stanza.

With Detroit now trailing 3-1 in the top of the ninth, heavy-hitting Willie Horton offered a glimmer of hope with his leadoff single. Two batters later, Jim Northrup drove him in with a triple that got past center fielder Cesar Tovar, who failed in his attempt to make a shoestring catch. "I always catch that kind of ball, but I know now I should have played it safe," admitted Tovar.[15] With one out and the tying run on third, both teams made strategic changes. Right-handed Twins reliever Stan Williams was brought in to face right-hander Elliott Maddox. Detroit countered by swapping Maddox for dangerous left-handed pinch-hitter Norm Cash, who promptly tied the game at 3-3 with a sacrifice fly scoring Northrup. Williams then ended the inning on Cesar Gutierrez's groundout.

Timmerman remained on the mound to face the Twins in the bottom of the ninth and retired the first batter, Cardenas, on a groundout. Oliva followed with a single and went to second when the normally sure-handed right fielder Al Kaline misplayed the ball. "The grass is new in right field," Oliva said of the poor turf conditions. "I knew that Al Kaline would have trouble handling the groundball I hit to him."[16] With a runner in scoring position and pull-hitting right-hander Harmon Killebrew coming to the plate, the Detroit infield employed the "Killebrew Shift."[17] The defensive strategy backfired, however, as the Twins slugger bounced a single – "like it had radar to guide it" – in the hole between first and second that scored Oliva to give Minnesota a 4-3 walk-off victory.[18] "That doesn't happen much more often than a batter striking out and finally being tagged out at third," quipped sportswriter Jon Roe of Killebrew's unlikely opposite-field hit.[19]

The lingering buzz from the near "Little League Home Run" largely overshadowed the Twins' victory and left Wilson still baffled after the game. "I don't know what happened," he admitted of his extra-base strikeout.[20] "I've never seen one like this, never been involved in one where a guy is running around the bases after the inning is over," said Alyea, whose delinquency in returning to the dugout helped him make the putout on Wilson – and made him fodder for wisecracks.[21] "If Alyea had been hustling, Earl might have made it," joked Tigers catcher Bill Freehan. "Tell him to start coming in and off the field a little quicker."[22]

MEMORABLE GAMES AT MINNESOTA'S DIAMOND ON THE PRAIRIE

SOURCES

The author accessed Baseball-Reference.com (baseball-reference.com/boxes/MIN/MIN197004250.shtml) for box scores/play-by-play information and other data as well as Retrosheet (retrosheet.org/boxesetc/1970/B04250MIN1970.htm). In addition to the sources cited in the Notes, the author also accessed GenealogyBank.com; NewspaperArchive.com; Newspapers.com; and Paper of Record.

NOTES

1. Wilson's home runs and wins above replacement (WAR) reflect those he achieved as a pitcher, pinch-hitter, and pinch-runner. His WAR uses the Baseball-Reference calculation methodology.
2. Bob Page, "Episode 80: Ty Cobb to Denny and HIS Generation: You Guys Suck!" *No Filter Sports with Eli Zaret, Denny McLain & Bob Page (Red Shovel Network)*, podcast audio, nofiltersportspodcast.com/2019/10/14/episode-80-ty-cobb-to-denny-and-his-generation-you-guys-suck/, October 14, 2019.
3. Jon Roe, "Twins Win 4-3 in Ninth," *Minneapolis Tribune*, April 26, 1970: 5I.
4. Dave Wright, *162-0: Imagine a Twins Perfect Season* (Chicago: Triumph Books, 2010): 32.
5. Mike Lamey, "Wilson Gets Three Bases on Whiff," *The Sporting News*, May 9, 1970: 25.
6. "Out Is an Out Is Finally an Out," *Minneapolis Tribune*, April 26, 1970: 1S.
7. "Out Is an Out Is Finally an Out."
8. Lamey.
9. Jim Hawkins, "Tiger Win Streak Ends at 8," *Detroit Free Press*, April 26, 1970: 1D.
10. Jim Hawkins, "'Grover Said Run, So I Ran' – Wilson," *Detroit Free Press*, April 26, 1970: 1D.
11. Associated Press, "Tiger Win Streak Snapped at Eight," *Times Herald* (Port Huron, Michigan), April 26, 1970: 1D.
12. "Out Is an Out Is Finally an Out," *Minneapolis Tribune*, April 26, 1970: 10S.
13. "Out Is an Out Is Finally an Out."
14. Hawkins, "Tiger Win Streak Ends at 8."
15. Roe.
16. Sid Hartman, "Sid Hartman," *Minneapolis Tribune*, April 26, 1970: 3S.
17. Roe.
18. Hawkins, "Tiger Win Streak Ends at 8."
19. Roe.
20. Lamey.
21. Associated Press, "Tiger Win Streak Snapped at Eight."
22. Lamey.

WILLIAMS AND QUILICI PICK OFF A WIN VERSUS CLEVELAND

APRIL 29, 1970: MINNESOTA TWINS 1, CLEVELAND INDIANS 0

By Tom Hawthorn

Stan Williams, a veteran right-hander, stood atop the mound at Metropolitan Stadium in the top of the ninth inning of a 1-0 game with runners at first and second and two out. At the plate stood pinch-hitter Vada Pinson, a dangerous batter and a new arrival in his first month with the Cleveland Indians after spending 12 seasons in the National League. Pinson was leading his teammates early in the season with a .352 batting average.

Pinson fouled off the first pitch. As Williams circled behind the mound rubbing a new ball, he shouted at second baseman Frank Quilici. "I yelled his name," Williams said, "and I whistled at him."

Later, the infielder shared what Williams had to say. "Stan yelled at me to be sure to knock down any groundball that came my way and keep it in front of me," Quilici said. "It's something a pitcher always says when the tying or winning run is on second base."

The pitcher also flashed a sign. "I thought it was the perfect situation to try our pickoff play," Williams said. "I thought everybody would be thinking about something else after the foul ball."[1]

The new ball rubbed and nestled in his glove, Williams looked toward the plate to get the sign from the catcher.

Less than two hours earlier, Jim Kaat threw the opening pitch on a warm Wednesday afternoon in Minneapolis. A strong wind blew in from right field at 24 to 36 miles per hour, the tail end of the previous day's storm. The wind promised to be a pitcher's helper, knocking down fly balls hammered to right.

Kaat cruised through the first inning, inducing three groundballs. In the second, he struck out the first two batters he faced, surrendered a double to Ray Fosse, then ended the inning with a third strikeout.

The top of the third inning was notable for three stellar defensive plays. Kaat himself knocked down Jack Heidemann's smash through the pitching box, pouncing on the slowly rolling ball behind the mound before wheeling to whip a strong underhanded throw to first. On opposing pitcher Rich Hand's short blooper beyond the infield, Quilici raced with his back to the plate to snag the ball. The inning ended when Quilici dived to grab Ted Uhlaender's hard drive toward right field, recovering from his dirt-eating snag to make the throw.

"It is just a do-or-die play," said Quilici, a utility infielder who started only because Rod Carew was nursing a rib injury. "Any time you can knock the ball down at second base you have a chance to throw the runner out."[2]

In the bottom of the inning, the Twins managed to score a run against the rookie Cleveland starter. Leo Cardenas singled and was forced at second by Tony Oliva, who then went to second on Harmon Killebrew's single. Rich Reese's spinning grounder befuddled Graig Nettles at third base. Oliva managed to race home to score an unearned run on the error. Hand halted the damage by inducing Brant Alyea to hit a routine groundball to second.

Kaat cruised through the fourth with a fly out and a pair of groundouts. In the fifth, Kaat got another groundball out before Fosse singled for his second hit and went to second on Eddie Leon's single. Heidemann then dropped a hit down the right-field line for Cleveland's third successive single. Oliva raced toward the line, fielding the ball on the hop before making a strong throw to Paul Ratliff at the plate to cut down Fosse for the inning's second out, preserving the lead. Fosse went flying in the collision, while Ratliff kept his feet. (Fosse would also be sent flying in a more memorable home-plate collision later in the season. He was infamously knocked down and injured by Pete Rose in the final play of the 1970 All-Star Game.) With runners on first and third, Kaat got yet another infield groundball, as Heidemann was forced, shortstop to second, to end the threat.

In the sixth, Kaat got groundball outs from shortstop to first and first unassisted before Ted Ford singled to left. The inning ended on yet another groundout, third to first.

The gusty wind led to a controversial play in the home half of the sixth. With one out, Reese drove a Hand pitch high and deep to right that seemed likely to go over the fence. Instead, the winds blew the ball back toward the field and Ford made a dive for the ball as it fell to the ground. "I caught it in the webbing," said Ford,[3] who got the start because Pinson was nursing a muscle strain in his leg. The scoreboard operator thought the ball had bounced out of the glove, as did Minnesota's first-base coach Vern Morgan, but second-base umpire George Maloney, in his sophomore American League season and working his 101st game, ruled the play a catch and Reese out. Morgan and Twins manager Bill Rigney argued their case with predictable results. The umpire told Rigney the ball never left Ford's glove. Replied Rigney, "Then there's got to be two of 'em, because I saw one movin' around out there."[4]

Kaat got three more groundouts in the seventh – third to first, short to first, third to first. He also had a one-two-three eighth with a flyout to right, a groundout third to first, and a called strike three on Uhlaender.

For the ninth, Rigney replaced Killebrew, who had six assists at third on the day, with Minnie Mendoza, a Cuban known for his fielding. Kaat was within an out of victory after getting Nettles to fly to center and striking out Ford. But then Tony Horton slashed a double to left and Roy Foster walked. Rigney dismissed Kaat in favor of the 6-foot-5, 230-pound Williams, the former Cleveland hurler, who was 2-0 and had yet to give up an earned run over 8⅔ innings in seven appearances.

Meanwhile, Cleveland manager Alvin Dark replaced Fosse with Pinson, who fouled off the reliever's first pitch.

As Williams prepared to throw his second pitch, Horton took a lead off second as Quilici snuck to the base. Williams spun, throwing to second as a desperate Horton dived for the bag. Umpire Maloney raised a right fist, ending the game.

"I tagged his hand," Quilici said. "I thought it was close enough to be called either way. It was just boom-boom that fast and just one of those things."[5]

Horton, who insisted the tag got him on the bicep, not the hand, rose from the dirt to argue with the umpire, who once again rejected the appeal on his original verdict.

"I didn't think I was out," Horton said. "I wouldn't have argued so much if I thought I was. It was a close play and it was my fault for making it so close."[6]

Cleveland's manager was forgiving in the wake of losing a 1-0 road game on a pickoff play. "This club is going to beat a lot of teams this season," Dark said. "Sure, they're going to make mistakes – a good player makes mistakes because he's trying to win any way he can. But you've got to go along with them when they hustle and that's what they're doing."[7]

It was a tough loss for the rookie Hand, who took his third defeat against no wins despite giving up just six hits and one walk over seven innings.

"I lost, so I didn't pitch well enough to win," Hand said. "That's life. The first win is always the toughest."[8] (The rookie would not get his first win until June 7, on a day he gave up three home runs, as Cleveland defeated the California Angels 6-4 in Anaheim.)

The game, which lasted 1 hour, 58 minutes, was seen by just 4,241 fans, among them Jackie Dark, the Cleveland manager's new bride, who spent her honeymoon touring American League cities. Wearing a floppy white hat, she sat in a box seat at Metropolitan Stadium alongside Cleveland owner Vern Stouffer and club President Gabe Paul.

After the game, Quilici explained his role on the Twins, where he was accustomed to giving Killebrew a

Bob Allison

late-inning respite at third. "You have to be a different breed to be a utilityman," he said. "You can't show you are envious of anyone, or say, 'Hey, I can do it better.' It happens to be a job I enjoy. I get the same satisfaction a coach gets when he watches his players execute well."9

Minnesota's manager had nothing but praise for his utilityman. "That Italian fellow may not have all the ability in the world, but he sure is inside the game all the time," Rigney said. "He's been making the double play for us and today he makes two super plays. He might make a good manager for somebody."10

Rigney added Quilici to his coaching staff the following season. After Rigney was fired midway through the 1972 season, Quilici, 33, was promoted to manager. Quilici had a 280-287 record as Twins manager before being replaced in 1975 by Gene Mauch. He was later a commentator on Twins radio broadcasts.

The 1-0 victory improved Kaat's record to 3-1. He gave up six hits, walked one, and struck out five. He limited Cleveland batters to just three fly-ball outs, while inducing 16 groundball outs.

"The only time I was in real trouble was when Oliva made that throw to home," Kaat said. "But anytime you're in a 1-0 game, you're in serious trouble as long as you're on the mound."11

In the Minnesota clubhouse, outfielder Bob Allison and pitcher Dave Boswell teased reporters for ignoring the starting pitcher in favor of talking to the reliever.

"Over here," Allison called out to the reporters. "This guy," he said, pointing to Kaat, "threw more than 100 pitches. He [indicating Williams] threw just one."

The reliever wished to correct the record.

"I threw two strikes," Williams insisted. "One each way."12

SOURCES

retrosheet.org/boxesetc/1970/B04290MIN1970.htm

baseball-reference.com/boxes/MIN/MIN197004290.shtml

Briere, Tom. "Mgr. Dark's Mgr. Is a Baseball Fan," *Minneapolis Tribune,* April 30, 1970: 30.

"Frank Quilici, Former Twins Player, Manager, Broadcaster, Dead at 79," *Minneapolis Star-Tribune,* May 16, 2018, *startribune*.com/frank-quilici-former-twins-player-manager-broadcaster-dead-at-79/482616621, accessed December 14, 2019.

NOTES

1 Jon Roe, "Twins' Kaat, Williams Halt Indians 1-0," *Minneapolis Tribune,* April 30, 1970: 29.

2 Mike Lamey, "'Caddy' Quilici Star Again,'" *Minneapolis Star,* April 30, 1970: 53.

3 Sheldon Ocker, "3 Glaring Mistakes Cost Tribe," *Akron (Ohio) Beacon Journal,* April 30, 1970: 56.

4 Ocker.

5 Ocker.

6 Ocker.

7 Ocker.

8 Ocker.

9 Lamey.

10 Roe.

11 United Press International, "Kaat Stops Indians 1-0," *St. Cloud* (Minnesota) *Times,* April 30, 1970: 28.

12 "Williams Pitched One Ball but 'Two Strikes,'" *Minneapolis Star,* April 30, 1970: 57.

BOMB THREAT PROVIDES EXTRA EXCITEMENT IN TWINS-RED SOX GAME

AUGUST 25, 1970: BOSTON RED SOX 1, MINNESOTA TWINS 0

By Stew Thornley

The 1970 Boston Red Sox had a trio of avid anglers—Reggie Smith, Carl Yastrzemski, and Gary Peters—who carried fishing tackle on road trips. An August swing through Minnesota gave the trio a chance to relax on a lake in Spicer, about 100 miles from Bloomington, Minnesota, where they would start a three-game series against the Twins the following night.[1]

It was an escape from baseball—the Red Sox were hopelessly out of the race for the American League East title—as well as from world events. That morning a bomb at the University of Wisconsin killed a graduate student, part of ongoing protests against the Vietnam War.

Minnesota had already experienced its own spate of bombings in the past week. One blast injured a woman at the Dayton's department store in St. Paul, and the Old Federal Building in Minneapolis had a bomb go off at 3 in the morning. The latter caused no injuries, but it set off a flurry of bomb threats to police departments and businesses,[2] and the events would intrude upon the Twins-Red Sox game on Tuesday, August 25.

The game started at 8:00 P.M., and starters Vicente Romo for Boston and Bill Zepp for Minnesota pitched scoreless ball into the bottom of the fourth.

With two outs, Tony Oliva on first base for Minnesota, and a 2-and-1 count on Rich Reese, first-base umpire Nestor Chylak ran in, waving his arms to stop play. The Longines clock atop the scoreboard showed the time as 9:15.

Fans wondered why Chylak called time and quickly found out as public-address announcer Bob Casey announced: "We have been informed an explosion will occur at 9:30. We ask you to please leave the stadium in an orderly fashion. There is plenty of time and no need to panic. If you will please leave the stadium, we will resume the game when possible."[3]

Someone had called the Bloomington police at 8:30 and said a bomb would explode at 9:30. The call was traced to a phone booth on the first deck of Metropolitan Stadium. Police and Twins officials began searching the stadium and made the decision to stop the game at 9:15 and clear people out.

The crowd of slightly fewer than 18,000 began heading toward the parking lot. The players went onto the field, presumably a safe place from an explosion.

At least one player opted for the parking lot, Bill Zepp. Zepp, in an interview 40 years later with Twins historian John Swol, said he recalled seeing owner Calvin Griffith in the dugout. "This was unheard of," Zepp said, adding that Griffith began talking to manager Bill Rigney. He soon understood the reason when the announcement were made. Rather than join the other players on the field, Zepp waited out the delay in

Fans wait out the bomb-threat delay on the field.

his car. "I didn't run but I walked briskly to get a dry shirt and go to the parking lot," he said.[4]

For some reason, ushers opened a gate by the Twins' first-base dugout and directed fans onto the field to join the players. The Twins later said that had been a mistake, but the result was that 1,000 or so fans, as well as vendors, got to mingle with the players during the delay.[5]

The atmosphere was so festive that many forgot the reason they were out there. One person shouted, "Hey, it's 9:30," causing people to look at the clock but not go into the fetal position many had learned in elementary-school air-raid drills during the height of the Cold War over the past decade.

Vendors hawked their wares the same as they did in the stands. One beer vendor set up shop on first base, quickly sold out, and lamented that he hadn't had the chance to get a couple more cases before the delay.

At 9:45 the all-clear was given, and fans were allowed back in the stands. Many who had gone to the parking lot had already departed, but the game resumed a few minutes before 10:00.

The 30-minute delay didn't affect Zepp, but Romo stiffened up a bit. He finished out the fourth inning with no damage. He was scheduled to lead off in the top of the fifth and came out to the on-deck circle. However, the trainer came out to talk to him, and manager Eddie Kasko decided to take him out. The fans, recognizing what had happened, gave Romo an ovation as he walked back to the dugout.

Zepp made it through seven innings before giving way to lefty Tom Hall, who retired the first two Red Sox in the eighth. Then the blast came—not an actual bomb but one off the bat of Tony Conigliaro that landed in the left-field bleachers to give Boston a 1-0 lead.

Ken Brett, who had relieved Romo, carried the shutout into the bottom of the ninth but gave way to right-hander Gary Wagner after a leadoff single by Tony Oliva. Harmon Killebrew hit a long drive to center. Reggie Smith caught it right in front of the 430-foot sign, a little to the left of straightaway center, and heaved a throw in. It was too late to get Oliva, who had tagged and advanced to second; it also caused Smith to come out of the game as he injured his arm making the throw.

Rich Reese walked to put runners on first and second, and pinch-hitter Jim Holt hit a hard grounder to second. Mike Andrews fumbled the ball, but recovered and threw to Rico Petrocelli to force Reese. With no chance to double up Holt at first, Petrocelli instead wheeled and fired to George Scott at third. Oliva had rounded the base and slipped; he was trapped and run down between third and home to end the game.

The loss was the third in a row for the Twins, continuing an August swoon that included a nine-game losing streak earlier in the month and was eroding their chances for a second straight division title. Minnesota's closest challenger at the time, the California Angels, had won in extra innings in Detroit to pull within 3½ games of first place. However, the Twins recovered and won the division easily, by nine games over Oakland.

The game also featured three of the league leaders in batting average—Oliva, Yastrzemski, and Smith (Luis Aparicio of Chicago was the other). Yaz and Smith were hitless, and Oliva's two hits put him and Yastrzemski atop the leaders at .321.

However, Oliva's gaffe to end the game loomed larger than his hits, and the bizarre event in the fourth inning dominated all the news coverage of the game.

Said Bill Rigney, "I've seen games rained out and postponed by power failures, but I've never been bombed out."[6]

The next night a copycat tried for a similar disruption at Sec Taylor Stadium in Des Moines, Iowa, calling before an American Association game between Indianapolis and Iowa and reporting that a bomb would go off at 8:15. Iowa owner Ray Johnson said, "The bomb threat was from a young boy. He phoned to say the bomb had been placed during the afternoon. But we had lots of personnel here all day, and no strangers had entered the park." Police and team personnel searched the stadium and decided not to evacuate the fans.[7]

Six years later—the Vietnam War over and a different mood prevailing in the country—another bomb threat was called in to Met Stadium. It happened during a game between the Angels and Twins on Saturday, September 26, 1976. This time the caller couldn't even get the satisfaction of clearing the stands and delaying the game; fans were told of the bomb threat and given the option of staying or leaving as the game continued.[8]

SOURCES

The sources cited in the Notes are supplemented by memories of the author, who was on the field during the delay, and the author's scorebook, which now contains autographs of Sonny Siebert, Mike Nagy, Carl Yastrzemski, Frank Quilici, and Rich Reese. The author also shook hands with Reggie Smith during the delay and was concerned that he squeezed too hard and later caused the injury that forced Smith out of the game. In addition to the sources cited in the Notes, the author also used the Baseball-Reference.com and Retrosheet.org websites.

MEMORABLE GAMES AT MINNESOTA'S DIAMOND ON THE PRAIRIE

NOTES

1. "Bosox Stars Take a Day Off" (Photo by Ron Schara), *Minneapolis Tribune*, August 26, 1970: 23; Ron Schara, "Walleyes Turn Backs on Yaz, Smith, Peters," *Minneapolis Tribune*, August 26, 1970: 27. The photo and story appeared in the Wednesday, August 26 *Tribune*, the morning after the game with the bomb threat. However, it is likely the photo was taken on Monday, August 24. Green Lake in Spicer is more than 100 miles from the Twin Cities, and the players probably would not have gone that far with a game that night. Boston had played Sunday afternoon in Kansas City and probably flew directly to Minneapolis, leaving a day off Monday that would have allowed enough time for a fishing trip that far from the Twin Cities.

2. "Bomb Threats Empty Buildings," *Minneapolis Star*, August 26, 1970: 4A.

3. Bob Fowler and Bob Whereatt, "In 4th Inning, Twins, Sox, Fans 'Bombed' Out at Met," *St. Paul Pioneer Press*, August 28, 1970: 1.

4. John Swol interview with Bill Zepp, June 2010, http://twinstrivia.com/interview-archives/bill-zepp-interview.

5. The number of fans who joined the players on the field was listed as anywhere from 1,000 to 4,000 depending on the news story.

6. Fowler and Whereatt, "In 4th Inning."

7. "Homers Only 'Bombs' in Stadium; Oaks Win," *The Sporting News*, September 12, 1970: 28.

8. Tom Briere, "Twins, Goltz Score 6-0 Win Over Angels" *Minneapolis Tribune*, September 26, 1976: 1C.

ROYALS' SIX-RUN NINTH INNING RUINS PERRY'S CHANCE FOR A 25-WIN SEASON

SEPTEMBER 29, 1970: KANSAS CITY ROYALS 14, MINNESOTA TWINS 13 (12 INNINGS)

By Bob Webster

Minnesota Twins manager Bill Rigney had a plan for the game on Tuesday against the Kansas City Royals. With three games to go in the regular season and the American League West title already clinched, Rigney wanted to get his players ready for the playoff opener Saturday against the AL East champion Baltimore Orioles.

His plan worked . . . for eight innings. "Head football coaches have game plans," said Rigney, "I had a game plan. Jim Perry was going to pitch five innings, Stan Williams three, and Ron Perranoski one. The game plan backed up a little bit."[1]

Perry was going for his 25th win of the season. He left the game with a 9-5 lead after five innings, and although he gave up five runs (four earned) on nine hits, his offense had given him the runs needed to qualify for the win. Williams did his part by pitching his three innings and surrendering only two hits. Perranoski came in, but couldn't put the Royals away, and with the help of two errors by Cesar Tovar, the Royals scored six runs in the ninth inning to give them an 11-9 lead. What was left of the 5,473 people in attendance had just witnessed the beginning of the wildness, which was capped when the tiebreaking run was driven home in the 12th inning by a Kansas City relief pitcher batting .125.

Amos Otis led off the game by lining out to Twins shortstop Leo Cardenas. George Spriggs singled, and Perry retired Lou Piniella and Ed Kirkpatrick to retire the side.

The Twins jumped all over Paul Splittorff, who relieved starter Al Fitzmorris before the latter even threw a pitch. Fitzmorris came up with a sore shoulder while warming up. Against Splittorff, Tovar walked, then came singles by Cardenas, Tony Oliva, and Harmon Killebrew. Cardenas and Tovar scored on Killebrew's hit. Splittorf grabbed Jim Holt's comebacker and started a 1-6-3 double play, then struck out Brant Alyea to limit the damage to two runs.

Bob Oliver led off the top of the second by hitting a single to left, but Perry retired Cookie Rojas, Bobby Floyd, and Tommy Matchick on fly balls to keep the Royals scoreless.

In the bottom of the second, George Mitterwald singled to center. Danny Thompson grounded into a 1-6 fielder's choice, retiring Mitterwald at second. Perry struck out. Tovar singled, Cardenas walked to load the bases, and Tony Oliva's single drove in Tovar, chasing Splittorff. Reliever Dave Morehead retired Killebrew, but the Royals were now down 4-0 after two innings.

The pitcher's spot was scheduled to lead off the top of the third, and Morehead stepped into the batter's box and struck out. Amos Otis followed with a double to left field. Pat Kelly ran for Otis and stayed there as Spriggs struck out and Piniella grounded to second. Kelly stayed in the game to play center.

Jim Holt led off the bottom of the third with a base hit to center but was erased when Alyea grounded to short for a 6-4-3 double play. Mitterwald walked, stole second, and scored on Danny Thompson's single to center. Perry singled to left and Tovar walked, filling the bases. Morehead got Tovar to ground out to second to again stop a big inning, but the Twins led 5-0 after three innings.

Kirkpatrick grounded out shortstop to lead off the Royals fourth and probably felt bad later when he discovered that of the first seven batters of the inning, he was the only one who did not hit a single. After Kirkpatrick's out, Oliver, Rojas, Floyd, Matchick, Billy Sorrell (pinch-hitting for Morehead), and Kelly all singled before Kelly was picked off first and

Spriggs grounded out to end the inning. The Royals scored five runs on six hits to tie the game, 5-5.

The Twins regained the lead in the bottom of the inning on a two-out, two-run double by Mitterwald. Perry faced the Royals' 3-4-5 hitters in the top of the fifth and retired them one-two-three.

Perry finished his five innings as planned, and Bob Allison batted for him to start the Twins' fifth. Allison reached second on an error by Kelly in center field. Two batters later, Cardenas singled in Allison. Oliva singled, and, with Ken Wright now pitching for the Royals, Killebrew reached on another error by Kelly in center with Cardenas scoring the second unearned run of the inning and giving the Twins a 9-5 lead.

Stan Williams pitched the next three innings, surrendering two singles. For the Royals, Wright pitched the sixth inning and Jim York pitched the seventh and eighth. They held the Twins to one hit in their 3⅔ innings on the mound.

After eight innings the Twins led 9-5 with their closer, Ron Perranoski, coming in to preserve Perry's 25th win of the season.

The Royals had other thoughts. Rojas and Floyd both singled to begin the top of the ninth. Matchick grounded out to first, moving the runners up. Sorrell singled to right, scoring Rojas and Floyd and cutting the Twins lead to 9-7. Jackie Hernandez, pinch-hitting for Kelly, singled to center. Rich Severson grounded into a fielder's choice with Sorrell taking third. Piniella grounded to Tovar at third, but he booted the ball. Sorrell scored and Severson took second. Kirkpatrick doubled to center, scoring Severson and Piniella, and Kirkpatrick took third on the throw home. Third baseman Tovar bobbled Oliver's grounder and Kirkpatrick scored. Rojas grounded out to end the inning, in which the Royals scored six runs to take an 11-9 lead.

Ted Abernathy came in with the save opportunity for the Royals in the bottom of the ninth. Carew struck out but Rich Reese walked. Frank Quilici ran for Reese. Paul Ratliff, pinch-hitting for Steve Brye, singled to right. Herman Hill ran for Ratliff. Tovar struck out, but Cardenas singled to center, scoring Quilici, and Charlie Manuel, pinch-hitting for Bill Zepp, singled to right to drive in Hill and tie the game, 11-11. Killebrew struck out to send the game into extra innings.

Both teams were scoreless in the 10th, then the Royals scored twice in the top of the 11th. Ellie Rodriguez walked and was sacrificed to second by Abernathy. Piniella singled Rodriguez home. Piniella stole second and took third on a bad throw by catcher Rick Dempsey. Kirkpatrick singled, driving in Piniella, giving the Royals a 13-11 lead.

With Abernathy still on the mound for the Royals in the bottom of the 11th, Quilici lined out to second. Cotton Nash walked. Tovar doubled to right, then Cardenas singled to center, scoring the two runners and tying the game again. It was Cardenas's fifth hit of the game. Manuel struck out looking and Jim Kaat, batting for Steve Barber, lined out to right.

Pete Hamm, relieving for the Twins, walked Floyd to lead off the 12th. With one out, Sorrell singled to right. Rodriguez popped out to first for the second out. With no position players left on the Royals bench, manager Bob Lemon let pitcher Abernathy bat, and he responded with a single to right, scoring Floyd and giving the Royals a 14-13 lead. Piniella flied out to end the inning.

After Jim Holt hit a leadoff single in the bottom of the 12th, Abernathy retired the Twins to preserve the victory.

The game lasted 4 hours and 5 minutes and set a major-league record by using 49 players, beating the old record by one. Of the 49 players in the game, 27 were Twins.[2] The two teams had 40 hits, 36 singles and four doubles.

"I didn't have any extras left," said Lemon. "All I had was starting pitchers. If Abernathy had given up one more hit, he would have been out of there."[3]

"It seems like quite a while since we've gotten a lot of runs," Rigney had said the day before after the Twins beat the Royals 1-0.[4]

The Baltimore Orioles, the Twins' playoff opponent beginning four days after this game, did not gain an advantage by Rigney's use of five relievers. The Orioles also had a long day, playing a doubleheader with both games going extra innings.

SOURCES

baseball-reference.com/boxes/MIN/MIN197009290.shtml

retrosheet.org/boxesetc/1970/B09290MIN1970.htm

NOTES

1. "Royals Foil Rigney's Game Plan," *St. Louis Post-Dispatch*, September 30, 1970: 23.
2. "Royals Foil Rigney's Game Plan."
3. "Royals Foil Rigney's Game Plan."
4. Dick Couch (Associated Press), "Twins Lose in 12th on Hit by Pitcher," *Kane* (Pennsylvania) *Republican*, September 30, 1970: 5.

SLAM, ERRORS GIVE ORIOLES PLAYOFF OPENER

OCTOBER 3, 1970: BALTIMORE ORIOLES 10, MINNESOTA TWINS 6

By Stew Thornley

The opening game of the 1970 American League playoffs[1] featured a pair of 24-game winners: Baltimore's Mike Cuellar, who had tied with Denny McLain for the Cy Young Award the year before, and Minnesota's Jim Perry, who would be the American League recipient in 1970.[2]

A 23-mile-per-hour wind blew out of the northwest at Minnesota's Metropolitan Stadium, and it may have affected both pitchers. Orioles manager Earl Weaver said, "The elements made it hard to get a grip on the ball."[3]

The Twins scored in the first on a single by Harmon Killebrew, but Paul Blair prevented further damage by tracking down a "savage liner"[4] to center by Tony Oliva. The Orioles loaded the bases with one out in the second; it looked like Perry might escape any damage when he got Mark Belanger to hit a grounder to shortstop Leo Cardenas. However, second baseman Danny Thompson skipped the relay to first in the dirt, allowing two runs to score. Cuellar followed with a popup in foul territory. Killebrew, playing third base, battled the wind and dropped the ball for an error. Cuellar struck out to end the inning, although it was an indication of how the wind was influencing the game.

Minnesota tied the game on a run-scoring groundout by Perry in the bottom of the second, but Baltimore got the lead back in the fourth on a sacrifice fly by Brooks Robinson and was threatening to get more. With two on and one out, Belanger hit a comebacker to Perry, another potential double-play grounder. Perry couldn't field the ball cleanly, though, and Belanger had an infield hit to load the bases.

Cuellar stepped in and hit a high fly down the right-field line that was clearly foul. Oliva ran over, in case it stayed in play. It didn't. Not only did the ball clear the short fence of the grandstand, the wind pushed it back to fair territory, and it landed with a resounding clunk on the metal decking just to the left of the foul pole. It took the stunned crowd, and the players, a moment to process that Cuellar had just hit a grand slam.

Cuellar had first stood at the plate and watched. He then started jogging in tandem with the drift of the ball toward fair territory. The runners had initially held up, and the foursome, bunched up, resembled a slow train in moving around the bases within the silent stadium.[5]

The carnage didn't stop. Don Buford pulled a home run to right. After a pitching change and strikeout, Boog Powell delivered a long home run to left-center to complete the seven-run inning.

The Twins got a run back in the fourth. Then Killebrew started the fifth with a home run to center measured at 437 feet,[6] and George Mitterwald delivered a two-run single with one out. Weaver came out to remove Cuellar, Dick Hall entered, and the tall reliever quickly ended the rally by getting Thompson to ground into a double play. "Hall, you hacker," one fan yelled as Hall trudged to the dugout.[7]

Fresh off the mound, Hall led off the top of the sixth with a single to left field and later scored on a single by Powell to increase the Baltimore lead to 10-6.

Hall allowed only one baserunner, a one-out single by Oliva in the seventh, but he was saved by another outstanding catch by Blair on the next batter, Brant Alyea, who hit a long drive to center. Blair got turned around as he raced back, but he was able to get his glove on the ball and flick it into the air. Still on the move as he approached the fence, Blair tried again and this time was able to corral the ball in his glove.

Minnesota manager Bill Rigney came out to argue that Blair had caught the ball off the fence, but Twins players and coaches in the right-center-field bullpen signaled to him that Blair had made the catch cleanly. Rigney threw up his arms as he saw the Twins' chance of a comeback evaporate.

MEMORABLE GAMES AT MINNESOTA'S DIAMOND ON THE PRAIRIE

"I turned to the right on the ball," said Blair of the catch. "When I looked over my left shoulder the ball was carrying more to right center. I finally caught up with it on the warning track. It hit the heel of my glove, popped up in the air, and I grabbed it again with my glove about a yard from the fence."[8]

Blair said the catch wasn't as difficult as the one he made in the first on Oliva's drive. "The first catch was the tougher," he explained, "because it was hit right at me and that's the toughest kind."[9]

After the 10-6 Baltimore win, Rigney dissected the missed plays by the Twins. Thompson had been playing shortstop for Evansville in the American Association when the Twins called him up after second baseman Rod Carew was injured. Playing out of position, Thompson never seemed comfortable in completing a relay from second, and Rigney referred to the "failure to complete a routine double play in the second inning." The manager also said, "I thought the ball Belanger hit off Jim Perry's glove in the fourth took us out of it. If Perry fields the ball, he gets out of the inning with a double play and we're only trailing 3-2. Instead, Belanger gets on to fill the bases for Cuellar's home run."[10]

The previous season Minnesota had opened the playoffs in Baltimore with two extra-inning losses. Hoping for a boost by starting at home in 1970, the Twins instead encountered an ill wind that left them on the short end of a slugfest.

SIDENOTES

In beating Minnesota, Baltimore won its 12th straight game, a streak that reached 17 as the Orioles finished off the Twins in two more games and won the first three games of the World Series, against Cincinnati. Baltimore beat the Reds in the World Series, 4 games to 1.

The game was played with fill-in umpires as the regulars – in Minnesota and in Pittsburgh for the National League playoffs – went on strike in search of higher pay for the All-Star Game, playoffs, and World Series. At Met Stadium two minor-league umpires, Bill Deegan of the Southern League and Darold Satchell of the International League, joined a pair of umpires on the league supervisory staff, Charlie Berry and John Stevens. Players and managers were advised to "go easy" on the replacements, and there were no incidents in the games.[11] It was the final umpiring assignment for Berry, who had last worked during the 1962 World Series. Stevens had also been serving as a swingman on crews and had umpired 24 games during the 1970 regular season. He continued to umpire in this manner the next few years.

The issue with the umpires was settled, and the regular umpires returned the next day for the second game of the series. Deegan was hired by the American League and became a regular starting the next season. He retired in 1980 but twice returned to fill in during labor disputes involving the umpires. For Satchell, along with three of the four National League replacements, it was his only game in the majors. One of the National League replacement umpires, Hank Morgenweck, was later hired by the American League and worked four seasons.[12]

Related link: Read all biographies from SABR's *Pitching, Defense, and Three-Run Homers: The 1970 Baltimore Orioles* at the SABR BioProject

SOURCES

Scorebook and memory of the author, who attended the game with his favorite cousin (who, more than a quarter-century later, was his best man).

https://www.baseball-reference.com/boxes/MIN/MIN197010030.shtml

http://www.retrosheet.org/boxesetc/1970/B10030MIN1970.htm

NOTES

1. Although it was officially called the American League Championship Series, the newspapers and fans generally used the informal term "playoffs" to refer to the series.

2. Perry had nearly become the second 25-game winner in Twins history (Jim Kaat in 1966 being the other), but the Minnesota bullpen blew a four-run lead in the ninth inning of Perry's final start of the season.

3. John Roe, "Orioles Breeze by Twins," *Minneapolis Tribune*, October 4, 1970: 1 Sports.

4. Lowell Reidenbaugh, "Orioles Polish Off Twins in Repeat Performance," *The Sporting News*, October 17, 1970: 8.

5. The home run was measured at 330 feet, as short as it could be in clearing the fence as the distance down the right-field line at Met Stadium was 330 feet.

6. At Met Stadium, home runs were measured to the spot they landed, not the projected distance that a ball would have traveled unimpeded.

7. Memory of the author, who interpreted the shout as more a frustrated sign of respect than an insult.

8. Tom Briere, "Wind Made Hit With Orioles," *Minneapolis Tribune*, October 4, 1970: 12 Sports.

9. Reidenbaugh.

10. "Rigney: Error Didn't Lose It," *Minneapolis Tribune*, October 4, 1970: 12 Sports.

11. Jerome Holtzman, "The Year in Review," *Official Baseball Guide for 1971* (St. Louis: The Sporting News, 1971), 287-290.

12. Retrosheet.org.

ORIOLES' BATS BLAST TWINS TO TAKE 2-0 ALCS LEAD

OCTOBER 4, 1970: BALTIMORE ORIOLES 11, MINNESOTA TWINS 3

By Stew Thornley

The 1969 expansion of the major leagues and the splitting of leagues into two divisions worked well for the Minnesota Twins, even though the front office was concerned about the impact on attendance by getting fewer games against popular teams like Detroit, Baltimore, New York, and Boston. However, the Twins were being placed in a division that contained both of the American League expansion teams as well as teams that weren't regarded as the best in the league.

The Twins' first decade in Minnesota was one of mostly competitive teams, including a pennant winner in 1965. The team had dipped in the standings in 1968, but fans had high hopes for the next season, when the Twins would be in a division with both of the expansion teams and only one team, Oakland, that had finished ahead of them in 1968. The Twins had won the West Division in 1969, the initial season of division play, but clearly weren't as good as the East Division champions, the Baltimore Orioles, who won 109 games during the regular season. The Orioles swept the Twins in the playoffs[1] although they were then upset by the New York Mets in the 1969 World Series.

The 1970 season mirrored the previous one in the American League. Minnesota won 98 games, 10 fewer than Baltimore. It could be argued that the Orioles were again the dominant team in the league, but a best-of-five series doesn't guarantee the better team will come out on top.

The 1970 series opened in Minnesota on Saturday, October 3, with the Orioles winning the first game 10-6, holding on in a slugfest thanks to the strong relief performance of Dick Hall. Substitute umpires had been used in the opening games of both leagues' playoffs—the regulars went on strike over the amount of money they would be paid for the games. It wasn't until late Sunday morning that the regular crews in both Minneapolis and Pittsburgh were told the issue had been settled and to report to the stadiums.

The Twins needed to win Game Two on Sunday to avoid having to sweep three games on the road, but the Orioles built a lead again.

Left-hander Tom Hall walked the first two Baltimore batters, Mark Belanger and Paul Blair. After Frank Robinson's fly to right sent Belanger to third, Tony Oliva misplayed a windblown fly by Boog Powell into a double.[2] Belanger could have tagged and scored even if Oliva had caught the ball, but it gave the Orioles runners on second and third with one out. Hall recovered to get Merv Rettenmund to look at a third strike and got Brooks Robinson to ground out.

Frank Robinson increased the lead with a long two-run homer to left in the third. The Orioles made it 4-0 in the fourth when Andy Etchebarren reached base with an infield single and advanced to second on an overthrow by shortstop Leo Cardenas. Dave McNally singled Etchebarren home and went to third on another hit, by Belanger. Bill Zepp relieved Hall with runners at the corners and one out. Blair hit a fly to right. Oliva made the catch and fired a strong throw to catcher George Mitterwald to nail McNally at the plate.

McNally, a southpaw who had won 24 games that year, allowed only a first-inning walk to Harmon Killebrew through three innings. He walked Cardenas to start the fourth, and Killebrew lined a home run to left. Oliva, going the opposite way, followed with another line-drive homer to left and the Twins were back in the game, trailing only 4-3.

Baltimore threatened to open it up again in the fifth, loading the bases with none out and prompting Minnesota manager Bill Rigney to go to the bullpen. The ovation Stan Williams received as he came in reflected the faith the fans had in the big right-hander to get out of the jam. Williams had produced a 10-1 won-lost record and a 1.99 earned-run average in 113⅓ innings that year, all in relief, and he did the job, retiring Brooks Robinson, Dave Johnson,[3] and Etchebarren without letting the runners advance.

Williams stayed in the game, batted, and walked with one out in the bottom of the inning and stopped at second on a single by Cesar Tovar. Cardenas singled to left, and Williams tried to score the tying run, but he was gunned out at the plate by Rettenmund.[4] Killebrew popped up to end the threat.

Williams shut down Baltimore over the next two innings and was lifted for a pinch-hitter in the bottom of the seventh. Ron Perranoski, Minnesota's other relief ace, entered in the top of the eighth and was greeted with a challenge by Baltimore manager Earl Weaver to check Perranoski for a "dark spot on the palm" of his pitching hand.[5] When Perranoski couldn't remove the spot with a towel, plate umpire Bill Haller sent him off to wash his hands.

When Perranoski returned, he derisively presented his clean hands to Weaver, who was lingering at home plate with Haller. After the game Perranoski said, "The very sight of Weaver upsets me."[6] Perranoski had been upset with Weaver after he wasn't picked for the American League All-Star team that season — Weaver had selected no relievers among his pitchers. According to Weaver, bullpen coach Jim Frey told him after Game One that he had seen Perranoski rub his hands with pine tar before he went into the game.[7]

Perranoski said the substance on his hand was "resin, dirt, and spit,"[8] not an uncharacteristic denial by a pitcher after being caught red- (or black-) handed. Haller wasn't fooled and said Perranoski's entire hand was black and determined it was pine tar. Asked why he didn't eject Perranoski, as the rules required, Haller replied, "You can go overboard with a rule. Just use common sense; have it taken off."[9]

Hands washed, Perranoski gave up a leadoff bunt single to Brooks Robinson, but Oliva made a nice play after trapping Johnson's liner to right. He came up throwing and forced Robinson at second. Etchebarren hit a comebacker to Perranoski, who started an inning-ending double play.

In the ninth, though, McNally led off with a double, and the Orioles loaded the bases with one out. Powell hit a ground-rule double to left for two runs and Rettenmund singled for another. Luis Tiant,[10] who had started the season for the Twins with wins in his first six decisions before breaking a bone in his shoulder, relieved and got Brooks Robinson to ground to short. Powell broke for home and scored when Cardenas's throw was high for an error. Johnson then finished the carnage with a three-run homer, giving the Orioles a seven-run inning for the second game in a row and an 11-3 lead in this game.

McNally, after Minnesota nearly tied the game in the fifth, gave the Twins few other opportunities. Mitterwald doubled with two out in the sixth, Bob Allison walked with one out in the seventh, and Brant Alyea walked with two out in the eighth. Now with an eight-run lead, McNally gave up a leadoff single in the ninth to Rick Renick, who was wiped out when Danny Thompson hit into a double play. Frank Quilici hit for Tiant and lifted a pop fly in foul territory on the right side. Powell drifted over and had the ball bounce off his glove, carom off his head, and roll down his chest before he corralled it against his stomach, a wacky play that seemed a fitting ending to this game.[11]

While the replacement umpires in Game One had generated no controversy — perhaps in part because of a request for the players and umpires to "go easy" on them[12] — the regulars in Game Two received no such courtesy, and Haller had several of his calls questioned. Blair, after being called out on strikes in the ninth, dropped his bat at Haller's feet. Haller, displaying the same restraint as he had when refusing to eject Perranoski, merely kicked the bat back in Blair's direction.

The Orioles completed the sweep of the series with a win the next day in Baltimore, giving them 14

Ron Perranoski

straight wins, including the final 11 of the regular season. They extended the streak to 17 before losing the fourth game of the World Series to the Cincinnati Reds but they won the next game to win their second world championship in five seasons.

The Twins completed a successful first decade in Minnesota with mostly competitive teams, one pennant, two division titles, and attendance that topped one million each year; the Twins led the American League in overall attendance from 1961 through 1970. No one knew it then, but the good times were ending as the Twins entered a long period of what ranged from bad to bland teams. The Minnesota Vikings, in a stretch that saw them going to the Super Bowl four times from 1969 through 1976, were taking over the sports interest in the state and the Twins reached one million in attendance only twice in their remaining 12 years at Metropolitan Stadium.

SOURCES

The author used his scorebook and memory of this game as well as Baseball-Reference.com in addition to the sources cited in the Notes.

https://www.baseball-reference.com/boxes/MIN/MIN197010040.shtml

http://www.retrosheet.org/boxesetc/1970/B10040MIN1970.htm

NOTES

1. Although it was officially called the American League Championship Series, the newspapers and fans generally used the informal term "playoffs" to refer to the series.
2. The wind had played a bigger role the previous day, but it was still a factor in Game Two. The weather, shown on the Twins-O-Gram on the scoreboard, had the game-time temperature as 73 with the wind out of the south-southwest at 17 mph.
3. "Dave," rather than the now more-familiar "Davey," is used here since that is what he went by at the time.
4. Despite Williams's fine relief work, manager Rigney focused on his inability to score on this play, telling Dan Stoneking of the *Minneapolis Star*, "I can score from second on that one." Dan Stoneking, "Twins' Williams to Ask 50% Pay Hike: Stan Stars in Relief Roles," *Minneapolis Star*, October 5, 1970: 12B.
5. Bill Hengen, "Perranoski Caught 'Hands Down,'" *Minneapolis Star*, October 5, 1970: 12B.
6. Tom Briere, "Perranoski Gets Pair of Clean Hands," *Minneapolis Tribune*, October 5, 1970: 29.
7. Briere. The bullpens at that time at Met Stadium were next to one another, beyond the fence in right-center field.
8. Briere.
9. Hengen.
10. Tiant was pitching his first and only season for Minnesota in 1970. He and Stan Williams were acquired in a December 1969 trade with the Cleveland Indians, where Tiant had pitched from 1964 through 1969. After his 6-0 debut with the Twins in 1970 he suffered a broken shoulder blade, missed two months of the season, and was less effective thereafter. Because of Tiant's injury and his age (30), the Twins failed to reach a contract agreement with him for 1971. He signed with the Boston Red Sox and pitched eight seasons there, winning 20 games on three occasions.
11. Memory of the author and also Dan Stoneking, "No Day for Glove Men," *Minneapolis Star*, October 5, 1970: 13B.
12. Jerome Holtzman, "The Year in Review," *Official Baseball Guide for 1971* (St. Louis: The Sporting News, 1971), 287-290.

TORNADOES DON'T TWIST TWINS' FORTUNES

JUNE 4, 1971: CLEVELAND INDIANS 4, MINNESOTA TWINS 2 (6 INNINGS)

By Gordon Gattie

The Minnesota Twins were competing with the Kansas City Royals for second place in the American League West Division as June 1971 arrived. After stumbling through a lackluster April, Minnesota went 16-12 in May and jumped from fourth place to second. The Twins were reigning AL West champions, winning both the 1969 and 1970 titles by nine games over the Oakland Athletics. Minnesota was selected to repeat as division champion in a poll of 307 members of the Baseball Writers' Association of America, edging out the California Angels and Athletics, but predicted to fall again to the Baltimore Orioles in the AL Championship Series.[1] The 1971 Twins' offense was led by future Hall of Famers second baseman Rod Carew and first baseman Harmon Killebrew, perennial All-Star outfielder Tony Oliva, and the underrated César Tovar. The pitching staff was anchored by veterans Jim Perry and Jim Kaat, with Bert Blyleven playing in his first full major-league season.

The Cleveland Indians were attempting to avoid the AL East basement after a dismal 6-14 April. The Indians improved in May and were percentage points behind the New York Yankees, fighting for fourth place in the division. Cleveland had finished next to last the previous season, 32 games out of first. The offense was led by All-Star catcher Ray Fosse, future star third baseman Graig Nettles, and veteran outfielder Vada Pinson, with stalwart veteran and five-time All-Star Sam McDowell spearheading the rebuilding pitching staff. Sportswriters had low expectations for the Indians, predicting another last-place finish.[2]

Twins manager Bill Rigney sent Blyleven to the mound. The right-hander had a 6-5 record and a 1.96 earned-run average. He had lost his last outing, against Baltimore, breaking a personal four-game winning streak. During those four starts, he had pitched at least eight innings, allowed one or no earned runs in each start, and struck out at least 11 batters three times. The

Collection of Stew Thornley

6-foot-3, 160-pound "Frying Dutchman" had been drafted two years earlier in the third round of the 1969 amateur draft.[3] He threw a devastating curveball, fastball, and changeup.[4]

Rigney changed his infield for the game. After playing 42 games at second base, Carew was moved from second base to third and Steve Braun shifted from third to second. Rigney told sportswriters, "We talked it over before, and Rod has been working out at third for several days. I would have started him there sooner, but I didn't want to have two men at new positions against teams like Baltimore and Detroit." Carew offered that he would play "wherever Rigney wants me."[5]

Indians manager Alvin Dark tabbed offseason acquisition Alan Foster for the matchup. Foster and Ray Lamb had been traded by the Los Angeles Dodgers to the Indians for Duke Sims in December.[6] The introspective Foster pitched one full major-league season for Los Angeles but never reached the Dodgers' expectations after his 1965 signing.[7] Dark, planning to use Foster third in the rotation, noted during spring training, "Alan is sneaky with good control, and most importantly, he knows how to pitch."[8] Through two months with Cleveland, Foster was 3-2 with a 3.54 ERA, though he was struggling with his control.

Blyleven struck out Nettles to start the game. With two strikes, he hit Pinson with a pitch. Fosse hit a tailor-made double play ball to shortstop Leo Cardenas; Pinson was out at second, but Braun's high throw on the double-play pivot pulled Killebrew off the bag and Fosse was safe.[9] Rookie Chris Chambliss had the game's first hit, and the Indians had runners on the corners. Chambliss, playing in his seventh major-league game, extended his hitting streak to include all six games he had played since taking over first base.[10] Ted Uhlaender singled to center field, scoring Fosse, and Ted Ford doubled to the wall into left field, scoring Chambliss and Uhlaender. A strikeout ended the inning with Cleveland ahead, 3-0.

Foster walked Tovar to start the Minnesota half. After two fly outs, Killebrew hit an infield single. Jim Holt put the Twins on the board by doubling to right, scoring Tovar and advancing Killebrew to third. After Braun was intentionally walked, Cardenas popped out to second, ending the inning with the score 3-1.

In the second inning, Blyleven improved upon his slow start by striking out the first two batters. He walked Nettles, the only walk he issued in the game, then picked him off for a quick inning. Foster also pitched better, allowing just a single by Tovar.

Both pitchers slightly switched gears while maintaining their effectiveness in the next two innings. Blyleven earned five of six outs on groundouts, with Fosse's right-field double the only baserunner for either team in the third and fourth innings. Foster got three fly outs and three strikeouts to retire the Twins in order. Both pitchers had one-two-three fifth innings.

Both offenses broke though in the sixth inning. With one out, Chambliss singled for Cleveland's first baserunner since Fosse's third-inning double. With Uhlaender up, Chambliss went to second on Blyleven's wild pickoff attempt. Uhlaender grounded out. Ford's single to left plated Chambliss as Cleveland regained its three-run lead. Eddie Leon grounded out, and the Indians led 4-1.

The crowd of 10,494 experienced a torrential 20-minute rain delay one pitch into the bottom of the sixth inning. Once play resumed, Oliva hammered his league-leading 12th homer, 443 feet into the bullpen area in right-center field.[11] After Killebrew grounded out and Holt flied to center, the heavy rain returned, and, with a 2-and-1 count on Braun, play was delayed another 43 minutes before the game was called on account of a tornado touchdown in nearby Burnsville.[12] Reports of tornado activity around the Twin Cities occurred throughout the evening, and about 60,000 homes lost electrical power.[13] Cleveland won the weather-shortened game, 4-2.

Both pitchers went the distance, Foster, the winner, allowed two runs on four hits with six strikeouts. Blyleven gave up four runs on six hits and struck out six. Ford and Chambliss paced Cleveland's offense, Ford with two hits and three runs batted in and Chambliss with two runs scored. Braun's errant throw helped set up Cleveland's three first-inning runs; he acknowledged his shortcoming by commenting, "I hurried my throw and should have taken more time."[14] Blyleven didn't blame Braun for the loss, saying, "Missing the double play in the first inning didn't shake me. I made some bad pitches. All their hits came on pitches above the belt. I've got to keep the ball down."[15]

Rigney planned to keep playing Carew and Braun at their new positions. "It will take both Braun and Carew time to make an adjustment at their positions, but Carew is missing Saturday and Sunday because of a service commitment," he said. "I'll use Harmon Killebrew at third base Saturday and use Rich Reese at first base."[16] The experiment lasted barely a week when Rigney returned both players to their original positions.[17]

MEMORABLE GAMES AT MINNESOTA'S DIAMOND ON THE PRAIRIE

The Indians won 15 of 31 games in June, then endured a July swoon and never recovered. Cleveland finished in the AL East basement with a 60-102 record, 43 games behind the division champion Orioles. Foster finished with an 8-12 record and 4.16 ERA in 181⅔ innings. Chambliss won the AL Rookie of the Year Award, earning 11 of 24 first-place votes.[18] Ford was the Indians' fourth outfielder that season and was traded to Texas the next year, his only full season in the majors.

The Twins struggled throughout the 1971 season. After spending two weeks in second place in May, they dropped to fourth place in mid-July and bounced between fourth and fifth for the rest of the season. Minnesota finished fifth with a 74-86 record, 26½ games behind Oakland and 5½ games ahead of the last-place Milwaukee Brewers.

Blyleven led all Twins players with 6.5 Wins Above Replacement (for his pitching only)[19] while leading the American League with a 3.797 strikeout-to-walk ratio. He finished fourth with 224 strikeouts, fifth with a 2.81 ERA, eighth with 17 complete games, and ninth with 278⅓ innings pitched, leading Minnesota pitchers in those categories. He compiled a 16-15 record in 38 starts in his first of 10 consecutive seasons pitching over 200 innings. Oliva led Minnesota hitters with a .337 batting average and a .915 OPS. Killebrew powered the offense with 28 home runs and 119 RBIs, while Tovar paced the Twins with 718 plate appearances and 18 stolen bases.

SOURCES

Besides the sources cited in the Notes, the author consulted Baseball-Almanac.com, and the following:

James, Bill. *The New Bill James Historical Abstract* (New York: The Free Press, 2001).

Ritter, Lawrence S. *Lost Ballparks: A Celebration of Baseball's Legendary Fields* (New York: Penguin Books, 1994).

Smith, Ron. *The Ballpark Book* (St. Louis: The Sporting News, 2000).

Thorn, John, and Pete Palmer, et al. *Total Baseball: The Official Encyclopedia of Major League Baseball* (New York: Viking Press, 2004).

NOTES

1. Chris Roewe, "Writers Predicting Repetition in Races," *The Sporting News*, April 10, 1971: 8.
2. Roewe: 8.
3. Gregory H. Wolf, "Bert Blyleven," Society for American Baseball Research BioProject, sabr.org/bioproj/person/86826f24. Accessed January 5, 2020.
4. Bill James and Rob Neyer, *The Neyer/James Guide to Pitchers: An Historical Compendium of Pitching, Pitchers, and Pitches* (New York: Fireside Books, 2004), 137.
5. Dick Gordon, "Carew, Braun Keep New Jobs," *Minneapolis Star*, June 5, 1971: 14.
6. Russell Schneider, "Tribe Trades Sims for 2 Hurlers," *Cleveland Plain Dealer*, December 12, 1970: 25.
7. John Wiebusch, "Dodgers Get Catcher Duke Sims in Trade," *Los Angeles Times*, December 12, 1970: 45.
8. Russell Schneider, "Loser Pascual Impresses Dark," *Cleveland Plain Dealer*, March 31, 1971: 43.
9. Tom Briere, "Cleveland Inundates Twins 4-2," *Minneapolis Star Tribune*, June 5, 1971: 11.
10. Russell Schneider, "Indians Jar Twins, 4-2," *Cleveland Plain Dealer*, June 5, 1971: 22.
11. United Press International, "Weather, Indians Halt Twins," *St. Cloud* (Minnesota) *Daily Times*, June 5, 1971: 9.
12. Gordon.
13. "Storm, Winds Strike Area; Damage Slight," *Minneapolis Star*, June 5, 1971: 1.
14. Gordon.
15. Briere: 12.
16. Briere: 11.
17. Tom Briere, "Kaat, Twins Bow 2-1 in 10," *Minneapolis Star Tribune*, June 10, 1971: 33.
18. Russell Schneider, "Chambliss Tops," *Cleveland Plain Dealer*, November 23, 1971: 37.
19. Baseball-Reference.com, "1971 Minnesota Twins Statistics," baseball-reference.com/teams/MIN/1971.shtml. Accessed January 10, 2020.

BLUE'S 13 STRIKEOUTS AND MITTERWALD'S ERRANT THROW SPARK OAKLAND WIN

JUNE 21, 1971: OAKLAND ATHLETICS 3, MINNESOTA TWINS 2

By Gordon Gattie

Vida Blue set the baseball world ablaze during the first Ahalf of the 1971 season. The 21-year-old Oakland Athletics left-hander from Louisiana was playing in his third big-league season. Blue debuted in 1969 but pitched less than 50 innings in the 1969 and 1970 campaigns. After a 1971 Opening Day loss to the Washington Senators, when he pitched only 1⅔ innings and walked four batters,[1] Oakland's young phenom won 10 consecutive decisions. Those victories included five shutouts and five additional complete games,[2] earning him an appearance on the cover of the May 31 *Sports Illustrated.* Heading into the Monday evening matchup against the Minnesota Twins, Blue was 14-2 with a microscopic 1.42 earned-run average and 133 strikeouts in 139⅓ innings. The lanky lefty threw a dynamic fastball, a good curveball, and an effective changeup.[3]

The Twins ended May 1971 with a 25-24 record, vying for second place, only percentage points behind the Kansas City Royals and seven games behind the American League West Division-leading Athletics. In a topsy-turvy three weeks in June, Minnesota went 3-8 from June 1 through June 13, then won six straight before losing the final game of a four-game series to the Chicago White Sox. As reigning AL West champion, the Twins had been selected to repeat as division winners in a spring-training poll of 307 members of the Baseball Writers' Association of America, edging out the California Angels and Athletics, though the Baltimore Orioles were favored to repeat as AL pennant winners.[4] However, Oakland was the dominant AL West team early in the season. After losing their first three games, the Athletics compiled a 17-8 April record and threatened to run away with the division title.

The Twins' potent offense was led by second baseman Rod Carew, who was just 25 years old and was on his way to his fifth All-Star selection in his first five years, and veteran first baseman Harmon Killebrew, who had moved with the ballclub from Washington in 1961. Perennial All-Star outfielder Tony Oliva and underrated César Tovar were enjoying stellar campaigns. The pitching staff was anchored by longtime Twins Jim Perry and Jim Kaat, with 20-year-old emerging ace Bert Blyleven pitching in his first full season.

The youthful Athletics led the AL West, seven games ahead of the second-place Royals entering the three-game series against Minnesota. Oakland manager Dick Williams was in his first year guiding the team after spending three seasons managing in Boston. The Athletics featured a balanced offensive attack behind slugging outfielder Reggie Jackson, with third baseman Sal Bando adding power and shortstop Bert Campaneris leading off. As the season started, Blue and Rollie Fingers were the top two starting pitchers, before Fingers became Oakland's closer.[5]

Twins manager Bill Rigney selected rookie right-hander Ray Corbin to face Oakland. Corbin was 4-3 with three saves and a 3.71 ERA in 43⅔ innings. He had debuted on April 6, but made his first start only four days earlier against the White Sox, when he allowed three runs and struck out six hitters in six innings, but didn't receive a decision as Minnesota won the game in extra innings. Rigney commented after that game, "I think I've found our fourth starter."[6] In 1970 Corbin led the Charlotte Hornets, Minnesota's Double-A affiliate, with 208 innings pitched and a 2.86 ERA. He impressed Twins coaches in spring training with a "good fast ball and good breaking stuff [but] he has been four years in the farm system."[7]

MEMORABLE GAMES AT MINNESOTA'S DIAMOND ON THE PRAIRIE

Oakland's veteran leadoff hitter Campaneris singled to center field. Joe Rudi sacrificed Campaneris to second base. Jackson and recent acquisition Mike Epstein both walked, and Corbin immediately experienced trouble with the bases loaded and one out. Bando hit a grounder to third baseman Killebrew, who elected to throw out Bando at first base instead of attempting to throw out Campaneris at home.[8] Corbin got Angel Mangual to ground out and escaped further damage.

Blue continued dominating AL hitters. Tovar, leading off in the Twins first, popped out to first base, and Carew and Killebrew struck out as Minnesota was quickly retired. In the second inning, both teams stranded a runner. The Twins reached Blue in the third frame. Rich Reese started the rally with a left-field triple. Corbin singled him home, earning his first major-league run batted in, to tie the score. Tovar forced Corbin, then stole second. Carew struck out a second time. Killebrew singled to left field, just past third baseman Bando, plating Tovar and giving Minnesota a 2-1 lead. Oliva walked, but a fly out ended the rally.

Over the next two innings, Corbin combined groundouts and lineouts to prevent Oakland from scoring. In contrast, Blue struggled with his curveball,[9] striking out three more hitters but also walking three in the fourth and fifth innings. Unable to pad their lead, Minnesota stranded two runners in each inning.

In Oakland's sixth with one out, Epstein doubled to right field. Bando singled to send Epstein to third. Corbin nearly wiggled out of another jam, striking out Mangual. However, Dave Duncan tied the score by singling home Bando. Blue regained his control in the bottom half, striking out the bottom third of Minnesota's lineup in order and reaching double digits in strikeouts for the fifth time in the season.

Corbin tired in the seventh inning. Blue, leading off, was hit on the left instep by a breaking pitch. Campaneris reached first on a failed sacrifice attempt as Blue was forced out at second. With one out, Rudi singled and Oakland had runners at the corners. Left-hander Tom Hall relieved Corbin to face lefties Jackson and Epstein. After Jackson popped out, Rigney addressed his pitcher and catcher George Mitterwald about holding the ball if Rudi attempted to steal second. On the third pitch to Epstein,[10] Mitterwald's throw to second base to catch Rudi on a delayed double-steal attempt sailed into center field, allowing Campaneris to score an unearned run and Rudi to reach second. Mitterwald's throw was likely influenced by his manager's words just before the play unfolded. "Something made me throw it. I knew I wasn't supposed to throw it. But something made me," he said after the game.[11] With Rudi in scoring position, Epstein flied out. Oakland was ahead 3-2.

The Twins' bats fell silent against Blue. He struck out Tovar, the hurler's fourth consecutive strikeout, and got two groundouts in the seventh inning. Hall was equally effective; he retired the remaining six batters he faced. In the bottom of the ninth inning, Reese led off with an infield popout. Pinch-hitter Steve Braun grounded out. Tovar walked, raising the fans' hopes, but Blue ended the game by striking out Carew for the third time as Oakland squeaked out a 3-2 victory.

Blue improved to 15-2, though the two runs he allowed increased his ERA from 1.42 to 1.46. His 13 strikeouts tied his season and career high to that point. (He struck out 17 Angels on July 9 when he pitched 11 shutout innings against California.) Blue was happy with his fastball but not his curveball, noting, "My fastball was humming in the last few innings. That carried me through."[12] Although Blue was halfway to a 30-win season, Williams downplayed the possibility of his reaching the mark. "We don't want to take any chances on ruining a young pitcher's career just to give him a chance to win 30," the manager said. "We'll give him his proper rest and an extra day when we can."[13]

The Twins struggled throughout the 1971 season. They fell to fourth place in mid-July and bounced between fourth and fifth for the rest of the season. They finished fifth with a 74-86 record, 26½ games behind Oakland and 5½ games ahead of the last-place Milwaukee Brewers.

After an incredible first half, Blue slowed during the second half. He started and earned the win for the AL squad in the 1971 All-Star Game.[14] In his first full major-league season, Blue went 24-8 with an AL-leading 1.82 ERA and eight shutouts in 312 innings pitched. His 301 strikeouts were a career best, and the only time he exceeded 200 strikeouts in a season during his career. He was second to Mickey Lolich, only seven behind Lolich's league-leading 308. Blue won the 1971 AL Most Valuable Player Award and the Cy Young Award; he finished with 14 first-place votes and 268 voting points, ahead of teammate Bando's 182 points.[15] Blue finished with 14 first-place votes for the Cy Young Award, narrowly ahead of Lolich.[16] Oakland's superstar was even featured on the cover of *Time* magazine's August 23, 1971, issue during his dream season.

METROPOLITAN STADIUM

SOURCES

Besides the sources cited in the Notes, the author consulted Baseball-Almanac.com, Baseball-Reference.com, Retrosheet.org, and the following:

Greene, Chip, ed. *Mustaches and Mayhem: Charlie O's Three-Time Champions: The Oakland Athletics: 1972-74* (Phoenix: Society for American Baseball Research, 2015): 37-43.

James, Bill. *The New Bill James Historical Abstract* (New York: The Free Press, 2001).

Thorn, John, and Pete Palmer, et al. *Total Baseball: The Official Encyclopedia of Major League Baseball* (New York: Viking Press, 2004).

NOTES

1. Ron Bergman, "Swingin' A's Get No Runs," *Oakland Tribune,* April 6, 1971: 45.

2. "Off to a Sizzling Start," *Sports Illustrated,* May 31, 1971: 18.

3. Bill James and Rob Neyer, *The Neyer/James Guide to Pitchers: An Historical Compendium of Pitching, Pitchers, and Pitches* (New York: Fireside Books, 2004), 136.

4. Chris Roewe, "Writers Predicting Repetition in Races," *The Sporting News,* April 10, 1971: 8.

5. Ron Bergman, "Blue Is Beautiful as No. 1 Resident on A's Hill," *The Sporting News,* April 17, 1971: 3.

6. Dan Stoneking, "Twins' Comeback Legion led by 'German General,'" *Minneapolis Star,* June 18, 1971: 30.

7. Bill Hengen, "Pitching Problem for Twins," *Minneapolis Star,* April 3, 1971: 14.

8. Ron Bergman, "Vida Fans 13, Wins 15th," *Oakland Tribune,* June 22, 1971: 39.

9. Bergman, "Vida Fans 13."

10. Jon Roe, "Blue Beats Twins for 15th Win," *Minneapolis Star Tribune,* June 22, 1971: 25.

11. Dan Stoneking, "'Something Made Me Throw,'" *Minneapolis Star,* June 22, 1971: 39.

12. "Vida Blue: The Big Difference?" *San Francisco Examiner,* June 22, 1971: 48.

13. Bergman, "Vida Fans 13."

14. Associated Press, "Reggie's Smash Turns It Around," *Oakland Tribune,* July 14, 1971: 41.

15. Ron Bergman, "Vida Adds MVP Award," *Oakland Tribune,* November 17, 1971: 53.

16. Ron Bergman, "Vida Wins Cy Award," *Oakland Tribune,* October 26, 1971: 37.

QUIET AS KITTENS AGAINST KAAT, NEW YORK ROARS BACK AGAINST MINNESOTA PEN TO BEST TWINS

JULY 30, 1971: NEW YORK YANKEES 11, MINNESOTA TWINS 9

By Mark S. Sternman

Jim Kaat knew how to win ballgames. In 1971 Kaat would win at least 10 games for the 10th straight year. From 1964 to 1970, he won 35 more games than he lost. The Twins had taken the first two American League West titles in 1969 and 1970 but struggled in 1971, falling out of first place on April 14 and never returning to the top spot. Pitching made the difference. Minnesota had the second best earned-run average in the AL in 1970 and the second worst in 1971.

Before taking on the Yankees on July 30, Kaat had won consecutive 2-1 victories against New York and Boston. He had yielded just 10 hits in his two complete games. A Twin Cities sportswriter explained Kaat's secret: "He had four of the staff's five previous complete games and said some of his success was due to a new pitch, a screwball."[1]

Expectations of a third straight close-fought win with Kaat on the hill did not come to fruition on July 30 at the Met. On this day, Minnesota fans would seemingly enjoy a rout ... and a trout, as the team put on a fishing-related promotion in the Land of 10,000 Lakes.

The Minnesota beat writer opened his game recap with a quip befitting both his name and the occasion. As Jon Roe wrote, "The 20 trout caught out of a tank at Fisherman's night at Metropolitan Stadium got off easy. ... There were 19,233 fans who got hooked, too. What those fans watched should have made the Twins want to dive in with the trout."[2]

After Kaat set down the Yanks in order in the top of the first, the Twins laced Stan Bahnsen early and often. Cesar Tovar had an infield single and scored on when Bahnsen made a wild throw on Rod Carew's bunt single. The miscue was something Bahnsen's more accomplished mound counterpart rarely committed. (Kaat won the American League Gold Glove Award for pitchers every year from 1962 to 1973.) Minnesota had manufactured an early run without the ball leaving the infield. Then Harmon Killebrew walked and Tony Oliva doubled in both of his future Hall of Fame teammates. With three runs on the board, none out, and a runner in scoring position, Kaat must have felt grateful for the unaccustomed run support. While Oliva did not score, the Twins led 3-0 after one.

The Twins helped New York get back into the game in the top of the second. With one out, Kaat walked Danny Cater. Kaat dialed up a grounder on a Ron Swoboda comebacker, but Leo Cardenas muffed the throw, putting runners at first and second. Horace Clarke singled in Cater to cut the lead to 3-1, a score that stood until the bottom of the fifth.

In this game Kaat may have expended more energy on offense than on defense. In the bottom of the second inning, he walked and stole second base, his second swipe of the year (tying the career high he set in 1965). In the fifth he legged out a double off Yankees reliever Al Closter.

After a quiet few innings, the Twins exploded for six runs in the bottom of the fifth on a rally that again started with an infield single by Tovar followed by a bunt single by Carew. Bahnsen wild-pitched the two speedy troublemakers to second and third. This time, he retired Killebrew, then walked Oliva intentionally to set up a double play. The stratagem for the Yankees blew up when the next three Twins had productive at-bats. Rich Reese singled in Tovar and Carew to give the Twins a 5-1 lead. Cardenas likewise singled to load the bases. Jim Nettles hit a sacrifice fly to put Minnesota up 6-1. George Mitterwald delivered what must have felt like a knockout blow with a three-run homer that gave the Twins a 9-1 edge and ended Bahnsen's bad day on the mound. Al Closter came on for Bahnsen. Kaat greeted the new pitcher with a double and Tovar reached on an error, but neither scored when Carew struck out.

Kaat relaxed, weakened, or both in the top of the sixth. Cater homered with one out to get New York a run closer at 9-2. With two outs, the Yanks scratched out an additional run on singles by John Ellis, Clarke, and Ron Hansen, who had pinch-hit for Closter. Still, Minnesota had a substantial six-run lead after 5½ innings.

The Twins could not tack anything on against the back end of the New York bullpen as Roger Hambright got through the home half of the sixth unscathed.

Bill Rigney, "the manager who had gained fame, and perhaps fortune, by manipulating relief pitchers,"[3] started to lift his regulars with Minnesota up by six runs. Jim Holt came in for Oliva, and, after Thurman Munson doubled to start the seventh, Ray Corbin relieved Kaat. Having waived the struggling Ron Perranoski to Detroit earlier in the day, Minnesota had one less veteran relief pitcher. Facing Corbin, Felipe Alou singled in Munson, but the Twins went into the stretch still up by five.

In the bottom of the seventh, shortstop Gene Michael's second error of the game and Munson's passed ball put a runner in scoring position. Feeling no need to extend his lead or tax his bullpen, Rigney let Corbin hit. The reliever struck out. Minnesota led 9-4 with just two innings to go.

Corbin quickly made Rigney regret his passivity by walking the bases loaded in the eighth. Stan Williams came in and walked Munson, forcing in a run. Down 9-5 but with the bases loaded and none out, the Yanks brought the tying run to the plate. Alou popped out, but Williams threw a wild pitch and then walked Roy White, so New York still had the bases loaded and now trailed 9-6 with the tying run at first. In the midst of a big day at the plate, Cater came through with a clutch bases-clearing double, the only hit and the only ball that left the infield during the five-run inning, to tie the score, 9-9. Managing aggressively now, Rigney yanked Williams and brought in Tom Hall, his best arm out of the bullpen. Hall threw a wild pitch, but Cater did not advance beyond third.

Following Rigney's lead, Yankee Manager Ralph Houk turned to his best reliever in the eighth, Jack Aker. Minnesota went back to its bread-and-butter offensive attack. Tovar got his third infield single of the game, and Carew bunted again. This time the Yankees retired Carew, who received credit for a sacrifice. Aker retired Killebrew and then had the easier task of facing Holt (who hit .259 in 1971) rather than Oliva (the eventual batting champion at .337). Aker got Holt on a fly ball and held the score at 9-9.

The Yankees played small ball to take the lead for the first time in the ninth inning. Clarke walked and Aker sacrificed him to second. Michael's single scored Clarke, breaking the tie, and Munson doubled in Michael. As Murray Chass of the *New York Times* opined, "Michael's hit was particularly gratifying . . . because the shortstop had been in a hitting and fielding slump. Including two errors he made [against the Twins], Michael had committed five in the last seven games. He had a total of only eight in all the others. At bat in the three previous games he had struck out seven times in eight trips."[4]

With New York leading 11-9, Aker stayed on to try to close the game. With two outs and none on, the Twins rallied. Nettles walked and Mitterwald singled. Pinch-hitter Steve Braun rolled one to Cater at first. In a fitting conclusion by the star of the game, Cater made the play himself, cementing the improbable comeback win by the Yankees, a feat made all the more improbable by its genesis against an accomplished pitcher like Jim Kaat.

NOTES

1   Bob Fowler, "Circus Act by Twins – But Rig's Not Laughing," *The Sporting News*, August 14, 1971: 29.

2   Jon Roe, "Twins, After Leading 9-1, Get 'Hooked' by Yankees 11-9," *Minneapolis Tribune*, July 31, 1971: 1B.

3   Bob Fowler, "Twins' Tortured Staff Due for a Major Overhaul," *The Sporting News*, August 21, 1971: 21.

4   Murray Chass, "Yanks Win, 11-9, From Twins," *New York Times*, July 31, 1971: 17.

WILLIE MAYS AND HARMON KILLEBREW DELIGHT TWINS FANS

AUGUST 9, 1971: MINNESOTA TWINS 5, SAN FRANCISCO GIANTS 2

By Thomas E. Merrick

Should a midseason exhibition be included among the greatest games in Metropolitan Stadium history? After all, as the United Press International wire service candidly pointed out, by the end of the game, "many of the Twins had left the dugout, showered and gone home."[1] If the players left early, how could the game be all that great?

But taking the entire night of baseball into consideration, it was an evening worthy of honor. The exhibition game between the Minnesota Twins and San Francisco Giants was just part of the festivities. A pregame home-run contest between Willie Mays and Harmon Killebrew was what made things special. Fans got to see, and salute, two of the game's greatest players. If baseball is at its best when it entertains us, and produces memorable moments, then this night at the Met delivered.

Players must have been dreading this August 9, 1971, exhibition. The Giants and Twins were forfeiting an offday that could have been used to rest minor injuries, or reconnect with family and friends. The Giants stopped off in Minnesota on their way home from five days on the road. They had spent a long afternoon in Chicago's Wrigley Field the day before, playing a total of 20 innings in their doubleheader against the Cubs. They were scheduled to face Montreal at Candlestick Park the following evening. The Twins had just arrived home after eight games in seven days against the White Sox, Royals, and Angels. They would battle the reigning world champion Baltimore Orioles the next three nights. No wonder players left the park early.

The fans, on the other hand, were eager to come to the ballpark. In fact, 24,719 of them showed up. Only three times all season did the Twins draw a larger audience.[2] The turnout was more than twice the overall season average of 11,910 per game,[3] and easily surpassed the next night's attendance of 15,881 against first-place Baltimore.

Baseball was far different in 1971, and those differences made this game appealing to Minnesotans. Interleague play did not begin until 1997, so fans ordinarily would not see Mays and the Giants in person. Furthermore, there was nothing like ESPN or the MLB Network to saturate homes with nightly games, exotic statistics, and highlight videos featuring every team.[4] Today we are awash in a sea of information and images, but at that time, people could only wonder about Killebrew versus Mays, and American League versus National League.

Another draw for some in attendance was the connection between Mays and Minneapolis. A precocious 20-year-old Mays toyed with American Association pitching while playing 35 games for the 1951 Triple-A Millers. He batted .477, drove in 30 runs, and slammed eight home runs in his brief Twin Cities stay.

The large crowd apparently caught the Twins off guard. The unexpected turnout delayed the start of the home run contest by 20 minutes to allow all the people to find their seats.[5] Once seated, the fans got their money's worth.[6]

The home-run contest called for three rounds of five fair balls for each batter.[7] A foul ball or a swing-and-miss would not count against him. The winner would be the hitter depositing the most of his 15 chances into the seats.

This was not the first home-run clash between these two stars. Mays and Killebrew squared off 11 years earlier while participating in the television show *Home Run Derby*.[8] The production was filmed in Los Angeles before the 1960 baseball season, and featured the top power hitters of the day. The televised contest had a much different format, but the same object: Hit as many pitches as possible over the fence. It awarded the winner $2,000 and the loser $1,000, and offered bonuses for three or more consecutive home runs. Killebrew earned $6,000 on *Home Run Derby* that winter,[9] a nice boost to his $20,000 Washington Senators salary.[10] He appeared on the show four times, winning two and losing two. Mays won three of his five televised home-run duels. In Episode 20 of the show, Mays rallied from a 5-3 deficit to defeat Killebrew 7-6.[11]

METROPOLITAN STADIUM

In this Metropolitan Stadium rematch, Mays and Killebrew needed no introduction to the man on the mound grooving pitches for them to hit. It was Minnesota native Paul Giel, who had been a teammate of Mays on the New York Giants in 1954 and 1955. After a stint in the Army, Giel rejoined Mays on the 1958 San Francisco Giants and briefly became Killebrew's teammate on the 1961 Twins. Giel showed his pitching impartiality by wearing a Twins uniform, but a Giants cap.[12] Four months later he was named athletic director of the University of Minnesota, a position he held until 1988.[13]

Both contestants were among the best home-run hitters ever. At the time, Mays – he turned 40 that May – had 643 career round-trippers, placing him second on the all-time home-run list behind only Babe Ruth.[14] Killebrew ranked 10th on the list, with 499 home runs.[15] The 35-year-old slugger had been stuck at 499 since July 25.[16] On the day of the exhibition, he admitted to columnist Sid Hartman that he had been pressing for two weeks.[17] His trek to the 500-home-run summit was further hindered by an injured right big toe, suffered on June 28 against Oakland, that required a special shoe to avoid aggravating the injury.[18] He hit only one home run in 31 games after suffering the injury.

In round one of the contest, Mays hit his first and third fair balls into the left-field stands. Killebrew hit his third and fourth into the same area, to tie the match at 2-2.[19] Mays outhomered Killebrew 2-1 in both the second and third rounds to win, 6-4.[20] For this Met Stadium showdown, no prize money was awarded. Each player did raise $250 for his favorite charity, courtesy of sponsor Harold Greenwood of Midwest Federal Savings and Loan.[21]

Mays and Killebrew continued to delight everyone once the game began. Mays "put on a show by playing center field in the first inning, then switching to first, second, shortstop, and third before retiring in the sixth."[22] He did not get a hit in three plate appearances, but in his final at-bat he sent Jim Nettles deep in center field to catch his long drive.[23]

Killebrew was the hero of the Twins' exhibition win. He ripped a game-winning three-run homer in the first inning that landed 422 feet away in the left-field stands.[24] The Twins added a run each in the fifth and the seventh – the latter a home run by Rich Reese – to claim a 5-2 victory. The Twins used 15 position players and four pitchers in the game.[25]

Since this was an exhibition, Killebrew's career home-run mark remained at 499 – but not for long. The next night against the Orioles, he hit number 500 in the first inning, and added number 501 in the sixth.[26] When he retired after spending 1975 with the Kansas City Royals, his home-run count had reached 573.

Minnesota ended the 1971 season 76-86 – fifth in the six-team American League West – 26½ games behind first-place Oakland. It was a disappointing outcome for the Twins, who had won the division handily in 1969 and 1970.

NOTES

1. "Twins Take Exhibition," *St. Cloud Times,* August 10, 1971: 12
2. Larger crowds were May 9 versus Washington (28,980); July 6 versus California (26,687); July 31 versus the New York Yankees (25,560). retrosheet.org/boxesetc/1971/VMIN01971.htm.
3. The 1971 Twins drew 940,858 for 79 home games. However, they played four single-admission doubleheaders at home in 1971, bringing the average per gate to 12,545.
4. ESPN's *SportsCenter* did not debut until September 7, 1979. en.wikipedia.org/wiki/History_of_ESPN. The MLB Network was founded in 1999.
5. Tom Briere, "Mays Wins Homer Duel, but Killebrew Saves One for Game," *Minneapolis Tribune,* August 10, 1971: 1C
6. Briere.
7. Briere.
8. wikipedia.org/wiki/Home_Run_Derby_%28TV_series%29.
9. wikipedia.org/wiki/Home_Run_Derby_%28TV_series%29.
10. baseball-reference.com/players/k/killeha01.shtml.
11. The episode can be seen on You Tube at: bing.com/videos/search?q=Home+Run+Derby+episode+20&&view=detail&mid=5D-6BE7FE0D4157D260D55D6BE7FE0D4157D260D5&&FORM=VRD-GAR&ru=%2Fvideos%2Fsearch%3Fq%3DHome%2520Run%2520Derby%2520episode%252020%26qs%3Dn%26form%3DQBVRM-H%26sp%3D-1%26ghc%3D1%26pq%3Dhome%2520run%-2520derby%2520episode%252020%26sc%3D0-25%26sk%3D%26c vid%3D239B57453B72463F81ECF13B421F820A. Accessed April 25, 2020.
12. Briere.
13. Cary Smith, "Paul Giel," SABRBioProject, sabr.org/bioproj/person/0b986aab.
14. Briere.
15. Briere.
16. Mike Lamey, "500th – No Pressure, Mays," *Minneapolis Star,* August 10, 1971: 1D.
17. Sid Hartman, "Sid Hartman," *Minneapolis Tribune,* August 11, 1971: 2C.
18. Hartman.
19. Briere.
20. Briere.
21. Briere.
22. "Killebrew Gets Back at Mays," *San Francisco Examiner,* August 10, 1971: 43.
23. "Twins Take Exhibition."
24. "Killebrew Gets Back at Mays."
25. "Box Score," *San Francisco Examiner,* August 10, 1971: 43.
26. retrosheet.org/boxesetc/1971/B08100MIN1971.htm.

KILLEBREW ENDS HOME RUN DROUGHT BY JOINING 500 CLUB

AUGUST 10, 1971: BALTIMORE ORIOLES 4, MINNESOTA TWINS 3

By Richard Cuicchi

Minnesota Twins slugger Harmon Killebrew was in an unusual home-run slump and appeared to leverage a late-season exhibition game and related home-run derby to get back on track. In dramatic fashion on the next day against the Baltimore Orioles, he slammed his 500th and 501st home runs to join an elite group of nine players who had previously attained this milestone.

The 35-year-old Killebrew had averaged nearly 40 home runs a season from 1959, his first season as a regular starter, through 1970. He had acquired his nickname, Killer, for good reason. During that period, he had hit more home runs (476) than anyone in the majors. (Hank Aaron was next with 452.) Killebrew had hit 11 home runs in five partial seasons prior to 1959 and, with 487 in his career through 1970, was closing in on the milestone. However, the 1971 season was uncharacteristic for him; he hit only 12 home runs through August 8. He had been without a homer in his previous 13 games (the last on July 25) and had only one in his last 36 games. For a feared hitter like Killebrew, his performance amounted to a season-long slump to that point.

While he remained at number 498 for a little over a month, Killebrew began to feel the tension of reaching the next milestone, because the Twins announced that commemorative mugs would be handed out to fans on July 6. They were predicting he would have reached 500 by then. But that didn't happen because Killebrew suffered a sprained right big toe and sat out several games. The Twins gave out the mugs anyway.[1]

Everyone was weighing in on why Killebrew couldn't break out of his drought. Twins owner Calvin Griffith offered, "Nobody can tell me it wasn't because of the pressure. Harmon had to be thinking about that. It is only natural that a man thinks about it, especially since everyone is talking about it."[2]

Killebrew acknowledged that he had felt the added pressure during the previous weeks, noting that every interview he conducted included questions about when he would finally achieve the milestone.[3]

On August 9 the Twins played a rare exhibition game during the regular season, against the San Francisco Giants. A home-run derby was staged before the game between Killebrew and Giants slugger Willie Mays, who had played with the Triple-A Minneapolis Millers in 1951. With each batter getting 15 fair balls, Mays outhit Killebrew in homers, 6-4. However, Killebrew also hit a homer during the game in which the Twins won, 5-2.[4] It turned out that the event served as a warm-up for Killebrew's next regular-season game, the following day.

The banter around the home-run derby contest centered on who was in the best position to chase Babe Ruth's home-run record. The 40-year-old Mays, who was in second place behind Ruth, suggested that Henry Aaron was the favorite to challenge the record. Killebrew said of his own case, "I'm just thinking about No. 13 this year, not Ruth's 714."[5]

The Twins began a three-game series with the Baltimore Orioles on August 10 with a night game at Metropolitan Stadium. The defending World Series champion Orioles held first place in the American League East Division with a 5½-game lead over Boston coming into the game, while the Twins were mired in fifth place in the AL West, 19½ games behind Oakland. The season's performance was a huge setback for the Twins, who had won their division in the previous two seasons.

The Twins' Tom Hall and the Orioles' Mike Cuellar drew the starting-pitcher assignments. Left-hander Cuellar had 13 wins, headlining a staff that included Jim Palmer, Dave McNally, and Pat Dobson. (Each would finish the season with 20 or more wins.) Hall was a part-time starter for the Twins, with four wins to his credit.

It had been two weeks since Killebrew's 499th home run, so it was a jubilant moment when he broke the slump in the bottom of the first with a solo home run to left field off Cuellar. Twins coach Frank Crosetti gave him a celebratory handshake as he rounded third base amid cheering fans who were aware of the significance of his hit. His teammates swarmed him as he arrived in the dugout, and they insisted that he take a bow in front of the crowd before teammate Tony Oliva stepped in the batter's box as the next hitter.[6]

The Orioles retaliated the next inning when Davey Johnson smacked a double scoring Boog Powell. Catcher Andy Etchebarren followed with a single that drove in a run to take the Orioles to a 2-1 lead.

The Orioles added a run in the third inning on Brooks Robinson's single off Hall that scored Merv Rettenmund, who had singled and gone to second on Frank Robinson's groundout.

The score remained 3-1 until Killebrew tied the score in the bottom of the sixth with his second home run off Cuellar. Cesar Tovar, who had singled, also scored.

Ray Corbin relieved Hall in the top of the eighth, while Cuellar was still in the game with the game tied after nine innings. Corbin yielded a leadoff solo home run to Rettenmund in the top of the tenth. Cuellar held the Twins scoreless in the bottom half to cinch the Orioles' 4-3 win.

In recording his ninth complete game of the season, Cuellar gave up seven hits and struck out five. Aside from the two round-trippers by Killebrew, he was in control of the rest of the game. Corbin took his ninth loss of the season. Twins pitchers gave up 11 hits and struck out seven. Etchebarren was the hitting star for the Orioles with two doubles and a single.

After the game Killebrew remembered some of the memorable home runs along his journey to 500. He said, "I remember the first homer I ever hit in the American League, when I was with Washington. It was Billy Hoeft of Detroit in 1955. There are other stickouts, like the one I hit over the roof at Detroit in 1962 off Jim Bunning, but most of the other homers become fuzzy in memory. I'll remember the one tonight."[7] Killebrew hit his 100th against the White Sox' Early Wynn in 1961, his 200th against Washington's Jim Duckworth in 1963, his 300th against the Yankees' Bob Friend in 1966, and his 400th against the White Sox' Gary Peters in 1969.

An oddity from Killebrew's milestone game was that umpire Bill Kunkel, who was behind the plate, had served up three home runs to Killebrew when he was pitching for the Kansas City A's in 1961.

Killebrew swapped an autographed Twins team baseball for the 500th home-run ball, which was caught by a fan. The fan was also invited to sit in the Twins owner's box for the balance of the game.[8]

President Richard Nixon made a congratulatory phone call to Killebrew days later. In lieu of an autographed baseball, Nixon offered to send personalized golf balls "guaranteed for a hole-in-one." Killebrew recalled that when he played for the Senators, Nixon, then the vice president, frequently attended Senators games.[9]

During his last 44 games of the season, Killebrew improved his home-run rate by hitting 14 for a season total of 28, still well below his average. He led the American League with 119 runs batted in. The season marked the beginning of a decline in his home-run output that continued over the next four seasons until he retired in 1975.

Killebrew finished his career with 573 home runs, fifth on the all-time list at the time. As of 2020 he was 12th on the list. During the 17 seasons (out of 22 total seasons) in which he was a regular starter, he led the American League in home runs in six seasons and finished in the top five in six other seasons. He was elected to the Baseball Hall of Fame in 1984.

The Twins finished fifth in the West Division in 1971 after having won the division in the previous two seasons. They wouldn't return to the postseason until 1987, when they won their first-ever World Series.

SOURCES

In addition to the sources cited in the Notes, the author consulted Baseball-Reference.com and the following:

Lamey, Mark. "Killebrew Reaches Elite Class With 500th Home Run," *The Sporting News*, August 28, 1971: 33.

NOTES

1. Bob Fowler. "Tension Broken – Killer Connects for 500th," *The Sporting News*, August 28, 1971: 7.
2. Steve Aschburner. *Harmon Killebrew: Ultimate Slugger* (Chicago: Triumph Books, 2012), 132.
3. Tom Briere. "Harmon Hits 500 and 501," *Minneapolis Star Tribune*, August 11, 1971: 1C.
4. Tom Briere. "Mays Wins Homer Duel, but Killebrew Saves One for Game," *Minneapolis Star Tribune*, August 10, 1971: 1C.
5. Briere. "Mays wins homer duel."
6. Tom Briere. "Harmon Hits 500 and 501."
7. Briere. "Harmon Hits 500 and 501": 2C.
8. Jim Elliott, "Twins Bow to Orioles in 10th, 4-3," *Baltimore Sun*, August 11, 1971: C4.
9. "Nixon Calls to Salute Killer for His 500 Feat," *The Sporting News*, August 28, 1971: 7.

KILLEBREW'S PINCH-HIT GRAND SLAM PROPELS TWINS TO 9-4 WIN OVER ATHLETICS

SEPTEMBER 3, 1971: MINNESOTA TWINS 9, OAKLAND ATHLETICS 4 (GAME 1)

By Doug Skipper

Harmon Killebrew's sixth-inning pinch-hit grand slam launched the Minnesota Twins to a 9-4 victory over the Oakland Athletics in the first game of a doubleheader at Metropolitan Stadium.

The first game of the twin bill was the makeup of a June 24 rainout. It preceded the scheduled Friday night game, which was designated Vida Blue Button Night. In a rare promotional event featuring a visiting team player,[1] the Oakland phenom scheduled to pitch that night, the Twins handed out blue buttons that read "Roses are red, my clothes were blue, when I was there to see Vida Blue."[2]

No attendance was announced for the makeup game, but the crowd swelled as fans arrived to watch the Twins take on the 21-year-old Oakland ace, who entered the evening with a 23-6 record, in the nightcap.[3]

Those who stayed late among the official announced crowd of 22,032 for the second game saw George Mitterwald smash a two-out ninth-inning solo home run into the left-field pavilion off Blue to lift Minnesota to a dramatic 2-1 victory and a sweep of the twin bill.

Those who arrived early enough were treated to Killebrew's game-breaking shot in the opener after the A's had taken an early lead.

Oakland jumped on Minnesota starter Jim Perry for two quick runs in the first, but it could have been more. Shortstop Bert Campaneris slapped a leadoff single to center, right fielder Reggie Jackson drilled a one-out double to left-center to drive in Campaneris, and third baseman Sal Bando singled to score Jackson. Trailing 2-0, Perry walked left fielder Adrian Garrett and catcher Gene Tenace to load the bases, but retired second baseman Dick Green on a groundout to short to avoid further damage.

The Twins quickly tied the score in the bottom of the inning with a little help. With one out, second baseman Rod Carew went to second when Oakland starting pitcher Diego Segui mishandled his grounder. After right fielder Tony Oliva drew a walk, first baseman Rich Reese singled to center to score Carew and move Oliva to third base. Left fielder Steve Brye forced Reese at second base, and Oliva scored. Segui picked Brye off first base to end the inning.

After Perry set the A's down in the top of the second, shortstop Steve Braun singled and third baseman Eric Soderholm, making his major-league debut, grounded to third to force out Braun. Soderholm took second on Phil Roof's single, then chugged around third on Perry's single to right. The rookie challenged the wrong outfielder. Jackson, who led American League right fielders with 15 assists in 1971 and amassed 133 in his 21-year Hall of Fame career, delivered a bullet to Tenace at the plate to retire Soderholm and preserve the tie.

After Perry set the Athletics down in order in the third inning, Carew opened the bottom half with a fly ball to right that Jackson chased and appeared to lose as it sailed over his head. On third with a triple, Carew scored one out later on Reese's groundout to first. Perry retired the A's in order in the fourth, and Soderholm launched his first career home run, a 378-foot one-out solo shot, to stake Minnesota to a 4-2 lead. The rookie had clubbed 22 home runs for the Pacific Coast League's Portland Beavers before his September call-up, "[b]ut I think I'll remember this one better."[4]

The Athletics trimmed the margin in half in the fifth. The speedy Campaneris beat out a bunt, swiped second (his 28th steal of the year), and scampered to third when Roof's throw went wild. With one out, he scored on Jackson's single off first baseman Reese's mitt to trim Minnesota's lead to 4-3.

Segui dispatched the Twins in the bottom of the fifth and in the sixth Tenace stroked a 381-foot one-out solo home run, his seventh of the season, to even the score at 4-4. Perry then surrendered a walk and two singles to load the bases, but again escaped a bases-loaded jam when he got Jackson to fly out to Brye in left field.

The outcome was determined in the bottom of the sixth. Brye slapped a one-out single behind second base, Braun doubled into the right-field corner, and Segui intentionally walked Soderholm. Twins manager Bill Rigney had planned to rest Killebrew in the opener against the right-handed Segui to be fresh for the nightcap against southpaw Blue.[5] But with the score tied, the bases loaded, one out, and his catcher, Roof, due up, Rigney sent up Killebrew to pinch-hit.

Oakland manager Dick Williams countered by relieving Segui with another righty, former Twins pitcher Mudcat Grant, Killebrew's teammate during the 1964-67 seasons. With the count 2-and-1, Grant offered up a fastball that Killebrew slugged 391 feet into Metropolitan Stadium's left-field seats.[6]

The home run was Killebrew's 19th of the season and the 506th of his career, the 10th most all-time then.[7] He finished his 22-year Hall of Fame career with 573. It was the 10th grand slam of Killebrew's career, the most among active major leaguers at the time. (He hit one more before wrapping up his career in 1975.) It was the third pinch hit home run of his career; he would hit four more. And it was the fifth pinch-hit grand slam by a Twin.[8]

Grant retired the next two hitters, but the Twins led 8-4.

When Mike Epstein led off the Athletics' seventh with a single, Rigney replaced Perry with Tom Hall. Hall retired two Oakland hitters, then surrendered singles to Tenace and Green. With the bases loaded and two outs, the Twins dodged danger for the third time when Hall struck out pinch-hitter Joe Rudi, who wasn't able to match Killebrew's heroics.

With the lead intact, the Twins added an insurance run in the bottom of the seventh. Carew greeted relief pitcher Jim Roland with a leadoff single to center and moved to second on Oliva's single to left. Two outs later, Braun drove in Carew with a single to right. After Roland plunked Soderholm with a pitch to load the bases, he struck out Mitterwald, who had replaced Roof at catcher, to end the inning with the Twins ahead 9-4.

That's the way it ended. Hall, making his first appearance in 24 days because of Marine Reserve duty,[9] retired Oakland in order in the eighth and ninth innings, striking out Bando and Garrett to end the game. Hall was awarded his seventh save. Perry improved to 16-14 for the season. Segui (9-6) was saddled with the loss. The game lasted 2 hours and 50 minutes.

With the sweep, Twins improved their record to 62-72, and staved off mathematical elimination in the American League West, while the Athletics fell to 88-49. However, the two teams were going in different directions. Minnesota, the two-time defending American League West champion, was eliminated from the race three nights later, and finished the 1971 season with a 74-86 record. The Athletics posted a 101-60 record to finish 16 games ahead of the nearest contender, Kansas City, and 26½ games ahead of the fifth-place Twins. The Athletics suffered a 3-0 sweep at the hands of the Baltimore Orioles in the AL Championship Series, but won the AL West five straight times (1971-75) and won three straight World Series titles (1972-74).

SOURCES

In addition to the sources cited in the Notes, the author accessed Retrosheet.org, Baseball-Almanac.com, Baseball-Reference.com, SABR.org, *The Sporting News* archive via Paper of Record, and the following articles on the SABR BioProject website:

Puerzer, Rich. "Vida Blue," sabr.org/bioproj/person/397acf10

Leavengood, Ted. "Reggie Jackson," sabr.org/bioproj/person/365acf13

Wancho, Joseph. "Mudcat Grant," sabr.org/bioproj/person/ba7b1b4d

Wancho, Joseph, "Harmon Killebrew," sabr.org/bioproj/person/55c51444

Wancho, Joseph. "Jim Perry," sabr.org/bioproj/person/f7911858

NOTES

1 Dan Stoneking, "Cliff-Edge Twins Still Hanging on," *Minneapolis Star*, September 4, 1971: 7A. Stoneking wrote, "The Twins players said it didn't bug them to have their front office stage such a promotion." He quoted George Mitterwald: "The idea is to put fans in the park and that's what it did. I wore one of those buttons before the game. So did my wife."

2 Tom Briere, "Twins Homers top Blue, A's," *Minneapolis Tribune*, September 4, 1971: 13. Briere quoted the button and a home-made button worn by a Twins fan that stated, "To heck with Blue, I'm for the 'Brew.'"

3 Stoneking reported, "Everyone showing up at the ballpark (and most of the fans came late) wearing blue received a button commemorating Vida's bid for a 24th victory."

4 Briere: 16.

5 Briere: 16.

6 Briere: 13; Deane McGowen, "Roundup: Killebrew Puts Pinch on A's with Slam," *New York Times*, September 4, 1971: 6.

7 Killebrew had hit his 500th home run less than a month earlier, one of two he hit off Baltimore's Mike Cuellar on August 8 at Metropolitan Stadium when he became just the 10th player to slug 500 career home runs.

8 Keith Sutton, "The Dream Hit: A Pinch Grand Slam," *1972 Baseball Research Journal*, sabr.org/research/dream-hit-pinch-grand-slam. Julio Becquer in 1961, Rich Reese in 1969 and 1970, and Rick Renick in 1970 had hit pinch-hit grand slams for the Twins. Only two players had accomplished the feat while the franchise was located in Washington, Cliff Bolton in 1934 and Hall of Fame Pitcher Early Wynn in 1946.

9 Stoneking.

RED ROSES, BLUE BUTTONS, AND A MITTERWALD WALK-OFF

SEPTEMBER 3, 1971: MINNESOTA TWINS 2, OAKLAND ATHLETICS 1 (SECOND GAME OF DOUBLEHEADER)

By Gordon Gattie

The Minnesota Twins occupied fifth place in the American League West Division when Labor Day weekend 1971 arrived in the Twin Cities. After spending most of June and early July in third place, the Twins dropped into fifth in a 13-15 August. Preseason prognostications placed Minnesota atop the AL West[1] after winning both the 1969 and 1970 titles by nine games over the Oakland Athletics. However, this year's team was not meeting expectations.[2] The Twins' offense was led by future Hall of Famers first baseman Harmon Killebrew and second baseman Rod Carew with perennial All-Star outfielder Tony Oliva vying for the batting title. The pitching staff was anchored by stalwart veterans Jim Perry and Jim Kaat, with Bert Blyleven playing in his first full major-league season.

The Oakland Athletics were poised to begin their AL West dominance. The Athletics led the AL West, 17½ games ahead of the second-place Kansas City Royals, entering the weekend series against Minnesota. Oakland was led by future Hall of Famers manager Dick Williams and slugging outfielder Reggie Jackson, with third baseman Sal Bando adding power and shortstop Bert Campaneris providing speed. All-Star youngster Vida Blue, pitching in his first full major-league season, led the league in several pitching categories and was considered an early favorite to win the Cy Young Award.[3]

Minnesota won the first game of Friday's doubleheader, 9-4. Both teams scored two runs in the first inning, and then Killebrew blasted a sixth-inning pinch-hit grand slam to break a 4-4 tie.[4]

Twins manager Bill Rigney selected rookie right-hander Ray Corbin to pitch the nightcap. Corbin was 7-10 with a 4.03 earned-run average in 111⅔ innings pitch. He last won six weeks earlier when he pitched seven scoreless relief innings and plated the tying run on a misplayed squeeze bunt.[5] Corbin led the Charlotte Hornets, Minnesota's Double-A affiliate, with 208 innings pitched and finished second with a 2.86 ERA in 1970. He impressed Twins coaches in spring training 1971 with a "good fast ball and good breaking stuff" though "he has been four years in the farm system."[6]

Oakland's budding superstar Blue faced Corbin. Although the game was hosted by Minnesota, the Twins front office promoted that evening as Vida Blue Button Night. The Blue button read, "Roses are red, my clothes are blue, when I was there to see Vida Blue!"[7] Anyone wearing blue clothes to the game received a Blue button. Blue was dominating baseball in 1971; through August, he was 23-6 with a 1.70 ERA and 274 strikeouts in 275⅓ innings pitched. The AL's starting pitcher in the 1971 All-Star Game, Blue pitched three innings and got the win, though he allowed two homers.[8] The lanky left-hander threw a dynamic fastball, a good curveball, and an effective changeup.[9]

Collection of Stew Thornley

Corbin quickly tamed Oakland's offense as the nightcap started. Athletics leadoff hitter Dwain Anderson, making his major-league debut, struck out in his first plate appearance. Joe Rudi and Jackson grounded out. In the Minnesota half, Cesar Tovar led off with a groundout. Carew singled and took second on a wild pitch but was stranded when Blue struck out Killebrew and Oliva. In the top of the second inning with two outs, Mike Hegan singled for Oakland's first baserunner. Dave Duncan grounded out, the fourth groundout Corbin induced in his first seven batters.

Twins rookie and Oakland native[10] Steve Brye led off Minnesota's second inning and blasted his first career home run, 346 feet off the left-field foul pole, to give Minnesota the lead.[11] Brye played in nine Twins games the previous season and made his 1971 Twins debut in the first game of the doubleheader after spending the season with the Triple-A Portland Beavers. He led Portland hitters with a .340 batting average and 14 stolen bases, and hit 13 homers. Brye commented after the game, "I've seen Blue pitch in Oakland when I've been home for Army Reserve meetings. Let alone this being my first major-league homer, having it come off Vida Blue has to be my biggest thrill ever."[12] Blue responded to Brye's blast by striking out Eric Soderholm. Catcher George Mitterwald singled and stole second, then went to third on Athletics catcher Duncan's wild throw. But Blue struck out the next two batters to strand Mitterwald.

The Athletics' Larry Brown started the third inning with a groundout, and Corbin struck out Blue. But Oakland fared better the second time through the order: Anderson and Rudi singled. Anderson scored on Jackson's single. Adrian Garrett grounded out to second, but Oakland had tied the game, 1-1.

After Tovar started the Twins' third inning with a groundout, Carew singled. Facing Minnesota's powerful number-three and -four hitters, Blue struck out Killebrew and Oliva for the second time. Corbin was equally effective: An Oakland leadoff hitter finally reached base in the fourth inning when Bando singled. With one out, Bando took third on a muffed groundball. With two outs and Blue hitting, Bando broke for home, but was out. The Twins also lost a runner in their half. Soderholm walked, the only walk Blue issued, then was caught stealing by Duncan.

In the fifth inning Oakland threatened with a pair of baserunners as Anderson and Rudi singled, repeating their third-inning at-bats. With one out, Jackson hit into a fielder's choice, and Garrett fouled out to end the threat. Blue cruised through Minnesota's hitters in the fifth with a foul pop fly, strikeout, and groundout. Both teams were retired in order during the sixth inning and the game remained deadlocked.

Larry Brown began the Oakland seventh with a single to left field. Blue sacrificed him to second. With two outs, Rudi walked, giving Jackson a third opportunity to bat with runners on first and second. He flied out to left field, and for the third time in the game, the Athletics stranded two runners. After the seventh-inning stretch, Brye led off with a single to left and stole second. But he remained there as Blue struck out two and got a fly out.

Adrian Garrett walked to open the A's eighth inning. Successive force outs and a stolen base put a runner at second with two down. Duncan walked, but pinch-hitter Rick Monday struck out to end Oakland's half with another missed opportunity. Blue also encountered trouble in the eighth. He started with a strikeout, but Tovar reached on an error and moved to second on Carew's third single. Killebrew flied out and Oliva grounded out. Both pitchers escaped their eighth-inning jams by stranding opposing runners on first and second.

Rookie right-hander Hal Haydel relieved Corbin for the ninth inning and thwarted Oakland hitters with a groundout and two strikeouts. Brye started the Minnesota ninth with a fly out to left field. Veteran George Thomas, appearing in the next to last game of his 13-year career,[13] grounded out to first base. Then George Mitterwald blasted a 1-and-2 Blue fastball into the left-field pavilion, giving Minnesota a dramatic 2-1 victory. Mitterwald exacted some revenge with his walk-off homer; in June against Oakland, his throwing error on a delayed double steal allowed the winning run to score in a Blue victory.[14] Losing manager Dick Williams lamented his slow hook: "That was going to be (Blue's) last inning. I was just then signaling for Rollie Fingers to get ready in the bullpen. (Blue) threw 142 pitches. He usually throws about 125."[15]

Besides each hitting a home run, Brye and Mitterwald also accounted for both Minnesota stolen bases. Reliever Haydel got his third win. Blue, who struck out 12 and walked one, was saddled with the loss, dropping his record to 23-7. Oakland squandered scoring chances, stranding 10 runners and hitting 1-for-8 with runners in scoring position. Williams noted, "We had plenty of opportunities tonight, but we just didn't get the big hit. In three of (Blue's) last four games, we've gotten him the grand total of one run."[16]

Minnesota swept the doubleheader attended by 22,032 fans, and eventually finished 1971 in fifth place

MEMORABLE GAMES AT MINNESOTA'S DIAMOND ON THE PRAIRIE

with a 74-86 record, 26½ games behind Oakland and 5½ games ahead of the last-place Milwaukee Brewers. The Athletics won the AL West with a 101-60 record, 16 games ahead of Kansas City. Blue received both the Most Valuable Player and Cy Young Awards.[17] Twins walk-off hero Mitterwald finished the season hitting .250 with 13 homers and 44 runs batted in 125 games.

SOURCES

Besides the sources cited in the Notes, the author consulted Baseball-Almanac.com, Baseball-Reference.com, Retrosheet.org, and the following:

James, Bill. *The New Bill James Historical Abstract* (New York: The Free Press, 2001).

Thorn, John, and Pete Palmer, et al. *Total Baseball: The Official Encyclopedia of Major League Baseball* (New York: Viking Press, 2004).

NOTES

1. Chris Roewe, "Writers Predicting Repetition in Races," *The Sporting News*, April 10, 1971: 8.
2. Bob Fowler, "Why Twins Shouldn't Fire Bill Rigney," *The Sporting News*, September 4, 1971: 12.
3. Wells Twombly, "Vida Blue, Newest Superstar," *St. Louis Post-Dispatch*, August 23, 1971: 36.
4. Tom Briere, "Twins' Homers Top Blue, A's," *Minneapolis Star Tribune*, September 4, 1971: 13.
5. Associated Press, "Corbin Hurls Twins Past Senators, 5-3," *Arizona Republic* (Phoenix), July 18, 1971: 27.
6. Bill Hengen, "Pitching Problem for Twins," *Minneapolis Star*, April 3, 1971: 14.
7. Briere: 13.
8. Phil Finch, "Spectacular Homers Save Vida Blue," *San Francisco Examiner*, July 14, 1971: 53.
9. Bill James and Rob Neyer, *The Neyer/James Guide to Pitchers: An Historical Compendium of Pitching, Pitchers, and Pitches* (New York: Fireside Books, 2004), 136.
10. Ron Bergman, "HRs Thwart Vida," *Oakland Tribune*, September 4, 1971: 13.
11. United Press International, "Twins Sweep Oakland," *St. Cloud* (Minnesota) *Times*, September 4, 1971: 12.
12. Bergman: 13.
13. Baseball-Reference.com, "George Thomas 1971 Game Log," baseball-reference.com/players/gl.fcgi?id=thomage01&t=b&year=1971. Accessed January 25, 2020.
14. Dan Stoneking, "Cliff-Edge Twins Still Hanging On," *Minneapolis Star*, September 4, 1971: 7.
15. Associated Press, "Mitterwald's Homer Bests A's and Blue," *Napa Valley Register* (Napa, California), September 4, 1972: 14.
16. Bergman: 13.
17. Ron Bergman, "Vida Adds MVP Award," *Oakland Tribune*, November 17, 1971: 53.

BREWERS, TWINS TAKE TWO DAYS, 22 INNINGS TO FINISH

MAY 12-13, 1972: MILWAUKEE BREWERS 4, MINNESOTA TWINS 3 (22 INNINGS)

By Stew Thornley

On Friday night, May 12, 1972, the focus of the baseball world was on the return of Willie Mays to New York. A trade between the San Francisco Giants and New York Mets just the day before was bringing the star back to the city where he had started his major-league career 21 years earlier, and a crowd of more than 44,000 was at Shea Stadium. Those fans were disappointed when Mays didn't get into the game.

Meanwhile, a much smaller crowd got more than it bargained for in the opening of a three-game series between the Milwaukee Brewers and Minnesota Twins. The weather was pleasant for baseball, and the cooler forecast for the next day was pleasant for an even bigger weekend event in Minnesota, the opening of fishing season.

The Twins, at 14-4, were leading the American League West Division with a strong start after a disappointing season. The Brewers were where they often were since coming into the league three years before as the Seattle Pilots—at the bottom of the standings in their division.

Despite the good beginning, a crowd of only 8,628 was at Met Stadium for the series opener. The fishing opener couldn't be blamed; in fact, the crowd was dotted with fishing enthusiasts who decided a quick ballgame would be the perfect preface for getting up early the next morning and heading for the lake.

The baseball buzz in Minnesota had been diminished after 1969 when manager Billy Martin was fired despite the Twins winning the division title. His successor, Bill Rigney, led the team to another first-place finish, but the team dropped to fifth place in 1971. The sports focus in the state had shifted to the Minnesota Vikings, a football team that was in the midst of a successful eight-season run that included four appearances in the Super Bowl. A players strike that delayed the start of the 1972 season didn't help, and the turnouts at the Met had been mostly sparse.

The temperature was 73 degrees with gusting winds out of the southeast when Dick Woodson delivered a strike to Dave May for the first pitch at 7:35 P.M. Woodson, looking for his fourth win of the season without a loss, put the Brewers down in order.

In the bottom of the inning the Twins got to Milwaukee starter Bill Parsons when Cesar Tovar lined a leadoff single to left, then stole second. After Danny Thompson struck out, Tovar scored on a ground-rule double to left by Rod Carew.

George Scott used his speed, such as it was, to tie the game in the fourth, singling with one out and, with two out, stealing second and scoring on Joe Lahoud's single.

Bobby Darwin

MEMORABLE GAMES AT MINNESOTA'S DIAMOND ON THE PRAIRIE

Tovar started another rally with one out in the fifth with a single. Thompson bunted, and catcher Darrell Porter's force attempt at second was too late; both runners were safe. Carew singled to center to score Tovar and send Thompson to third. Harmon Killebrew walked to load the bases, and a walk to Bobby Darwin forced Thompson in and Parsons out of the game. Earl Stephenson relieved and got Steve Braun to ground into a double play, preventing any more runs.

John Briggs walked to start the top of the seventh and went to third on a double by Lahoud. Woodson got a break when Billy Conigliaro's comebacker deflected off his glove to Thompson. The shortstop was able to both hold Briggs at third and throw out Conigliaro at first. Porter worked a walk on a full count to load the bases. Bill Voss was announced as a pinch-hitter for Rick Auerbach. When Rigney went to the bullpen for Dave LaRoche, Milwaukee manager Dave Bristol sent up right-handed-hitting Tom Reynolds to hit for Voss. Reynolds grounded a single to left, good for two runs and a 3-3 tie.

That was the last scoring of the night. Both teams called on their relief aces – Ken Sanders for Milwaukee and Wayne Granger for the Twins – and each threw five scoreless innings. Others followed for varying stints.

Walks were plentiful in the game, including intentional passes. Tovar singled with one out in the 14th, stole second, and went to third on an overthrow by Porter. Thompson grounded out to pitcher Frank Linzy as Tovar held. Bristol then had Linzy intentionally walk Carew and Killebrew to bring up the struggling Darwin. The strategy worked as Darwin struck out on a ball in the dirt.

Bristol tried it again two innings later with Jim Colborn on the mound. Tovar led off with his fourth single of the game, and Thompson sacrificed. Colborn intentionally walked Carew to get to Killebrew, who flied out. Darwin ended the inning with his fifth strikeout of the game.

Friday night was becoming Saturday morning when Bob Gebhard took the mound for the Twins in the top of the 18th, his first appearance of the season. He quickly got into trouble, giving up singles to May and Bob Heise. Gebhard worked out of it, though, and also survived a threat in the 19th when Colborn tripled with one out. He got Ron Theobald on a comebacker, intentionally walked May, and got Heise to force May at second.

During the extended innings the crowd thinned out with some of the remaining ones moving into better seats. "Hey, Rigney, I'm gotta go fishing in the morning," yelled one stalwart, refusing to leave even though it would mean little sleep for him. "Billy Martin [Rigney's predecessor as manager] never did this!"

The fans who hung around were having a good time, and some didn't care how long the game continued. There was a limit, however, not imposed by anyone's bat but by an American League curfew that didn't allow an inning to start after 1:00 A.M.

The teams reached the curfew in the 21st inning, and the Twins made a push to end rather than suspend the game. With one out Carew doubled, his fifth hit of the game, and Killebrew was intentionally walked to get to Darwin.

Darwin had come up as a pitcher with the Los Angeles Angels in 1962; unable to make it on the mound, he switched to hitting and did better. The Twins gave up outfielder Paul Ray Powell to the Los Angeles Dodgers after the 1971 season, and Darwin was an early sensation with the Twins, homering in four of the first five games in 1972. Trouble hitting curveballs sent him into a slump, and fans were demonstrating their frustration at watching him flail against breaking pitches.

As he came up in the bottom of the 21th, he was 0-for-8 in the game with five strikeouts. He made contact this time, but it was a grounder to third baseman Mike Ferraro, who started a double play that sent the fans out of the ballpark at 1:05 A.M.

The game resumed 12 hours and 10 minutes later. The starters for the scheduled game that day—Bert Blyleven of Minnesota and Jim Lonborg of Milwaukee—first pitched the resumption of the suspended game. The temperature was nearly 20 degrees cooler than when the game had begun, and an even smaller crowd—some back from the night before but otherwise mostly different fans—was in the stands.

Theobald opened the 22nd with a single and May sacrificed. Heise popped out, and Scott was intentionally walked. Ferraro then grounded a single to right-center, off Carew's glove, and Theobald scored the first run in 15 innings.

Braun grounded a single to right to start the bottom of the inning. Steve Brye bunted down the first-base line. Scott slipped fielding the ball and was charged with an error as both runners were safe. Rick Dempsey sacrificed, putting runners on second and third. Eric Soderholm hit for Blyleven and made good contact, but right at Ferraro, who caught his line drive for the second out.

Tovar had a chance to tie a major-league record with 11 at-bats in a game, but Milwaukee manager Bristol went to an effective strategy—the intentional walk—and had Lonborg put him on. With the bases loaded, Thompson grounded to Heise, who threw to Theobald at second to force Tovar and end the game, 17 hours and 57 minutes after it had started.

The combined playing time was 5:47. Colborn, who pitched from the 15th to the 21st, was the deserving winning pitcher. Milwaukee pitchers walked 12, five intentionally, and the Twins walked eight, two intentionally. The Brewers left 16 runners on base, the Twins 23; 86 batters came to the plate for Milwaukee and 92 for Minnesota.

After a break, the regular game began with Lonborg and Blyleven pitching. Neither made it to the end of this one, which went 15 innings with the Twins winning.

Coming away with a split, Milwaukee and Minnesota played 37 innings in fewer than 24 hours.

SOURCES

The author used his scorebook and memories of the game for this account.

The BaseballReference.com and Retrosheet.org websites were used to confirm all data.

JULY 7, 1972: KILLEBREW'S HOMER WINS QUILICI DEBUT

MINNESOTA TWINS 5, NEW YORK YANKEES 2

By Dana Yost

On Friday, July 7, 1972, presidential candidates arrived in Miami for the 1972 Republican National Convention that nominated Richard Nixon. Billie Jean King won the women's title at Wimbledon. And, that night at Metropolitan Stadium, two Twins greats did what they could so well: Harmon Killebrew slugged a go-ahead home run and Rod Carew drove in two runs with an infield single.

But the biggest headline in the next day's *Minneapolis Tribune* belonged to neither Killebrew nor Carew. Instead, it went to a man who had backed them up in the Twins' infield for a half-dozen years, Frank Quilici.

"Twins Win 5-2; Quilici Record 1.000," the headline the next morning read.[1]

The Twins defeated the New York Yankees 5-2 in Quilici's debut as a major-league manager in front of 19,514 fans, to that point the Twins' largest home crowd of the season.

The likable Quilici was greeted with a "standing ovation ... when he brought the lineup card to home plate at the start of the game."[2]

Fans weren't the only ones excited about Quilici's debut.

"Do I feel more anxious to play?" Carew said. "Only about 200 percent more."[3]

At 33, Quilici became the youngest manager in the major leagues. He replaced Bill Rigney, who was fired after the Twins finished a dreary road trip 1-5, including losing their last four in a row. Not only were they losing, their offense was nearly impotent: In the five losses, they'd scored a total of four runs and were shut out in back-to-back games in the last two. Not that things had gone much better at home: In their previous homestand, the team's attendance was as anemic as the hitting had been on the road. The Twins drew late-June crowds of 12,803, 6,815, 6,475, 12,668 (for a doubleheader), and 5,099, as they fell out of the American League West race.

After leading the American League in attendance in their first decade (1961-1970), they'd failed to draw 1 million fans for the first time in 1971. In midsummer 1972, they were becoming an attendance afterthought, something owner Calvin Griffith couldn't abide. He knew the Twins needed a jolt.

Although well-liked by players and fans and a link to past Twins glory, Quilici was not necessarily the obvious choice to replace Rigney. After he retired in 1970, he was largely given a "cheerleader role," as a

Frank Quilici

coach without portfolio – a loosely fitting position that basically gave him a uniform and paycheck but no duties and did not count toward his major league pension.[4] But he had played in all seven games of the 1965 World Series, was on the 1969 and 1970 American League West Division championship teams, and "was as well-known in this state as Hubert Humphrey,"[5] according to Griffith. The young Quilici was considered a good communicator who could be fiery when needed, and his youth was in his favor. After thinking it through, Griffith decided Quilici might inspire the Twins.

"We believe this is a team with a lot of potential," Griffith said in a news conference to announce the managerial change, with a smiling Qulici at his side. "We have better players than we had last year. Our pitching is much better and our hitters aren't the worst in the American League. I think we're fifth in team batting."

"This move has been going through my mind for a couple of weeks. I haven't been able to sleep well the past two nights, though. . . . I think Frank can stimulate the players and give baseball back to the fans. I hope he has better luck than Rigney."[6]

Quilici said he wanted players who would hustle and dedicate themselves to the game, and planned on using his open brand of communication.

"I don't think managing in my first major-league game compares to anything else that's happened to me," he said. "I think I've had enough time to have the importance of the job register, but I certainly am starting to feel the challenge of the job – what it can mean to our team, the organization, the people in the stands."[7]

As Quilici's first game started, the Twins looked more like they had in their losing road trip than anything fresh: They trailed 2-1 through six innings and had left eight runners on base. Quilici was getting nervous.

"I told the guys on the bench that this was a lot of fun," Quilici joked. "Hey, [here] we're losing the game. I sensed that maybe they were trying too hard to give me a win in my first game."[8]

With two outs in the bottom of the seventh, Carew singled to center field. The next batter, Killebrew, homered off starting and losing pitcher Fritz Peterson to turn the game around, giving the Twins a 3-2 lead. Not a surprise: Killebrew always hit Peterson well. His .324 lifetime average against Peterson was the best of the 20 pitchers he had the most plate appearances against. But Killebrew didn't hit for much power against Peterson – only three doubles, two home runs and a .485 slugging average.[9] But one of those home runs came here and, from Quilici's perspective, was well-timed.

"I wanted to jump through the roof of the dugout," Quilici said. "The first thing I thought of when Harmon hit that ball was [the home run] he got against the Yankees in 1965, right before the All-Star Game." The 1965 homer helped propel the Twins to the American League pennant. "I don't know why I thought of that particular hit, but maybe it's because I was down at Denver [in the minor leagues] right then and a few days later I joined the Twins. Maybe, too, it's right around the All-Star break now."[10]

"Killebrew smiled when told of Quilici's remark. 'I hope that means we can do the same thing again this year.'"[11]

Killebrew said the home run "meant a little something extra 'because Frank and I have been close friends for a long time.'"[12]

Along with Killebrew's homer, "some dipsy-do, in the eighth inning, provided Quilici with the victory."[13]

In the eighth, the Twins had George Mitterwald on third base and speedy Cesar Tovar on second base with one out. A nervous Quilici whiffed on calling for a squeeze bunt with Danny Thompson at the plate, and Thompson ended up flying out. Carew was up next and hit a slow roller down the first-base line. "He dipped around Felipe Alou's tag – in the view of umpire Bill Kunkel – and grabbed the bag with an outstretched dive."[14]

Mitterwald scored and Tovar "kept streaming around third base" and scored, too, while Alou "discussed" the play with Kunkel.[15] The two runs gave the Twins a 5-2 lead and made a winning pitcher of reliever Wayne Granger, who threw three scoreless innings to finish the game.

Carew said of the play at first base, "Normally I try to run with long strides. But last night I really tried to burn it down the line. You try to do everything to win [for Quilici], I guess."[16]

Carew had three hits to go with his two runs batted in. "Everyone wanted to get off on the right foot for Quilici. ... I busted my butt to try to help Frank win his first game."[17]

Griffith, who'd been so unhappy with the team's performance that he could barely sleep, liked what he saw in Quilici's debut.

"It was a different type of hustle. They looked like a different team to me."[18]

MEMORABLE GAMES AT MINNESOTA'S DIAMOND ON THE PRAIRIE

The Twins' attendance bump continued for the rest of the Yankees series, with a crowd of 14,866 the next day and 19,613 for the finale.[19]

Yet for the season, the Twins didn't prove any more successful under Quilici than under Rigney. They were 41-43 under Quilici after going 36-34 for Rigney. Their total home attendance was 797,901 in the strike-shortened year. Quilici lasted as manager until the end of the 1975 season, when he was fired with a career record of 280-287.[20] He became a Twins broadcaster for a time and a longtime goodwill ambassador for the team.

NOTES

1 Jon Roe, "Twins Win 5-2; Quilici Record 1.000," *Minneapolis Tribune*, July 8, 1972: 1B.

2 Roe.

3 "For Quilici, 1st Day Means Meetings, TV and Tipped Cap," *Minneapolis Tribune*, July 8, 1972: 3B.

4 Bob Fowler, "Quilici Leads with Gentle Talk – or Left Hook," *The Sporting News*, July 29, 1972: 31.

5 Bob Fowler, "Cal Expects Quilici to Lure Fans Back to Twins," *The Sporting News*, July 22, 1972: 19.

6 Bob Fowler, "Cal Expects Quilici to Lure Fans Back to Twins."

7 "For Quilici, 1st Day Means Meetings, TV and Tipped Cap."

8 Roe.

9 baseball-reference.com, Killebrew vs. opposing pitchers.

10 Roe.

11 Roe.

12 Sid Hartman, "Twins Worked Harder for New Pilot Quilici," *Minneapolis Tribune*, July 8, 1972: 3B.

13 Roe.

14 Roe; retrosheet.org.

15 Roe.

16 Roe.

17 Hartman.

18 Hartman.

19 baseball-reference.com.

20 All statistics in this paragraph from baseball-reference.com.

YANKEES' BERNIE ALLEN DOES IN FORMER TEAMMATES

JULY 8, 1972: NEW YORK YANKEES 1, MINNESOTA TWINS 0 (11 INNINGS)

By Stew Thornley

Bernie Allen was well-known in Minnesota, for bad and good reasons to fans in the state.

In 1960 he was the quarterback, kicker, punter, and a defensive back for a Purdue team that upset the Minnesota Gophers and kept them from winning the Big Ten title outright. (The Gophers still tied for the conference championship and were voted college football national champions at the end of the regular season.)

After the game Minnesota fans congratulated Allen as he walked to the Purdue bus. He said that was a reason he chose to sign with the Minnesota Twins rather than take a large bonus from the New York Mets. "I was a quiet kid then, and New York scared the hell out of me. I remembered the Gophers fans and felt Minnesota was a place that I could be comfortable."[1]

Allen became the regular second baseman for Minnesota in 1962, playing 159 games and hitting 12 home runs in helping the Twins finish second, five games behind the New York Yankees. In 1964 Allen was injured at second base, tearing ligaments in his knee. He said he sought his own surgeon, who repaired his knee, a procedure Minnesota owner Calvin Griffith didn't sanction. Griffith paid for the surgery but, according to Allen, cut his salary by a corresponding amount before the next season.[2]

"I liked everything about Minnesota except Calvin," said Allen. "In fact, he's the reason I was a player representative later in my career. I was there for Marvin Miller's first union meeting."[3]

The surgery allowed Allen to play for nine more seasons and gave him the chance to be around long enough to vex Griffith one more time.

It was Saturday, July 8, 1972, a day when it looked as though no baseball would be played. The matchup of aces Mel Stottlemyre of the Yankees and Bert Blyleven of the Twins was enough to keep most fans hanging around Metropolitan Stadium even though the start of the game was delayed 2 hours and 7 minutes by rain.

By 1972 Allen was a Yankee, having been traded in December 1966 to the Washington Senators and then in December 1971 by the Texas Rangers to the Yankees.

During the rain New York pitcher Mike Kekich walked down the left-field line and began running wind sprints toward center field. A bored bunch of Knothole Day kids found some amusement by jeering Kekich. Kekich responded by completing one of his sprints with a belly flop and slide on the wet grass. The jeers turned to cheers and got louder when Kekich repeated the stunt, this time by stroking his arms as though he were swimming on the turf. As Kekich walked back to the foul line, he stopped in front of the bleachers and led one section against another in trying to produce the loudest cheers. For years after, Twins announcer Herb Carneal said he always had a soft spot in his heart for Kekich because of the entertainment he provided for the young fans.[4]

Ray Christensen of WCCO Radio broadcasts a game from the Met in the 1970s.

MEMORABLE GAMES AT MINNESOTA'S DIAMOND ON THE PRAIRIE

The entertainment finally moved to the pitcher's mound when the rain let up. Neither team could break through although both had chances.

Roy White of the Yankees doubled with two out in the top of the fourth. After a walk to Ron Blomberg, Allen hit a low liner to the right side. Rod Carew moved left from his second-base position and snared the ball for the final out.

In the last of the fifth, the Twins' Charlie Manuel and Bobby Darwin led off with singles. Eric Soderholm forced Darwin at second as Manuel moved to third. Stottlemyre got out of the jam by striking out George Mitterwald and getting Blyleven to foul out to Rusty Torres in right.

The Yankees produced their best chances in the later innings. White led off the seventh with a bunt single through Carew and went to third when Blomberg lined a single off Harmon Killebrew's glove at first. Allen struck out, and Celerino Sanchez walked to load the bases. Jerry Kenney went down swinging for the second out and Stottlemyre grounded Blyleven's next pitch up the middle. Shortstop Danny Thompson dived, gloved the ball behind second base, and flipped to Carew to force Sanchez.

Blyleven put down the top of the New York order in the eighth but got in trouble again when he walked White to start the ninth. Blomberg was rung up by plate umpire Bill Kunkel (a former Yankees pitcher), but White was off on a 0-and-1 pitch to Allen, who poked a single through the vacated spot at short, sending White to third. Sanchez grounded to Eric Soderholm at third, and White got caught in a rundown as he tried to come home. Felipe Alou hit for Kenney and struck out.

No longer wanting to rely on his mates to produce a run, Stottlemyre lined a double to left-center to lead off the 10th, and Torres walked. Thurman Munson was called out on strikes and Bobby Murcer forced Torres at second. Blyleven then issued his sixth walk of the game, to White to load the bases, and fell behind 2-and-0 to Blomberg, who then hit a grounder to right. Carew went well to his left to field it and threw to Blyleven covering to get the right-hander out of another inning.

Rich Reese hit for Blyleven with one out in the last of the 10th and singled, but Cesar Tovar grounded into a double play, sending the game into the 11th.

Allen was the first batter in the 11th inning, against Wayne Granger, and the count reached 2-and-2 before Allen got under an inside sinker and sent it into the right-field seats. "It might have been a ball," he said, "but I had two strikes on me and couldn't afford to take a chance."[5]

As Allen watched the ball sail out, he tripped over first base and sprawled face-first into the ground. Allen got up and continued his journey around the bases for the only run of the game. "That's how I used to avoid big linemen at Purdue," Allen said. "Duck under them."[6]

In the days when starters were often completers, Stottlemyre took the mound in the bottom of the 11th even though he had already delivered 132 pitches. Only after he gave up a single to Thompson, the first batter in the inning, did manager Ralph Houk signal to the bullpen for Sparky Lyle. Lyle had been fantastic for the Yankees after coming to New York in a late spring training trade with Boston. Coming into the Minnesota game with an earned-run average of 0.91 over 49⅓ innings, Lyle was a fireman who often pitched more than three innings when it was necessary.

Houk didn't consider using Lyle until Thompson's leadoff single. Lyle needed only nine pitches to lock down the win, getting Carew on a comebacker as Thompson went to second and striking out Killebrew and pinch-hitter Steve Brye.

Whether disappointed or elated by the outcome, those who stayed through the delay and more than three hours of play had seen a great contest. Harmon Killebrew summed it up: "That's the kind of game where both pitchers should get a win."[7]

SOURCES

The author's scorebook contains the account of the game. Baseball-reference.com and Retrosheet.org were used to determine Sparky Lyle's ERA and innings coming into the game.

NOTES

1. Patrick Reusse, "Minnesota Was a Good Fit for Bernie Allen of the '65 Twins," *Minneapolis Star Tribune,* July 30, 2015, http://www.startribune.com/minnesota-was-a-good-fit-for-bernie-allen-of-the-65-twins/319761501/.
2. Author conversation with Bernie Allen, September 12, 1999.
3. "Minnesota Was a Good Fit."
4. Herb Carneal with Stew Thornley, *Hi Everybody!* (Minneapolis: Nodin Press, 1995).
5. Joseph Durso, "Stottlemyre Is 1-0 Victor on Allen's Wallop in 11th," *New York Times,* July 9, 1972, sec. 5: 1.
6. Jon Roe, "Yankees Dampen Twins," *Minneapolis Tribune,* July 9, 1972: 1C.
7. "Yankees Dampen Twins."

REESE'S PINCH GRAND SLAM LEAVES TWINS SHORT OF VICTORY

JULY 9, 1972: NEW YORK YANKEES 9, MINNESOTA TWINS 6

By Stew Thornley

Rich Reese could deliver in the pinch.

He had two important pinch-hit two-run homers within a two-week span in 1967, one off Fred Talbot to beat the Yankees in New York and the other against Moe Drabowsky in the last of the ninth for a 10-9 win over Baltimore.[1]

In 1969 Reese started hitting them with the bases full. On August 3 he hit for Jim Kaat and sent a grand slam over the left-field fence that saddled Baltimore's Dave McNally with his first loss of the season after 15 wins. His grand slam on June 7, 1970 — hitting for announced pinch-hitter Bob Allison — broke a 3-3 tie in Washington.

Reese wasn't in the lineup against Steve Kline of the Yankees in the rubber game of a series at Metropolitan Stadium on July 9, 1972, not that anyone noticed. The attention was on Kline, who came into the game with an earned-run average (ERA) of 1.86, the best in the majors among qualifying pitchers.

Fans were starting to come back to the Met, in part because of Frank Quilici, who took over as Minnesota manager before the beginning of the weekend series.

Twins owner Calvin Griffith didn't have much success with his gate receipts over the first half of the season. The team's season opener had been scheduled for what was a beautiful day for baseball on April 6 – except that there was no baseball as a players' strike wiped out the opener plus six more home games.

When the strike ended, the Twins were set to open at home on Saturday, April 22, but the game was postponed by rain. The opener finally occurred the next day, but with the temperature 44 degrees and a northwest wind of 12 miles per hour, the crowd was a little under 18,000. Even though Minnesota won 23 of its first 35 games, the attendance didn't pick up, and when the success on the field started to wane, manager Bill Rigney was sent packing.

Quilici had been a popular player with the Twins and served as a coach under Rigney starting in 1971. Griffith was up front about picking Quilici over third-base coach Ralph Rowe, who had 10 years of managing experience in the minor leagues, including as the skipper of Minnesota's top farm team in Portland, Oregon, in 1971. Quilici, who lived year-round in Minnesota, traveled through the region to promote the Twins in the offseason, and Griffith hoped he could stimulate the fans as well as the players.[2]

The managerial change seemed to have an effect in the Friday-night opener of the series, drawing a season-high crowd of 19,514 as Harmon Killebrew's two-run homer in the seventh gave Quilici a win in his debut. Rain kept some fans away on Saturday as the Yankees won 1-0 on an 11th-inning homer by Bernie Allen, but a sunny Sunday brought them back, and attendance topped that of Friday night by 99 (19,613).

Unfortunately for the locals, the Twins played one of their poorer games of the season and fell in a hole quickly. Ron Blomberg put the Yankees ahead in the first with a two-out, two-run double off the fence in right. The next inning Horace Clarke's two-run double, followed by a run-scoring single by Thurman Munson, made the score 5-0 and sent Minnesota starter Ray Corbin to the showers. New York added a run in the fifth.

As for Steve Kline, five scoreless innings shrank his ERA to 1.77. But the Twins got a run in the sixth on doubles by Jim Nettles (who was pinch-hitting) and Rod Carew.

The game got completely away from the Twins, artistically and competitively, in the top of the seventh, starting with a popup by Bobby Murcer. Third baseman Eric Soderholm called for it but appeared to be having trouble, perhaps with the sun. Shortstop Danny Thompson didn't call him off, and at the last instant Soderholm let the ball drop and was charged with an error. Roy White doubled, and Blomberg hit a fly to right. Cesar Tovar got a bad jump, allowing the ball to drop and then skip past him. Murcer scored and White, who had to hold until the ball landed safely, hustled for home as Tovar made a wild heave that sailed past catcher George Mitterwald.

Kline took the 9-1 lead into the bottom of the seventh and got leadoff batter Charlie Manuel to pop out before Bobby Darwin beat out an infield hit. Soderholm followed with a single and Mitterwald walked to load the bases. Manager Ralph Houk decided that was enough for Kline and called for Lindy McDaniel as Reese came out of the dugout to hit for pitcher Bob Gebhard.

Like many other batters in the league, Reese didn't like dealing with McDaniel's forkball, and he found a way to get around it. After McDaniel missed with his first two pitches, Reese said, he looked to third and pretended that Rowe had given him the take sign on 2-and-0. "I gave him a disgusted look and said, 'Take'?" His intent was to fool McDaniel into thinking he wouldn't be swinging at the next pitch.[3]

Reese was determined to go after only a fastball and that's what he got, sending the pitch into the bleachers in right field. Reese said the Yankees weren't enamored of his theatrical antics, especially catcher Thurman Munson, who gave Reese an earful when he completed his circuit and crossed home plate.[4]

In the stands, two teenagers – one a Yankees fan, the other a Twins fan – looked at each other and said simultaneously, "There goes Kline's ERA."[5]

Reese's third career pinch-hit grand slam set an American League record and tied him with Ron Northey for the major-league mark. (Since then, Willie McCovey hit his third pinch slam, all of them coming in the National League, and Ben Broussard tied Reese for the American League record as well as the others for the major-league record.)[6]

The blast at least gave the Twins fans something to cheer about, although their team's sloppiness continued through the rest of the game. Sparky Lyle relieved McDaniel in the last of the eighth after Killebrew singled. Lyle got Steve Brye to ground into a double play with Killebrew's takeout slide comically coming in five feet short of second base.

Soderholm made another error in the ninth when he couldn't hold a throw from Darwin in center that had beaten Felipe Alou at third. The Twins managed to get out of the inning and got a run off Lyle in the bottom of the ninth, but even this didn't please Quilici as Soderholm scored despite running through Rowe's stop sign.

The Yankees won 9-6. Though their ERAs both suffered, Kline got his eighth win of the year and Lyle his league-leading 19th save.

While the historic feature of the game was Reese's grand slam, the immediate focus after the game was on the poor showing by the Twins. "What a shame it is to get a good crowd like we did today and then play that kinda game," Quilici said. "It kinda sours it all."[7]

SOURCES

The author's scorebook contains the account of this game. In addition to the sources cited in the Notes, the author used the Baseball-Reference.com and Retrosheet.org websites for material pertinent to this article.

NOTES

1   Reese's homers came on August 18, 1967 against Talbot and August 31, against Drabowsky.

2   Tom Briere, "Griffith Says Quilici Was Stunned by Promotion," *Minneapolis Tribune*, July 7, 1972: 1C.

3   Author interview with Rich Reese, August 1, 2015.

4   Reese interview.

5   The author was one of the teenage fans (not the Twins fan).

6   Keith Sutton, "The Dream Hit: A Pinch Grand Slam," *Baseball Research Journal*, Society for American Baseball Research, 1972; David Vincent, SABR Home Run Log.

7   Jon Roe, "19,613 See Yanks Rip Twins," *Minneapolis Tribune*, July 10, 1972: 1C.

EDDIE BANE MAKES MAJOR-LEAGUE DEBUT FOR TWINS IN INDEPENDENCE DAY SELLOUT

JULY 4, 1973: KANSAS CITY ROYALS 5, MINNESOTA TWINS 4

By Steve Smith

In 1972 the Minnesota Twins' attendance hit a low of 797,901. In late June of 1973, the Twins were on pace to draw less than that of 1972. On June 27 the Twins played the Texas Rangers in Arlington before a crowd of 35,698, far above the average Rangers crowd of 8,470. The stimulus for the large crowd was the major-league debut of David Clyde, a left-handed pitcher who was the first pick in the 1973 draft on June 5 and came directly to the majors for his debut.

Twins owner Calvin Griffith took notice and the following day it was announced that Eddie Bane would be the Twins starter for the July 4 game at Metropolitan Stadium against Kansas City. Bane, like Clyde a left-handed pitcher, was the Twins' first-round pick in the 1973 draft. He was a college All-America at Arizona State, had a collegiate record of 40-4 and was 1973 college player of the year. His ASU team lost the 1973 College World Series championship game to USC.[1] Three days after that game, he signed a $55,000 contract with the Twins. Like Clyde, Bane would come directly to the major leagues to make his July 4 debut.

The Twins were hoping to attract a crowd of 30,000, far above their 1973 average attendance. As added inducements, they also announced they would pass out 30,000 photos of Bane to fans attending the game and would have a fireworks display after the game.

The game was successful beyond the Twins' expectations. A crowd of 45,890 flocked to Metropolitan Stadium on a beautiful July 4 evening. The late-arriving crowd was not expected by Twins officials,[2] so fans had difficulty getting parked and into their seats by game time. The Twins decided to delay the start of the game by 15 minutes. "I was well into my warmup when they said the game would be delayed," Bane said. "I didn't care but Kitty [Jim Kaat] went crazy. He was yelling, 'You can't do this to the kid. He's already loose, sweated up.'"[3]

The start of the game was pushed back, but it didn't bother Bane. He allowed only one run in seven innings. The first batter he faced, Freddie Patek, flied out to center field. Cookie Rojas then walked but was forced at second on a grounder to short by Amos Otis. Otis was then thrown out when he attempted to steal second.[4] Bane went three up, three down in the second inning, including his first major-league strikeout — Lou Piniella.

Bane allowed his only run in the third on a single by Hal McRae and a double by Fran Healy. He allowed a single in the fourth inning by Kurt Bevacqua, who was then erased in a double play. Bane retired the side in order in the fifth and sixth innings.

In the seventh inning, Piniella reached on an error by third baseman Steve Braun and was sacrificed to second. Paul Schaal walked. Bane got out of the jam by striking out McRae and getting Jim Wohlford on a liner to left.

Meanwhile the Twins were held scoreless by Royals starter Dick Drago for the first seven innings. Although the Twins accumulated eight hits and two walks off Drago, they were unable to push across a run.

Twins manager Frank Quilici brought in Ray Corbin to start the eighth. Corbin pitched a scoreless inning.

In the bottom of the eighth the Twins erupted for three runs off Drago on a double by Braun followed by Larry Hisle's single scoring Braun and a home run by first baseman Joe Lis to take a 3-1 lead. However, in the top of the ninth, Kansas City mounted a comeback off Corbin. After striking out Piniella, Corbin allowed a single to Bevacqua, then walked Schaal and pinch-hitter John Mayberry to load the bases. Pinch-hitter Gail Hopkins hit a foul pop to third on which Bevacqua was able to score. Corbin fell behind in the count to pinch-hitter Ed Kirkpatrick to load the bases and then fell behind in the count to Patek. Bill Hands relieved and completed the walk to Patek, which forced in the tying run.[5] Rojas followed with a two-run single that gave the Royals the lead. Steve Hovley flied out to left to end the inning.

The Twins led off the bottom of the ninth with singles by Rod Carew and Jerry Terrell. Gene Garber relieved Drago and gave up a fly ball to designated hitter Tony Oliva on which Carew scored. With the Royals leading 5-4, Garber struck out Bobby Darwin, allowed a single to Braun, and got Larry Hisle to fly to center to end the game.

Drago got the win and Corbin took the loss. The game was played in 2 hours and 58 minutes.

Bane went on to start five more games with the Twins in 1973 and relieve in 17 games. He finished 1973 with a record of 0-5 and a 4.92 earned-run average (ERA) in 60⅓ innings pitched. He spent all of 1974 and most of 1975 at Tacoma, the Twins' Triple-A affiliate. In September 1975 he was called up by the Twins, started four games and finished with a 3-1 record and a 2.86 ERA in 28⅓ innings. In 1976 he again started the season at Tacoma, was called up in June and started 15 games for the Twins, finishing 4-7 with a 5.11 ERA in 79⅓ innings pitched.

After spending 1977 with Tacoma, Bane was released by the Twins. Although he attempted comebacks with the White Sox and Royals, he never pitched in the major leagues again.

In 1984 Bane accepted an offer to scout for the Cleveland Indians. He turned that job into a career, working for the Dodgers, Rays, Angels, Tigers, and Red Sox. He was scouting director for the Angels from 2004 to 2010 and was the man responsible for making Mike Trout the 25th selection in the 2009 draft.

The July 4, 1973, crowd established the regular-season attendance record for the Twins in Metropolitan Stadium.[6] "They announced 45,000 but the crowd had to be 250,000, from the conversations I've had," Bane said.[7]

"I remember after I pitched that night, the people gave me a standing ovation. And at the time, there weren't such things as curtain calls like they have now. Jim Kaat told me to go out of the dugout and tip my hat so I did. I think that was a pretty neat deal for the people there to do that for me."[8]

AUTHOR'S NOTE

The author attended this game and was inspired to write this article after reviewing his scorecard and his Eddie Bane picture received at the game.

SOURCES

Sources consulted include Retrosheet.org, Baseball-Reference.com, *The Sporting News*, and the *Minneapolis Star Tribune*.

NOTES

1. Bane did not pitch in the championship game. He pitched the semifinal game, defeating the Dave Winfield-led Minnesota Gophers. Winfield was the fifth pick of the 1973 draft by the San Diego Padres. Bane was the 11th pick.
2. Only 12,000 advance tickets had been sold.
3. Patrick Reusse, "Happy 40th Anniversary Eddie Bane," *Minneapolis Star Tribune*, July 4, 2013.
4. Otis was ejected from the game for arguing the call.
5. Hands relieved Corbin with a 2-and-0 count on Patek and completed the walk, which was charged to Corbin.
6. The record was broken on June 26, 1977, with a crowd of 46,963 inspired by a jersey day promotion.
7. Reusse.
8. Jim Walsh, "Bane Fondly Remembers Standing Ovation in Debut for Twins," *Minneapolis Star Tribune*, April 19, 1987.

KAAT DEFEATS FORMER TEAMMATES IN COMPLETE-GAME DUEL WITH ALBURY

JUNE 22, 1974: CHICAGO WHITE SOX 3, MINNESOTA TWINS 1 (10 INNINGS)

By Richard Cuicchi

Jim Kaat's previous outing for the White Sox on June 18, 1974, was a red-letter day: He got his 200th major-league win. Perhaps it contributed to his confidence in his next game, on June 22, when he went 10 innings to claim his next victory. Kaat's mound opponent, Vic Albury, didn't make it easy for him though, since the Twins left-hander was also at the top of his game that day, matching Kaat's 10 innings.

The 1974 season was like riding on a roller-coaster for Kaat. He had his share of ups and downs during the season, experiencing multiple winning and losing periods. The Minnesota Twins had given up on him late in the 1973 season, and the White Sox claimed him off waivers in August for barely the waiver price. The 35-year-old Kaat was now in his second season with the White Sox. It appeared that the White Sox had gotten a bargain when he won four of his first five decisions. But his season began to fall apart in mid-May when he suffered a five-game losing streak, and he started questioning whether his career was fizzling out.

During his career, Kaat had pitched through some tough periods before, but he always seemed to rebound. Before coming to the White Sox, he had played 15 seasons for the Twins, winning 190 games, the most by any Twins pitcher at the time. Included were 12 seasons with double-digit wins.

He pitched only 23⅓ innings in those five losses, and had a 7.33 earned-run average. Only once did he get past the seventh inning. Consequently, White Sox manager Chuck Tanner had to make the tough decision to remove the veteran from the starting rotation.

Was this the beginning of the end of Kaat's illustrious career? He said, "You begin saying to yourself, 'Well this must be the end.' You worry about it. But it's a strange thing. Age isn't that much of a factor. Sometimes you can pitch as well, or better, at 35 than you did at 25.'" He added, "When you're young and doing poorly, you never think of those things. When you're 22 and get kicked around, you still have a future. But when you're 35, you've got to turn it around a lot quicker."[1]

However, Kaat did turn things around. He broke his losing streak by picking up his 199th career win in a relief appearance on June 7. His start on June 18, his first since June 2, was celebrated with his 200-win milestone, a complete-game victory over Cleveland.

The Twins had roughed up Kaat with four runs in 2⅔ innings in his first outing against them in early April, so he was looking to get revenge against his former teammates.

Without a left-hander in the starting rotation for the Twins, Albury had been pressed into service as a starter in late April. A first baseman when he signed with Cleveland in 1965, he had converted to pitching after serving two years in the military. The starting role was new to him: In his rookie season, 1973, his 14 appearances were all in relief, with an impressive 2.70 ERA. Joining the rotation in 1974, he posted effective outings in three of his first four starts. Despite his initial success, he was anxious to return to his reliever role. He said, "I don't dislike being a starter, but I like being a relief pitcher better."[2] But then he ran into difficulty, recording five consecutive losing decisions before his start on June 22. His 2-6 record reflected his regression.

Coming into the game, the White Sox were in fourth place in the American League West, but just three games behind the first-place Oakland A's. The Twins were in fifth place in the six-team division, five games behind the White Sox. Their lineup featured potent hitters like Rod Carew, Harmon Killebrew, Tony Oliva, Bobby Darwin, and Larry Hisle.

MEMORABLE GAMES AT MINNESOTA'S DIAMOND ON THE PRAIRIE

Jim Kaat was an outstanding pitchers for the Twins in the 1960s and 1970s before being sent to the Chicago White Sox in 1973. The following year he beat the Twins with a 10-inning complete game.

Chicago scored in the first and last innings of the game but couldn't manage to put up a run in between. The White Sox' run in the first inning came on a walk to Brian Downing, a single by Jorge Orta, a wild pitch, and a groundout by Ron Santo.

Albury held the White Sox in check for the next eight innings, allowing only one runner to reach second base, in the fifth inning.

The Twins tied the game in the bottom of the eighth when Eric Soderholm led off with a single. Glenn Borgmann bunted him to second, Danny Thompson's grounder to second base moved him to third, and Steve Brye's single scored Soderholm.

The Twins had a chance to win the game in the bottom of the ninth, when Larry Hisle drove a 430-foot shot over center fielder Ken Henderson that appeared to be headed for extra bases. However, Henderson retreated in time to make a lunging catch that took him against the bullpen gate.

In the top of the 10th, Downing singled off Albury with two outs. Orta followed with his fourth home run of the season to make the score 3-1. Kaat retired the side in order in the bottom half to claim the victory. It was the third game of the season in which Orta's hit won a contest in extra innings.

Kaat, who was wearing an old Bert Blyleven T-shirt under his uniform for good luck, was stingy with the Twins hitters when it came to allowing baserunners; they managed only five singles and a walk. Excluding the White Sox' two run-scoring innings, Albury kept the game close, effectively silencing their bats with a lone single and three walks. Altogether, he yielded five hits and four walks for the entire game.

Albury expressed frustration about how his season was going. He said, "I guess I keep wondering when I'm going to win one. But I try not to let it bother me when I'm out there pitching. I never think I'm going to lose while the game is going on." He added, "But when it's over, it seems like I just can't get a win. There's nothing I can do but go back out and try my hardest again next time."[3]

Kaat sympathized with Albury, "I know he's been having rough luck," the ex-Twin said. "He certainly deserved to win this game, too, but it was the kind of game where a break could win it, and I'm glad we got the break. Except for three feet [a reference to Hisle's drive that Ken Henderson corralled], we might have lost this one in nine innings."[4]

Kaat's winning decision brought his record to 7-6. It was his third victory in a row, and he would go on to win seven straight. But his season took another turn for the worse in August when he lost six of eight starts.

He experienced another resurgence in his season by finishing with a seven-game winning streak. Kaat yielded only two earned runs in his last 60⅔ innings pitched. His final record was 21-13; it was the second 20-win season of his career.

Albury had a revival of his own, going 6-2 record the rest of the season, primarily as a starter. He pitched two more seasons in the majors, eventually getting his wish to return to the reliever role.

Pitching coach Johnny Sain was a calming force for Kaat during his rough spots. Kaat's previous work under Sain in Minnesota allowed him to be comfortable putting his career in Sain's hands. He attributed his turnaround to a change in his pitching motion. "You might say it goes against everything you're taught. But I'm throwing more with my arm and less with my body," he said. "Johnny Sain feels that this delivery suits me better at this stage of my career."[5]

Kaat was hardly finished at age 35. He won 20 games the next season, earning a fourth-place finish in the Cy Young Award voting. He went on to pitch in the majors until age 44, retiring after the 1983 season. He ended his career with 283 wins, 21st on the all-time leader list at the time.

METROPOLITAN STADIUM

SOURCES

In addition to the sources cited in the Notes, the author consulted Retrosheet and Baseball-Reference.com:

retrosheet.org/boxesetc/1974/B06240KCA1974.htm

baseball-reference.com/boxes/MIN/MIN197406220.shtml

NOTES

1. Jerome Holtzman, "Slumping Kaat Knows Value of Self-Discipline," *The Sporting News*, June 22, 1974: 17.
2. Bob Fowler, "Albury, Successful as Starter, Longs for Bullpen," *The Sporting News*, May 25, 1974: 10.
3. John Gilbert, "10th Inning Orta Homer Tips Twins," *Minneapolis Tribune*, June 23, 1972: 3C.
4. Gilbert.
5. Richard Dozer, "Vet Kaat Proving Chisox Can Spot a Pitching Bargain," *The Sporting News*, August 31, 1974: 3.

HISLE HOMER HELPS BLYLEVEN OVERCOME RANGERS ON INDEPENDENCE DAY

JULY 4, 1974: MINNESOTA TWINS 3, TEXAS RANGERS 1

By Frederick C. Bush

An Independence Day crowd of 21,008, the largest gathering of the season at Metropolitan Stadium to that point, came to see the Twins' 23-year-old pitching ace, Bert Blyleven, take on the Texas Rangers in the finale of a four-game series. Blyleven had been battling a back injury and hard luck for much of the season. After winning 20 games the previous year, he had lost 10 of his first 16 decisions in 1974, including two tough 1-0 contests. As part of an effort to turn around his fortunes, he had enrolled in a course that was "supposed to teach [him] to relax and enjoy [his] work more."[1] Blyleven apparently was a quick learner: He turned in a one-hit performance on Independence Day, "although it did test his patience to the limit" since he had to wait until there were two outs in the bottom of the ninth to see his pitching gem result in victory.[2]

Both Blyleven and the Rangers' Jim Bibby came out gunning. Each hurler retired the first seven batters he faced, with Blyleven recording four strikeouts and Bibby three. The first hit in the game was Texas shortstop Toby Harrah's one-out solo homer to right field in the top of the third inning. Although Twins center fielder Steve Brye said that Harrah's ball "hit the post on the top of the fence and barely bounced out of the park," the result was still a 1-0 Texas lead.[3]

Harrah's homer was his 12th of the season, only one fewer than the 13 he had accumulated over the previous three campaigns. Harrah's newfound power stroke had made him a thorn in the Twins' side all season. He had hit exactly half of his homers against Minnesota and already had victimized Blyleven with two round-trippers on June 24, although the Twins had prevailed, 8-4, in that game in Arlington, Texas. After the July 4 game, Blyleven confessed, "Catcher Phil Roof had called for a curve and I shook him off and threw the fast ball that Harrah hit out."[4] For most of the evening, it looked as though that lone mistake would result in Blyleven's third 1-0 loss of the season.

Bibby gave up his first hit in the bottom of the third – a single by Roof – but that was all the Twins could muster, and the two big right-handers continued to stifle the opposing lineups. After Harrah's homer, Blyleven retired nine consecutive Rangers before he allowed the second Texas baserunner of the game via a one-out walk to catcher Jim Sundberg in the sixth. However, that was to be all the base traffic for Texas until the eighth inning.

Bert Blyleven

Minnesota Twins

Bibby allowed two-out doubles in the sixth and seventh innings, but escaped unscathed on both occasions. In the sixth inning, designated hitter Tony Oliva became the first Twins batter to reach second base when, according to a Texas news article, he "was given a double by the charitable home town official scorer."[5] Left fielder Alex Johnson had caught up to Oliva's fly ball at the warning track, "but it glanced off his glove and the scorer called it a hit instead of an error."[6] It mattered not, as the next batter, Bobby Darwin, flied out to right field.

In the bottom of the seventh inning, Larry Hisle hit a no-doubt double to left-center field after Steve Braun and Jim Holt had been retired. This time around, Minnesota manager Frank Quilici sent Harmon Killebrew to the plate to pinch-hit for Roof. "Killer" quickly flied out to right field on Bibby's first pitch to him to quash the Twins' hope for a tie or the lead.

Although Blyleven allowed Texas no further hits, he put himself in a jam via walks in the top of the eighth. Jim Spencer, leading off, drew the second walk issued by Blyleven in the game. Lenny Randle's sacrifice advanced Spencer to second, and then Blyleven walked Harrah to put two runners on with one out. Blyleven bore down and induced successive fielder's-choice grounders by Sundberg and César Tovar to keep the score 1-0.

After Bibby set the Twins down in order, Blyleven again put himself in a "two-on and one-out" jam in the top of the ninth. With one out, he hit Johnson with a pitch and then walked right fielder Jeff Burroughs, the eventual 1974 American League Most Valuable Player. Blyleven extricated himself from this mess of his own making by getting Mike Hargrove to ground into a 4-6-3 double play. Now it would be up to the Twins batters to bail out Blyleven.

A new hope arose in the Twins and their fans when Bibby walked the leadoff batter, Oliva. Jerry Terrell ran for Oliva. Although it was only the second walk Bibby had issued, to go along with a mere four Twins hits, Texas skipper Billy Martin pulled his starter and inserted relief ace Steve Foucault. The move looked like another of Martin's shrewd decisions when Foucault struck out the first batter he faced, Darwin.

Suddenly, however, Martin's move backfired. Braun singled to right field, and Terrell stopped at third base. Holt lofted a sacrifice fly to Tovar in left field that drove in Terrell to tie the game. Tovar made an ill-advised late throw to home on the play that allowed Braun to take second base. Hisle now stepped up to the plate and sent Foucault's first offering, a curveball, over the left-field fence for a 3-1 Twins triumph that started the Fourth of July fireworks early in Minneapolis.

Hisle said of his game-winning blast, "I figured that he'd throw me a curve ball, and I was geared for it. ... I never hit Foucault much last year, but I've done better against him this year. I hit one off him in Texas with two on during our last trip. Yup, a curve ball."[7]

There was irony in Hisle having become the hero of the game, a fact that was not lost on the man of the hour himself. Hisle conceded, "I'm sure that if Eric Soderholm would not have had an injured foot I wouldn't have been in the lineup. I've not been swinging the bat very good of late and I can't blame Frank Quilici for not playing me."[8] On this night, Hisle was 2-for-3 with a double, a homer, and a walk, and two runs batted in. By season's end, he had appeared in 143 games and had batted .286 with 19 home runs and 79 RBIs.

As for Blyleven, whose mound acumen had kept the Twins in the game, he also claimed to have known what was coming, just as Hisle did in his at-bat. Blyleven asserted, "I told Eric Soderholm in the dugout about the fourth inning that we'd win 2-1 in the ninth inning, but Hisle's home run made me a one-run liar."[9]

Whether or not Blyleven was clairvoyant, he pointed out the reasons for his renewed success on this day. He explained, "I was more relaxed on the mound than I have been lately. I think the self-motivation course I've been taking is helping me. ... It also was my first game in quite a while that I haven't had to wear a brace on my back. I hurt my back earlier in the year, but it feels good now."[10] It felt so good that Blyleven overcame his 6-10 start to the season and finished at 17-17. While a .500 pitching record may not seem impressive, it was not an accurate reflection of Blyleven's stellar 2.66 earned-run average over 281 innings pitched. Instead, as was often the case during Blyleven's Hall of Fame career, it was more reflective of the fact that he played on an average team; in this instance, it was the 1974 Minnesota Twins, a squad that finished with an 82-80 record.

NOTES

1. Fred McMane, "'Self-Motivation Class' Pays Off for Blyleven," *St. Cloud* (Minnesota) *Times*, July 5, 1974: 21.
2. McMane.
3. Sid Hartman, "Big Hit for Hisle," *Minneapolis Star Tribune*, July 5, 1974: 2C.
4. Hartman.

5 Harold McKinney, "Twins Stun Foucault with Late Home Run," *Fort Worth Star-Telegram*, July 5, 1974: 31, 35.

6 McKinney.

7 Tom Briere, "Twins Win 1-Hitter," *Minneapolis Tribune*, July 5, 1974: 2C.

8 Hartman.

9 Briere: 1C.

10 McMane.

THREE EXTRA-INNING COMEBACKS AND WIN FOR LOCAL PITCHER IN BIG-LEAGUE DEBUT

SEPTEMBER 10, 1974: MINNESOTA TWINS 8, CHICAGO WHITE SOX 7 (15 INNINGS)

By Gordon Gattie

The Minnesota Twins were tied with the Kansas City Royals for third place in the American League West Division, one game under .500 with a 70-71 record, as they prepared for the Chicago White Sox, who were only a half-game behind the two teams. Minnesota had played sub-.500 baseball nearly all season; the team last attained a .500 winning percentage on May 7 when it was 12-12 after shutting out the Milwaukee Brewers. The Twins' first winning month was July, which was highlighted by a five-game winning streak and a three-game winning streak featuring three consecutive walk-off wins. Throughout the summer months, rumors circulated about the Twins potentially leaving the Twin Cities.[1] The Minneapolis and St. Paul Chambers of Commerce authorized a Stadium Task Force to investigate the stadium situation and in their report urgently stated, "The Minnesota Vikings … and the Minnesota Twins … will relocate their franchises from the Twin Cities … if improved sports facilities are not available."[2]

Minnesota scored three eighth-inning runs and defeated the White Sox 3-1 on September 9 to open a nine-game homestand.[3] Frank Quilici, who played his entire major- and minor-league career with Minnesota, guided the Twins in his second full season as manager.[4] Future Hall of Fame second baseman Rod Carew was vying for his third consecutive AL batting title[5] as the centerpiece of the Twins' offense. Third baseman Eric Soderholm, with outfielders Larry Hisle and Bobby Darwin, added power to Minnesota's offense. Bert Blyleven and Joe Decker were Minnesota's top two starting pitchers.

Chicago was playing the final game of its nine-game road trip on September 10. The White Sox' offense included veteran sluggers Dick Allen and Ken Henderson, with youngster Jorge Orta hitting over .300 since late June.[6] Chicago's pitching staff featured durable veteran starting pitchers Wilbur Wood and Jim Kaat, with youngsters Terry Forster and future Hall of Famer Rich Gossage anchoring the bullpen. Unfortunately for manager Chuck Tanner, the White Sox played without notable regulars Allen, catcher Ed Herrmann, third baseman Bill Melton, and left fielder Carlos May that evening.[7] Although unknown at the time, Allen had already played his last game for Chicago before leaving the team in mid-September.[8] The others were dealing with various injuries: Melton suffered a pulled leg muscle the previous weekend, Herrmann contended with sore knees, and May limped badly on heavily-taped ankles.[9]

Vic Albury started for Minnesota. The 6-foot left-hander was pitching his first full season in the majors. After an August demotion to the bullpen, Albury returned to the rotation as the fourth starter. He had last pitched five days earlier against the Royals when he threw a six-hitter.[10] Entering the contest, Albury was 6-8 with a 4.74 earned-run average in 133 innings pitched.

Wood started for Chicago. The durable knuckleballer had led the American League or tied for the lead the past two seasons in wins (24 each season), games started (49 in 1972, 48 in 1973), and innings pitched (376⅔ in 1972, 359⅓ in 1973). He finished fifth in Cy Young Award voting in 1973, and was an All-Star team selection in 1974. Chicago's ace carried a 20-17 record and a 3.64 ERA in 294⅓ innings pitched into Tuesday's game; he had endured a rough April but pitched better starting in mid-May.[11]

Albury started quickly; Chicago leadoff hitter Lee Richard flied out and Orta grounded out. Henderson delivered the evening's first hit by singling to left field. Ron Santo grounded out to end Chicago's first frame. The Twins struck in their half. Steve Brye singled and Carew bunt singled. Wood nearly escaped trouble when Hisle grounded into a double play as Brye reached third. Darwin launched his 24th homer over the left-field wall to give Minnesota a 2-0 lead. Killebrew grounded out to end the first inning.

The White Sox responded in the second. Brian Downing walked, Jerry Hairston doubled, and Tony Muser singled, scoring Dowling. With runners at the corners and no outs, Bucky Dent hit into an unconventional double play: He attempted a squeeze, and Minnesota first baseman Craig Kusick ran Hairston down off third base, then Dent was caught in a rundown between first and second base and tagged out by center fielder Brye.[12] Bill Sharp flied out as Chicago pulled within a run.

Minnesota threatened in the bottom of the second, but with runners on first and second and one out, Phil Roof hit into a double play. Fans subsequently witnessed little action on the basepaths from the third inning through the sixth as both pitchers established their rhythms. In the third inning, Chicago's Orta singled but was caught stealing as Henderson struck out. Minnesota had runners on in the third and fifth innings, but neither traveled beyond first base.

The offenses awakened in the late innings. In the seventh, Minnesota's Danny Thompson blasted a solo shot into left field. In the eighth, Soderholm walked with the bases loaded and two outs to score Carew, who reached base on a third-strike passed ball. The Twins carried a 4-1 lead into the ninth inning.

Bill Campbell, who relieved Albury starting the eighth inning, allowed a leadoff single by Henderson in the ninth. Pinch-hitter Nyls Nyman, in his first major-league plate appearance, doubled to right, bringing the tying run to the plate with no outs. Downing launched his 10th homer into the night sky, tying the game, 4-4. Hairston singled and Campbell's night was finished. Reliever Tom Burgmeier allowed a Muser single, sending Hairston to third and poising the White Sox to grab the lead. However, a fly out, groundout, and strikeout ended the threat. In the bottom half, White Sox reliever Terry Forster relieved Wood and retired the Twins on two groundouts and a lineout, and the game headed into extra innings for the 3,285 attending fans.[13]

Downing singled to start the Chicago 11th. Hairston sacrificed him to second. After Muser struck out, Dent plated Downing with a single to center field. The White Sox missed an opportunity to extend their lead when Eddie Leon fouled out with runners on first and second.

Coming to bat in the bottom of the inning, Minnesota wasted no time tying the score; leadoff hitter Kusick belted his eighth homer of the season 404 feet to left field to tie the game, 5-5. Forster retired the next three hitters and the contest moved into the 12th inning. Minnesota threatened in the 12th; with no outs, Carew walked, stole second, and went to third on a wild pitch. But Forster struck out Hisle and Darwin, then Killebrew grounded out.

Chicago pulled ahead in the 13th inning when Dent's single plated Hairston. Minnesota countered in the bottom of the inning on Glenn Borgmann's single driving in Soderholm. (Another Twins baserunner, Jerry Terrell, was thrown out at home by left fielder Hairston.) The teams exchanged runs again in the 14th; for the White Sox, Orta singled, moved to second on an errant pickoff attempt by reliever Tom Johnson, took third on a groundout, and scored on Nyman's single. For the third time during extra innings, the Twins rallied: Soderholm singled with two outs and scored on pinch-hitter Tony Oliva's left-field double.

In the 15th inning, Johnson retired Chicago in order. For Minnesota, Carew walked with one out. He stole second base, his 35th of the season, then scored the winning run on Hisle's bad-hop single that bounced over White Sox third baseman Leon's head. Hisle's hit also ended his 0-for-12 slump.[14] After three extra-inning comebacks, 4 hours and 7 minutes, and six extra innings, the Twins prevailed, 8-7.

Johnson, a native of St. Paul,[15] made his major-league debut and won his first game with two effective innings, allowing only an unearned run. Gossage absorbed the loss. Carew scored twice with three walks and three stolen bases while Brye banged out three hits from the leadoff spot. Downing went 3-for-6 and scored three runs while Henderson and Hairston also had three hits for the White Sox. The Twins finally reached .500 again, and eventually finished third in the AL West with an 82-80 record, one game ahead of Chicago. Quilici commented after the game, "This is just like beating Cincinnati in the seventh game of the World Series. These guys ... these guys . . . just never quit."[16]

After much speculation regarding the Twins' future in the Twin Cities, the franchise remained in Minnesota. Carew won his fourth batting title and finished seventh in the Most Valuable Player voting. His 7.5 Wins above Replacement led AL position players and his 38 stolen bases were second in the league.

Hisle finished second on Minnesota with 19 homers and 79 runs batted in, and ninth in the AL with a .465 slugging percentage.

SOURCES

Besides the sources cited in the Notes, the author consulted Baseball-Almanac.com, Baseball-Reference.com, Retrosheet.org, and the following:

James, Bill. *The New Bill James Historical Abstract* (New York: The Free Press, 2001).

Thorn, John, and Pete Palmer, et al. *Total Baseball: The Official Encyclopedia of Major League Baseball* (New York: Viking Press, 2004).

NOTES

1 Bob Fowler, "Sagging Gate Spurs Rumors of Move by Twins," *The Sporting News*, September 28, 1974: 18.

2 Dan Stoneking, "Stadium Report: Twins, Vikings to Move Unless …" *Minneapolis Star*, September 10, 1974: 35.

3 Dan Stoneking, "Killebrew Homers So … Goltz' Faith Rewarded," *Minneapolis Star*, September 10, 1974: 35.

4 Tom Briere, "Quilici to Emphasize Execution as Twins Open Training on Monday," *Minneapolis Tribune*, February 24, 1974: 32.

5 Dan Stoneking, ".400 for Carew: Impossible Dream?" *Minneapolis Star*, September 2, 1974: 22.

6 John Hillyer, "Orta His Own Severest Critic as .315 Hitter," *The Sporting News*, August 31, 1974: 3.

7 Richard Dozer, "Twins Beat Sox in 15th," *Chicago Tribune*, September 11, 1974: 74.

8 Richard Dozer, "Last Allen Sox Trip: a Walk," *Chicago Tribune*, September 15, 1974: 75.

9 Chicago Tribune Press Service, "Angels, Tanana End Sox' Win Streak at 4," *Chicago Tribune*, September 7, 1974: 88.

10 Associated Press, "Dad 'Gives' Albury Jr. Twin Win," *Minneapolis Star*, September 6, 1974: 22.

11 Jerome Holtzman, "Chisox Owner Allyn Gets Assist in Wood Comeback," *The Sporting News*, May 25, 1974: 10.

12 Tom Briere, "Twins Hit .500 Mark," *Minneapolis Star Tribune,* September 11, 1974: 25.

13 Dan Stoneking, "Twin Rallies Do It," *Minneapolis Star,* September 11, 1974: 55.

14 Tom Briere, "Twins hit .500 mark," *Minneapolis Tribune,* September 11, 1974: 28.

15 Stoneking, "Twin Rallies."

16 Stoneking, "Twin Rallies."

PETE MACKANIN SAVES OFFICIAL SCORER'S DILEMMA

OCTOBER 1, 1974: MINNESOTA TWINS 6, TEXAS RANGERS 0

By Stew Thornley

Pete Mackanin has spanned the Western Hemisphere as a player, coach, and manager from Canada to Venezuela. He may be best remembered as manager of the Philadelphia Phillies from 2015 to 2017, although Bob Fowler of the *Minneapolis Star* once referred to him as a "non-fiction Casey at the Bat" for a feat Mackanin performed early in his playing days.[1]

During the period when the Base Ball Writers Association of America provided official scorers for games, columnists and beat writers often did double duty, picking up extra dollars by making judgments on hits and errors while also covering the games for their newspaper. Eventually active writers were removed from scoring duties because of a conflict of interest between the roles. On October 1, 1974, Fowler experienced the conflict.

The Texas Rangers had clinched a second-place finish in the American League West Division as they came to Minnesota for a season-ending two-game series in 1974. Only personal milestones were on the line for Texas players. Jim Bibby was set to try for his 20th win in the series opener, but he was scratched because of illness and replaced by David Clyde.

Clyde didn't last long. He gave up a two-run single to Twins third baseman Eric Soderholm in the first and was charged with three more runs in the third as Soderholm started a rally with a leadoff walk.

Soderholm's name loomed large in the game, not because of what he did at the plate but because of what he didn't do in the field. Toby Harrah, the second batter of the game, hit a two-hopper off Soderholm's glove. Shortstop Danny Thompson fielded the carom but had no play. To the surprise of some, perhaps many (although not too many as the attendance that day was 2,274 at Metropolitan Stadium), Fowler credited Harrah with a hit.

Harrah took his spot at shortstop in the bottom of the first, but Pete Mackanin replaced him in the second inning. Texas manager Billy Martin had started Harrah only to allow him to have played in every game of the season. (Martin did the same thing the next day in the season finale.)

Twins starter Dave Goltz retired Texas in order from the second inning through the seventh before walking Tom Grieve in the eighth. By this time the phone was ringing in the press box, calls from the Minnesota dugout asking if Fowler would change Harrah's first-inning hit to an error. Minnesota coach Bob Rodgers told Fowler that Martin had called from the Texas dugout and said he would have no problem if Harrah's hit were changed from a hit to an error on Soderholm.[2]

Dave Goltz

Minnesota Twins

Rodgers asked Fowler if he could change his decision. "I can," Fowler replied. "But I won't."

Others in the press box were having fun with Fowler's predicament. They asked if Fowler would be interviewing Goltz after the game and, when told he would be, one said, "Looks like I'll be writing a fight story."[3]

In the ninth Bill Fahey flied out and Mike Cubbage grounded out. Mackanin, playing in his first game of the season after being called up from the minors the week before, stepped in. He had played briefly for the Rangers the previous season and had a career batting average of .098. An unlikely savior, Mackanin swung and sent a drive off the fence in left-center. He legged it to third, and his triple brought great relief to Fowler. Tom Robson then grounded out to end the game, a 6-0 Twins win.

After the game, Goltz said, "If I'd have gone through without another hit, I was going to ask the official scorer to change it after the game. ... Maybe a black eye might have changed it, but honestly I was glad I hung that slider to Mackanin in the last inning. Then we didn't have to go through all of that after the game about the no-hitter."

Said Soderholm, "I booted the ball, plain and simple, on Harrah in the first inning, and the manager [Frank Quilici] chewed me out for it when I came to the dugout. I wanted to call the official scorer in mid-game and ask him to change it to an error. Finally, coach Bob Rodgers called the official scorer in the press box in the eighth inning before the only legitimate hit and the scorer said he wouldn't change it."[4]

Soderholm told another reporter, "The best you could say of the way I played that ball was that I played it into a hit. But realistically, I let the ball play me. I should have made the play all the way and didn't. I should have gotten an error."[5]

As for Harrah, he said, "It was an either-or play, but if it had been the only hit and they had asked me after the game, I'd have said — make it an error, Goltz deserved a no-hitter the way he pitched."[6]

Five years later, the Twins acquired Mackanin in a trade. A few days later Fowler devoted his column to how Mackanin had saved his hide, writing, "He can produce in a pressure situation, he can hit in the clutch. ... If you doubt that, I've got the sweat-stained scorecard to prove it."[7]

SIDENOTES

Goltz, according to sportswriter Chan Keith, threw only 70 pitches in the game.[8] The win evened his record at 10-10 for the season. Goltz pitched eight seasons with the Twins (1972-1979) and never had a losing record.

The original pitching matchups for the series were Jim Bibby vs. Dave Goltz and Ferguson Jenkins vs. Joe Decker. Clyde replaced Bibby, who was projected as the starter for the next day if he recovered from his illness. If not, reported the October 2 *Minneapolis Tribune*, Steve Hargan would start while Jenkins, with 321⅓ innings pitched that season, would "rest for the winter."[9] Instead, in the season finale Jenkins pitched against Jim Hughes, who started in place of Decker, who was scratched with a sore elbow. With nothing more on the line than a 25th victory for Jenkins, Martin let the pitcher hit for himself, eschewing the designated hitter. Hughes took a no-hitter into the sixth inning when, you guessed it, Jenkins led off with an infield single off, you guessed it, Soderholm's glove. There was no controversy with the official scorer's call on this one, Jenkins came around to score the first run of the game, and Texas beat the Twins 2-1. With two out in the bottom of the ninth, Harmon Killebrew pinch-hit in what many figured (correctly) would be his last time up with the Twins. Steve Foucault struck out Killebrew to end the game and the season.

It was déjà vu all over again for Goltz two years later. On September 25, 1976, Goltz gave up a hit to Dave Collins, the first batter of the game, who reached when Goltz was late in covering first base and dropped a throw from Rod Carew. Official scorer Patrick Reusse, who covered the game for the *St. Paul Pioneer Press*, received the same pressure Fowler had experienced as the hit lingered as the only one off Goltz into the ninth. With two out, it was Mario Guerrero who eliminated any controversy with a single to right-center field. Like Fowler, Reusse wrote about the situation years later and concluded his column with, "I love Mario Guerrero. Always have, always will."[10]

AUTHOR'S NOTE

I was at this game to do play-by-play announcing for a sports broadcasting course, but I was in in a different booth, away from the activity surrounding Fowler. My opinion — that of an armchair official scorer before becoming a real one later (and discovering there is a difference between the armchair and the hot seat) — was that Soderholm should have been charged with an error.

SOURCES

In addition to the sources cited in the Notes, the author also consulted Baseball-Reference.com and Retrosheet.org.

NOTES

1. Bob Fowler, "Twins New Player Has a Fan for Life," *Minneapolis Star*, December 10, 1979: 8B.
2. Chan Keith, "Goltz Almost Had 'Perfect' Day," *Minneapolis Star*, October 2, 1974: 1D.
3. Fowler.
4. Tom Briere, "Goltz Just Misses No Hitter; Twins Beat Texas, Clinch 3rd," *Minneapolis Tribune*, October 2, 1974: 1C.
5. Briere.
6. Briere.
7. Fowler.
8. Keith.
9. Briere.
10. http://milkeespress.com/officialscorers.html.

JENKINS FOILS HUGHES'S NO-HIT BID AS RANGERS TAKE 1974 FINALE FROM TWINS

OCTOBER 2, 1974: TEXAS RANGERS 2, MINNESOTA TWINS 1

By Frederick C. Bush

A paltry crowd of 2,570 fans showed up at Metropolitan Stadium as the two franchises formerly known as the Washington Senators squared off in their 1974 season finale. Neither team was playoff bound, though the Texas Rangers had challenged the Oakland A's in the American League West for much of the season, and the pitching matchup seemed actually to be a mismatch in favor of Texas. The Twins sent September call-up Jim Hughes to the mound to make only his second major-league start, against 1971 National League Cy Young Award winner Ferguson Jenkins, who was resurgent after being shipped to Texas by the Chicago Cubs after a subpar 1973 season. On this day, Hughes exceeded expectations as he took a no-hit bid into the top of the sixth inning, until the future Hall of Famer Jenkins gave his team the edge with ... his bat.

Texas manager Billy Martin had intended to start Jim Bibby on this day, so that the big right-hander could have a shot at his 20th victory of the season, but Bibby came down with the flu and Jenkins was pressed into duty.[1] Martin also made the now-unorthodox move – in the American League, anyway – of letting Jenkins bat. Jenkins became the first AL pitcher to hit for himself from the beginning of the game and the first Rangers pitcher to hit for himself since the junior circuit had instituted the use of the designated hitter in 1973.[2]

Hughes showed that he was not intimidated by such a formidable foe as Jenkins, though his day hardly got off to an auspicious start. Speedy Dave Nelson drew a walk to lead off the game, took second on Lenny Randle's grounder, and made it to third when Hughes uncorked a wild pitch with Jim Spencer at bat. Hughes extricated himself from danger by inducing consecutive groundouts by Spencer and Tom Grieve that denied Nelson the opportunity to score. After that, the Minnesota rookie settle into a groove and allowed only one additional baserunner – via a walk to Jim Sundberg in the third – for the next four innings. Though a perfect game had been out of the question from batter number one, Hughes had "Ranger hitters look[ing] like they were wearing cast iron underwear" as he flirted with a no-hitter.[3]

Jenkins, on the other hand, breezed through three Twins batters in the first but then had to navigate around traffic on the bases in the second and third innings. Craig Kusick led off the Twins' half of the second with a single but was retired at second on Eric Soderholm's fielder's-choice grounder. After Larry Hisle flied out, Danny Thompson stroked a base hit to right field that advanced Soderholm to third base. Jenkins squelched the Twins' hopes of breaking on top by striking out Luis Gomez.

In the bottom of the third, Steve Brye knocked a one-out double to left field and went to third on Steve Braun's grounder. Martin had Jenkins issue an intentional walk to Tony Oliva, putting runners at the corners with two out. The strategy worked as Kusick hit a grounder to short that forced Oliva at second base to end the inning. After that, Jenkins settled into a pitchers' duel with Hughes as he set the Twins down in order from the fourth inning through the sixth.

Jenkins' task was made easier by the fact that Rod Carew, having already sewed up the AL batting title, was given the day off by Minnesota manager Frank Quilici. With his 1974 batting crown in hand, Carew had become the first AL player to win three consecutive batting championships since Ty Cobb had pulled off the feat from 1917 through 1919. Carew's .364 batting average in 1974 also was the highest in the AL since Ted Williams batted .388 in 1957.

In the absence of the game's premier hitting star, Jenkins, who had struck out in his first at-bat, took the opportunity to display some batting prowess of his own and rained on Hughes' no-hit parade in the top of the sixth. In truth, Jenkins' hit "was hardly a lethal shot."[4] His grounder up the third-base side "hit a divot left over from last Sunday's Minnesota Vikings game" and took a bad bounce over the third baseman Soderholm's head.[5] Nonetheless, Hughes' no-hitter was gone and the shutout would soon follow.

Nelson laid down a sacrifice bunt, but Hughes – who had fielded the ball cleanly – hesitated on the throw, which arrived at second base too late to retire Jenkins. Now Hughes momentarily lost his composure and, with Bob Jones at the plate, was called for a balk that allowed both Jenkins and Nelson to advance one base. Both runners had to hold as Jones grounded out to Kusick at first base, but then Spencer lined a single to center that drove in Jenkins for the first run of the game. Texas tried for another run via a suicide squeeze, but the result was a rally-killing, inning-ending double play as both Nelson and Spencer were thrown out.

The Rangers' third and final hit off Hughes turned out to be the decisive blow of the contest as Grieve led off the top of the seventh inning with a solo home run to increase Texas's lead to 2-0. From that point forward, Hughes allowed only one additional baserunner for the remainder of the game – Sundberg, who drew his second walk in the eighth – but the deficit was too much to overcome as the Twins scored their lone run on Soderholm's solo homer in the bottom of the seventh.

Martin lifted Jenkins for pinch-hitter Mike Cubbage in the top of the eighth and then sent Steve Foucault to the hill to finish the final two innings. Foucault picked up seamlessly where Jenkins had left off and retired all six Twins batters he faced, striking out three of them. The final batter he faced was Harmon Killebrew, pinch-hitting for Larry Hisle, who struck out looking. After the game, "Killer" was asked if this had been his last game in a Twins uniform, to which question he responded, "I hope not. I said at the start of the season I'd know at season's end if I wanted to play another year. I do, and I hope it's with the Twins, but I guess [owner] Mr. [Calvin] Griffith has the final say on that."[6] As it turned out, Killebrew, who had spent his entire career with the Washington/Minnesota franchise, ended up playing his 22nd and final season with the Kansas City Royals.

After Foucault set Killebrew down on strikes to earn his 12th save, the season was over for both teams. All that was left was for each to find the highlights of a campaign that ended without participation in the postseason. Jenkins had set a career high with 25 victories while striking out 225 batters and posting a 2.82 ERA over 328⅓ innings for the 84-76 Rangers. Texas skipper Martin asserted, "I'm voting for Ferguson Jenkins over Jim Hunter of Oakland for the Cy Young Award and I'm voting for Billy Martin as manager of the year."[7] While neither of those awards went to Martin's selections, he had reason to be optimistic. Jenkins did receive the AL's Comeback Player of the Year award, outfielder Jeff Burroughs was voted the AL MVP, and first baseman Mike Hargrove was named the AL Rookie of the Year.

Other than Carew's batting crown, the outlook was not as rosy in the Twin Cities. Minnesota finished with an 82-80 overall record that was good for third place behind the Oakland A's and Texas in the AL West. They were 48-33 at the Met, but drew only 662,401 fans in 77 dates, which put their attendance dead last in the AL. Griffith made pitching coach Bob Rodgers into a scapegoat and fired him. Quilici was so upset over the firing of Rodgers that he considered resigning in protest. He revealed, "Bobby [Rodgers] and I talked about that [resigning], but he said that I had a job to do here, and I have."[8] It was true that Minnesota's pitching was average, but it was hardly the team's primary shortcoming. Most notably, clutch hitting was in short supply as the 1974 Twins left 1,263 runners on base over the course of the season.[9]

Based upon his complete-game performance in 1974's finale, Hughes was a potential bright spot for the future. He finished the 1975 season with a 16-14 ledger and a 3.82 ERA under the tutelage of new pitching coach Lee Stange, but stardom was not in the cards and the Twins released him in November 1977.

SOURCES

The author consulted baseball-reference.com for the game box score and both team and individual player statistics.

NOTES

1. Mike Shropshire, "Jenkins Gives Texas 2-1 Finale," *Fort Worth Star-Telegram*, October 3, 1974: 40.
2. "Fergie Foils No-Hitter Bid," *Dayton* (Ohio) *Journal Herald*, October 3, 1974: 22; Merle Heryford, "Martin Rates Rangers Better With Winning Spirit for '75," *The Sporting News*, October 19, 1974: 29.
3. Shropshire.
4. Shropshire.

MEMORABLE GAMES AT MINNESOTA'S DIAMOND ON THE PRAIRIE

5   Shropshire.

6   Tom Briere, "Twins Drop Finale – and Coach," *Minneapolis Star Tribune*, October 3, 1974: 35.

7   Briere.

8   Briere: 33, 35.

9   Briere: 35. The 1975 edition of *The Sporting News Official Baseball Guide* supports the figure given here; however, baseball-reference.com lists the figure as 1,262, a minor discrepancy that does not detract from the fact that the Twins had trouble bringing runners home in the 1974 season.

MAY 4, 1975: TWINS RETIRE KILLEBREW'S NUMBER BEFORE BEATING ROYALS

MINNESOTA TWINS 6, KANSAS CITY ROYALS 3

By Thomas J. Brown Jr.

Harmon Killebrew spent 21 seasons starting with the Washington Senators and then the Minnesota Twins after they moved to the Twin Cities. The Twins released him at the end of the 1974 season, and Killebrew signed with the Kansas City Royals. The early May series between the two teams marked the first time that Killebrew appeared at Metropolitan Stadium as a visiting player.

The Twins announced that May 4 would be Harmon Killebrew Day. Yet only 14,805 spectators showed up on a cool, windy afternoon to see Killebrew take the field against his former team. The Twins retired his number 3 during a pregame ceremony, and Twins owner Calvin Griffith presented Killebrew with his old uniform.

Killebrew told the crowd that among his baseball accomplishments "this was one that I was not looking forward to. But I'm grateful to Mr. Griffith, Mr. Ossie Bluege [the scout who signed him to a Washington contract in 1954] and the fans of this area who have been so good to me over the previous 14 years."[1]

Twins manager Frank Quilici sent Vic Albury to the mound. Albury had lost his last outing, failing to go past the fourth inning in a 7-2 loss to Texas. The Twins hoped he would rebound from that start and help the team beat the Royals in the final game of the series. A victory would give the Twins a sweep of the series, making up for the three-game sweep they suffered in Kansas City in April.

After Amos Otis hit a one-out double in the first, Albury struck out John Mayberry. Hal McRae hit a groundball to third baseman Eric Soderholm, who threw the ball away. Otis scored and McRae ended up on second.

Killebrew stepped to the plate amid scattered applause from the fans. Then he hit Albury's first pitch into the left-field bleachers. The ball was measured at 380 feet, which meant that Killebrew didn't need the shorter fence in order to treat his fans to another powerful home run.[2] His homer put the Royals ahead 3-0. Albury continued to struggle, allowing the next two batters to reach base before he got Frank White to pop out for the third out.

Chan Keith, writing in *Minneapolis Star*, wrote: "When it was suggested at that point to club president Griffith he might also like to retire Albury's uniform ... with Victor still in it, generally jovial Calvin did not laugh."[3]

The Royals started Al Fitzmorris. He entered the game with a 3-1 record that included a complete-game victory against the Twins on April 11. After the Twins had beaten the Royals' other top starters in the first two games of the series, Kansas City manager Jack McKeon was hoping that Fitzmorris would shut down the Twins again to prevent the team from being swept.

But the Twins wasted no time jumping on Fitzmorris in their half of the first. With one out, Sergio Ferrer doubled to right field and Steve Brye singled him home. Fitzmorris walked Bobby Darwin to put Brye in scoring position, and Brye came home when Steve Braun singled. Darwin also scored when left fielder Al Cowens tried to throw him out at third but his throw couldn't be handled by third baseman George Brett. (The error was charged to Cowens.) When the dust settled and Fitzmorris finally got the third out, the Twins had tied the score.

Albury continued to struggle in the second, walking two of the five batters he faced, but kept the Royals from scoring. But when he walked Killebrew, the first batter he faced in the third, Quilici lifted him and summoned rookie Jim Hughes from the bullpen.

MEMORABLE GAMES AT MINNESOTA'S DIAMOND ON THE PRAIRIE

Hughes had lost his first start of the season, on April 20. He had pitched two innings a week earlier in a 7-2 loss to the Texas Rangers. Although Hughes walked two of the five batters he faced in the third to load the bases, the Twins batters couldn't get the ball out of the infield and Hughes kept them from putting any runs on the scoreboard.

Meanwhile, Fitzmorris continued to struggle. Dan Ford led off the bottom of the second with a single. Rod Carew followed with a double to center field that brought Ford home and gave the Twins a 4-3 lead. Carew moved to third on Ferrer's second hit of the game. McKeon reached into his bullpen and brought in Dennis Leonard to relieve Fitzmorris. McKeon later said, "Certainly the pitching isn't very good right now. But that's the way this game goes. You win some and you lose some. It'll straighten itself out over a number of games."[4]

When Brye flied out to right field against Leonard, Carew tagged up but was thrown out at home by Cowens. At the time, "the hot line into all major league parks spread the news that the next run would make history."[5] Moments later, Carew tested one of the best throwing arms in baseball and failed. If he had been safe, he would have scored baseball's one millionth run.

"I knew it was the millionth run if I made it," Carew said later. "But I couldn't get past the catcher's shin guards. I didn't run for that reason, but they hollered from the dugout and I knew I had a chance to be the millionth."[6] Shortly afterward, Major League Baseball announced that Houston Astro Bob Watson had scored the milestone run on Milt May's three-run homer in San Francisco.

Hughes pitched solid baseball after he took over from Albury. Over the next six innings, he allowed just four Royals hits, two each in the eighth and ninth. All told, nine Royals reached base against Hughes, but the only one who made it past second was Killebrew. The slugger was hit by a pitch in the fifth. Hughes said later that "[the] pitch got away from me. I meant to throw it down and away but I got it up and in."[7] Killebrew advanced to third on two groundouts but was stranded there when White hit a pop fly for the third out.

Hughes faced Killebrew twice more in the game and struck him out both times. Killebrew looked at three curveballs in the seventh and never even swung his bat. Hughes repeated his strategy in the ninth, throwing two curveballs before tossing a slider that Killebrew finally swung at and missed.

Hughes said after the game, "In the late innings I was just trying to remember what I'd done with each hitter earlier in the game. I had some luck with the breaking pitch against Harmon so I decided to stay with it."[8]

The Twins added two more runs in the fifth inning. With Leonard still on the mound, Eric Soderholm walked. Craig Kusick then hit a 413-foot home run into the left-center-field seats to put the Twins up 6-3.

Those insurance runs would not be needed: Hughes shut down the Royals the rest of the way. Quilici was delighted with his performance, telling reporters after the game, "He was great. He was in trouble a couple of times late in the game, but I'm not going to be too smart and take the guy out of the game when he hasn't allowed a run."[9] Killebrew also complimented the rookie after the game, saying, "We didn't exactly wear him out. I thought he had really good stuff."[10]

Killebrew left his mark on Metropolitan Stadium when he was with the Twins. His return as a Royal allowed him to do that one more time. His home run made his homecoming memorable for the fans who showed up to see the slugger from Payette, Idaho. Always a winner, Killebrew said, "It will go down as one of my more memorable home runs but like so many that have gone before – it doesn't mean much when you lose."[11]

SOURCES

In addition to the sources cited in the Notes, I used the Baseball-Reference.com, and Retrosheet.org websites for box-score, player, team, and season pages, pitching and batting game logs, and other material pertinent to this game account.

baseball-reference.com/boxes/MIN/MIN196706030.shtml

retrosheet.org/boxesetc/1967/B06030MIN1967.htm

NOTES

1. Tom Briere, "Twins Blast Royals 6-3," *Minneapolis Star Tribune*, May 5, 1975: C1.
2. Briere. In 1975 the Twins installed a fence in front of the regular fence in left field to enhance the frequency of home runs. Many, including Killebrew's this day, made it into the permanent bleachers.
3. Chan Keith, "No. 3 Retired," *Minneapolis Star Tribune*, May 5, 1975: 26.
4. Brent Kallestad, "Twins Sweep Royals Series Despite Killebrew Homer," *Bemidji* (Minnesota) *Pioneer*, May 5, 1975: 7.
5. Briere.
6. Keith.
7. Keith.
8. Keith.
9. Keith.
10. Keith.
11. Briere.

CAREW STEALS HOME AS HUGHES OUTDUELS PERRY IN WHITEWASH OF INDIANS

MAY 14, 1975: MINNESOTA TWINS 3, CLEVELAND INDIANS 0

By Frederick C. Bush

The Minnesota Twins started 23-year-old righty Jim Hughes on May 14 in an early clash with the Cleveland Indians at a "nearly deserted Metropolitan Stadium."[1] Hughes had made two starts the previous September and had fired a three-hitter in a tough 2-1 loss to the Texas Rangers and 1971 National League Cy Young Award winner Ferguson Jenkins in the final game of the season. In spite of that promising performance, the Twins envisioned Hughes more as a long reliever; however, a spate of injuries to the starting staff – Dave Goltz, Joe Decker, and Vic Albury all missed time with various ailments – forced Hughes into the rotation.[2] Hughes was coming off a complete-game victory over Baltimore on May 9 in which he had allowed only one earned run (two total) and had lowered his season earned-run average to 2.31. Now, in only the fifth start of his young major-league career, his mound opponent was another former Cy Young Award winner, the venerable greaseballer Gaylord Perry, who had claimed the American League award in 1972. Hughes seemed to pitch up to the level of his competition and, on this day, he had his best outing to date.

Although Hughes's performance became the positive story of the game, another event that occurred early on ended up garnering most of the press coverage. Hughes surrendered a leadoff triple to John Lowenstein but managed to escape unscathed before part one of the game's "incident" took place in the bottom of the first. Perry, too, allowed the leadoff batter to reach base as Steve Braun singled to right field. Four-time AL batting champ Rod Carew grounded into a fielder's choice and then decided he needed to get into scoring position since Braun had been forced at second. With Larry Hisle at the plate, Carew stole second and went to third when Indians second baseman Jack Brohamer was unable to corral catcher John Ellis's throw and was charged with an error.

At this point, Perry practically dared Carew to steal home as he continued to pitch from the windup rather than from the stretch. After Hisle struck out, the temptation became too much for Carew as Bobby Darwin batted. Carew explained after the game, "Gaylord was just slow in his windup. ... I saw I could get that far off, so I decided to go on the third one [pitch]."[3] Darwin stepped aside as Carew slid into the plate for his first steal of home since 1973 and a 1-0 Twins lead.[4] As for Darwin's alertness on the play, Carew said, "I gave Bobby a signal that I was coming. I hit my belt and pointed to my eye this time."[5] Darwin walked, but

Rod Carew

Perry bore down and fanned Eric Soderholm to end the inning.

After that, all was quiet on the basepaths for a time as both pitchers set down the side in order over the next two innings. However, part two of the "incident" took place as Carew came to bat with two outs in the bottom of the third. Perry threw Carew a bit of old-fashioned chin music in retaliation for the latter's steal of home in the first inning. On the very next pitch, an agitated Carew swung and missed and intentionally let go of his bat, which landed to the right of the mound. Perry stood still and stared at the bat while Brohamer and first-base umpire Nestor Chylak rushed between Carew and the mound to prevent any potential fisticuffs. According to Carew, Chylak asked him, "Is the bat slippery?" to which he responded, "Did you ask Gaylord if the ball was slippery?"[6]

Carew's sarcasm notwithstanding, Chylak's quick action prevented the situation from escalating and no warnings were issued to either side. Perry remained calm in the moment and refused to comment afterward, but Carew was still livid at game's end, asserting, "If it ever happens again, I'll do it [let his bat fly] again or I'll do something to get back. ... I just don't like being thrown at. Too many guys have been hurt by things like that. A batter can freeze when a pitcher's throwing at him intentionally and he can really be injured."[7] Carew likely got his message across to Perry, but he also became the Cleveland starter's third strikeout victim in the at-bat.

On the heels of such hubbub, Hughes almost lost his shutout in the top of the fourth. Frank Duffy led off with a double and advanced to third on George Hendrick's grounder. Boog Powell hit a grounder that first baseman Craig Kusick scooped up and rifled home to catcher Glenn Borgmann, who tagged Duffy out at the plate. Hughes then walked Rico Carty, which put Powell in scoring position, but Ellis flied out to right field to end the threat.

In the bottom of the inning, Hisle greeted Perry with a leadoff solo homer that made it a 2-0 game. Soderholm drew a one-out walk but overplayed his hand when he tried to steal second and was gunned down by Ellis for the second out. Steve Brye's grounder was out number three, and then Hughes had a one-two-three top of the fifth, courtesy of a 4-6-3 double play.

Perry ran into another jam in the bottom of the fifth and was fortunate to escape it without allowing another Twins runner to cross home plate. Borgmann drew a one-out walk but was erased at second on Sergio Ferrer's grounder; Ferrer's ball should have resulted in a double play, but Powell dropped the ball at first for an error and Ferrer was safe. Braun singled to put runners at first and second as Carew came to bat for the third time. This time the ball truly did slip out of Perry's hand and he was charged with a wild pitch that allowed both runners to advance. Perry then issued an intentional walk to Carew that loaded the bases, but he was able to breathe a sigh of relief when Hisle popped out to Brohamer.

By this point in the game, Hughes was on autopilot. He retired the Indians in order in the sixth, seventh, and ninth innings and allowed only a harmless two-out single by Brohamer in the eighth. Perry continued to scuffle, though his outing was hardly disastrous. He allowed Minnesota's third and final run on Darwin's solo homer to lead off the bottom of the sixth. The Twins had one last scoring opportunity in the seventh, which came when Braun struck a two-out single and pinch-runner Dan Ford stole second base. Now it was a case of déjà vu all over again (as Yogi Berra may or may not have said) as Perry intentionally walked Carew and induced a pop fly by Hisle to end the inning.

Hughes put an exclamation point on his first career shutout when he struck out Powell, the slugger who had won the AL Most Valuable Player Award in 1970 as a member of the Baltimore Orioles, to end the game. It was the first time in six games that Minnesota had defeated Perry since he had come to the AL in 1972.[8] Hughes, who had been a 33rd-round draft choice in 1969, was ecstatic as he said, "I was so psyched up pitching against a name like Gaylord Perry, probably as high as I've ever been. I knew I'd probably have to pitch a shutout to win tonight."[9] After his sterling effort, Hughes sported a 3-1 record and 1.67 ERA for the young season.

Twins manager Frank Quilici was effusive in his praise and asserted, "I think Hughes's use of his changeup will provide a good mental lesson for the rest of our staff. They'll recognize the value of an offspeed pitch."[10] Hughes's changeup was a palmball that he had begun to test out during offseason workouts in December 1971. Hughes described the pitch, saying, "I tucked the ball into the palm of my right hand and threw it as hard as a fastball."[11] The result of such experimentation was "an offspeed pitch that dropped."[12]

For a brief period during the 1975 season, Hughes harnessed his palmball and the rest of his arsenal as he went on a six-game winning streak. The May 14 shutout of Cleveland was his second of five consecutive

METROPOLITAN STADIUM

complete games and first of two consecutive shutouts. Although injuries initially gave Hughes his opportunity to start in 1975, Quilici said, "We'll be using a five-man rotation because we have so many games in June, July, and August. And anyone who pitches the way Hughes has been pitching will be in that rotation."[13] Hughes's magic ran out, but he still had his finest season in the majors, finishing at 16-14 with a 3.82 ERA over 249⅔ innings for a Twins team that finished in fourth place in the AL West with a 76-83 record.

SOURCES

Baseball-reference.com was consulted for the game box-score and play-by-play as well as for player and team statistics.

Retrosheet.org was also consulted for the game box score and play-by-play.

NOTES

1. Tom Briere, "Hughes, Speed, Power Lead Twins to 3-0 Win," *Minneapolis Star Tribune*, May 15, 1975: 39. Only 3,176 fans were in attendance at the game.
2. Bob Fowler, "Hughes Palm Ball a Handy Twin Pick-Me-Up," *The Sporting News*, May 31, 1975: 12.
3. "Cleveland Indians Notebook: Rod Carew 'Talks' with Theft of Home," *Mansfield* (Ohio) *News-Journal*, May 15, 1975: 30.
4. Briere.
5. "Cleveland Indians Notebook."
6. "Cleveland Indians Notebook."
7. "Carew Warns Gaylord Perry," *St. Cloud* (Minnesota) *Times*, May 15, 1975: 33.
8. "Hughes Handles Indians," *St. Cloud Times*, May 15, 1975: 33.
9. Briere.
10. Briere.
11. Fowler.
12. Fowler.
13. Fowler: 30.

KILLEBREW HITS FINAL HOME RUN

SEPTEMBER 18, 1975: KANSAS CITY ROYALS 4, MINNESOTA TWINS 3

By Paul Hofmann

Harmon Killebrew was the face of the Minnesota Twins during the team's first 14 years in the Twin Cities. He hit 475 home runs as a member of the Twins, 244 of which came at Metropolitan Stadium.[1] On this day, Killebrew was making his final appearance in Minnesota, wearing an unfamiliar Kansas City Royals uniform. Killebrew had hoped he would be an everyday player with the Royals, but he was relegated to serving as a designated hitter against left-handed pitching, leaving him unsure he would return for the 1976 season.[2] "It's been a long season," Killebrew said. "I can't tell you right now if I'll be playing another year."

Killebrew's departure from the Twins was not what one would expect for a player with the legacy of being the franchise's most prolific power hitter. After two injury-plagued seasons (1973 and 1974), the Twins offered Killebrew a position as a player-coach or manager of the Triple-A Tacoma Twins. Feeling he was not yet done playing, Killebrew rejected the offer and signed a free-agent contract with the Royals. That spring, longtime teammate and former Twins left-hander Jim Kaat quipped, "The Cardinals made a vice president out of [Stan] Musial and the Twins wanted to send you to Triple-A."[3]

The Royals entered the September 18 game against the Royals with a record of 84-67, eight games behind the three-time defending World Series champion Oakland Athletics in the AL West. The Twins were 71-77, 19½ games off the pace and playing out the string.

Twenty-five-year-old right-hander Doug Bird started for the Royals. He was making his third consecutive start after 47 appearances out of the bullpen. He entered the game with a record of 9-6 and a 3.39 earned-run average. He was opposed by 5-foot-9-inch left-hander Eddie Bane. The Twins' number-one pick in the 1973 amateur draft was making his second start after being recalled from Triple-A Tacoma, where he had gone 15-11 with a 4.03 ERA. He was 1-0 with a 5.87 ERA with the Twins.

A couple of late-morning showers passed through the Twin Cities, contributing to the sparse turnout of 3,201 for the Thursday matinee. The temperature was 67 degrees under mostly cloudy skies when Bane delivered the game's first pitch to Royals center fielder Amos Otis. The temperature felt even cooler with the 20-mph wind that was blowing in from right field toward the third-base line.

Before the seats were even warm, Otis deposited his ninth home run of the year into the left-field stands. Cookie Rojas followed with a single but was thrown out trying to steal second by Twins catcher Glenn Borgmann. Bane then retired George Brett on a fly ball to left and struck out John Mayberry.

Bird retired the first two batters in the bottom of the first before giving up a single to Rod Carew, who took second when right fielder Al Cowens mishandled the ball. Carew's single, one of his two hits in the game, proved harmless when Tony Oliva lined out to Briggs.

The Royals increased their lead in the second inning. With one out, the 39-year-old Killebrew, who entered the game with a .200 batting average, homered to left to make the score 2-0. It was Killebrew's 14th home run of the season and 573rd (and final) homer of his Hall of Fame career. With two out Jim Wohlford and Buck Martinez singled to put runners at the corners. Bane struck out Otis to end the inning and retired the Royals in order in the third, fourth, and fifth innings.

Bird held the Twins off the scoreboard until Carew, the new face of the franchise, who was on the way to his fourth consecutive American League batting title, led off the bottom of the fourth with a home run to right field, his 14th of the season.

The score remained 2-1 until the bottom of the sixth. Johnny Briggs reached on an error by Bird and stole second. Dave McKay walked and Danny Thompson moved the runners along with a well-placed sacrifice bunt to third. Jerry Terrell tied the game with a single to right that scored Briggs. When Terrell was caught in a rundown between first and second, McKay tried to score but was thrown out at the plate.[4] Borgman walked, moving Terrell to second, and rookie Lyman Bostock singled to put the Twins ahead, 3-2.

The Twins uprising prompted Royals manager Whitey Herzog to replace pitcher Bird with left-handed veteran Ray Sadecki. The 34-year-old, acquired two weeks earlier from Atlanta, was making his fourth appearance for the Royals. After walking Steve Braun to put runners on first and second, Sadecki retired Carew on a groundout to second to end the inning.

The Royals answered in the seventh when Bane turned into "his own worst enemy."[5] Killebrew started the rally by drawing a walk. Rodney Scott ran for him. Freddie Patek reached when Bane fielded his bunt and threw wild to first. Wohlford also bunted and Bane made a wayward throw to third, leaving the bases loaded with no outs. The pair of errors spelled an end to Bane's afternoon; Twins manager Frank Quilici called on right-hander Bill Campbell to relieve him. Campbell was 4-6 with a 3.99 ERA.

Vada Pinson, pinch-hitting for Martinez, hit a sacrifice liner to left to score Scott with the tying run. Patek scored the go-ahead run when Otis singled to right field. At the end of 6½ innings, the Royals led 4-3.

Sadecki retired the first batter in the bottom of the seventh before being replaced by rookie George Throop. The 6-foot-7-inch right-hander had been called up to the Royals when rosters expanded in September. Throop, who had gone 12-9 as a starter at Triple-A Omaha, was making his fifth relief appearance for the Royals.

The score remained 4-3 as Throop and Campbell navigated their way through varying degrees of trouble from the bottom of the seventh to the top of the ninth. In the bottom of the ninth, Throop retired Carew on a fly ball to center and Oliva on a pop fly to short, then struck out Dan Ford to end the game.

The time of the game was 2 hours and 40 minutes. The victory went to Sadecki, whose record improved to 4-3. It was his only victory for the Royals. Throop was credited with the save, his second for the Royals. The loss went to Bane, evening his record at 1-1.

Killebrew finished the season with a .199 batting average, 14 home runs, and 44 runs batted in. At the end of the season, the up-and-coming Royals released Killebrew, who at the time ranked fifth in career home runs. On March 3, 1976, the slugger formally announced his retirement.[6]

After Killebrew's death in 2011, Twins President David St. Peter summarized what he meant to the Twin Cities:

"No individual has ever meant more to the Minnesota Twins organization and millions of fans across Twins Territory than Harmon Killebrew. Harmon will long be remembered as one of the most prolific home run hitters in the history of the game and the leader of a group of players who helped lay the foundation for the long-term success of the Twins franchise and Major League Baseball in the Upper Midwest. However, more importantly, Harmon's legacy will be the class, dignity, and humility he demonstrated each and every day as a Hall of Fame-quality husband, father, friend, teammate, and man."[7]

Metropolitan Stadium was demolished in January 1985.[8] The site became the location of the gigantic Mall of America. Along the south side of the mall runs Killebrew Drive, and a red chair was bolted along a wall marking the approximate spot where Killebrew's 520-foot home run in 1967 landed.

It was only appropriate that Killebrew's final home run came at Metropolitan Stadium.

SOURCES

In addition to the sources cited in the Notes, the author consulted Baseball-Reference.com and Retrosheet.org.

baseball-reference.com/boxes/MIN/MIN197509180.shtml

retrosheet.org/boxesetc/1975/B09180MIN1975.htm

NOTES

1. Killebrew hit two home runs at Metropolitan Stadium for the Royals. He hit the first was on May 4, 1976, the day on which the Twins retired his number 3. The second was in this game, the final game he played at Metropolitan Stadium.
2. Patrick Reusse, "Noncommittal on 1976: Killebrew Stings Twins," *St. Paul Pioneer Press,* September 17, 1975: 20.
3. Joseph Wancho, "Harmon Killebrew," SABR BioProject.
4. Del Black, "Royals Win Sloppy Game," *Kansas City* (Missouri) *Times,* September 19, 1975: 40.
5. Black.
6. "Killebrew Retires to Do TV," *Minneapolis Star Tribune,* March 4, 1976: 35.
7. "MLB: Quotes About the Death of Twins Great Harmon Killebrew," Associated Press, May 17, 2011. Retrieved from legacy.com/obituaries/name/harmon-killebrew-obituary?pid=178604108.
8. "Metropolitan Stadium," Retrieved from ballparksofbaseball.com/ballparks/metropolitan-stadium/.

TWINS FANS BOO BLYLEVEN IN FINAL START BEFORE TRADE, BLYLEVEN MAKES OBSCENE GESTURE

MAY 31, 1976: CALIFORNIA ANGELS 3, MINNESOTA TWINS 2

By Mike Lynch

On May 23, 1976, Minnesota pitcher Bert Blyleven beat the Kansas City Royals, 3-1, and won his 99th career game, all with the Twins, for whom he debuted as a 19-year-old on June 5, 1970. He had a solid rookie season, going 10-9 with a 3.18 earned-run average in 27 games, all but two as a starter, and quickly established himself as the Twins' ace. From 1971 to 1975, Blyleven led Minnesota's rotation in ERA four times and had the sixth-best earned-run average among all major-league starters.[1] Pitching for a Twins team that played at a .489 clip, however, had his career record only 10 games over .500.

Blyleven regularly clashed with team owner Calvin Griffith over salary and became fed up when he lost his arbitration case in 1975 and earned only $10,000 more than he had made in 1974. When Los Angeles Dodgers pitcher Andy Messersmith was granted free agency after the 1975 season and signed a four-year deal with the Atlanta Braves worth $1.1 million, Blyleven refused to sign his contract, hoping to eventually cash in as well.[2]

Rumors circulated that Blyleven was demanding $1.2 million over four years or a trade.[3] Blyleven denied that he had asked for that much and was only speculating what he could get on the open market, but the horse was already out of the barn and fans turned on him.

After a failed attempt on May 27 to beat the A's in Oakland for his 100th win thanks to a costly error by third baseman Steve Braun, Blyleven "sulked and complained about his lack of support," a valid criticism considering the Twins' offense averaged fewer than three runs a game when Blyleven started.[4]

Minnesota hosted the Texas Rangers for a three-game set that began on May 28. Two days later, Rangers owner Brad Corbett met Blyleven in the Twins' clubhouse, and they agreed on a three-year deal worth approximately $420,000.[5] The only question was what the Twins would receive in return.[6]

On May 31 Blyleven took the mound at Metropolitan Stadium to face the California Angels and 22-year-old lefty Frank Tanana, a flamethrower who led the American League with 269 strikeouts in 1975 in only his second full season and finished in a fourth-place tie with former Twin Jim Kaat in AL Cy Young Award voting.

Tanana was roughed up in his first three outings and had a 6.35 ERA on April 19, but he quickly turned things around and pitched to a 1.97 ERA in his next eight starts. Tanana was on a five-game winning streak going into his matchup with Blyleven and had held opposing batters to a .192 average since April 26. Blyleven was having a typical season, leading the Twins' rotation in ERA at 3.13 but sitting at .500 with a 4-4 record thanks to anemic run support and shoddy defense that led to six unearned runs in his first 11 starts.

The last-place Angels, who at 18-30 were already 10½ games behind the first-place Kansas City Royals, sent Jerry Remy, Bob Jones, and Bobby Bonds to the plate to start the contest in front of 8,379 fans, a paltry crowd for a night game on Memorial Day. "As a lynch mob it would have been strictly a warmup act in the days of Marie Antoinette," wrote Jim Klobuchar in the *Minneapolis Star*.[7]

Blyleven made quick work of them, striking out Remy and Bonds, and getting Jones on a grounder to short. The third-place Twins, who at 21-20 were only four games out of first, countered with Steve Brye, Rod Carew, and Larry Hisle in the bottom of the first. Brye singled to center and Carew bunted perfectly down the third-base line for an infield hit, and both moved up a base on catcher Andy Etchebarren's passed ball. Hisle popped out to first and Tanana hit Dan Ford with a pitch to load the bases, but the southpaw fanned Craig Kusick and got Phil Roof to ground out to first to end the threat.

The Angels scored a run in the top of the second when Bruce Bochte led off with a double to left and came home on Bill Melton's soft single to left. Joe Lahoud walked and Ron Jackson struck out before Etchebarren singled to load the bases.[8] However, Blyleven retired Dave Chalk on a popup to third and Remy on a grounder to first.

Tanana surrendered two more hits in the bottom of the second but worked his way out of the jam without allowing a run. Bob Randall followed a Dave McKay fly out with a single, but Etchebarren threw him out trying to steal with Luis Gomez at the plate. Gomez followed with a single before Tanana struck out Brye to end the inning.

Blyleven retired Jones,[9] Bonds, and Bochte in the third on a fly out to left, a strikeout, and a groundout to first; Tanana got Carew to ground to second, Hisle to ground to short, and Ford to fly out to center. Blyleven set the Angels down in order again in the fourth with help from his defense. Melton's liner between third and short was stabbed out of the air by a diving McKay, and then Lahoud was thrown out at first by Carew, who made a nice diving stop and threw from his knees. Blyleven fanned Jackson to close out the frame.

Tanana retired the Twins in order in the bottom of the inning, striking out Kusick, getting Roof on a fly out to center, and coaxing McKay to ground to third. Blyleven retired his ninth straight batter when he struck out Etchebarren leading off the top of the fifth, but he hit Chalk with a pitch to end his streak. Blyleven got Remy on a fly out to left and fanned Jones for his seventh strikeout of the game and the 1,400th of his career.[10]

Tanana had been virtually unhittable since the second inning, and he set down his ninth straight batter in the bottom of the fifth when he retired Randall on a fly to right, Gomez on a popup to first, and Brye on a grounder to third. Blyleven continued to battle, though, and with a little help from Roof he escaped a minor jam after Bonds walked to lead off the top of the sixth and went to second on Bochte's sacrifice. Bonds tried to steal third with Melton at the plate, but Roof gunned him down for the second out of the inning. Melton flied out to left, and the game remained 1-0 in favor of the Angels.

Tanana rediscovered his curveball in the bottom of the sixth and continued his mastery over the Twins in impressive fashion. He not only struck out the side, he got Carew, Hisle, and Ford on called third strikes. "I didn't have control of my curve early in the game," Tanana explained. "But I found it in the sixth inning and it was just curveball, fastball the rest of the way."[11]

The Angels extended their lead to 2-0 in the top of the seventh when Jackson followed a Lahoud strikeout with a single to left, then came around to score when Etchebarren hit a blooper to center that eluded Brye's dive and rolled to the warning track for a triple. Etchebarren was overly aggressive and was tagged out by Carew after a brief rundown. Blyleven then finished the inning by getting Chalk to ground to third.

Tanana began the bottom of the inning by fanning Kusick for the third time and got Roof to ground to third before striking out McKay to set down his 16th straight batter. When Blyleven took the mound for the eighth, angry fans greeted him with a "beery farewell serenade" that went, "Good Night, Bert: It's Nice to See You Go."[12] California scored another run when Bochte drove in Remy with a single after Remy walked, stole second, and went to third on a sacrifice bunt.

Minnesota finally broke through in the bottom of the eighth when Randall led off with a triple and scored on Rod Carew's two-out single to center. Blyleven set the Angels down in order in the top of the ninth before fans loudly booed as he left the mound. Just before entering the dugout, Blyleven made an obscene gesture, "an arm signal that will never appear in the Boy Scouts' manual," wrote Klobuchar.[13]

Twins fans got a second gesture from a player when Kusick, who was booed lustily for fanning three times, launched a 407-foot bomb into the left-field bleachers, then mimicked Blyleven while he trotted down the third-base line. However, that was as close as the Twins would get. Tanana buckled down and struck out Roof and McKay, his 11th and 12th victims, to close out a 3-2 win.

SOURCES

In addition to the sources cited in the Notes, the author accessed Retrosheet.org, Baseball-Reference.com, and SABR.org.

MEMORABLE GAMES AT MINNESOTA'S DIAMOND ON THE PRAIRIE

NOTES

1 Blyleven's ERA was sixth among pitchers with a minimum of 700 innings pitched.

2 Bob Fowler, "Blyleven: $1.2 million, 4 years," *Minneapolis Star*, May 26, 1976: 71.

3 Fowler."

4 "Blyleven-to-Rangers Swap Nearly Set," *Santa Ana* (California) *Register*, June 1, 1976: 25. In 12 starts for the Twins in 1976 before they traded him to the Texas Rangers on June 1, Blyleven got 2.8 runs of support per start. Eight pitchers made at least 12 starts for the Twins in 1976 and Dave Goltz, who finished seventh on the staff in run support, got 4.0 runs of support per start. Eddie Bane made 15 starts for Minnesota that year and got 5.7 runs of support per start.

5 The *Santa Ana Register* reported that the deal was worth $700,000 and the *Minneapolis Star* reported it at $500,000, but according to Baseball-Reference.com and a *Sporting News* salary survey, the Rangers paid Blyleven $140,000 in 1976. He was able to strike a deal with the Rangers after Calvin Griffith gave him permission to field offers from other teams.

6 "Blyleven-to-Rangers Swap." Texas sent third baseman Mike Cubbage, shortstop Roy Smalley, pitchers Bill Singer and Jim Gideon, and $250,000 to Minnesota for Blyleven and shortstop Danny Thompson.

7 Jim Klobuchar, "A Lack of Daintiness at the Park," *Minneapolis Star*, June 1, 1976: 9.

8 Joe Soucheray, "Blyleven Edged by Angels 3-2," *Minneapolis Tribune*, June 1, 1976: 19. Baseball-Reference.com and Retrosheet.org have Bill Melton's hit as a single to center, but Soucheray wrote, "Melton singled, softly, also to left" following Bruce Bochte's double to left.

9 When Blyleven retired Jones for the first out of the third inning, he recorded his 1,700th career inning pitched.

10 Other pitchers who reached 1,400 career strikeouts in 1976 were Texas Rangers hurler Bill Singer on May 1 when he struck out Boston's Denny Doyle in the top of the eighth inning; Atlanta Braves pitcher Andy Messersmith on May 7 when he struck out Pittsburgh pitcher John Candelaria in the bottom of the second; Houston Astros pitcher Larry Dierker on May 9 when he fanned St. Louis's Vic Harris in the bottom of the seventh; Baltimore Orioles pitcher Jim Palmer on May 25 when he struck out Cleveland's Charlie Spikes in the top of the sixth; and New York Mets hurler Jerry Koosman on September 6 when he fanned Cubs center fielder Joe Wallis in the bottom of the sixth.

11 "Blyleven Gets the Gate from Angels," *San Pedro* (California) *News-Pilot*, June 1, 1976: 10.

12 Soucheray; Klobuchar."

13 Klobuchar. Blyleven's gesture was described as an "Italian Salute."

YOUTH IS SERVED AS TIGERS TOP TWINS 7-3

JUNE 20, 1976: DETROIT TIGERS 7, MINNESOTA TWINS 3

By Bill Schneider

As the Detroit Tigers and the Minnesota Twins prepared to square off at Metropolitan Stadium on Sunday, June 20, 1976, neither team had particularly distinguished itself to that point in the season. The Tigers, at 26-33, were at least so far staying out of the American League East basement, where they had finished every year since Billy Martin was fired during the 1973 season. The Twins were two games under the .500 record they always seemed to hover around in the early to mid-1970s (1972: 77-77, 1973: 81-81, 1974: 82-80, 1975: 76-83).

The Twins franchise was in the midst of significant changes. They had hired veteran manager Gene Mauch to replace Frank Quilici after the disappointing 1975 campaign. Already bearing his "Little Genius" nickname, Mauch's was expected with his dugout savvy to elevate the team's fortunes. Interestingly, Quilici had joined the Twins broadcast team, where he presumably had the opportunity to second-guess the moves made by his successor.

More significantly, on June 1, 1976, the Twins had traded longtime staff ace Bert Blyleven, as well as infielder Danny Thompson, to the Texas Rangers for a package including pitchers Bill Singer and Jim Gideon, infielders Roy Smalley and Mike Cubbage, and $250,000. While none of the players the Twins received had the pedigree of Blyleven, each nonetheless represented a reasonable return for a star player unlikely to sign with Twins after his contract expired at the end of the 1976 season. In fact, Blyleven had made his feelings toward the Twins organization well known the day before he was traded. After a 3-2 loss to the Angels at Metropolitan Stadium on May 31, Blyleven made an obscene gesture to the Twins home crowd. When questioned afterward, Blyleven said, "I couldn't care less about the fans. Maybe I should flip them every game and that would bring in more fans to the park. Maybe that fat bastard [owner Calvin] Griffith would have some money to pay us."[1]

The other Twins development was much more positive. A rookie, 20-year-old Butch Wynegar, had emerged as the Twins starting catcher early in the season, and had conjured up hope for a possible All-Star berth as he delivered a slash line of .295/.402/.440 to this point of the season. Despite the fact that he was the youngest player in the major leagues at the time of the game, Harold Delano Wynegar Jr. (Butch was a nickname bestowed by his grandmother) had established a veteran-like reputation for perseverance and dedication to his craft. Mauch commented, "Adversity never fazes him. He just keeps grinding away."[2]

Wynegar was joined in the staring lineup by another youngster, second-year outfielder Lyman Bostock, as well as longtime Twins stalwarts Steve Braun, Larry Hisle, and Rod Carew. The 25-year old Bostock was hitting a strong .327 to go with a .375 on-base percentage as the teams took the field.

Change was in the offing for the Tigers as well. Two 21-year-old rookies, starting pitcher Mark Fidrych and first baseman Jason Thompson, had emerged as significant contributors to the team. Thompson, after hitting three home runs in four games to start the 1976 season at Triple-A Evansville, had seized the first-base job and had already hit seven homers in the majors. It was Fidrych, though, who had emerged as a revelation for the Tigers.

The 6-foot-3 redhead had pitched reasonably well in the minors in 1975 (11-10, 3.21 earned-run average), but had given little indication of the level he would pitch at in 1976. Fidrych made his first start of the 1976 season on May 15, a game he would win 2-1 over the Indians while pitching a complete game. In his five subsequent starts, he had completed every game while going 4-1. In fact, he entered the June 20 game with a 5-1 record and a minuscule 1.86 ERA. He had

240

MEMORABLE GAMES AT MINNESOTA'S DIAMOND ON THE PRAIRIE

attracted significant attention for his antics on the mound as well. As Ron Fimrite of *Sports Illustrated* later recapped, Fidrych "ran to his position, uncommonly eager to get on with the game. He knelt on the mound to pat the earth in front of him and smooth out the opposing pitcher's spike holes. He bolted from the mound to shake the hands of fielders whose play behind him seemed to call for some demonstration of his gratitude. And – the coup d'estime – he talked to the baseball! You could see him standing out there on the mound, holding that ball before him and actually speaking to it, as if he were Hamlet addressing poor Yorick's skull."[3]

Squaring off against Fidrych was recently acquired Twins hurler Bill Singer. Singer had not pitched particularly well for the Twins in his three starts since coming from the Rangers in the Blyleven trade, but the 32-year-old veteran was hoping to change his fortunes.

Tigers outfielder Ron LeFlore led off the game with a single off Singer but would get no further than second base when the half-inning ended. Bostock similarly led off for the Twins with a single, but was nabbed attempting to steal second by Tigers catcher Bruce Kimm. One batter later, Carew also singled, but he too was thrown out by Kimm as he attempted to steal second.

In the second, the Tigers got on the board. Alex Johnson singled to center with one out, advanced to second on a wild pitch, and scored when Aurelio Rodriguez doubled. Singer was able to strand Rodriguez at second as he dispensed with the bottom of the Tigers order.

The Tigers lead didn't hold up for long. With two out, Fidrych gave up back-to-back walks to Hisle and Steve Brye. Shortstop Jerry Terrell then singled Hisle home and second sacker Bob Randall also walked. Bostock grounded out to end the threat, so the game was tied 1-1 entering the third inning. Entering the game, Fidrych had generally exhibited good control (he had walked 10 in 58 innings), so three walks in the span of four batters was unusual.

The Tigers offense continued to reach Singer in the third. With one out, Tom Veryzer and Dan Meyer singled. After Rusty Staub fouled out, Thompson blasted his eighth homer of the season, to left-center, before Singer could end the threat. The Tigers now led 4-1.

After the Twins went quietly in the bottom of the third, the Tigers in the fourth scored for the third inning in a row. With two out, Kimm walked and was doubled home by LeFlore. The Tigers were now up 5-1.

The fifth and the top of the sixth were uneventful, but in the bottom of the sixth the Twins got to Fidrych again. Wynegar led off with a single (his second hit of the game). Fidrych issued his fourth walk of the game to the recently acquired Cubbage to put runners on first and second. Wynegar advanced to third on Hisle's fly out. Veteran Brye singled Wynegar home to narrow the Tigers lead to 5-2, but Fidrych coaxed a double-play ball from Jerry Terrell to end the inning.

This was not Singer's day, though. LeFlore led off the top of the seventh with a single and Singer hit Veryzer with a pitch. Meyer flied out, but Singer then balked the runners to second and third. Staub hit a sacrifice fly to score LeFlore, and Thompson singled Veryzer home. The inning ended with the Tigers up 7-2.

Fidrych disposed of the Twins in the bottom of the seventh, and the Tigers failed to dent reliever Steve Luebber in the eighth after Mauch mercifully ended Singer's day. His final line stood at seven runs allowed on 10 hits in seven innings. It's safe to stay that Singer had not yet made Twins fans forget Blyleven, as he had now allowed 18 runs in his 24⅔ innings of work as a Twins starter since coming from the Rangers.

In the bottom of the eighth, Fidrych's control once again deserted him. Wynegar failed in his bid to get his third hit of the day, but Cubbage and Hisle walked. Brye then doubled to right to score Cubbage. At this point, Tigers manager Ralph Houk ended Fidrych's complete-game streak at six. Houk called on veteran fireman John Hiller to end the threat, and he was able to get to out of the inning without yielding another run. The Tigers now held a 7-3 lead.

After a quiet Tigers ninth, the Twins again threatened. Phil Roof singled, and with one out Wynegar got his third hit of the day, a double to right. Hiller was able to strand the runners, though, and pick up his sixth save of the season as the Tigers won 7-3.

After the game, both Fidrych and Houk acknowledged "The Bird's control problems." Fidrych said, "I walked six guys and somehow got away with it."[4] Houk added, "He didn't pitch like Fidrych. He normally has very good control."[5]

While the game was not particularly close, the 11,916 fans who visited Metropolitan Stadium got to see a showcase of the teams' precocious rookies. In addition to Fidrych's sixth victory of the young season, Jason Thompson was 2-for-5 with a homer and four runs batted in, and hometown favorite Butch Wynegar raised his batting average over .300 with his 3-for-5 performance.

METROPOLITAN STADIUM

NOTES

1. John Snyder, *Twins Journal: Year by Year and Day by Day with the Minnesota Twins since 1961* (Covington, Kentucky: Clerisy Press, 2010): 121.
2. Douglas S. Looney, "He's Catching on Real Fast," *Sports Illustrated*, June 21, 1976: 47.
3. Ron Fimrite, "He's Not a Bird, He's a Human," *Sports Illustrated*, April 11, 1977: 45-46.
4. Associated Press, "Fidrych Wins 6th," *Adrian* (Michigan) *Daily Telegraph*, June 21, 1976: 10.
5. "Fidrych Wins 6th."

BLYLEVEN TRIUMPHANT IN RETURN TO THE MET

JULY 26, 1976: TEXAS RANGERS 3, MINNESOTA TWINS

By Bob Wood

Bert Blyleven was drafted by the Minnesota Twins in the third round of the 1969 free-agent Draft (number 55 overall)[1] as an 18-year-old graduate of Santiago High School in Garden Grove, California. Born in the Netherlands (April 6, 1951), the right-hander advanced quickly through the minor leagues, making his debut as a 19-year-old on June 5, 1970. His 10 wins helped Minnesota win the West Division title, and he pitched in relief against the Baltimore Orioles in the playoffs.

Blyleven peaked at 20 wins in 1973, when he made the All-Star team. With a wicked curveball, he annually registered over 200 strikeouts. Contract negotiations with owner Calvin Griffith after his 20-win All-Star season were contentious. The next season saw Blyleven lose in arbitration and go on the disabled list for the first time (21 days in June 1975) with a sore shoulder. With the Peter Seitz arbitration hearing forever changing the game, Blyleven formally requested a trade after the 1975 season and refused to sign a contract, playing out his option, under the renewal clause,[2] for the 1976 season.

On May 23, 1976, Blyleven won the 99th game of his career. After losing in Oakland on May 27, he had a chance to win his 100th game in front of Minnesota fans on May 31 against California but lost 3-2 to Frank Tanana.

With trade rumors swirling, the fans serenaded Blyleven in the eighth and ninth innings "Goodbye Bert ... we're glad to see you go!" After retiring the Angels in order in the ninth, Blyleven raised his left arm, grabbed it with his right, and extended a finger to the choir, as he headed to the dugout for the final time as a Twin.[3]

This resulted in a fine and an apology, but the big news the next morning was the consummation of Blyleven's trade to the Texas Rangers.

Infielder Danny Thompson, who was also playing out his option, was traded with Blyleven to Texas for Bill Singer, Roy Smalley, Mike Cubbage, Jim Gideon, and $250,000.

Eight weeks later, the Rangers came to Minnesota, and sent Blyleven to the mound on July 26 to face Dave Goltz and the Twins.

The Twins promoted the return of Blyleven, their former ace, with newspaper and radio ads, but only 9,184 turned out to see him pitch for the Rangers against the Twins. His return was marked by jeers, the same as his final appearance for the Twins on May 31. Every time Blyleven walked to the mound, the fans let him have it. He responded by doffing his cap and pitching one of the best games of his career.[4]

After the Rangers were retired in the first inning, Blyleven took the mound for the first time as a visitor in Minnesota. He handled a comebacker for the first out, then struck out Smalley, who had not only been a part of the trade for Blyleven, but was the nephew of Twins manager Gene Mauch. Rod Carew then bounced out to second base.

Texas took the lead on a two-out error by Twins second baseman Bob Randall in the second inning, and Blyleven quickly got three more groundouts in the home half. In the Twins third inning, Blyleven induced three groundballs to shortstop Toby Harrah, who then led off the Rangers fourth inning with a home run, making the Texas lead 2-0.

Steve Braun became the first Twins baserunner when he singled leading off the bottom of the fourth inning. Blyleven again struck out Smalley and again got Carew to bounce to second base, this time for a fielder's choice. Carew, who had 36 stolen bases already this season, tried to steal second base but was thrown out by catcher Jim Sundberg. Carew argued the call and was ejected by second-base umpire Jim Evans. Craig Kusick replaced Carew as the Twins first baseman.

Minnesota failed to get the ball out of the infield again in the fifth inning as Blyleven sandwiched a groundout between a pair of strikeouts. In the sixth inning, the Twins batters were again dominated, producing only a groundball to third base with two more strikeouts.

Goltz continued to keep the game close, and after another scoreless frame, Texas sent Thompson to play second base, replacing Lenny Randle. Thompson, the other player traded by Minnesota with Blyleven, had won the Hutch award in 1974 for overcoming his diagnosed leukemia. The former Oklahoma State All-American would not survive the calendar year, however, as he lost his battle to the disease on December 10 at the Mayo Clinic in Rochester, Minnesota, after undergoing spleen surgery the week before.

The Twins brought the top of the order up after the seventh-inning stretch. Braun, who had their only hit, lifted a fly ball to center field, the longest drive yet against Blyleven, for the first out. Another groundball produced the second out, bringing Kusick (Carew's replacement) to the plate for the first time. Kusick singled to center, but Butch Wynegar was called out on strikes to end the inning.

In the eighth inning Blyleven got yet another groundout before walking Mike Cubbage, who had been one of the players involved in the trade, but Larry Hisle bounced into a 4-6-3 inning-ending double play.

Goltz was removed in the top of the ninth, after allowing an RBI single to Sundberg. Tom Burgmeier replaced him on the mound and retired Juan Beniquez and Gene Clines to end the inning.

Dan Ford struck out to start the bottom of the ninth. Tony Oliva batted for Bob Randall and bounced out to first base. That brought Steve Braun to the plate for the fourth time. With a single and a fly out, Braun had hit the ball better than any other Twin, but Blyleven struck him out to end the game.

It was a two-hit shutout for Blyleven, his third shutout of the season, and the 102nd victory of his career. He struck out nine batters, and the team had 17 assists. Besides the two singles, only one ball left the infield for Minnesota (Braun's fly to center field in the seventh inning).

The game took 2 hours and 17 minutes with Greg Kosc calling the balls and strikes behind the plate. The rest of the crew was second-base umpire Evans, Nestor Chylak (first base), and Joe Brinkman (third base).

SOURCES

In addition to the references cited in the Notes, the author consulted the following:

Baseball-reference.com

Retrosheet.org

Fowler, Bob. "Twins' Price Too High for Blyleven and Carew," *The Sporting News,* November 8, 1975: 51.

Newberg, Jamey. "Swapping Stories: The Bert Blyleven Trade of 1976," MLB.com/blogs, May 24, 2007: newberg.mlblogs.com/swapping-stories-the-bert-blyleven-trade-of-1976-66faee78bd8a

Wolf, Gregory H. "Bert Blyleven," sabr.org/bioproj/person/bert-blyleven/

NOTES

1. baseball-almanac.com/draft/baseball-draft.php?yr=1969.
2. Bob Fowler, "Blyleven Points West," *The Sporting News,* June 5, 1976: 52.
3. Bob Fowler, "Fans Gave Blyleven Musical Farewell," *The Sporting News,* June 19, 1976: 28.
4. Bob Fowler, "Twin Hurlers Running Toward Walk Record," *The Sporting News,* November 8, 1975: 51.

SINGER SETS STAGE FOR BAD NIGHT WITH ANTHEM FLUB

AUGUST 17, 1976: BALTIMORE ORIOLES 10, MINNESOTA TWINS 3

By J. G. Preston

It was "Bloomington Night" at Metropolitan Stadium on August 17, 1976, when the Twins paid tribute to their home community as part of their game against the Baltimore Orioles. The reigning Miss Bloomington – Stephanie Nilson,[1] a 19-year-old college student and aspiring opera singer – was invited to sing the national anthem a cappella before the game.

"She got through 'the rockets' red glare, the bombs bursting in air' just fine," according to the *Minneapolis Tribune*, "but she didn't make it past 'gave proof through the night.' She lost the tempo, then the tune, then stopped.

"'Aaaaw rats!' Miss Nielsen [*sic*] said, and walked off."[2]

"She smiled graciously, bowed, and a sympathetic audience applauded," according to an Associated Press report.[3]

Stephanie was thrown off by a delayed echo from the public-address system. "I wasn't ready for that," she said when she looked back on her performance in 2015. "Nobody told me about the echo. I reached that point where I couldn't think of where I was as it was coming out of my mouth, and I just totally lost it. What I did, throwing my hands up in the air and saying, 'oh, rats' was, thankfully, instinctively correct. I could have said other things, but I wasn't a cusser, so I'm thankful that didn't come out."[4]

Her gaffe made headlines across the country, some of them quite amusing: "Singer loses perilous fight with anthem"[5]... "National anthem infested by rats"[6] … "Anthem gets new ending"[7] … "Star-spangled boner."[8]

Among those who heard about Stephanie's misadventure was Ted Turner, who just seven months earlier had bought the attendance-starved Atlanta Braves. Turner was willing to stage just about any stunt to attract attention and, perhaps, paying customers, including ostrich racing (Ted himself participated) and "Headlock and Wedlock Day," featuring weddings at home plate before the game and professional wrestling on the field afterward.

Turner invited Stephanie to sing the national anthem before the Braves' nationally televised game on August 23, and she did, turning in what was described as a "flawless performance."[9] That also made newspapers nationwide, this time with pictures of Stephanie celebrating her success. And on August 30, the Twins invited Stephanie back to Met Stadium to try again before their game with the Milwaukee Brewers, and she "came through unscathed."[10]

On August 17, the sound of Stephanie Nilson's "aw, rats" had hardly faded before the Orioles pounced on Twins pitcher Tom Johnson, making what would be the only start of his major-league career.[11] After Al Bumbry struck out to lead off the game, Bobby Grich singled and stole second, Reggie Jackson walked, and designated hitter Lee May crushed a 384-foot home run into the left-field bleachers for a 3-0 Baltimore lead.

"That home-run pitch was a mistake," May said afterward. "It was a slider he got out over the plate."[12] The homer was May's 22nd of the season, putting him one behind Oakland's Sal Bando for the American League lead. "When May's hot, he's as tough as there is," said Minnesota manager Gene Mauch, who had also managed against May when both were in the National League.[13]

Johnson settled down after that, allowing just two more hits, both singles, and one walk through five innings. Meanwhile, however, his teammates had little success against Baltimore pitcher Rudy May; the Twins collected three singles and a walk in the first five innings and did not get a runner past second base. May was helped by an unusual double play in the fourth inning: After Dan Ford singled, first baseman Tony Muser caught a foul popup off the bat of Steve

Brye and threw to catcher Rick Dempsey, who had run to first base, to double up Ford.[14]

The Orioles' bats came alive again in the sixth inning. Jackson led off with a double, Lee May followed with a triple, and Ken Singleton singled to make the score 5-0. After Muser struck out, Doug DeCinces singled to right, and when Ford mishandled the ball, the runners advanced to second and third.

Jim Hughes relieved Johnson, and the first batter he faced, Mark Belanger, hit a shot that bounced off Hughes's foot. Shortstop Roy Smalley retrieved the ball and threw to catcher Glenn Borgmann, who got Singleton in a rundown between third and home. Borgmann wound up tagging Singleton out, with DeCinces moving to third and Belanger taking second.[15] Hughes walked Dempsey to load the bases, then Bumbry delivered a single to center that scored DeCinces and Belanger, giving the Orioles a 7-0 lead.

Rudy May took his shutout into the seventh inning, when singles by Ford, Brye, and Smalley gave the Twins a run. Another run followed in the bottom of the eighth, again requiring three singles, this time off the bats of Rod Carew, Ford, and Brye. Rudy May exited the game after Brye's hit, with Dyar Miller coming on to get pinch-hitter Steve Braun to pop up for the final out of the inning.

In the top of the ninth, the Orioles roughed up Hughes, a 16-game winner as a rookie in 1975 who struggled in his second season. Dempsey led off with a single and was forced out by Bumbry, who moved up on a wild pitch. After Grich walked, Jackson singled to score Bumbry and Lee May singled to bring home Grich, May's fifth run batted in of the game. (He would end the season with 109 RBIs to lead the league.) Jackson stopped at second on May's hit, then moved to third on Singleton's fly ball to left field and scored on Hughes's second wild pitch of the inning, making the score 10-2, Baltimore.

The Twins did get another run in the bottom of the ninth on doubles by Smalley and Larry Hisle and had runners on first and third when Craig Kusick flied out to end the game, with the final score Baltimore 10, Minnesota 3.

When it was over, Stephanie Nilson's singing was about the only thing Twins fans had to smile about ... and even she had a tough night.

SOURCES

Game stories from the *Minneapolis Tribune* and *Baltimore Sun* were accessed via Newspapers.com.

NOTES

1. Her name was misspelled "Stephany Nielsen" in early newspaper accounts.
2. "Singer Loses Perilous Fight with Anthem," *Minneapolis Tribune*, August 18, 1976: C-1.
3. "National Anthem Infested by Rats," *Bangor (Maine) Daily News*, August 19, 1976: 22.
4. The author interviewed Stephanie, now Stephanie Askew, in 2015 for a blog post, "From 'aw, rats' to redemption: Miss Bloomington sings the National Anthem at two ballparks in 1976."
5. *Minneapolis Tribune*, August 18, 1976: C-1.
6. "National Anthem Infested by Rats."
7. *St. Petersburg (Florida) Times*, August, 18, 1976: 4-C.
8. *State Journal-Register*, Peoria, Illinois, August 20, 1976.
9. Associated Press, "No Cues This Time," *Ithaca (New York) Journal*, August 24, 1976: 15. Stephanie wasn't Turner's only pregame attraction that night. He also staged a pregame "Baseball Olympics" (it was an Olympic year, after all) in which one of the events saw Turner and Phillies pitcher Tug McGraw compete to see who could push a baseball from third base to home plate the fastest using their nose. Photos of that also found their way onto sports pages across the country.
10. Gary Libman, "Twins Crush Brewers, End Losing Streak," *Minneapolis Tribune*, August 31, 1976: 5C.
11. Johnson was one of the game's top relief pitchers in 1977, with a 16-7 record and 15 saves in 71 appearances. But all that work took a toll on his arm; he appeared in only 18 games in 1978, and after surgery to repair a torn rotator cuff in March 1979, he never pitched in the majors again. Jim McKernon, "Tom Johnson," Society for American Baseball Research Baseball Biography Project, sabr.org/bioproj/person/1362d95c.
12. Associated Press, "Baltimore Steps on Twins," *Bemidji (Minnesota) Pioneer*, August 18, 1976: 8.
13. Joe Soucheray, "Baltimore Clobbers Twins 10-3," *Minneapolis Tribune*, August 18, 1976: 1C.
14. "Lee May Drives in 5 as Orioles Rip Twins, 10-3," *Baltimore Sun*, August 18, 1976: C5.
15. "Twins Scorecard," *Minneapolis Tribune*, August 18, 1976: 2C.

LATE SEASON OFFICIAL SCORING CONTROVERSY ENDED BY NINTH-INNING HIT

SEPTEMBER 25, 1976: MINNESOTA TWINS 6, CALIFORNIA ANGELS 0

By Sarah Johnson

A bouncer to the first baseman leading off the game called a hit. This judgment call remains the only hit until two out in the ninth inning when the potential last batter singles to right, replacing the lonely '1' that had sat on the scoreboard for more than two hours. "That's about as far down the plank as you can walk as the OS," said Patrick Reusse, a staff writer for the *St. Paul Pioneer Press* and the official scorer for the game on Saturday, September 25, 1976, at Metropolitan Stadium, who began to get an earful from a multitude of sources as the innings rolled by.[1] In addition to this controversial midmorning decision, the late-season contest won 6-0 by the Minnesota Twins over the California Angels also included a future Hall of Famer becoming the first major-league pitcher to strike out more than 300 hitters in four different seasons.

A sparse crowd (officially recorded as 4,942) was in attendance for the first game of this two-game series during the last homestand of the season. The Twins went on to finish the 1976 campaign with a record of 85-77, good enough for third place out of six teams in the American League West and five games behind the division-winning Kansas City Royals. California ended up in fourth place in the same division, 14 games behind the Royals at 76-86. It was a normal fall day in Minnesota with temperatures in the low 60s.[2]

The pitching matchup featured Twins right-hander Dave Goltz, the native Minnesotan who finished the season with 14 wins and a 3.36 earned-run average, and California's Nolan Ryan, the fireballing right-hander who came into the game needing nine strikeouts to reach 300 for the season.

Angels left fielder Dave Collins led off the game with a chopper to Twins first baseman Rod Carew. Dave Goltz, late in covering first base, dropped the underhand throw from Carew, allowing Collins to reach safely. "Collins was a speedy guy," Reusse remembered. "I thought he was going to beat it out so I called it a hit. It wasn't immediately a controversy."[3]

After the single, Collins was caught stealing and Goltz went on to have four one-two-three innings. The Twins took the lead in the bottom of the third on a solo home run by right fielder Dan Ford. His hit went into the temporary bleachers set up in left field for Minnesota Vikings football games, prompting Ford to say, "Bring back the porch in 1977."[4] The Twins added three more runs in the third and fourth innings, aided by four walks issued by Ryan. Ryan threw 160 pitches and walked eight over seven innings to lose his 18th game of the season. He struck out 11, including a called third strike on Twins second baseman Bob Randall to end the sixth inning for number 300. "It's nice anytime to get into the record books," Ryan said. "They pay you for wins. It's been a frustrating season."[5]

The only Angels threat during the game came in the top of the sixth when Goltz walked Collins to lead off the inning and California second baseman Jerry Remy reached on an error, putting runners on first and second with no one out. But Goltz struck out center fielder Bob Jones and first baseman Tony Solaita and got designated hitter Mario Guerrero to ground into a force out to end the inning. Although Goltz struck out eight, he also walked four, including catcher Terry Humphrey in the second inning.

Angels right-hander Gary Wheelock gave up two runs in the eighth inning, including a run-scoring double by Twins left fielder Larry Hisle, and Minnesota won easily, 6-0, in a game that lasted 2 hours, 28 minutes. The California offense struggled during the season, with Reusse writing in his game story about the two additional runs, "The runs were merely insurance. Goltz was coasting through the

Angels – a collection which carries a .235 team batting average."[6] In the top of the ninth, the last chance to take the official scorer off the hook, Jones struck out and Solaita flied out before Guerrero hit a single to right, ending an afternoon of drama.

The game started at 10:30 A.M. to accommodate WCCO, the team's flagship radio station, which also held the rights to broadcast University of Minnesota football and had a game nearby at Memorial Stadium that afternoon. As the baseball game progressed with the sole Angels hit, the pressure increased in the press box. In a 2013 blog on the *Star Tribune's* website, Reusse, now a *Minneapolis Star Tribune* sports columnist, wrote: "By mid-game, messages started to arrive from Calvin Griffith family members that the Collins chopper in the first must be changed to an error in the name of justice. There was a call from the dugout to the press box, with the message: 'Tell Reusse that Carew says that was an error.'"[7] Reviewing the play wasn't an option – "The thing to remember is in those days there were no replays – only some of the games were even on TV – so you really had to pay attention," Reusse said.[8]

"The crowd was so small I could hear fans yelling at me," Reusse told the author in 2019. "The press box wasn't very crowded – most reporters were off covering the Vikings or Gopher football – and it was a lot more irreverent back then than it is today. I remember when Guerrero got the hit I stood up and yelled, I was the happiest person in the ballpark. When people ask me who my favorite player is and I say Mario Guerrero they usually go, 'Huh?' I tell them he got the biggest hit of my career."[9]

At the time, local sportswriters also served as official scorers, which could make for some uncomfortable situations: The scorer making a judgment call during the game potentially affecting a player's statistics could also be dependent on that player for a postgame interview. In his game story, Reusse included quotes from both Goltz and Minnesota manager Gene Mauch about Collins's hit. "It makes no difference now because they got another hit, but that was an error on me," said Goltz. "I beat him to the bag but I dropped the throw." "Dave got a terrible jump off the mound, but he was still a couple of steps ahead of Collins," said Mauch. "Until there were two outs in the ninth, it was as easy a no-hitter as I've ever seen."[10]

The *Orange County Register* did not mention the controversy, covering the first-inning play only by reporting, "The first hit off Goltz was by leadoff hitter Collins in the opening inning. Collins tapped a ball to first baseman Rod Carew, but Goltz was unable to get to first in time to make the play. Mario Guerrero singled in the ninth for the Angels' other hit."[11]

In the Twin Cities, the rival newspaper for the *Pioneer Press,* the *Minneapolis Tribune* (later the *Star Tribune*), named Reusse as the official scorer in its game story. "Umpire Dave Phillips called Collins safe and official scorer Pat Reusse ruled a hit. Mario Guerrero of the Angels finally took the scorer off the hook when he lined a single to right field with two out in the ninth inning for the first legitimate hit to remove any no-hit controversy," wrote the *Tribune's* Tom Briere.[12]

"You didn't have to do it, they would ask if you wanted to be an official scorer, but I wanted the extra money," said Reusse. "We were paid by [Major League Baseball] for scoring games. I don't remember any controversies with guys telling me they wouldn't talk to me because of one of my calls and I never made a call because I thought a player would be mad at me and maybe not talk to me if I called a play a certain way."[13]

The tradition of having writers scoring and covering the game was phased out during the late '70s. "At the end of last season [1978] all Twin Cities newspapers closed down on official scoring," wrote *Minneapolis Tribune* columnist Dick Cullum on July 5, 1979.[14]

This game is inextricably linked with two others in Twins history. Two years earlier in a late-season matchup against the Rangers, it was also Dave Goltz on the mound when the second batter of the game hit a groundball to Twins third baseman Eric Soderholm. The official scorer that day, Bob Fowler of the *Minneapolis Star,* called it a hit and took his own place on the hot seat as Goltz held Texas hitless until a two-out, ninth-inning triple by shortstop Pete Mackanin relieved him of the same controversy. More than 20 years later, Twins starter Eric Milton no-hit the Angels (then called the Anaheim Angels) in another September morning start necessitated by the Gopher football schedule.[15]

SOURCES

In addition to the sources cited below, the author consulted Baseball-Reference.com and Retrosheet.org.

baseball-reference.com/boxes/MIN/MIN197609250.shtml

retrosheet.org/boxesetc/1976/B09250MIN1976.htm

MEMORABLE GAMES AT MINNESOTA'S DIAMOND ON THE PRAIRIE

NOTES

1 Patrick Reusse, telephone interview, August 28, 2019 (hereafter Reusse interview).
2 Weather Report, *Minneapolis Star*, September 24, 1976: 12A.
3 Reusse interview.
4 Patrick Reusse, "Twins, Goltz Handcuff Angels," *St. Paul Pioneer Press*, September 26, 1976: 1 – Sports Section.
5 "Ryan Likes Strike Outs," *Orange County Register* (Anaheim, California), September 27, 1976: C2.
6 Patrick Reusse, "Twins, Goltz Handcuff Angels."
7 Patrick Reusse, "The Day That Mario Guerrero Saved My Bacon," *Star Tribune*, startribune.com/reusse-blog-official-scoring-the-day-mario-guerrero-saved-my-bacon/216343301, accessed September 2, 2019.
8 Reusse interview.
9 Reusse interview.
10 Patrick Reusse, "Twins, Goltz Handcuff Angels."
11 "Goltz Upstages Ryan's Record," *Orange County Register,* September 26, 1976: D4.
12 Tom Briere, "Twins, Goltz Score 6-0 Win Over Angels," *Minneapolis Tribune,* September 26, 1976: 10C.
13 Reusse interview.
14 Dick Cullum, *Minneapolis Tribune*, July 5, 1979: 3D.
15 By the time of the Milton no-hitter (1999) both the Twins and the Gopher football team played at the Metrodome. When games were scheduled on the same day, the Twins played in the morning and the Gophers in the evening, allowing time to change the field from a baseball to a football layout.

ADAMS'S EIGHT RBIS, CAREW'S FIVE RUNS LEAD TWINS IN SLUGFEST

JUNE 26, 1977: MINNESOTA TWINS 19, CHICAGO WHITE SOX 12

By Jim McKernon

In baseball nothing is inevitable. All the right ingredients can turn into the most boring of games. But every once in a while those ingredients mixed just right turn into a memorable feast. Maybe not a subtle, nuanced meal that requires a discriminating palette but a long, raucous Sunday-afternoon backyard barbecue potluck with the family and neighbors where everyone eats too much and maybe one or two of the adults overindulge. Such was the June 26, 1977, game between the Minnesota Twins and visiting Chicago White Sox. As host Gene Mauch started from the first-base dugout to hand his lineup card to home-plate umpire Steve Palermo, the Twins' ticket booth workers were turning away out-of-luck fans. The Twins' "Jersey Day" promotional giveaway, a Twins tee-shirt emblazoned with the number "29" of its perennial all-star Rod Carew, was partially responsible for the large crowd but didn't tell the whole story.

The Twins entered the weekend series in second place in the American League West Division with a record of 38-30, a mere two one-thousandths of a percentage point behind the division-leading White Sox (37-29). The Friday night game was prelude to Sunday's affair in many ways as the Twins claimed first place with a 7-6 victory thanks to Lyman Bostock's eighth-inning solo home run. Meeting Mauch and Palermo at the plate on Sunday was White Sox manager Bob Lemon, whose slugging South Side Hitmen had taken back first place the previous night with an 8-1 victory. That gave the White Sox 28 runs against the Twins in just four games in 1977. Sprinkle in 90-degree heat, clear blue skies, and a strong breeze blowing out to the left-field bleachers, and the party was on.

The Twins had surprised everyone by putting together an excellent start to the 1977 season. Pitching and fielding certainly weren't their forte. Mauch had made a point of trying to improve the defense during spring training after his club led the AL in errors the previous season. Having lost All-Star reliever Bill Campbell to free agency, an already-suspect pitching staff was also dealt a serious blow in April when pitchers Mike Pazik and Don Carrithers were seriously injured in a car accident. The Twins were relying on the likes of outfielders Larry Hisle, Bostock, Disco Danny Ford, sophomore All-Star catcher Butch Wynegar, and, of course, Carew to carry them. As Mauch explained to Larry Keith of *Sports Illustrated*, "I just tell the starters to bust it for as long as they

Glenn Adams

MEMORABLE GAMES AT MINNESOTA'S DIAMOND ON THE PRAIRIE

Among the wackiness during the Twins' 19-12 win over the White Sox was a fan who climbed the left-field foul pole.

can, and then I go to the bullpen. We want to contain the other team long enough for us to get our offense in operation."[1]

On the South Side of Chicago the equally surprising White Sox had slugged their way to the top of the division. The White Sox were not relying on pitching and defense either. The second season of the free-agency era saw owner Bill Veeck employ a "rent-a-player" strategy in hopes of making the team competitive. Veeck had traded for unsigned option-year players Oscar Gamble and Richie Zisk before the season. He also added free-agent third baseman and former Twin Eric Soderholm, a player coming back from knee surgery, to bolster a lineup that already included Ralph Garr, Chet Lemon, Jim Spencer, and Brian Downing.

Starting in right field for the Twins that afternoon was Glenn Adams. Adams, a nine-year pro, had come to the Twins after stints in the Astros' minor-league system and with the Giants in the majors. Describing his National League experience, Adams said, "Well Houston only wants outfielders who can run the 100 in 9-flat and the Astros don't care if they can hit or not. The Giants just thought they had better players."[2] The former Pacific Coast League batting champ[3] was available and Mauch, also a former National Leaguer, knew he could hit. In December 1976 the Twins paid the Giants $50,000 for his rights.[4] Although he was hitting .329 as he divided his time among designated hitter, right field, and pinch-hitter, nobody anticipated what was to happen this Sunday.

The first four innings saw the Twins plate 15 runs and Adams had a hand in many of them. He came to the plate in the first inning with the bases loaded and doubled to right-center to drive in Carew and Bostock. In the second, it was, as Yogi Berra would say, déjà vu all over again with the bases jammed with Twins. Adams's grand slam off starter Steve Stone made the score 8-1 and brought Dave Hamilton in from the bullpen to finish the inning. Lemon lamented after the game, "Our pitchers don't dare pitch up, but everybody was up today."[5]

Twins starter Bill Butler didn't fare much better than Stone. In the third with one out, Chet Lemon singled and Lamar Johnson homered. A walk to Richie Zisk and a home run by Soderholm ended Butler's day. Mauch summoned Twins closer Tom Johnson. The Twins' answer to the loss of Bill Campbell, Johnson entered the game with an ERA of 1.82 and eight wins in his 32 appearances. He gave up two more runs before the end of the inning, and by the time the Twins batted again in the bottom of the third, the White Sox had narrowed the margin to 8-7.

After a walk, two singles, a groundout, then another single in the Twins' third, Adams singled to drive in Wynegar for his seventh run batted in (RBI). The score now stood at 12-7. In the seventh, again the sacks were full of Twins as Adams made his way to the plate. (Adams told *St. Paul Pioneer Press* writer Patrick Reusse after the game: "Well, a guy could knock in 300 runs if the bases were loaded every time he came to the plate.")[6] Adams's sacrifice fly netted his eighth RBI of the afternoon, a Twins record. Gene Mauch described the day this way, "It was a great day for hitting and there were some very good hitters swinging the bat. Some very good hitters and one unreal hitter."[7] That "unreal hitter" was Rod Carew. Carew entered the game on a torrid streak, and his batting average at .396. Since June 1, he was 40-for-87, a .459 average. The day before the start of the White Sox series, Mauch commented, "I've never seen anything like it. The year (1957) Ted Williams hit .388, I knew I would never see anything like it again. I was wrong."[8] Twins shortstop Roy Smalley said wryly, "My goal is to hit 100 points less than Rodney."[9]

A double in the first followed by a single in the second inning put Carew at an even .400. As the Twins flashed the news via the scoreboard to the capacity crowd of 46,463, they rose for the first of three standing ovations. In the fourth, after Carew singled in Bob Randall with the Twins' 14th run, the crowd, including 20,000 youngsters either wearing or holding jerseys of their hero, rose again to show its appreciation. Carew tipped his hat to acknowledge the cheers. Wynegar singled home Carew and the inning ended with the Twins enjoying a 15-8 lead. The White Sox added solo home runs by catcher Jim Essian and Lemon in the fifth to make it 15-10, but Carew and the partisans would have the last word.

In the eighth the crowd went absolutely crazy when Carew collected his fourth hit and sixth RBI of the day on a two-run home run to left field off Larry Anderson. That made the score 17-10, and raised Carew's average to .403. "I've never seen anything like it," Carew said. "To tell you the truth, I'm a little embarrassed because I didn't know how to react."[10] The manager knew what to do. "I told Rod to go out and tip his cap. And only because it is him. The fellows in the other dugout know that. That crowd wants the reaction from Carew. They know he isn't trying to show anyone up. After all there is only one Rodney."[11]

When Johnson got Chet Lemon to fly out for the final out and his ninth win, the score stood 19-12. The Twins were back in first place and their record book needed some updating. In addition to the new regular-season attendance mark and Adams's RBI record, Carew's five runs scored was a record. The Twins' 19 runs scored and the 31 runs by both teams were also new records. In addition to those records, the *St. Paul Pioneer Dispatch* reported that Met Stadium ushers and Bloomington police also had to reunite almost 100 lost children with their families and deal with more than a few cases of inebriation.[12] In the fourth inning a fan climbed the left-field foul pole and had to be talked down. (That fan was future SABR member Stew Thornley.[13])

Mauch summed it all up: "I've never had a game like this. Not anything close."[14]

NOTES

1   Larry Keith, "Minny Gets the Max From a Minimum," *Sports Illustrated*, June 20, 1977: 22.

2   Patrick Reusse, "Record Crowd Watches As Twins Bomb Chisox," *St. Paul Pioneer Press*, June 27, 1977: 17.

3   Playing for Phoenix, Adams led the Pacific Coast League with a .352 batting average in 1974.

4   Sid Hartman, *Minneapolis Tribune*, June 27, 1977: 2C.

5   Richard Dozer, "Twins Devour Sox Pitching," *Chicago Tribune*, June 27, 1977: Sec. 6, page 1.

6   Reusse, "Record Crowd Watches As Twins Bomb Chisox."

7   Pat Thompson, "Met Is Noisy House That Rodney Filled," *St. Paul Pioneer Press*, June 27, 1977: 17.

8   Patrick Reusse, "Hitting, Pitching Mesh as Twins Drub Texas 12-2," *St. Paul Pioneer Press*, June 24, 1977: 22.

9   Reusse, "Hitting, Pitching Mesh as Twins Drub Texas 12-2."

10 Reusse, "Record Crowd Watches Twins Bomb Chisox"

11 Thompson, "Met Is Noisy House That Rodney Filled."

12 Pat Thompson, "Twins Recapture First Place," *St. Paul Pioneer Press*, June 27, 1977: 22.

13 Interview with fan who climbed the foul pole, July 17, 2019.

14 "Biggest Regular Season Crowd Ever Sees Twins Win 19-12," *Minneapolis Tribune*, June 27, 1977: 1.

LARRY HISLE'S BUNT HELPS DAVE GOLTZ BEAT NOLAN RYAN

JULY 21, 1977: MINNESOTA TWINS 3, CALIFORNIA ANGELS 2

By Thomas E. Merrick

With Dave Goltz pitching for the Twins, and Nolan Ryan going for the Angels, a savvy fan entering Metropolitan Stadium on July 21, 1977, might well expect to witness a pitchers' duel. And that is exactly what the 21,239 in attendance did see – after the first inning.

Both teams were sending their best to the mound. At age 30, Ryan was nearing legendary status. He could claim four no-hitters and had topped the league in strikeouts for four of the previous five seasons, including a record 383 strikeouts in 1973. In 1977 he was leading the league in wins (13) and strikeouts (234), averaging over 11 strikeouts per nine innings.[1] While Goltz was less fearsome, he had registered 14 wins in each of the previous two seasons and already had 10 wins this year. The Minnesota native was enjoying his finest season, which would culminate with 20 wins.

California quickly scored off Goltz. Jerry Remy struck out to begin the game, but Rance Mulliniks reached base when Twins shortstop Roy Smalley booted his grounder.[2] Bobby Bonds followed with a home run over the fence in left-center to stake the Angels to a 2-0 lead.[3] Goltz responded by striking out Tony Solaita but surrendered a single to Don Baylor before retiring the Angels with another strikeout.

Despite striking out three Angels, Goltz had encountered the sort of first-inning problems that had plagued him recently.[4] The opposition had scored in the first inning of eight of his last 12 starts, including six consecutive starts from June 15 to July 5. When Goltz was asked afterward about this recurring problem, he quipped, "Maybe we should start these games at 8:45 instead of 7:30."[5]

The Twins' first inning started with a single by Mike Cubbage.[6] After a fly out, Rod Carew drew a walk, putting runners at first and second. Up stepped Lyman Bostock, who tripled off the right-field fence to score Cubbage and Carew and tie the game.[7] Afterward, Ryan commented on Bostock's triple, "I gave him a pitch to hit ... and he hit it. You don't make a mistake against that type of hitter, and I made a mistake."[8]

Next, Butch Wynegar sent a grounder to second baseman Remy, who checked Bostock back to third before retiring Wynegar. That brought Larry Hisle to the plate for what proved to be the key play of the game.

Hisle had been battling Ryan since joining the Twins in 1973, with Ryan usually getting the better of it. Ryan had struck out Hisle 23 times in their rivalry,[9] victimizing Hisle more times than any other pitcher did.[10] For the season, Hisle had mustered just two hits off Ryan in 12 at-bats.[11] According to Hisle, "I just don't hit him that well. So, I went to the plate telling myself that I was going to try a bunt."[12] A bunt? With two outs? From the player leading his team in home runs, and the league in runs batted in?

Later, Hisle explained his thinking: "I figured my chances of bunting for a hit were better than my chances of swinging for one. I knew the third baseman (Dave Chalk) would be playing back, but I also knew that if I tried to bunt on the first pitch and missed, he

Lyman Bostock

Minnesota Twins

253

would move in a few steps on ensuing pitches and take that play away from me."[13] Hisle needed a first-pitch strike from Ryan. If he got one, with the element of surprise on his side, a properly executed bunt might work.

Hisle got the strike he wanted, and bunted it down the third-base line for a single. "It was perfect," said Angels manager Dave Garcia. "There was nothing Dave Chalk could do about it."[14] Bostock scored on the play to give the Twins a 3-2 lead.[15] "Hisle has knocked in a lot of big runs this season with some long hits," said Twins manager Gene Mauch, "But tonight, he drove in a very big run with one that went 26 feet."[16] It was a big run indeed, ultimately giving the Twins a win.

The third inning presented Minnesota with an opportunity to extend its lead. After retiring the first two Twins batters, Ryan walked Wynegar. Hisle followed with another single – this one a more conventional hit to left field – sending Wynegar to third base. Another walk loaded the bases, but Smalley, batting next, grounded out to end the threat.

No Angels reached base in either the second or third inning and Goltz notched two more strikeouts. The Angels' fourth inning began with Solaita hitting a grounder to Carew, which he took to first unassisted. Goltz had now retired eight consecutive batters.

Then suddenly, the Angels threatened to retake the lead. Baylor stroked his second single of the night and advanced a base when Twins second baseman Mike Cubbage muffed Chalk's grounder. With runners now at first and second, Danny Goodwin hit a hard grounder "that seemed headed for center field,"[17] but Smalley atoned for his first-inning error and third-inning groundout by gloving the ball and beating Chalk to second base for a force out.[18] Goltz struck out Danny Briggs – his sixth strikeout of the game – to end the inning. Garcia cited this inning as the game's turning point.[19]

Smalley also figured prominently in the Twins' final scoring opportunity. He walked to begin the sixth and advanced to second when Ryan issued a walk to Rob Wilfong. Cubbage moved Smalley to third and Wilfong to second with a sacrifice bunt. But the scoring opportunity was squandered when Glenn Adams hit a grounder toward first that Solaita fielded and threw home for the tag on Smalley. Carew flied out to end the inning, and Ryan, finally harnessing his control, did not allow another Twins baserunner.

Meanwhile, Goltz was holding California at bay. The Angels had one baserunner in both the sixth and eighth, and two Angels reached base in the seventh, but no one went beyond second base. In the ninth, Goltz coaxed three "meek groundballs" to complete a 3-2 Minnesota victory.[20]

Good pitchers can shut down opponents even when they are not at their best. That was evident in this game. Ryan did not have good command and admitted he had no faith in either his fastball or curve.[21] He struck out just four – far below his norm – threw a wild pitch, walked eight batters, and balked, yet he pitched a four-hitter, and no one crossed home plate after the first inning. Likewise, Goltz pitched from behind in the count most of the night,[22] which usually leads to defeat. Even so, he got steadily better as the game went on, and "slammed the door" on the Angels in the ninth.[23] As Mauch emphasized after the game, "Dave Goltz has learned how to win."[24]

Larry Hisle

NOTES

1   234 strikeouts in 190⅔ innings.

2   "Angel Scorecard," *Los Angeles Times,* July 22, 1977, Section III: 6.

3   "Angel Scorecard."

4   Bob Fowler, "Hisle's winning bunt emphasizes his value," *Minneapolis Star,* July 22, 1977: 7B.

MEMORABLE GAMES AT MINNESOTA'S DIAMOND ON THE PRAIRIE

5   Fowler.
6   "Angel Scorecard."
7   Don Merry, "One Bad Inning One Too Many for Ryan, Angels," *Los Angeles Times,* July 22, 1977, Section III: 1.
8   Merry.
9   Fowler.
10 Over Hisle's career, Ryan struck him out 29 times in 67 at-bats (and 77 plate appearances). baseball-reference.com/play-index/batter_vs_pitcher.cgi?batter=hislela01.
11 Fowler.
12 Fowler.
13 Fowler.
14 Merry: 6.
15 Fowler.
16 Fowler.
17 Merry: 6.
18 Merry: 6.
19 Merry: 6.
20 Max Nichols, "Mauch: Goltz Learns to Win," *Minneapolis Star,* July 22, 1977: 7B.
21 Merry: 1.
22 Fowler: 9B.
23 Nichols.
24 Nichols.

JULY 27, 1978: CUBBAGE HITS FOR THE CYCLE; PERZANOWSKI GETS HIS ONLY COMPLETE-GAME VICTORY

MINNESOTA TWINS 6, TORONTO BLUE JAYS 3

By Dan Levitt

Even with Dave Goltz, the Twins' best pitcher, on the mound, on Wednesday, July 26, 1978, the Twins lost the first of a two-game midweek series with the Toronto Blue Jays, baseball's most hapless team. The Twins were now 12½ games out of first place in the American League Western Division, and getting back in the division race seemed a long way off. Moreover, they were starting Stan Perzanowski, a 27-year-old journeyman who had last pitched in the majors with Texas in May 1976. His career record of 3-4 with a 5.02 earned-run average did little to inspire confidence.

After California had released him from its organization in August 1977, Perzanowski, cousin of one-time Twins reliever Ron Perranoski, called around for a job. Minnesota farm director George Brophy decided to take a flier on the sinkerball pitcher, sending him to the Twins' Triple-A farm club in Toledo. In his first 24 games, Perzanowski was 5-1 with a 2.46 ERA, and Twins manager Gene Mauch decided to give him a start with the big-league club. Perzanowski responded by pitching the best game of his career, hurling his only complete-game victory.

Despite this performance, Perzanowski was overshadowed by his one-time Texas and minor-league teammate, third baseman Mike Cubbage. Cubbage became the fifth Twin to hit for the cycle, joining Rod Carew, Cesar Tovar, Lyman Bostock, and Larry Hisle.[1] "I used to hit a few for Perzanowski when we were at Spokane in the Pacific Coast League," Cubbage said. "We both belonged to Texas then. I know that Perzanowski can pitch; he'll help us up here."[2]

For this Thursday day game, the Twins drew 18,285 fans, a large turnout for the time. (Attendance was only 6,014 the night before.) Against the Twins, Toronto manager Roy Hartsfield called on 22-year-old right-handed pitcher Jim Clancy, who would go on to a nice career. Hosken Powell led off for the Twins in the bottom of the first and reached on an infield single. Roy Smalley singled him to third, and Powell scored when Carew hit into a double play, giving Minnesota a 1-0 lead.

Cubbage led off the second inning with the Twins ahead 1-0 and belted the ball to right field but was thrown at third trying to stretch his hit to a triple, earning a stare-down from Mauch.[3] The Blue Jays tied the score in the third when Luis Gomez scored on a double by Rick Bosetti. In the fourth Cubbage homered to right after Dan Ford walked, giving the Twins a 3-1 lead. After another hit and a walk, Hartsfield replaced Clancy with lefty Jerry Garvin.

The Blue Jays made it a one-run game again in the top of the fifth with a walk and two singles. In the bottom of the inning, Powell again singled and eventually scored on a sacrifice fly by Dan Ford. With Cubbage due up next, Mauch left him in the game. Cubbage had been platooning with Larry Wolfe, but the righty had been struggling and was hitting only .223, while Cubbage had only slightly cooled off from the .325 he was hitting at the All-Star break. With two well-struck balls so far, Mauch hoped Cubbage could stay hot. "I wanted to see what he could do," Mauch said. "He's been stroking the ball very well."[4] Cubbage rewarded his manager with a hard single off Garvin's glove that bounded to third.

In the bottom of the seventh with the Twins still up 4-2, Powell led off with his third single in three at-bats. (He had one walk.) With two out and Powell on second, Hartsfield intentionally walked Ford to get to Cubbage. Cubbage hit the ball off the center-field fence, scoring both Powell (his third run of the day) and Ford. In going for the catch, center fielder Bosetti hit the wall and fell down, giving Cubbage time to get to third for a stand-up triple and the cycle.[5]

In the ninth Toronto scored one more run on two hits to make the final score 6-3. Perzanowski's sinker held the Blue Jays to six hits and 21 groundouts. The 19 assists by the Twins set a team record, and Carew's 21 putouts set a team record and fell just one short of the major-league record for a first baseman.[6]

"It's a pleasure to be in the major leagues again," Perzanowski said after the game. "To win and to pitch when you can put the ball right where you want it. That's pretty much my style, sink the fastball low and get the groundball. Today I had the curve and the forkball for a changeup."[7] He also remembered how hard the last two years had been, "You better believe it's easier pitching up here than it is to get back up here."[8]

Mauch responded by putting Perzanowski into the rotation. "I love groundball pitchers who can throw strikes," Mauch said. "He'll get another start in the first game (Tuesday night) in Seattle."[9] But Perzanowski could not duplicate his performance and was pulled from the rotation several weeks later, going 1-7 with a 5.66 ERA subsequent to his complete-game victory.

Cubbage thought his performance might earn him more starts against lefties: "I hope this will help me stay in the lineup all the time. I always believed that I can hit left-handers."[10] Mauch mostly kept his third-base platoon during August but gave Cubbage a few more opportunities; he had 101 plate appearances, well more than any other month. Cubbage hit .220 for the month, however, and in September his playing time fell more in line with previous months; for the season Cubbage faced lefties in 47 plate appearances. Overall, Cubbage hit .282 with an on-base plus slugging percentage (OPS) of .749, his best year in the majors.

The next season the Twins promoted third baseman John Castino, co-recipient of the 1979 Rookie of the Year Award. Cubbage remained a semi-regular, receiving some platoon at-bats with the right-handed Castino and at designated hitter. In 1980, Cubbage's final season in Minnesota, Mauch moved him to first base, where he partially platooned with Ron Jackson.

On the broader team level, the victory was insignificant. The Twins remained 12½ games out of first and in fifth place.

SOURCES

In addition to the sources mentioned in the notes, the author consulted baseball-reference.com and retrosheet.org. He would also like to thank his brother, fellow SABR member Jed Levitt, who was at the game and still had his scorebook.

NOTES

1. Since Cubbage, six Twins have hit for the cycle: Gary Ward, Kirby Puckett, Carlos Gomez, Jason Kubel, Michael Cuddyer, and Jorge Polanco.
2. Tom Briere, "New Twin Finds Life in Majors a Winner," *Minneapolis Tribune*, July 28, 1978.
3. Author interview with Mike Cubbage, January 17, 2020.
4. Associated Press, "Cubbage Hits for Cycle; Twins Whip Blue Jays," *Eau Claire* (Wisconsin) *Leader-Telegram*, July 28, 1978.
5. Author interview with Mike Cubbage, January 17, 2020.
6. Bob Fowler, "Toledo a Start for Stan," *Minneapolis Star*, July 28, 1978; "Twins Tales," *The Sporting News*, August 19, 1978; Briere.
7. Briere.
8. "Twins 6, Blue Jays 3," *Des Moines Tribune*, July 28, 1978.
9. Bob Fowler, "Toledo a Start for Stan," *Minneapolis Star*, July 28, 1978.
10. "Cubbage Hits for Cycle; Twins Whip Blue Jays."

DISCO DAN'S BLUNDER HANDS TROUT FIRST MAJOR-LEAGUE VICTORY

SEPTEMBER 5, 1978: CHICAGO WHITE SOX 4 MINNESOTA TWINS 3

By Paul Hofmann

Despite a balmy 81-degree game-time temperature and a promotion in which the Twins gave away a car at the game, the Tuesday evening game between the Chicago White Sox and Minnesota Twins drew a sparse turnout of 3,630. Those who decided not to come to the ballpark not only missed out on an opportunity to win a new car, they also missed one of the most bizarre plays in Metropolitan Stadium history that left members of both teams "saying they'd never seen a play like it."[1]

The sixth-place White Sox were 57-80, 18 games behind the American League West-leading Kansas City Royals. After hovering around the .500 mark as late as mid-June, the team had fallen out of contention and was in the process of auditioning late-season call-ups with an eye on next season. The fifth-place Twins were 62-76, 13½ games off the pace. The team had fallen out of contention when it lost 11 of 13 to close out the month of April.

Twenty-one-year-old rookie left-hander Steve Trout got the start for the White Sox. The son of right-hander Dizzy Trout, who won 170 games for the Tigers and Red Sox between 1939 and 1952, he was making his first major-league start.[2] He was opposed by another rookie, Roger Erickson. The 22-year-old right-hander entered the game with a record of 13-9 and 4.15 earned-run average.

Trout and Erikson both tossed two hitless innings before the White Sox broke through in the top of the third. Catcher Bill Nahorodny led off with a single to center. After shortstop Don Kessinger flied out to center, Claudell Washington hit a two-run homer to deep right field. It was his fourth of the year. Erickson retired the next two hitters to retire the side and at the end of 2½ innings the White Sox led 2-0.

The Twins threatened in their half of the third. Bombo Rivera reached on an infield single and went to third when first baseman Craig Kusick singled to center field. With runners at the corners and no one down, it appeared the Twins were on the verge of a big inning. But Trout struck out Butch Wynegar and got out of the inning when Roy Smalley hit a comebacker that the hurler turned into a 1-6-3 double play.

The White Sox added a run in the fourth. Lamar Johnson grounded out to second to start the inning, then Chet Lemon tripled high off the left-center-field wall and scored on Eric Solderholm's sacrifice fly to right. Greg Pryor doubled to left but was stranded when Nahorodny struck out to end the inning.

Gene Mauch

Minnesota Twins

MEMORABLE GAMES AT MINNESOTA'S DIAMOND ON THE PRAIRIE

Trout continued to stymie the Twins. Including the last batters of the third inning, he retired 13 of 14 hitters, giving up a lone leadoff single to José Morales in the bottom of the fifth. Left-handed rookie Darrell Jackson relieved Erickson to start the fifth for the Twins. Jackson entered the game with a record of 4-4 and 4.76 ERA.

Jackson held the White Sox scoreless for two innings before they extended their lead with another run in the seventh inning. With one out, Pryor doubled to left field. One out later, Kessinger singled to left to score Pryor.

Heading into the bottom of the seventh with a 4-0 lead, Trout and the White Sox seemed to be in control. After Willie Norwood struck out to start the inning, the Twins loaded the bases on back-to-back singles by Dan Ford and Morales and a walk to Larry Wolfe. White Sox manager Larry Doby, who had replaced Bob Lemon earlier in the season, called on left-hander Rich Hinton to relieve the tiring Trout. Rivera greeted Hinton with a single to center that should have scored two runs, but Ford, who could have scored easily from third, trotted down the line and turned backward to wave Morales home. The *Minneapolis Star* described what happened next:

> "But (Ford) stopped in the right-handed batter's box, signaled to Morales to score standing up and slapped his palm a few feet from home. Then after Morales scored, Ford flinched, as if realizing what had occurred and sheepishly touched the plate with his toe.
>
> Umpire Joe Brinkman quickly called Morales out for passing Ford on the basepath. Instead of trailing 4-2 with one out and runners at first and third, the Twins were behind 4-1 with two on and two out."[3]

After the play, Twins manager Gene Mauch came out of the dugout to ask Brinkman for an explanation of the play. Ford, who stood nearby listening, "looked at the ground and headed back to the dugout without protest."[4] After Kusick popped out to Mike Squires at first to end the inning, Mauch told Ford to "take a hike."[5]

Mauch's banishment of Ford required him to quickly rearrange the entire outfield. Rivera moved from right field to left, Norwood moved from left field to center, and Hosken Powell, who replaced Ford in the fourth spot of the batting order, came in to play right field.

After Jackson pitched a scoreless eighth, 25-year-old right-hander John Sutton came on in relief in the ninth. Sutton, enjoying his second and last cup of coffee in the majors, was making his 16th appearance of the season. He pitched a scoreless ninth to keep the score at 4-1.

The Twins staged a last-gasp rally in the bottom of the ninth. With one out, pinch-hitter Glenn Borgmann doubled to center field and scored on Morales' double to right field. Wolfe singled to right with Morales stopping at third. Left-hander Pablo Torrealba was brought on to relieve Hinton, and Rob Wilfong ran for Wolfe. Rivera greeted Torrealba with a single to center that scored Morales to cut the White Sox lead to 4-3. Wilfong and Rivera advanced a base when center fielder Thad Bosley bobbled the ball. Torrealba intentionally walked Kusick to load the bases before Doby called on right-hander Lerrin LaGrow to close the door.

Close the door he did. LaGrow struck out pinch-hitter Rod Carew, who was on his way to his seventh and final American League batting title, and retired Smalley on a fly ball to center field to leave the bases loaded and end the game.

The victory, his first major-league decision, went to Trout. He won his final two starts of the season and finished the year with a record of 3-0 and a 4.03 ERA.[6] The loss dropped Erickson to 13-10. He was 1-3 in four games against the White Sox and allowed 31 hits, including six home runs, with an earned run average of 9.35 in 17⅓ innings. LaGrow earned his 15th save of the season. The time of the game was 2 hours and 27 minutes.

After the game, an aggravated Mauch told reporters, "I don't know what to say because I've never had this feeling before. All I know is that he will not be paid for today's game."[7] This was the first time in Mauch's tenure as Twins manager that he fined a player.[8] The fine amounted to $370 of Ford's estimated $60,000 salary that season.

Twins President Calvin Griffith echoed the skipper's frustration in his postgame comments. "We've got 24 guys trying to catch Oakland and Texas in the standings, and he's so nonchalant it's unbelievable," Griffith said.[9]

Griffith's comments indicated that Ford's time with the Twins might be coming to an end. During the offseason the Twins traded him to the California Angels for Danny Goodwin and Ron Jackson.

Mauch and Ford were briefly reunited when Mauch replaced Jim Fregosi as Angels manager in May 1981.

METROPOLITAN STADIUM

In January 1982 Ford was traded to the Baltimore Orioles for Doug DeCinces and Jeff Schneider, dispelling the age-old adage that time heals all wounds.

SOURCES

In addition to the sources cited in the Notes, the author also consulted Baseball-Reference.com and Retrosheet.org

baseball-reference.com/boxes/MIN/MIN197809050.shtml

retrosheet.org/boxesetc/1978/B09050MIN1978.htm

NOTES

1. Gary Libman, "Ford Recalled After Stopping on Freeway," *Minneapolis Tribune*, September 6, 1978: C1.
2. Trout had made his major-league debut on July 1, when he worked the eighth inning of a 10-0 Twins victory at Metropolitan Stadium.
3. Bob Fowler, "Ford Falls Off the Tightrope," *Minneapolis Star*, September 6, 1978: 1D.
4. Libman.
5. Fowler.
6. Trout finished his 12-year major-league career with a record of 88-92 and a 4.18 ERA.
7. Fowler.
8. Fowler.
9. Fowler: 4D.

ALL ABOUT RODNEY

APRIL 17, 1979: CALIFORNIA ANGELS 6, MINNESOTA TWINS 0

By Bob Tholkes

Signed as an 18-year-old amateur free agent by the Twins in 1964, Rod Carew became the Twins' second baseman in 1967 and was named Rookie of Year and an American League All-Star. He won seven batting titles as a Twin from 1969 through 1978, and in 1977, when he flirted with the .400 mark and finished at .388, was named the American League's Most Valuable Player and appeared on the cover of Time. All of which explains why his initial appearance at Metropolitan Stadium as a visiting player, in the Twins' home opener of April 17, 1979, turned into a Rodney-fest. A Rod Carew Day was declared by the Minnesota State Senate, and he was the subject of photos, headlines, and sports columns in the *Minneapolis Tribune*, *Minneapolis Star*, *St. Paul Dispatch*, and *St. Paul Pioneer Press*.

The Twins' all-time (well, 19 seasons) attendance record for a home opener had been set in 1961, their first season in town, at 24,606. By April 17, 14,000 tickets had been sold for Carew's return, with hopes, given that the Twins had won seven of their first nine and that the temperature was expected to exceed the average high of around 50 degrees ("I hope it doesn't rain," said Twins' owner-general manager Calvin Griffith).[1] Yielding to unbridled optimism, Twins ticket manager Dave Moore told the Tribune's Tom Briere that that all-time record for the home opener might be threatened.[2]

The sun shone brilliantly. The mercury hit 67 degrees. And 37,529 attended, obliterating the old record. It was not matched in the two seasons remaining at the Met. Would it have happened without Carew's departure and return? The Tribune, at least, gave him the largest share of the credit.[3]

Carew, of course, should have followed up, especially since he reacted to his overwhelmingly friendly reception by greeting fans and signing autographs on the sidelines before the game, by playing a key role in a close, exciting contest, but no ... another future Hall of Famer, Nolan Ryan, scattered four hits and three walks and struck out 10 for his second dominant win against the Twins within a week. Twins starter Dave Goltz yielded the eventual winning run in the first on Rick Miller's leadoff triple and Don Baylor's two-out single, and was knocked out during the Angels' four-run fifth. Willie Mays Aikens led off the inning with a solo home run, followed by back-to-back triples by Brian Downing and Bobby Grich, a sacrifice fly by Rance Mulliniks, and a single by Miller, which turned into a run when center fielder Willie Norwood let the ball go through his legs, allowing Miller to complete a circuit of the bases. A single run in the seventh, off Pete Redfern when Grich doubled and later scored on another sacrifice fly by Mulliniks, closed the scoring.

Carew settled for a single in four at-bats. Interviewed extensively after the game, he radiated contentment, following up his comment on arrival the previous day that it was "nice to get away from Calvin"[4] by expressing his pleasure with his reception by the fans, which included a standing ovation during pregame player introductions, and with the talent he now found himself surrounded by on the Angels; he wished the Twins well.

Carew's reception was part and parcel of the increasingly unsettled environment in which Griffith and the Twins were trying to find a way forward, a stew of Griffith's financial limitations (self-imposed, to an extent), the beginning of player free agency in 1976, and the local campaign to move the club to an indoor ballpark in downtown Minneapolis designed to be shared with the National Football League's Minnesota Vikings. At 67, Griffith ultimately couldn't or wouldn't adjust successfully. He sold his controlling interest in the club to Twin Cities banking magnate Carl Pohlad in 1984, less than three seasons after the Twins moved downtown and indoors to the Hubert H. Humphrey Metrodome.

The contrast between the joys of watching baseball on the warmest day in six months in the Twin Cities and the prospect of indoor baseball on such days were not lost on the pundits and fans present on April 17. "I won't go to any baseball game in a stadium with a dome," one fan was quoted as promising.[5] The Tribune's Bob Lundegaard, after emphasizing the glorious weather, reminded his readers that Metropolitan Stadium was "undomed," and the paper accompanied his lead article with a photo of bare-chested fans soaking up the sun.[6] Lundegaard's fellow on the Tribune, M. Howard Gelfand, was more explicit: "It was such a perfect day that only advocates of a domed stadium could have found misery under the cloudless sky. Now a stadium was something to play ball in, not to put a roof over."[7]

Depressing both the fan base and the Twins' prospects of building another winner on the field more immediately was professional baseball's altered labor-relations landscape – player free agency – which had revolutionized player compensation, converting the Griffith-family-owned operation, which was completely dependent on the Twins, from an outmoded outlier in a landscape of independently wealthy major-league club owners to a financial dinosaur staring extinction in the face. Calvin Griffith had long been a bitter resister of changes in players' status and was notorious as a tough negotiator of player salaries. His early years in Minnesota, when he could maintain a competitive payroll level, had departed and would not return while his remained a family-operated franchise dependent on its baseball income and operating in a comparatively small market lacking a major-league tradition of long standing. Since 1976, when his stars could begin contemplating free agency, future Hall of Famers Carew and Bert Blyleven, middle-of-the-order regular Larry Hisle, and young star Lyman Bostock had departed, either by free agency or by trades engineered to prevent their loss without compensation.

Fans and the local press reacted predictably to the departures and the unpromising outlook under the Griffith ownership, as typified by comments published on the occasion of Carew's return with the Angels on April 17. Acerbic St. Paul Pioneer Press columnist Don Riley presented a laundry list of blameworthys that fans could choose to "hate": The California Angels, for signing Carew; Carew, for leaving; the Twins and/or Griffith, for letting him go; Gene Autry, the Angels' owner, for throwing outrageous sums at Carew and others; greedy players in general; and the whole system, where loyalty to fans and teams was now taking a back seat.[8] Most other commentaries took sides: While Carew was the object of a prolonged standing ovation at the beginning of game (which he explained by noting that "the people here know I gave them 12 years of good baseball"[9]), Charley Walters of the Pioneer Press led off his article with a reference to "Millionaire Rod Carew"[10]; a fan wrote to the Minneapolis Star to complain, "Rod Carew sold out to the California team last winter. ... [H]ow come the constant, everyday pictures and stories?"[11] a "Carew the Capitalist" banner appeared in the left-field pavilion;[12] and the applause for Carew faded away by his last plate appearance. Others were differently inclined: "Trade Calvin Griffith" buttons appeared on fans tailgating in the stadium parking lot;[13] "Cal Griffith Fan Club" was inscribed on bags that a few wags wore over their heads;[14] a fan was quoted as observing that "It's Griffith who should be traded";[15] and Lundegaard reported, "Minnesota governor Al Quie threw out the first ball. ... 'If that picture of him next to Calvin gets in the paper,' muttered a nearby fan, 'it'll cost him 30,000 votes.'"[16]

As Griffith mostly remained in his box during the April 17 game, anti-Calvinists refocused on a striking symbol of the changes in the Twins' fortunes: young outfielder Willie Norwood, who followed up on his team-record 14 errors in 1978 by letting a groundball single go through his legs, to the accompaniment of raucous jeers. Naturally, Norwood led off the home half of the same inning, singled, and was promptly picked off first base, with departed hero Carew applying the tag.

The Minneapolis Tribune's sports-section headline of April 18 appeared to capture the day's essence: "Perfect baseball day has flaws."[17]

NOTES

1. Charley Walters, "Carew an Opponent for Twins' Opener," *St. Paul Pioneer Press*, April 17, 1979: 14.

2. Tom Briere, "Carew Comes Home Carrying Enemy Colors," *Minneapolis Tribune*, April 17, 1979: 1C.

3. Bob Lundegaard, "Calvin Has Full House, but Twins Lose," *Minneapolis Tribune*, April 18, 1979: 1A.

4. Walters, "Carew an Opponent for Twins' Opener."

5. Sean T. Kelly, "Baseball Buffs Abound at Record Twins Opener," *St. Paul Dispatch*, April 18, 1979: 1.

6. Lundegaard, "Calvin Has Full House, but Twins Lose," *Minneapolis Tribune*, April 18, 1979: 1A.

7. M. Howard Gelfand, "Perfect Baseball Day Has Flaws," *Minneapolis Tribune*, April 18, 1979: 1C.

8. Don Riley, "Don Riley's Eye Opener," *St. Paul Pioneer Press*, April 17, 1979: 14.

MEMORABLE GAMES AT MINNESOTA'S DIAMOND ON THE PRAIRIE

9   Joe Soucheray, "Joe Soucheray,", *Minneapolis Tribune*, April 18, 1979: 1C.

10 Walters, "Carew an Opponent for Twins' Opener."

11 "Fan Opinion,"*Minneapolis Tribune*, April 17, 1979: 8C.

12 Charley Walters, "Rod Good Hitter, Poor Guesser," *St. Paul Pioneer Press*, April 18, 1979: 17.

13 Kelly, "Baseball Buffs Abound at Record Twins Opener."

14 Paul Levy, "Baseball Fans Special, and So's Opening Day," *Minneapolis Tribune*, April 18, 1979: 9B.

15 Kelly, "Baseball Buffs Abound at Record Twins Opener."

16 Lundegaard, "Calvin Has Full House, but Twins Lose."

17 Gelfand, "Perfect Baseball Day Has Flaws."

KOOSMAN REACHES 20-WIN PLATEAU FOR SECOND TIME

SEPTEMBER 30, 1979: MINNESOTA TWINS 5, MILWAUKEE BREWERS 0

By Brian Wright

When Jerry Koosman took the mound at Metropolitan Stadium for the final game of 1979, a sense of déjà vu must have been felt.

Three years before, he made good on his chance to achieve a milestone every starting pitcher aims for when the schedule begins: 20 wins. He'd finish that 1976 season with 21, but victories would soon be much harder to come by.

As the Mets franchise fell on hard times in the wake of the Tom Seaver trade, Koosman was too often on the short end of his team's ineptness. A year after winning 20, he lost 20 – just among a handful in baseball history to have that dubious honor. Yet he finished with a 3.49 earned-run average, proof that he failed to get respectable run support.

The Seaver deal – on top of management's indifference regarding free agency – indicated that if Koosman wanted to be on a winner, he'd best go somewhere else. After the 1978 season, in which his record was a meager 3-15 but his ERA under 4.00, the 35-year-old left-hander requested – and was granted – a trade to his home state.

Raised in Appleton, Wisconsin, where he spent much of his childhood working with his father and brothers on a farm, Koosman returned with a wealth of pitching experience in tow. As he wrapped up his first season in Minnesota, he became one of a handful to attain 20 victories in each major league. But this one had a different feeling.

"The first time I won 21 was a special experience," Koosman said. "But any time you win 20 games when you're pitching with a new ballclub is hard to beat. It's just great. The guys just played super ball all year behind me."[1]

Jerry was pretty superb at the outset of the '79 season, showing he could adjust quickly to American League batters by winning his first seven decisions. And for a welcome change, he got plenty of runs from the Twins offense. But this early-season success was countered by a monthlong winless drought that saw him lose six times.

The roller coaster continued: he won four in a row, then lost four straight, then was victorious in six consecutive outings to bring his ERA down to 3.35. After dropping three of his next four decisions, the pendulum had seemingly swung in favor of a win streak when he notched his 19th at County Stadium in Milwaukee.

Jerry Koosman

Minnesota Twins

MEMORABLE GAMES AT MINNESOTA'S DIAMOND ON THE PRAIRIE

LAST MET STADIUM PLAYERS STANDING

Of all who played at Metropolitan Stadium, who was the last player active in the major leagues?

Rickey Henderson first played at Met Stadium on August 10, 1979. His last game at the Met was August 12, 1981. Henderson played in the major leagues for more than 22 years beyond that, his last game being September 19, 2003.

Mike Morgan is the runner-up. Morgan first pitched at Metropolitan Stadium in the first game of a doubleheader on August 10, 1979 (also Henderson's first game at the Met). Morgan, who played for 12 different teams, including the Twins, made his final appearance in the majors on September 2, 2002.

Honorable mention goes to **Harold Baines**, who made his Met Stadium debut on May 26, 1980, and played through the 2001 season (final game September 27).

And One Who Missed

A second-round draft pick of the Twins in January 1978 who debuted in the majors the following season, **Jesse Orosco** lasted longer than any of the above players, last pitching in the majors on September 27, 2003. However, in 1979 Orosco was gone from the Twins, having gone to the New York Mets in a deal that brought Jerry Koosman to Minnesota. Orosco pitched for nine teams in the majors, the last one being the Twins.

Koosman's chance to lock up number 20 in his second-to-last start of the year was placed into the hands of reliever Mike Marshall. Protecting a 5-3 lead with one out in the eighth, Marshall let the Twins' lead on the White Sox slip away before relinquishing the winning run in the 10th.

As was the case in 1976 with the Mets, Koosman had another shot at the milestone. But unlike '76, he couldn't rely on his next start if it fell through again. His team had something to play for too. A victory would ensure a winning record.

If Koosman and the Twins were to do it, they both would earn it against the team with the fourth-best offense in the American League and Koosman's last victim.

The Milwaukee Brewers, a team stocked with young talent like Robin Yount, Paul Molitor, and Cecil Cooper, were concluding a second straight season of at least 93 victories and a runner-up finish in the American League East.

The 36-year-old Koosman pitched around potential trouble in the early innings. Despite allowing hits to the first two batters – Jim Gantner and Yount – Koosman escaped trouble with the help of his defense. Hosken Powell turned Dick Davis's fly ball into a double play when he nailed Gantner trying to advance to third.

Koosman prevented a second-inning threat by picking off Jim Wohlford at first base. Lenn Sakata's subsequent double was rendered less important – more so when he was left stranded. Gantner opened the third with a walk, but Koosman induced an inning-ending double play.

"In the first three innings I was wild and didn't have my good stuff," he said. "I really had to work to get things back together."[2]

Milwaukee continued to threaten. But true to his veteran status, Koosman's command held the Brewers in check.

The Twins, meanwhile, didn't get a hit until the fourth. But in the fifth, the offense broke out. Three singles and a groundout against Brewer starter Lary Sorensen produced five runs, not to mention Sorensen's ouster.

That was all the scoring the Twins would produce. And as it turned out, that would be more than Koosman needed.

He retired the side in the sixth and yielded only a single in the seventh. Koosman finished the eighth when he got Gorman Thomas looking for his 157th and final strikeout of the season. It was also a league-high

175th whiff for Thomas, who was quite displeased by the result. He flung his bat and helmet before being tossed by home-plate umpire Derryl Cousins.

"It was a good pitch," Koosman recalled. "The pitch had the whole plate."[3]

As he came out to pitch the ninth, the Met Stadium crowd sensed the moment. The paid attendance was barely over 10,000, but chants of "Koos … Koos … Koos" were clearly audible throughout the park and reached a crescendo as the inning played out.[4]

A 20th victory seemed all but certain. Koosman could do it in style: A 10th complete game and second shutout were within reach. The Brewers, though, threatened both of those. But thanks to the glove work of rookie third baseman John Castino, the shutout was kept intact. Don Money's attempt at a leadoff hit was squelched when Castino backhanded Money's grounder and threw across the diamond for the first out.

After catcher Ray Fosse legged out a triple, Castino's defense came to Koosman's aid once more. On a groundball by Wohlford, Castino trapped Fosse between third base and home and turned him into the second out, eliminating a runner from scoring position. Koosman then got Sakata to fly out to secure the 5-0 victory.[5]

"You go into a game like that knowing you have to put your best game on the line and hope things work out," Koosman said.[6]

"When [he] got to the Minnesota Twins' clubhouse," wrote Ken Feaster in the *Winona Daily News*, "there was a present waiting for him from teammate Dave Goltz – a bottle of champagne."[7]

Jerry had plenty of reasons to celebrate. He led all Twins players for 1979 with a 7.2 WAR (Wins above Replacement), which was also tied for the best among all American League pitchers; was fifth in strikeouts; and finished sixth in the American League Cy Young Award balloting. The blanking of the Brewers, the only time Milwaukee was shut out all year,[8] lowered his ERA to 3.38.

Koosman lasted two more seasons in Minnesota. Although his first year with the Twins was his best, he followed up his 20-victory campaign with 16 wins and 149 strikeouts in 1980 while also serving an occasional role in the bullpen. The Twins sent Koosman to the Chicago White Sox at the trading deadline on August 30, 1981. After three years in the Windy City and two more after that in Philadelphia, Koosman retired with a record of 222-209, a 3.36 ERA, 140 complete games, 33 shutouts, and a WHIP of 1.26.

Not bad for a former Minnesota farm boy.

NOTE

If not for Koosman's pitching, along with Castino's determination to preserve the shutout in the ninth, the Brewers would have become only the second team to go an entire season without being shut out. The New York Yankees did it in 1932.

Koosman set a team record with 14 pickoffs when he picked off Wohlford in the second.

SOURCES

In addition to the references cited in the Notes, the author consulted Baseball-Reference.com and Retrosheet.org.

NOTES

1   Ken Feaster, "Koos Praises Castino," *Winona Daily News,* October 1, 1979: 8.

2   Ken Feaster, "Jerry Koosman Pockets 20th Victory," *Winona Daily News.* October 1, 1979: 8.

3   "Jerry Koosman Pockets 20th Victory."

4   "Koos Wins 20 – Ponders '80 at Season End," *Minneapolis Star.* October 1, 1979: 48.

5   "Koos Praises Castino."

6   "Jerry Koosman Pockets 20th Victory."

7   "Koos Praises Castino."

8   Bob Fowler, "Koosman Wins 20th in 1979 Finale," *Minneapolis Tribune.* October 1, 1979: 23.

GROUND GEOFF

JULY 5, 1980: MINNESOTA TWINS 2, TEXAS RANGERS 1

By Bob Tholkes

"More than 50 percent, and you're a ground-ball pitcher. More than 55 percent and you're an *extreme* ground-ball pitcher."[1]

By baseball analyst Rob Neyer's research-based formulation above, the Texas Rangers were the victims, and the 9,398 spectators in attendance the accidental onlookers, of *extreme* baseball extremism on July 5, 1980, at the hands of the seemingly mild-mannered Minnesota Twins left-hander Geoff Zahn.

Zahn was a product of the Dodgers' farm system who found himself as a major-league pitcher at age 32 in 1977 with the Twins, after brief tenures with the Dodgers and Cubs. He was a bargain, averaging 13 wins per year from 1977 to 1979 and adding 14 more in 1980. His start on July 5 found him with 6 wins, 10 losses, and a less-than-satisfactory 4.13 earned-run average. The Twins were in fifth place in the American League West Division, with a record of 33 wins and 44 losses, 12½ games behind Kansas City. They were in decline compared with 1979, when they were eight games over .500 at the same stage. The club's hemorrhaging of free agents had continued in the offseason, when 20-game winner Dave Goltz, despite being a Minnesota native, left for the Dodgers.

The local press still paying attention to the beleaguered franchise was nonetheless, at least for the time being, in an optimistic frame of mind. Sid Hartman's July 5 column in the *Minneapolis Tribune* reprinted manager Gene Mauch's upbeat assessment of the club's play in recent weeks, including wins in four of its last six games and his hopes that Zahn and Jerry Koosman, a 20-game winner in 1979, would heat up.[2]

Zahn may have been pleased to see the Texas Rangers come to town. His record against Texas was a cumulative four wins and no losses. Also, he told the *Tribune's* Tom Briere, since the Twins had pitched another lefty, Darrell Jackson, against the Rangers the previous night, a 4-3 loss in 12 innings in which Jackson stymied Texas for seven innings, he was able to update his strategy for facing their hitters by watching the video.[3]

The Rangers were otherwise not every pitcher's delight. Their team batting average of .276 at game time ranked fourth in the league. Al Oliver and Buddy Bell were All-Stars near the top of the league in batting, and Mickey Rivers and Bump Wills supplied speed at the top of a lineup of savvy veterans. Nevertheless they were bumping along at 37 wins and 40 losses, second in the West Division but 8½ games back. More veterans inhabited their pitching staff, led by Zahn's opponent, future Hall of Famer Ferguson Jenkins, who began the day with seven wins, five losses, and an ERA of 3.14.

Texas scored in the top of the first with two out, on Oliver's walk and singles by Bell and Richie Zisk. More portentously, as it turned out, all three outs in

Roy Smalley

their inning were recorded on groundouts. Texas's second inning produced three more of the same. Jenkins, meanwhile, kept the Twins off the scoreboard until the fourth, as Rick Sofield was caught stealing after a single in the first and Hosken Powell, after hitting a triple, was erased on an unsuccessful squeeze attempt in the third.[4] Then Sofield singled again in the fourth, and Roy Smalley Jr. followed with a two-run home run, a liner that nicked the right-field foul pole.

Zahn still had jams to work out of. The Twins' infield made an adventure of the sixth, loading the bases with one out on two errors and a walk before converting a groundball third-to-second-to-first double play. In the eighth Rivers and Wills singled with one out, again putting the tying run on third, but Zahn helped himself by picking Wills off first base. Zahn's groundball outs meanwhile continued to mount, and when John Ellis closed the ninth and the contest by grounding into the Twins' third double play, the total had reached 19, 70 percent of the Rangers' outs in the game.

Zahn's performance was encouraging, but the relatively small turnout for a midseason Saturday matinee was probably more on the minds of Twins brass. The Twins' attendance was the lowest in the major leagues. On July 6 the *St. Paul Pioneer Press* printed the results of a survey of "*Pioneer Press* Super Fans" on the question, "What do (the Twins) need to do – other than win – to attract some customers?" Noted the first respondent: "A team lacking a superstar which plays poorly in a ballpark of minimal attractiveness is in trouble. … Since most Twins stars seem to disappear via the free agency route, these attendance boosters are not available." The same respondent thought that contemporary players deserved blame, describing them as "arrogant businessmen at war with management." Another thought the Twins could take fans' minds off the quality of the team with "extra entertainment or incentives," such as ladies' nights, free admission for kids, and reduced-price or free parking. Yet another called on the club to take better care of the fans who did show up, by making sure that there were enough vendors on hand and plenty of ticket-sellers and ticket-takers. A final interviewee didn't think giveaways or new faces on the roster would help long-term and simply felt that more fans were needed who would be loyal regardless of the club's fortunes on the field.[5]

Discouragingly for the Twins and their fans, answers were not found in 1980. The team resumed its struggles on the field, Mauch resigned in August, and after the season Zahn joined the exodus of free agents, departing for the California Angels.

NOTES

1. Rob Neyer, "What We Talk About When We Talk About Ground-Ball Pitchers," *Baseball Nation*, 2012.
2. Sid Hartman, "Sid Hartman," *Minneapolis Tribune*, July 5, 1980: 2C.
3. Tom Briere, "Twins Beat Texas with Zahn Rerun," *Minneapolis Tribune*, July 6, 1980: 1C.
4. Briere.
5. "Poor Attendance: Any Solution?" "SuperFans," *St. Paul Sunday Pioneer Press*, July 6, 1980: Sports 2.

CLUTCH HOMERS BY HATCHER AND SMALLEY LEAD TWINS TO WIN OVER RED SOX

MAY 12, 1981: MINNESOTA TWINS 4, BOSTON RED SOX 3 (10 INNINGS)

By Brian M. Frank

Roy Smalley was off to a solid start to the 1981 season for the struggling Minnesota Twins. John Bierig of the *Minneapolis Star* wrote that he'd been "the only bright spot in a dismal season" for the ballclub.[1] Smalley, fresh off signing a four-year contract extension in the offseason, was hitting .294 with 6 home runs, 19 walks, and 19 runs batted in when he injured his right shoulder in a game against Baltimore on May 6. Since his injury, he'd been relegated to pinch-hitting duties; his shoulder injury prevented him from making the throws necessary to play shortstop. After he had precautionary x-rays, the *Minneapolis Tribune* reported that Smalley was not expected to play in the opening game of a three-game series with the Boston Red Sox.[2]

Smalley's teammate, center fielder Mickey Hatcher, was also not in good health. Hatcher, acquired from the Dodgers in an offseason trade, was hitting .276 but was battling a virus that caused him to have a sore throat, congestion, and an upset stomach. He reported vomiting "several times" the day the Twins were to open their series against the Red Sox.[3]

Surprisingly, despite their ailments, both Smalley and Hatcher were in the lineup for the series opener against Boston, Hatcher in center field and Smalley as the designated hitter.

The Twins had been struggling with a 10-17 record and were 12 games back in the American League West. They'd lost five of their last six games. However, right before that rough stretch, they'd gone into Fenway Park and swept a four-game series from Boston. Meanwhile, the Red Sox had won five in a row to climb back to a .500 record at 13-13 and were 3½ games out of first place in the American League East.

Minnesota sent right-hander Roger Erickson to the mound to face Boston lefty John Tudor. Both pitchers were off to rough starts. Erickson was 1-3 with a 4.08 earned-run average in five starts, while Tudor was 1-1 with a 4.84 ERA in three starts.

Only a smattering of fans were on hand for the night game. The announced crowd was 3,572. The low attendance was due in large part to the fact that many fans stayed home to watch the National Hockey League's Minnesota North Stars play the New York Islanders in their first Stanley Cup Finals game in franchise history.

Boston threatened to score in the second inning when Tony Perez and Carney Lansford singled with one out. But a nice play by first baseman Ron Jackson helped keep the game scoreless. Jackson made a diving stop on Rick Miller's hard groundball and flipped to Erickson covering at first for the second out. Erickson then struck out Glenn Hoffman to end the inning.

Hatcher, still struggling with his illness, raced into the clubhouse to vomit after hitting a double in the fourth inning. He was able to remain in the game.

Both pitchers entered the middle innings with shutouts intact, before Boston broke through against Erickson in the sixth. Jerry Remy led off with a single and went to third when Dwight Evans singled. Carl Yastrzemski, who was in a horrendous slump, hitting just .175 entering the game, singled to bring Remy home and send Evans to third. Jim Rice followed with a sacrifice fly and the Red Sox took a 2-0 lead.

Tudor entered the seventh inning having allowed only three hits and three walks. He'd used a lively fastball to shut down Twins hitters. "I didn't really know where it was going," Tudor said after the game.[4] Minnesota finally broke through against the lefty with a big blast in the seventh. Smalley led the inning off with a single. After Tudor retired the next two batters, Ron Jackson lined a ball over the left-field fence to tie the game.

Erickson gave up a single to Remy and a walk to Yastrzemski to put two men on with one out in the eighth. Minnesota manager Johnny Goryl brought Doug Corbett in from the Twins' bullpen. Corbett struck out Rice and got Perez to fly out to end the inning and keep the game knotted at 2-2.

Tudor gave way to Bob Stanley to start the bottom of the eighth. Stanley breezed through his first inning of work, retiring the side in order. But in the ninth, after Smalley flied out, Pete Mackanin and Hosken Powell, hitting for Dave Engle, both singled. After getting Ron Jackson to ground into a force at third base, Stanley walked Sal Butera to load the bases with two down. St. Paul native Tom Burgmeier came out of the Red Sox bullpen and needed only one pitch to get Rob Wilfong to fly out and end the inning without any runs crossing the plate.

Boston regained the lead in the top of the 10th. Remy and Evans singled with one down, and Yastrzemski cashed in his second RBI of the day with a sacrifice fly to give the Red Sox a 4-3 lead.

Things weren't looking good for the Twins in their half of the 10th. Burgmeier remained in the game for Boston and retired Gary Ward on a groundout and John Castino on a pop foul to start the inning and put the Twins' backs to the wall.

Ailing Mickey Hatcher stepped in against Burgmeier with the Twins down to their final out. He took Burgmeier's first delivery for a strike, and then drilled the next pitch deep to left field. Hatcher later said of the pitch: "It wasn't that far in on me. It was a slider that started out over the plate, then broke down over it and kinda hung."[5] Hatcher sent the ball sailing into the left-field seats to tie the game 3-3.

As on-deck hitter Roy Smalley watched the ball go out, he thought Burgmeier "might not be quite so invincible as he had been. I thought, 'Maybe I've got a chance,'" he told reporters.[6] Having had only a couple of pinch-hit at-bats the last few games while he rehabilitated his shoulder, Smalley was feeling much more comfortable at the plate after being the designated hitter for an entire game. "It helps to be in a game where you know you're going to get four at-bats," he said, "and where if you make an out you know you're going to get another at-bat." He added, "I kind of straightened out during the game."[7]

Smalley followed up Hatcher's home run by hitting one of his own, this one to left-center for a walk-off win. "I just figured I would go after him," Smalley said. "The pitch was outside and at the knees, but I got a good piece of it."[8]

The unlikely duo of Hatcher and Smalley had combined for back-to-back home runs and led the Twins to a come-from-behind 4-3 victory. Hatcher battled through his sickness to finish the game 2-for-5 with a double and his clutch game-tying home run in the 10th. Smalley, playing with a sore shoulder, had gone 2-for-3 with two walks and the game-winning homer.

The Red Sox were in disbelief after letting a game slip away after they seemed to have it in their grasp. "I can't believe it," Boston manager Ralph Houk said. "This was a bad game to lose."[9]

Meanwhile, the Twins were ecstatic at the dramatic turn of events, especially after their recent struggles. "It sure is a good feeling," said Goryl. "We ain't won too many like this."[10] The win was just the Twins' second in their last seven games. "I hope this picks us up," Smalley said. "I hope it gives us a little emotion about winning. If it doesn't, there's something wrong with us."[11]

SOURCES

In addition to the sources cited in the Notes, the author consulted Baseball-Reference.com and Retrosheet.org.

NOTES

1 Joel Bierig, "Goryl Wonders Just How to Make These Pieces Fit," *Minneapolis Star*, May 11, 1981: 10C.

2 "Tonight/Twins vs Boston," *Minneapolis Star Tribune*, May 12, 1981: 5C.

3 Gary Libman, "Hatcher, Smalley Homers Trip Sox in 10th," *Minneapolis Tribune*, May 13, 1981: 1C.

4 Peter Gammons, "Twins Homers Trip Sox in 10, 4-3," *Boston Globe*, May 13, 1981: 72.

5 Gammons.

6 Libman.

7 Libman.

8 Associated Press, "Twins' Homers Tip Boston," *St. Cloud (Minnesota) Daily Times*, May 13, 1981: 4D.

9 Gammons.

10 Associated Press, "Twins' Homers Tip Boston."

11 Libman: 2C. The Twins lost their next eight in a row, leading to the firing of manager Johnny Goryl.

TWINS DOWN A'S TO TAKE '81 'REOPENER'

AUGUST 10, 1981: MINNESOTA TWINS 6, OAKLAND ATHLETICS 1

By Peter Seidel

"If you think what goes on between the white lines has anything to do with running a baseball team today, you've got a lot to learn."

– Clark Griffith, Twins executive vice president and son of owner Calvin Griffith[1]

Entering the 1981 season an ongoing labor dispute between owners and players lingered over the issue of free-agent compensation. The owners demanded compensation for losing free-agent players. "I think compensation is basically mandatory," asserted Giants owner Bob Lurie. "When a team like San Diego loses a player the caliber they did [Dave Winfield], they're entitled to get something more than they did, an amateur draft choice."[2] The players maintained that any form of compensation undermined the value of free agency.

The result of this unresolved dispute led the players union to vote unanimously on May 29 for a strike, which began on June 12. On July 31 a compromise was reached under which a team that lost a premium player could be compensated by selecting a "nonprotected" player from any team. But the strangest part of the agreement to resume play was that the season was broken into two halves. The Yankees, Athletics, Dodgers, and first-time defending World Series champion Phillies, which were the division leaders when the strike began, were all guaranteed postseason berths. They would face the division winners of the second half of the season in best-of-five Division Series with the winners squaring off in a best-of-five League Championship Series.

The A's were enjoying a renaissance thanks largely to an aggressive style of play dubbed implemented by their manager, Billy Martin, and dubbed Billy Ball. For the last-place Twins, losers of 39 out of 56 games and 18 games behind the division-leading A's, it was a fresh start. "I think a lot of players feel as I do," said designated hitter Glenn Adams, "that the first half of the season is like last year. This is almost like 1982, only the season is only seven or eight weeks long."[3]

In their first game back after the strike ended, the Twins sent 24-year-old right-hander Roger Erickson against Oakland, while the A's countered with Rick Langford, who led the American League in complete games in 1980 and 1981. The game didn't start well for the host Twins: Rickey Henderson smacked the first pitch from Erickson into right field for a single. Henderson attempted to steal his league-leading 34th base, and catcher Butch Wynegar's throw to second would have nailed him had shortstop Roy Smalley held on to the ball. With Henderson on second and no outs, "I said to myself, 'Jeez, here we go,'" said

Billy Gardner

Minnesota Twins

Erickson.[4] Dwayne Murphy grounded the next offering from Erickson to first baseman Danny Goodwin, who tossed to Erickson covering first base for the first out of the game as Henderson took third. Erickson walked Wayne Gross to put runners at the corners but escaped without any damage by striking out slugger Tony Armas and inducing Jim Spencer to fly out to left field.

After that there was not much action until the top of the fourth inning, when Oakland's Gross led off with a line drive that right fielder Hosken Powell tried to make a shoestring catch on. The ball got past him for a triple. Gross scored on Spencer's sacrifice fly to center field. The A's added another run off Erickson in the top of the fifth when Mark Budaska led off with a double, went to third on Keith Drumright's single to center, and scored on Rob Picciolo's 1-6-3 double play. Erickson could have easily nailed Budaska at the plate but chose to go for the double play.

The Twins struck back with a vengeance in the bottom of the fifth. Goodwin and Wynegar led off with singles. Ron Jackson's bunt moved them up a base, and Powell's single to right field scored both runners and tied the game, 2-2. Rob Wilfong's single to center field advanced Powell to third. Mickey Hatcher hit a grounder to third that Gross bobbled; Powell scored to give the Twins a 3-2 lead. Smalley walked, loading the bases. Adams lined a single to left, scoring Wilfong and Hatcher and putting the Twins up 5-2. Martin did something he rarely did while managing the A's; he pulled starter Langford out of the game for reliever Jeff Jones to face John Castino. Castino lined a shot just out of the reach of Henderson for a double, scoring Smalley and extending the Twins' lead to 6-2. Martin quickly replaced Jones with Tom Underwood, who struck out Goodwin and got Wynegar to fly out to right field for the final out of the inning.

It was an unexpected offensive explosion by one of the least explosive offenses in the American League; the Twins had sent 11 batters to the plate in the inning and scored six runs (five earned) on six hits. The Twins as a team ranked next to last in the American League in every major offensive category, including runs scored, team batting average, on-base percentage, slugging percentage, and home runs (47). Their rare offensive outburst allowed the Twins to accomplish something else that was uncommon for them in 1981: recover from a two-run deficit, something they had accomplished only twice before in the season. "It's hard to express what it means, to me, to the team," said Powell. "We're not going to let the little things get us down anymore. We don't want to beat ourselves anymore."[5]

Perhaps the "reopener" was just what the Twins needed to exorcise their poor start to the 1981 season. Smalley told *Minneapolis Star* beat writer Paul Levy after the game that the 15,414 in attendance at Metropolitan Stadium were "a lot louder and more enthusiastic than the crowd of 42,658 that attended the home opener on April 9."[6]

"Based upon what I saw tonight, I think our players realize they have a unique opportunity," said Twins manager Billy Gardner. "It is a fresh start. They will wake up tomorrow with a share of first place. It is a nice feeling. It is up to them how they wake up two months from now."[7]

SOURCES

In addition to the sources cited in the Notes, the author consulted Baseball-Reference.com, Retrosheet.org, and the following:

Back To Baseball: backtobaseball.com/playballregularseason.php?page=45&IDindex=MIN198108100&date=August+10%2C+1981.

Verducci, Tom. "Inside the Chaos of 1981 – MLB's Last Severely Shortened Season." *Sports Illustrated*, May 29, 2020: si.com/mlb/2020/05/29/pete-rose-1981-baseball-strike.

Bumbaca, Chris. "Explaining the 1981 MLB Season: How Baseball Survived Shortened Year," *USA Today*, March 15, 2020: usatoday.com/story/sports/mlb/2020/03/15/1981-mlb-season-coronavirus-delay-baseball/5054780002/.

NOTES

1. Michael Lenehan, "The Last of the Pure Baseball Men," *The Atlantic*, August 1981: theatlantic.com/magazine/archive/1981/08/the-last-of-the-pure-baseball-men/305825/.
2. MLB Network. Baseball's Seasons 1981 "A Season Interrupted." Retrieved via YouTube April 26, 2020: youtube.com/watch?v=SAbPlbbrb9E.
3. Dan Stoneking, "6-2 Victory Means One Game … and More," *Minneapolis Star*, August 11, 1981: 9B.
4. Paul Levy, "Opener II: Twins' Play Eclipses Fireworks," *Minneapolis Star*, August 11, 1981: 9B.
5. Levy.
6. Levy.
7. Levy.

TWINS OVERSHADOWED BY THE PAST

AUGUST 15, 1981: SEATTLE MARINERS 6, MINNESOTA TWINS 0

By Bob Tholkes

A forgettable year for the Minnesota Twins, 1981, stands out in that it was the final season of Metropolitan Stadium. Even a finale couldn't be properly planned for the ballpark, which opened in 1956 and was used by the minor-league Minneapolis Millers until the Washington Senators moved to Minnesota.

A game on June 11 drew some curious onlookers, just in case this was the final game because major-league players were scheduled to go on strike the next day. At the time, no one was sure if they would return that season.

At the time of the strike, the Twins had already seen manager Johnny Goryl fired (in May) in favor of the feistier Billy Gardner, but had regardless settled into seventh and last in the American League West Division with a record of 17 wins and 39 losses.

One game was planned – an annual Old Timers event, which the Twins announced would take place on Saturday night, August 15, regardless of whether the regulars were back or not for their scheduled game against the Seattle Mariners. As it turns out, they were.

The strike was settled with barely a week to spare, and the season resumed. A split-season format was adopted, calling for division winners from the first half (before the strike) to be matched against the champions of the second half in each division. Minnesota celebrated a "reopener" on August 10 in beating Oakland before more than 15,000 fans, only the fourth crowd of more than 10,000 at the Met that season.[1]

But the promise of a look at stars of the past drew 17,831 for a pregame exhibition that featured future Hall of Famer Harmon Killebrew and Tony Oliva, Zoilo Versalles, Bob Allison, Earl Battey, Mudcat Grant, Cesar Tovar, Jim Perry, Bernie Allen, Jerry Kindall, Al Worthington, Frank Quilici, Don Mincher, Dick Stigman, Rich Reese, Ted Uhlaender, Dave Boswell, and Camilo Pascual from the 1965 pennant winners as well as Gardner, Bob Gebhard, George Thomas, Charley Walters, Tom Lundstedt, Mike Poepping, Greg Thayer, Chuck Nieson, Lenny Green, Jim Lemon, Fred Bruckbauer, Bill Dailey, and batboy Mark Stodghill.[2]

The chance to see revered players make their last romp on Met Stadium turf was the highlight for many, especially when the game that followed produced its share of lowlights.

Twins starter Brad Havens was a promising rookie with 17 innings under his belt, a respectable earned-run average of 3.71, and zero wins against two losses. Seattle started veteran Glenn Abbott, an original Mariner (1977) with two 12-win seasons in his past but in 1981 only an occasional starter with a current record of one win and four losses. Offensive fireworks were nonetheless not to be expected; the Mariners ranked 11th in batting average in the 14-team league, while the Twins were a notch lower at 12th and on their way to posting, at .241, the lowest team home batting average in their 21 seasons in Minnesota. The Twins averaged 3.44 runs per game in 1981, third worst in the majors.

A single and a double – by the eight and nine hitters in Seattle's order – gave the visitors the first run of the game, in the third. The same dynamic duo, center fielder Joe Simpson and shortstop Jim Anderson, who combined for six hits in eight at-bats in the game, produced Seattle's second run in the fifth on another single and double, the latter a routine fly to center lost in the gray sky by Mickey Hatcher. Two additional Mariners singles to start the sixth finished Havens' night, Seattle's third run scoring on a subsequent double-play grounder off reliever Fernando Arroyo.

The Twins knocked Abbott out in the sixth, loading the bases with one out, but Hatcher's liner behind second base off rookie left-hander Bryan Clark was grabbed by Anderson, who stepped on second for the double play.

Seattle picked up an unearned run in the seventh, and two singles and a walk chased Arroyo in the eighth, when the final two runs were plated. Clark, meanwhile, finished up the Mariners' four-hit shutout, concluding a game played in the tidy elapsed time of 2 hours and 17 minutes.

The Twins moved, for better or worse, into the Metrodome in Minneapolis to begin 1982, which would be still drearier. The full schedule would be played, and the Twins embarked on a full-fledged youth movement, sending veterans Roy Smalley and Butch Wynegar to the Yankees in separate deals in April and May, and going on to lose 102 games. The help that would eventually propel them to the surprise championship of 1987 had already started arriving before 1981 ended, however, as Kent Hrbek, Tim Laudner, and Gary Gaetti made their debuts. Meanwhile, with the club moving to its downtown ballpark from suburban Bloomington, the *Minneapolis Star* and the *Minneapolis Tribune* were playing nice about the disappointing season, but sports columnist Patrick Reusse of the *St. Paul Dispatch* felt fully able to swing away at the team and its owner, Calvin Griffith.

On the following Monday, after the Twins had finished losing four of five games at home to also-lowly Seattle, Reusse commented in his column, "It has taken the Griffith organization 21 years, but it has presented Minnesota ... with the genuine article, the product that symbolized the Griffiths in Washington: Our very own, authentic, last-place team ... The only reminders this weekend (of the past Twins contenders that the old timers played for) were the line drives off the bat of Tony Oliva and the anticipation when Harmon Killebrew came to the plate. ... Oh, yes, this team used to be that good. The words to describe it now are more appropriately inscribed on the walls of public lavatories. ... the absence of the Twins for two months really was the only bonus of this wet, dreadful summer. ... "[3]

The uninspired effort of August 15 included such reviews as:

Billy Gardner: "We looked like horsepoop." (Probably not his exact words).

Mickey Hatcher: "I know I played with my head up my butt." (Also perhaps not his precise verbiage).

"We Want Killebrew!" (A chant heard from fans in the right-field stands in the ninth inning).[4]

The Twins, though they finished the year with the worst overall record in the division, still were given permission to print World Series tickets, as the split-season format kept them in the second-half race into the final week. They weren't mathematically eliminated until September 30, when they lost to the Kansas City Royals, perhaps appropriately in the final baseball game at Metropolitan Stadium.

POSTSCRIPT

Why include this uninspiring example from Metropolitan Stadium's last season in a collection of its most memorable games? The author was part of a contingent of members who, earlier that day, had attended the first Minnesota gathering of Society for American Baseball Research members. From such modest roots came the organization's model regional organization, the Halsey Hall Chapter of SABR.

SOURCES

retrosheet.org

NOTES

1. The other crowds in five figures to that point were on Opening Day, for a Sunday doubleheader in late April, and for a game against Milwaukee just before the strike.

2. "Names of Ex-Twins at Old Timers Game," *Minneapolis Tribune,* August 16, 1981: 8C.

3. Patrick Reusse, "It was a Weekend to Try to Forget the '81 Twins," *St. Paul Dispatch,* August 17, 1981: 5B.

4. Jay Weiner, "Twins Lose to Seattle: Fans Call for Harmon," *Minneapolis Tribune,* August 16, 1981: 8C.

THE MET CLOSES WITH A LOSS

SEPTEMBER 30, 1981: KANSAS CITY ROYALS 5, MINNESOTA TWINS 2

By Joe O'Connell

It was a bad day.

The weather was drab, home plate was missing, and the Minnesota Twins lost their last game ever at Metropolitan Stadium.

When the grounds crew reported for work they discovered that vandals had gotten into the ballpark and had sliced through the rubber tarpaulin that covered the home-plate area and removed the plate. Fortunately, the grounds crew supervisor, Ed Weller, had a spare plate installed before the game.[1]

Twins manager Billy Gardner, reflecting after his team's 5-2 loss to the Kansas City Royals, suggested it was the Royals who had swiped the base. "They stole everything else," the skipper said.[2]

The date was September 30, 1981, the final scheduled home game for the Twins, who were moving to the Hubert H. Humphrey Metrodome in 1982.

Twins owner Calvin Griffith was not excited about the end of Metropolitan Stadium, claiming that if the first and second decks had been completed down the third-base line to the left-field corner, he would never have agreed to move his team to a new ballpark.[3]

Griffith asserted that Met Stadium was one of the best parks in the country to watch a ballgame.[4]

Roy Smalley has just popped up on the final pitch thrown at Met Stadium.

While history treats Met Stadium well, the ballpark was not without its detractors.

Calvin's son, Clark, was a vice president at the time. "The ballpark was never really completed," he said. "There were some bad design decisions made back in 1955-56.

"They should have made the stadium eight feet deeper to accommodate more box seats between first and third base. Major parts were cracking. It wasn't a question of making repairs. We would have needed to tear it down and start over."[5]

Team management, despite a disappointing season, expressed optimism about the final game at the ballpark that greeted the team on its arrival from Washington in 1961.

A players strike had wiped out the middle two months of the 1981 schedule, and the season was divided in half. The Oakland A's had won the first-half title in the American League West Division, and the Royals were in first place in the second half when they met the Twins that day.

Although the Twins, who finished the first half with a 17-39 record, were 23-26 in the second half, they still had an outside chance of winning the division and making the playoffs. Expectations were for a crowd of 25,000 to 30,000, but only 15,900 showed on a damp and rainy day with a high temperature of 56 degrees. It was a time before metal detectors, but many in the crowd came armed with hammers, screwdrivers, and shovels ... intent on taking souvenirs home with them.

Fernando Arroyo delivered the first pitch at 1:24 P.M., and Willie Wilson hit a grounder to shortstop Roy Smalley, whose long throw from the hole was high. Wilson was on with a base hit and stopped at second when Frank White dropped a single into left with the dangerous George Brett coming up. However, Brett fouled to third baseman Gary Gaetti in foul territory, and Willie Aikens grounded into a double play to end the threat.

The bottom of the Kansas City order got a rally going in the second. With one out, Hal McRae singled to center and, one out later, went to third on John Wathan's single to right. Wathan was running on a pitch to U. L. Washington, who grounded a single inside third to score McRae and send Wathan to third. Wilson dropped a Texas Leaguer into left to drive in Wathan and give the Royals a 2-0 lead.

Lefty Larry Gura retired the first five Twins batters before giving up a single to Gaetti. Pete Mackanin hit the next pitch to left and was credited with a game-tying home run, although it appeared that a fan had reached over the fence and touched the ball. According to Dan Stoneking in the *Minneapolis Star,* Wilson, the Royals left fielder, decided not to argue with second-base umpire Joe Brinkman, explaining after the game, "You think they are going to take away a home run from the home team on the last game ever in their park?"[6]

Kansas City knocked Arroyo out of the game in the fourth. After McRae led off with a single, Clint Hurdle lined a 1-and-1 pitch into the bleachers in right. The ball caromed off one of the wooden slats and back onto the field. Dave Engle picked it up and disgustingly heaved it back into the seats. Wathan singled for the second time but was thrown out trying to stretch the hit by left fielder Mark Funderburk. After giving up his fourth straight hit, a double to right-center by Washington, Arroyo was relieved. Wilson singled on Bob Veselic's first pitch to bring home Washington.

Gura had all the runs he needed. After Mackanin's home run, he gave up an infield single to Ron Washington with two out in the third and then retired the next 16 batters.

As the day wore on, the skies got darker and the mood gloomier, not so much because the Twins were losing 5-2 as because each out was a step closer to the death of baseball at the Met.

In the middle of the ninth, the fans perked up, perhaps helped by the organist playing the Minnesota Rouser, the fight song for the University of Minnesota, and a fan in a Richard Nixon mask danced on top of the Royals dugout.[7]

Gary Ward responded by lining the first pitch in the bottom of the ninth to right for a single, the Twins' first baserunner since the third. Ron Washington flied out. Dave Engle, with a 15-game hitting streak on the line, hit a grounder off Gura's glove that deflected to White at second. As White flipped to shortstop U. L. Washington to force Ward, it appeared that this

Although the final baseball game was played at the Met September 30, the final event was a football game between Minnesota and Kansas City December 20, 1981. Fans grabbed souvenirs after the game.

could finally be it. However, Engle beat the relay to first, giving the ballpark one last reprieve.

As the Longines clock atop the scoreboard in right-center field crawled past 4:00, Smalley swung at a 0-and-2 pitch and hit a soft popup to the left side. Washington moved a little to his right and gloved it for the final out.

Asked about the final game, Smalley laughed and said, "I made the last out. That's what a lot of people remember." Nearly 40 years after that, game Smalley admitted he wanted to go out with a bang.

"I can admit now that I was trying to hit a home run," he said, "but the best I could do was a fly out to left field. It was a great hitter's ballpark, but the field could get really tough from being used by the Twins, the Vikings, and Kicks and Minnesota weather."[8]

Smalley's teammates shared his mixed emotions for their home field.

Reserve catcher Sal Butera said that moving downtown might end a bad era for the team. "The

MEMORABLE GAMES AT MINNESOTA'S DIAMOND ON THE PRAIRIE

Joe O'Connell

new domed stadium might create new interest and excitement for the fans," he said.[9]

Laurel Prieb, Major League Baseball vice president for special projects in 2020, was a Twins public-relations intern to Tom Mee at the time and said she had fond memories of Met Stadium. "I remember that even though it was a crummy day a lot of fans stuck around after that last game," he said. "There were a lot of great memories in that ballpark."[10]

Indeed. The Twins had hosted both the All-Star Game and the World Series in 1965 and won the American League West Division title in 1969 and 1970. The Twins had the best overall attendance in the American League in their first decade in Minnesota.

If nothing else, the loss to the Royals ensured that there would be no playoff games at the Met. The Twins were formally eliminated from the race while the win clinched a playoff spot for Kansas City.[11]

Minneapolis Star columnist Doug Grow in a farewell to the Met recalled that in 1956 Commissioner Ford Frick said to Minnesota sportswriter Halsey Hall of Met Stadium, "Damn, what a beautiful park."[12]

Praise had flowed when the ballpark opened. National League President Warren Giles said of the Met, "It's out of this world. I always wanted to sit in a ballpark that didn't have a post. Now that I've seen it, it's really something."[13]

His American League counterpart, Will Harridge, also was impressed. "You haven't overlooked a single detail to make this the last word in stadium construction," he said.[14]

By the end, however, Metropolitan Stadium was running down. Plagued by mostly noncontending teams since they won a division title in 1970, the Twins drew more than a million fans only twice in their final 11 seasons. They drew only 469,090 fans at home in the strike-shortened 1981 season, worst in the major leagues.

The Minnesota Vikings of the National Football League had been the catalyst for a new stadium, and the Twins went along with them for a new multipurpose facility that would have its roof inflated for the first time only two days after the final game at the Met.[15]

TWINS TOPICS:

Two members of the Twins 1961 starting lineup, Gardner and Jim Lemon, were also on the field for the final game at Met Stadium. Gardner, the original second baseman, was the team's manager, and left fielder Lemon was the first-base coach.

The Twins finished their 21 years at Met Stadium with a record of 910-759-5.

Seating capacity for the 1961 opener was 30,637. It was 45,919 by the time the team left. The team led the American League in attendance in 1963 and 1965 and finished last in both 1980 and 1981.

The location of the Met's home plate is marked in Nickelodeon Universe in the middle of the Mall of America while a seat on the northern wall represents the spot where future Hall of Famer Harmon Killebrew hit the longest home run in Met Stadium history, 520 feet, on June 3, 1967.

Fans attending the final Twins game did relatively little damage in their search of souvenirs in contrast to what happened after the last Minnesota Vikings home game later that year.

Met Stadium stood empty for more than three years before being demolished in January 1985.

SOURCES

Baseball-Reference.com

Retrosheet.org

retrosheet.org/boxesetc/1981/B09300MIN1981.htm

baseball-reference.com/boxes/MIN/MIN198109300.shtml

NOTES

1   Dan Stoneking, "Baseball at the Met: History Comes to Bat – and Humbly Flies Out, *Minneapolis Star,* October 1, 1981: 1A, 4A.

2   Joe Soucheray, "Between the Rain and the Rain, the Met Was Good Place to Be," *Minneapolis Tribune,* October 1, 1981: 1A.

3   Conversation with Calvin Griffith, circa 1983.

4   Associated Press, "Twins, Fans Say Good-bye to Met Stadium," *St. Cloud* (Minnesota) *Times,* October 1, 1981: 1D.

5   Telephone interview with Clark Griffith, June 2020.

6   Stoneking: 4-5A.

7   Stoneking: 5A.
8   Telephone interview with Roy Smalley, June 2020.
9   *St. Cloud Times*.
10 Telephone interview with Laurel Prieb, June 2020.
11 The win did not clinch first place for Kansas City, which had a 1½-game lead over Oakland at the end of the day. However, if Oakland had won the second-half title in addition to the first-half title, the Royals, as the second-place team in the second half, would have made the playoffs.
12 Doug Grow, "Met's Farewell: Twins' Home Went from the Best to an Anachronism in 25 Years," *Minneapolis Star*, September 30, 1981: 14B.
13 Grow.
14 Grow.
15 Ron Meador, "Stadium's First Big Fans Give Shape to Downtown Dome," *Minneapolis Tribune*, October 3, 1981: 1A.

CONTRIBUTOR BIOGRAPHIES

Rich Arpi has been a SABR member since 1982 and has been active in the Halsey Hall Chapter. He has given numerous presentations and written several articles on Minnesota baseball teams, players, and events.

Nathan Bierma is a SABR member and SABR Games Project contributor living in Grand Rapids, Michigan. His writing has appeared in the *Chicago Tribune, Chicago Sports Review,* and *Detroit Free Press* as well as in SABR's volumes on the greatest games at Wrigley Field, Comiskey Park, and Shibe Park, among others. He is the author of *The Eclectic Encyclopedia of English: Language at Its Most Enigmatic, Ephemeral, and Egregious.* His website is nathanbierma.com.

Thomas J. Brown Jr. is a lifelong Mets fan who became a Durham Bulls fan after moving to North Carolina in the early 1980s. He was a national board certified high-school science teacher for 34 years before retiring in 2016. Tom still volunteers with the English Language Learner students at his former high school, serving as a mentor to those students and the teachers who are now working with them. He also provides support and guidance for his former ELL students when they embark on different career paths after graduation. Tom has been a member of SABR since 1995 when he learned about the organization during a visit to Cooperstown on his honeymoon. He has become active in the organization since his retirement and has written numerous biographies and game stories, mostly about the New York Mets. Tom also enjoys traveling as much as possible with his wife and has visited major-league and minor-league baseball parks across the country on his many trips. He also loves to cook and makes all the meals at his house while writing about those meals on his blog, Cooking and My Family, cookingandmyfamily.wordpress.com.

Frederick C. "Rick" Bush joined SABR in March 2014. Since that time, he has written articles for more than two dozen SABR books and additional pieces for both the Biography and Games Projects. Together with Bill Nowlin, he has co-edited three SABR books about the Negro Leagues: *Bittersweet Goodbye: The Black Barons, the Grays, and the 1948 Negro League World Series* (2017); *The Newark Eagles Take Flight: The Story of the 1946 Negro League Champions* (2019); and *Pride of Smoketown: The 1935 Pittsburgh Crawfords* (2020). Rick lives with his wife, Michelle, their three sons – Michael, Andrew, and Daniel – and their border collie mix, Bailey, in the greater Houston area, and he teaches English at Wharton County Junior College's satellite campus in Sugar Land.

Ralph Caola is from Troy, New York, where he grew up playing baseball and listening to Yankees games with his father. After a lack of talent ended his collegiate baseball career, he played softball for 30 years. In 2003 he wrote a series of articles titled "Using Calculus to Relate Runs to Wins," which appeared in SABR's Statistical Analysis Research Committee newsletter, *By the Numbers.* He also wrote the SABR Biographies of Bobby Bonds and Nomar Garciaparra. The retired engineer and businessman now spends his summers in Troy and winters in Port Charlotte, Florida, playing tennis and golf.

Alan Cohen has been a SABR member since 2010, and he attended his first SABR convention in 2012 in Minneapolis. By then Metropolitan Stadium had become the Mall of America. His first presentation at a SABR convention pertained to players who homered in the same ballpark in the majors and minors. Twenty-nine players, including Harmon Killebrew, did it at Metropolitan Stadium. He serves as vice president-treasurer of the Connecticut Smoky Joe Wood Chapter and is datacaster (MiLB First Pitch stringer) for the Hartford Yard Goats, the Double-A affiliate of the Colorado Rockies. His biographies, game stories, and essays have appeared in more than 60 SABR publications. Since his first *Baseball Research Journal* article appeared in 2013, Alan has continued to expand his research into the Hearst Sandlot Classic (1946-1965), from which 87 players advanced to the major leagues. He has four children and eight grandchildren and lives in Connecticut with his wife, Frances, their cats Morty, Ava, and Zoe, and their dog, Buddy.

Richard Cuicchi joined SABR in 1983 and is an active member of the Schott-Pelican Chapter. Since his retirement as an information technology executive, Richard authored *Family Ties: A Comprehensive Collection of Facts and Trivia about Baseball's Relatives.* He has contributed to numerous SABR BioProject and Games publications. He does freelance writing and blogging about a variety of baseball topics on his website, TheTenthInning.com. Richard lives in New Orleans with his wife, Mary.

Greg Erion (1947-2017) joined SABR in 1980 and was an accomplished author and historian. Since 2015, he served as project leader for the fledgling SABR Games Project and helped this new initiative thrive, building a solid team of editors and contributors, overseeing the production of five SABR Digital Library books, and providing a sense of stability, leadership, and direction for the entire effort. He also contributed many stories of his own to the Games Project and BioProject, including a biography of his favorite player, one-time NL batting champion Debs Garms. He was born on August 11, 1947, and was in the first four-year graduating class at El Camino High School. He earned a degree in transportation from San Francisco State University and served with distinction in the US Army in Thailand during the Vietnam War. He worked for many years as an executive with the Western Pacific and Southern Pacific railroads. He earned two master's degrees, one in business and another in history, and taught history classes at Skyline College.

T.S. Flynn is a White Sox fan living in Twins Territory. He's an educator and member of the Halsey Hall SABR Chapter.

Brian Frank is passionate about documenting the history of major- and minor-league baseball. He is the creator of the website The Herd Chronicles (herdchronicles.com), which is dedicated to preserving the history of the Buffalo Bisons. His articles can also be read on the official website of the Bisons. He was an assistant editor of the book *The Seasons of Buffalo Baseball, 1857-2020,* and he's a frequent contributor to SABR publications. Brian and his wife, Jenny, enjoy traveling around the country in their camper to major- and minor-league ballparks and taking an annual trip to Europe. Brian was a history major at Canisius College, where he earned a bachelor of arts degree. He also received a Juris Doctor from the University at Buffalo School of Law.

Gordon J. Gattie is a lifelong baseball fan and SABR member since 1998. Currently a civilian US Navy engineer, he includes among his baseball research interests ballparks, historical trends, and statistical analysis. Gordon earned his Ph.D. from SUNY Buffalo, where he used baseball to investigate judgment performance in complex dynamic environments. Ever the optimist, he dreams of a Cleveland Indians-Washington Nationals World Series matchup, especially after the Nationals' 2019 World Series championship. Lisa, his wonderful wife who roots for the Yankees, and Morrigan, their beloved Labrador retriever, are looking forward to resuming their cross-country travels visiting ballparks and other baseball-related sites. Gordon has contributed to many SABR publications, including several issues of *The National Pastime*, and the Games Project.

Steve Ginader is a retired logistics manager living in Minnesota. He and his wife, Julie, travel in a teardrop camper visiting national and state parks throughout the United States. They are parents of two grown children and one grandchild. He has written articles for the SABR games project and several book reviews for the Deadball Era newsletter.

Gene Gomes has a family connection to professional baseball in Abner Powell, his great-grandfather, who was a nineteenth-century player, manager, team owner, and innovator. Gene was born in New Orleans on April 15, 1952 (Opening Day). The first major-league game he attended was played on July 23, 1963, in Dodger Stadium. He graduated from Louisiana State University and follows their baseball and football teams closely. Gene coached all his children's baseball teams for many years in New Orleans and Minneapolis, where he now lives, and he hopes to pass on his love of baseball to each of his seven grandchildren. A dentist for 42 years, Gene now dabbles in baseball research.

Bruce Harris has been a SABR member since 2006. He has written three biographies (Bob Tufts, Pete Craig, and Bob Saverine) for the SABR BioProject. He has also contributed several essays to the Games Project. His 2007 article, "Baseball and Briar," was published in the *Baseball Research Journal*.

Tom Hawthorn is an author and journalist who lives in Victoria, British Columbia. His most recent book was *The Year Canadians Lost Their Minds and Found Their Country: The Centennial of 1967.*

Paul Hofmann, a SABR member since 2002, is the associate vice president for international affairs at Sacramento State University and a frequent contributor to SABR publications. Paul is a native of Detroit and a lifelong Detroit Tigers fan. He lives in Folsom, California.

Mike Huber has been rooting for the same American League East team for over 50 years. The first game he ever saw in person involved the Orioles and the Twins. He is the former chair of SABR's Games Project Committee and enjoys writing about rare events in baseball, such as hitting for the cycle or slugging two grand slams in the same game.

Sarah Johnson is a Minnesota-based sports statistician and writer/researcher. She has contributed to many SABR initiatives, including the Bio Project, the Games Project and the *Baseball Research Journal*.

Norm King (1957-2018) of Ottawa joined SABR in 2010 and became a prolific contributor to the SABR BioProject and Games Project until his death from a rare form of bile duct cancer in 2018. He was the lead editor and author of *Au jeu/Play Ball: The 50 Greatest Games in the History of the Montreal Expos,* published in 2016, and wrote chapters for a number of other SABR books, including *Thar's Joy in Braveland: The 1957 Milwaukee Braves; Winning on the North Side: The 1929 Chicago Cubs;* and *A Pennant for the Twin Cities: The 1965 Minnesota Twins.* He was an active member of SABR's Quebec Chapter and a friendly face at the SABR national convention each year.

Dave Lande, a SABR member since 2009, grew up in western North Dakota listening to many Minnesota Twins games on the radio. As a teenager, he saw his first major-league baseball game in person at Met Stadium on Labor Day weekend, 1966. Fifteen years later, in 1981, he was in attendance for the last baseball game played at Met Stadium. In between those years, he saw numerous baseball games at Met Stadium, a few football games (including one as a member of a college marching band), and at least one soccer game. The story for the first Twins opener at Met Stadium in 1961 is his first SABR article. An active member of the Halsey Hall Chapter, he is a two-time chapter president.

Len Levin is a longtime newspaper editor in New England, now retired. He lives in Providence with his wife, Linda, and an overachieving orange cat. He now (Len, not the cat) is the grammarian for the Rhode Island Supreme Court and edits its decisions. He also copyedits many SABR books, including this one. He is just down the interstate from Fenway Park, where he has spent many happy hours.

Dan Levitt is the author of several baseball books and numerous essays. He is a longtime SABR member and a recipient of the Davids Award and the Chadwick Award. His books have won the Larry Ritter Book Award and the Sporting News-SABR Baseball Research Award, and have twice been finalists for the Seymour Medal.

SABR member and Massachusetts native **Mike Lynch** is the founder of Seamheads.com and the author of five books, including *Harry Frazee, Ban Johnson and the Feud That Nearly Destroyed the American League,* which was named a finalist for the 2009 Larry Ritter Award and was nominated for a Seymour Medal. His most recent work includes a three-book series called *Baseball's Untold History* and several articles that have appeared in SABR books. His collaboration with others on Negro Leagues history earned him the 2019 Tweed Webb Lifetime Achievement Award from SABR's Negro Leagues Research Committee. He lives in Roslindale, Massachusetts, with Catherine and their cats, Jiggs and Pepper.

Jim McKernon is a librarian. Born and raised in St. Paul, he lives in Minneapolis. His first baseball memory was listening to a home-run derby between Harmon Killebrew and Willie Mays prior to a 1971 in-season exhibition game. His greatest baseball thrill was attending Game One of the 1987 World Series.

Tom Merrick is a retired North Dakota District Court judge and an Air Force veteran, currently living in Buffalo, Minnesota. He has been a SABR member since 2000 and frequently contributes essays to the SABR Games Project. His article "Swede Risberg's journey to Jamestown" appeared in the June 2019 *Black Sox Scandal Research Committee Newsletter.* Among his many blessings are his wife, Pamela, their three children, and their two granddaughters.

Dave Mona covered the Minnesota Twins as the beat writer for the *Minneapolis Tribune* in the 1968 and 1969 seasons. He has co-hosted the Sunday Sports Huddle talk show on WCCO Radio with *Tribune* columnist Sid Hartman since 1981. His book, *Beyond the Sports Huddle: Mona on Minnesota,* was published in 2008. In 1986 he co-authored (with Dave Jarzyna) *Twenty-five Seasons,* a history of the Minnesota Twins.

Chad Moody is a nearly lifelong resident of suburban Detroit, where he has been a fan of the Detroit Tigers from birth. An alumnus of both the University of Michigan and Michigan State University, he has spent 25 years working in the automotive industry. Chad's first foray into formal baseball research occurred as a teenager, when he had a letter published in *Baseball Digest.* From that humble beginning, he has since frequently contributed to SABR's BioProject and Games Project. Chad and his wife, Lisa, live in Northville, Michigan, with their children, Jacob and Jessica, and dog, Daisy.

Bill Nowlin was pleased to be asked to write something related to Ted Williams, a subject of particular interest to this longtime SABR board member. He saw Williams play the last four years of his storied career. Bill lives in Cambridge, Massachusetts, and was a co-founder of Rounder Records in 1970. He has written several hundred articles for SABR and has helped edit a considerable number of SABR's books.

Joe O'Connell has been a SABR member since 1985 and is a charter member of the Halsey Hall Chapter. He enjoys researching the American Association St. Paul Saints from before the arrival of the Minnesota Twins. He also has interest in the Twins and the Metropolitan Stadium years.

A lifelong Indians fan, **Tim Otto** grew up 40 miles east of Cleveland and attended his first Indians game in 1960. In the early '60s he rooted for Tribe players such as Vic Power, Dick Stigman, Jim Perry, Jerry Kindall, and Jim Grant, all of whom were later traded by Cleveland to the Twins. He was excited to have the opportunity to write about Jack Kralick's no-hitter, a game highlighted prominently on Kralick's 1963 Post Cereal baseball card that was part of Tim's collection as a kid.

J.G. Preston lives in Santa Fe, New Mexico, but he spent nearly 30 years in Minnesota and saw several games at Metropolitan Stadium during his college years. While he was there he covered the Twins as sports director of the Minnesota News Network (1983-88) and hosted a Twins call-in show on the Twins radio network; edited the Twins program magazine (1988-90), contributed articles to the Twins program and yearbook in later years; and wrote the scripts for two Twins season highlight films (1988-89) and for a video biography of Kirby Puckett that was narrated by Bob Costas. He's also contributed biographies and game stories to a number of other SABR publications.

Carl Riechers retired from United Parcel Service in 2012 after 35 years of service. With more free time, he became a SABR member that same year. Born and raised in the suburbs of St. Louis, he became a big fan of the Cardinals. He and his wife, Janet, have three children, and he is the proud grandpa of two.

Joel Rippel, a Minnesota native and graduate of the University of Minnesota, is the author or co-author of 10 books on Minnesota sports history and has contributed as a writer to several books published by SABR.

Bill Schneider is a SABR member.

Peter Seidel has been a member of SABR since 2014. A lifelong Yankee fan, Pete grew up a short ride from the Stadium in southern Westchester County. After earning a master's degree from Harvard University, Pete relocated to the Dallas-Fort Worth area with his two children for his day job as a business development executive for AT&T. Pete has contributed to several SABR books starting with the Mike Sandlock book in 2016 as well as many articles to the SABR Baseball Games Project. Aside from being a diehard Yankee fan, Pete enjoys spending time with his teenage kids, bicycling, hiking, kayaking, and playing guitar in whatever spare time he has.

Andrew Sharp grew up in the D.C. area as a fan of Washington Senators I and II, and spent 30-plus years in the wilderness as a New York Mets fan before happily regaining a Washington team to support. A retired newspaper editor, he began writing BioProject essays in 2017 and has written SABR's ownership histories of the Griffith era and the expansion Senators.

Doug Skipper has contributed to a number of SABR publications, presented research at national and regional conventions, and written more than two dozen player, manager, and game profiles for the SABR Baseball Biographical Project. A SABR member since 1982, he served as president of the Halsey Hall Chapter in 2014-2015, is a member of the Deadball Era Committee, and chairs the Lawrence Ritter Award Committee. He is interested in the history of Connie Mack's Philadelphia Athletics, the Boston Red Sox, the Minnesota Twins, and old ballparks. A market research consultant residing in Apple Valley, Minnesota, Doug is also a veteran of father-daughter dancing. Doug and his wife, Kathy, have two daughters, MacKenzie and Shannon.

Steve Smith is a retired certified public accountant who has been a SABR member since 2000. His primary passion is researching the baseball history of his hometown, Keokuk, Iowa. He has been a Twins fan since moving to Minnesota in 1972. He spends his winters in Englewood, Florida, near the Tampa Bay Rays' spring-training site in Port Charlotte.

Mark S. Sternman made his first-ever trip to the Twin Cities to see his beloved Harvard women's hockey team win the national championship on March 27, 1999, at the University of Minnesota's Mariucci Arena thanks to freshman Jennifer Botterill's overtime goal. He has returned countless times since then for baseball, hockey, and Surly's Beer Garden. Sternman looks forward to a post-pandemic return so he can visit the site where George Floyd was murdered, a horrific event that has resulted in a much-needed reevaluation of the racist realities that permeate U.S. society.

Bob Tholkes is a longtime SABR member.

Stew Thornley is an official scorer for Minnesota Twins home games and is a member of the Major League Baseball Official Scoring Advisory Committee. He has been a SABR member since 1979.

Bob Webster grew up in northwest Indiana and has been a Cubs fan since 1963. Now living in Portland, Oregon, he earned an accounting degree from Linfield College and an MBA from Maryhurst University. He is retired from Intel Corporation as a construction and facilities contract manager as well as a government contracts analyst. In addition to researching and writing for various SABR projects, Bob is currently researching and documenting the history of the Northwest League and was a Gameday Stats Stringer for the Hillsboro Hops for three seasons. He is a member of the Northwest Chapter of SABR and on the Board of Executives of the Old-Timers Baseball Association of Portland.

Steve West is a freelance writer in Texas. He has written a number of articles for the BioProject, and was co-editor of the SABR book *Whales, Terriers and Terrapins: The Federal League 1914-15*.

Gregory H. Wolf was born in Pittsburgh, but now resides in the Chicagoland area with his wife, Margaret, and daughter, Gabriela. A professor of German studies and holder of the Dennis and Jean Bauman Endowed Chair in the Humanities at North Central College in Naperville, Illinois, he has edited a dozen books for SABR. He is currently working on projects about Shibe Park in Philadelphia and Ebbets Field in Brooklyn. Since January 2017 he has been co-director of SABR's BioProject, which you can follow on Facebook and Twitter.

Bob Wood is an Ohio native who has lived in Lansing, Illinois, since 1978, four blocks from where his wife, Jean, grew up. Proud father of a son, John, and an Australian daughter, MaryJo, and grandfather of Hoosier Ryan and Aussie Tesla, he celebrates his 47th year of marriage while continuing to serve on the local school board and as a church trustee. A former Little League and Babe Ruth manager, Bob umpired high-school baseball for many years. A member of the Twentieth Century Baseball Association (TCBA), he enjoys APBA replays and the annual TCBA convention. He has enjoyed contributing to the SABR Games Project and Oral History Project.

Brian Wright has authored two books on the New York Mets: *Mets in 10s: Best and Worst of an Amazin' History*, which was released in April 2018 from The History Press, and *The New York Mets All-Time All-Stars*, which came out on February 24, 2020, from Lyons Press. He currently serves as a historian for Metsmerized Online, contributing weekly features on notable Mets moments and players. He was managing editor for *Met-rospectives*, a publication from the Society for American Baseball Research chronicling the greatest games in franchise history and has contributed to other books, including the most memorable moments at Wrigley Field, Comiskey Park, and for the San Diego Padres.

Dana Yost was an award-winning daily newspaper journalist for 29 years, mostly at papers in Minnesota. Since 2008, he has published six books and is working on his first novel. He has lived his entire life in the Upper Midwest, and has been around as long as the Twins have: he was born in 1961.

SABR Books on the Negro Leagues and Black Baseball

From Rube to Robinson: SABR's Best Articles on Black Baseball

From Rube to Robinson brings together the best Negro League baseball scholarship that the Society of American Baseball Research (SABR) has ever produced, culled from its journals, Biography Project, and award-winning essays. The book includes a star-studded list of scholars and historians, from the late Jerry Malloy and Jules Tygiel, to award winners Larry Lester, Geri Strecker, and Jeremy Beer, and a host of other talented writers. The essays cover topics ranging over nearly a century, from 1866 and the earliest known Black baseball championship, to 1962 and the end of the Negro American League.

Edited by John Graf; Associate Editors Duke Goldman and Larry Lester
$24.95 paperback (ISBN 978-1-970159-41-7)
$9.99 ebook (ISBN 978-1-970159-40-0)
8.5"X11", 220 pages

Pride of Smoketown: The 1935 Pittsburgh Crawfords

The 1935 Pittsburgh Crawfords team, one of the dominant teams in Negro League history, is often compared to the legendary 1927 "Murderer's Row" New York Yankees. The squad from "Smoketown"—a nickname that the *Pittsburgh Courier* often applied to the metropolis better-known as "Steel City"—boasted four Hall-of-Fame players in outfielder James "Cool Papa" Bell, first baseman/manager Oscar Charleston, catcher Josh Gibson, and third baseman William "Judy" Johnson. This volume contains exhaustively-researched articles about the players, front office personnel, Greenlee Field, and the exciting games and history of the team that were written and edited by 25 SABR members. The inclusion of historical photos about every subject in the book helps to shine a spotlight on the 1935 Pittsburgh Crawfords, who truly were the Pride of Smoketown.

Edited by Frederick C. Bush and Bill Nowlin
$29.95 paperback (ISBN 978-1-970159-25-7)
$9.99 ebook (ISBN 978-1-970159-24-0)
8.5"X11", 340 pages, over 60 photos

The Newark Eagles Take Flight: The Story of the 1946 Negro League Champions

The Newark Eagles won only one Negro National League pennant during the franchise's 15-year tenure in the Garden State, but the 1946 squad that ran away with the NNL and then triumphed over the Kansas City Monarchs in a seven-game World Series was a team for the ages. The returning WWII veterans composed a veritable "Who's Who in the Negro Leagues" and included Leon Day, Larry Doby, Monte Irvin, and Max Manning, as well as numerous role players. Four of the Eagles' stars—Day, Doby, Irvin, and player/manager Raleigh "Biz" Mackey, as well as co-owner Effa Manley—have been enshrined in the National Baseball Hall of Fame in Cooperstown. In addition to biographies of the players, co-owners, and P.A. announcer, there are also articles about Newark's Ruppert Stadium, Leon Day's Opening Day no-hitter, a sensational midseason game, the season's two East-West All-Star Games, and the 1946 Negro League World Series between the Eagles and the renowned Kansas City Monarchs.

Edited by Frederick C. Bush and Bill Nowlin
$24.95 paperback (ISBN 978-1-970159-07-3)
$9.99 ebook (ISBN 978-1-970159-06-6)
8.5"X11", 228 pages, over 60 photos

Bittersweet Goodbye: The Black Barons, The Grays, and the 1948 Negro League World Series

This book was inspired by the last Negro League World Series ever played and presents biographies of the players on the two contending teams in 1948—the Birmingham Black Barons and the Homestead Grays—as well as the managers, the owners, and articles on the ballparks the teams called home. Also included are articles that recap the season's two East-West All-Star Games, the Negro National League and Negro American League playoff series, and the World Series itself. Additional context is provided in essays about the effects of baseball's integration on the Negro Leagues, the exodus of Negro League players to Canada, and the signing away of top Negro League players, specifically Willie Mays. Many of the players' lives and careers have been presented to a much greater extent than previously possible.

Edited by Frederick C. Bush and Bill Nowlin
$21.95 paperback (ISBN 978-1-943816-55-2)
$9.99 ebook (ISBN 978-1-943816-54-5)
8.5"X11", 442 pages, over 100 photos and images

Friends of SABR

You can become a Friend of SABR by giving as little as $10 per month or by making a one-time gift of $1,000 or more. When you do so, you will be inducted into a community of passionate baseball fans dedicated to supporting SABR's work.

Friends of SABR receive the following benefits:
- ✓ Annual Friends of SABR Commemorative Lapel Pin
- ✓ Recognition in This Week in SABR, SABR.org, and the SABR Annual Report
- ✓ Access to the SABR Annual Convention VIP donor event
- ✓ Invitations to exclusive Friends of SABR events

SABR On-Deck Circle - $10/month, $30/month, $50/month

Get in the SABR On-Deck Circle, and help SABR become the essential community for the world of baseball. Your support will build capacity around all things SABR, including publications, website content, podcast development, and community growth.

A monthly gift is deducted from your bank account or charged to a credit card until you tell us to stop. No more email, mail, or phone reminders.

Join the SABR On-Deck Circle

Payment Info: _____Visa _____Mastercard   ○ $10/month

Name on Card: _____   ○ $30/month

Card #: _____   ○ $50/month

Exp. Date: _____ Security Code: _____   ○ Other amount _____

Signature: _____

Go to sabr.org/donate to make your gift online

Society for American Baseball Research
Cronkite School at ASU
555 N. Central Ave. #416, Phoenix, AZ 85004
602.496.1460 (phone)
SABR.org

Become a SABR member today!

If you're interested in baseball — writing about it, reading about it, talking about it — there's a place for you in the Society for American Baseball Research.

SABR memberships are available on annual, multi-year, or monthly subscription basis. Annual and monthly subscription memberships auto-renew for your convenience. Young Professional memberships are for ages 30 and under. Senior memberships are for ages 65 and older. Student memberships are available to currently enrolled middle/high school or full-time college/university students. Monthly subscription members receive SABR publications electronically and are eligible for SABR event discounts after 12 months.

Here's a list of some of the key benefits you'll receive as a SABR member:

- Receive two editions (spring and fall) of the *Baseball Research Journal*, our flagship publication
- Receive expanded e-book edition of *The National Pastime*, our annual convention journal
- 8-10 new e-books published by the SABR Digital Library, all FREE to members
- "This Week in SABR" e-newsletter, sent to members every Friday
- Join dozens of research committees, from Statistical Analysis to Women in Baseball.
- Join one of 70+ regional chapters in the U.S., Canada, Latin America, and abroad
- Participate in online discussion groups
- Ask and answer baseball research questions on the SABR-L e-mail listserv
- Complete archives of *The Sporting News* dating back to 1886 and other research resources
- Promote your research in "This Week in SABR"
- Diamond Dollars Case Competition
- Yoseloff Scholarships

- Discounts on SABR national conferences, including the SABR National Convention, the SABR Analytics Conference, Jerry Malloy Negro League Conference, Frederick Ivor-Campbell 19th Century Conference, and the Arizona Fall League Experience
- Publish your research in peer-reviewed SABR journals
- Collaborate with SABR researchers and experts
- Contribute to Baseball Biography Project or the SABR Games Project
- List your new book in the SABR Bookshelf
- Lead a SABR research committee or chapter
- Networking opportunities at SABR Analytics Conference
- Meet baseball authors and historians at SABR events and chapter meetings
- 50% discounts on paperback versions of SABR e-books
- Discounts with other partners in the baseball community
- SABR research awards

We hope you'll join the most passionate international community of baseball fans at SABR! Check us out online at SABR.org/join.

SABR MEMBERSHIP FORM

	Standard	Senior	Young Pro.	Student
Annual:	☐ $65	☐ $45	☐ $45	☐ $25
3 Year:	☐ $175	☐ $129	☐ $129	
5 Year:	☐ $249			
Monthly:	☐ $6.95	☐ $4.95	☐ $4.95	

(International members wishing to be mailed the Baseball Research Journal should add $10/yr for Canada/Mexico or $19/yr for overseas locations.)

Participate in Our Donor Program!
Support the preservation of baseball research. Designate your gift toward:
☐ General Fund ☐ Endowment Fund ☐ Research Resources ☐ _____
☐ I want to maximize the impact of my gift; do not send any donor premiums
☐ I would like this gift to remain anonymous.

Note: Any donation not designated will be placed in the General Fund.
SABR is a 501 (c) (3) not-for-profit organization & donations are tax-deductible to the extent allowed by law.

Name _____

E-mail* _____

Address _____

City _____ ST _____ ZIP _____

Phone _____ Birthday _____

* Your e-mail address on file ensures you will receive the most recent SABR news.

Dues $ _____
Donation $ _____
Amount Enclosed $ _____

Do you work for a matching grant corporation? Call (602) 496-1460 for details.

If you wish to pay by credit card, please contact the SABR office at (602) 496-1460 or sign up securely online at SABR.org/join. We accept Visa, Mastercard & Discover.

Do you wish to receive the *Baseball Research Journal* electronically? ☐ Yes ☐ No
Our e-books are available in PDF, Kindle, or EPUB (iBooks, iPad, Nook) formats.

Mail to: SABR, Cronkite School at ASU, 555 N. Central Ave. #416, Phoenix, AZ 85004

www.ingramcontent.com/pod-product-compliance
Lightning Source LLC
Chambersburg PA
CBHW081344070526
44578CB00005B/712